BATMAN

ARKHAM UNHINGED

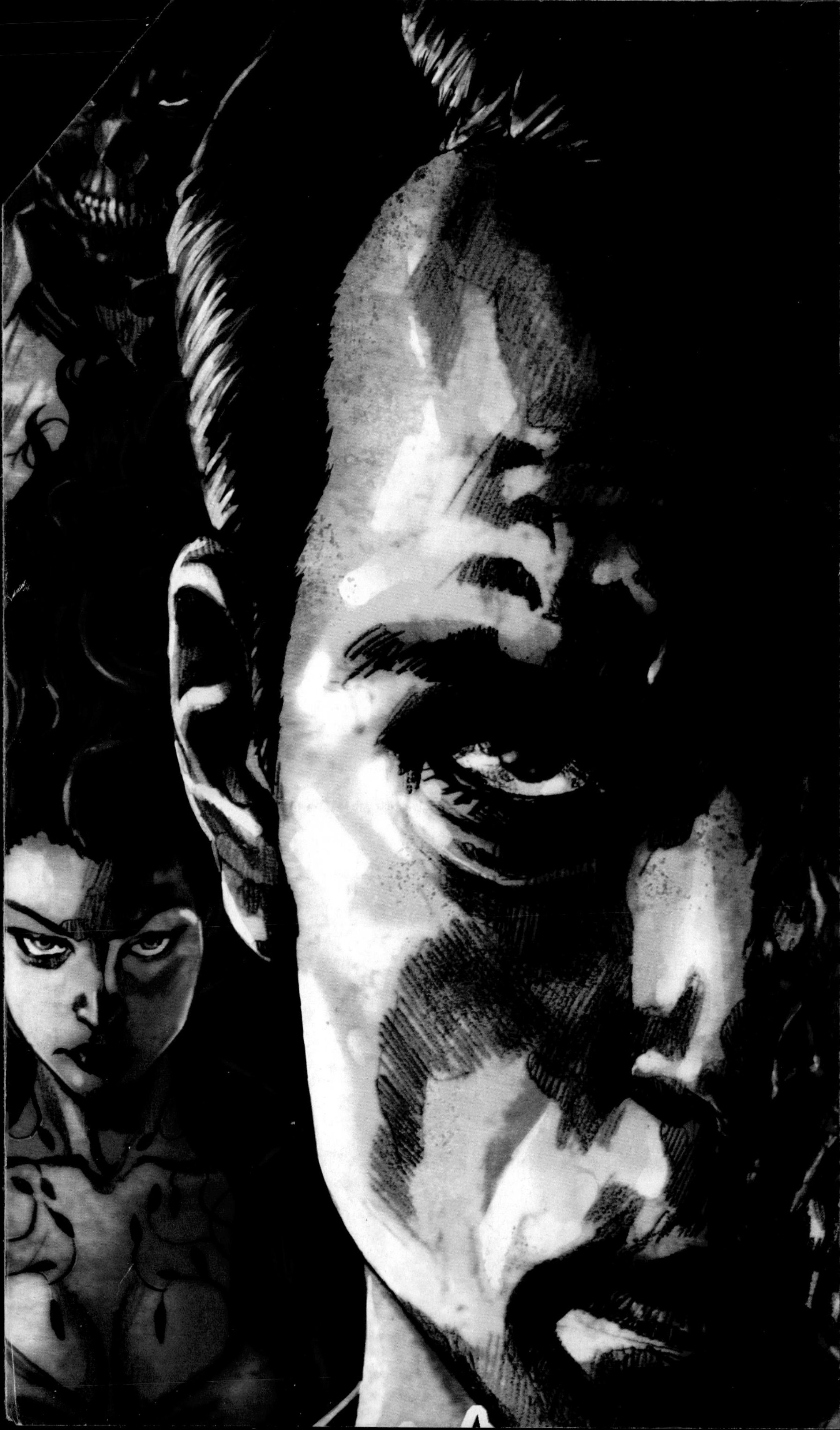

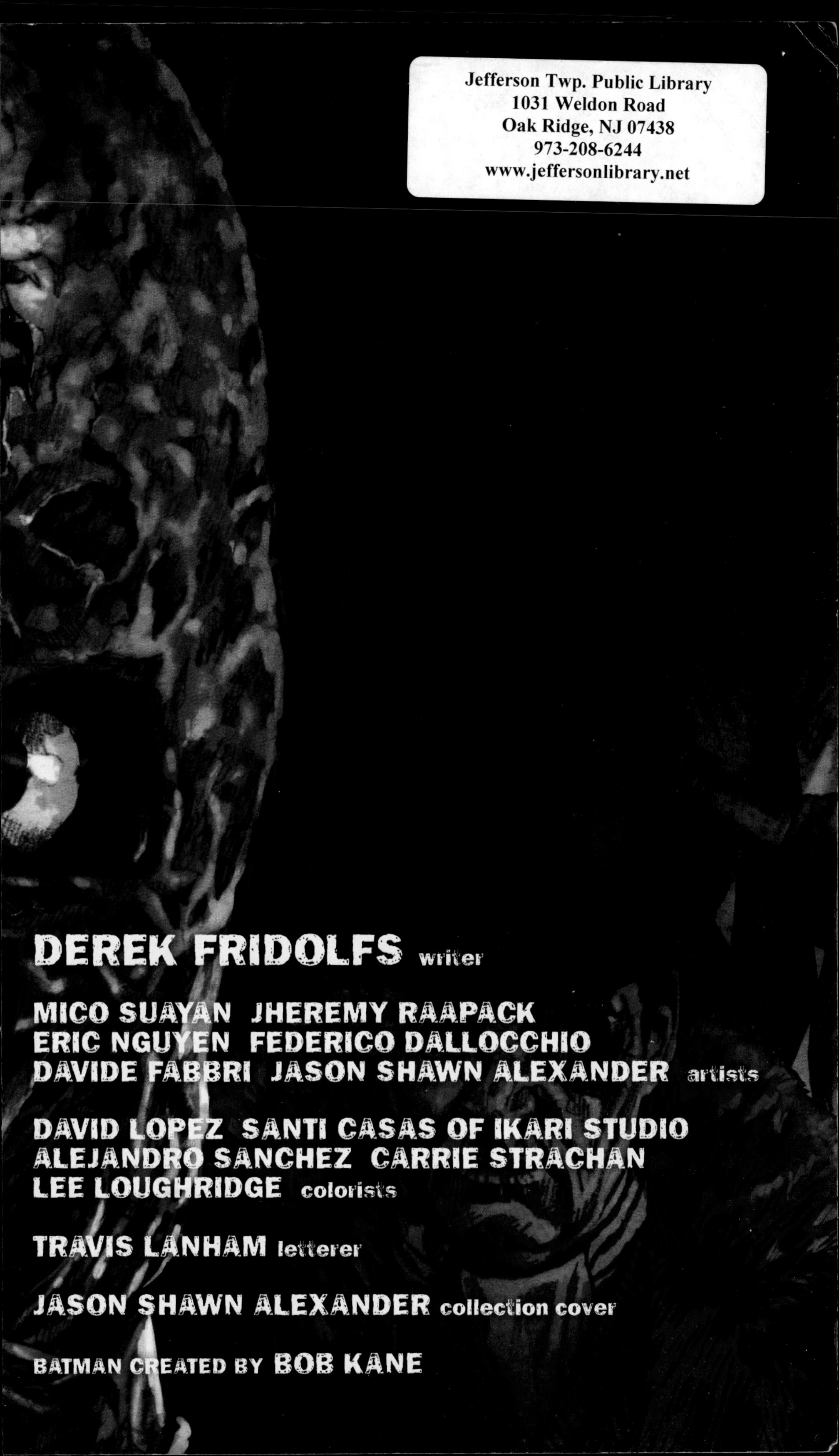

DEREK FRIDOLFS writer

MICO SUAYAN JHEREMY RAAPACK
ERIC NGUYEN FEDERICO DALLOCCHIO
DAVIDE FABBRI JASON SHAWN ALEXANDER artists

DAVID LOPEZ SANTI CASAS OF IKARI STUDIO
ALEJANDRO SANCHEZ CARRIE STRACHAN
LEE LOUGHRIDGE colorists

TRAVIS LANHAM letterer

JASON SHAWN ALEXANDER collection cover

BATMAN CREATED BY **BOB KANE**

Jim Chadwick Editor – Original Series
Sarah Gaydos Assistant Editor – Original Series
Robin Wildman Editor
Robbin Brosterman Design Director – Books
Louis Prandi Publication Design

Hank Kanalz Senior VP – Vertigo and Integrated Publishing

Diane Nelson President
Dan DiDio and Jim Lee Co-Publishers
Geoff Johns Chief Creative Officer
Amit Desai Senior VP – Marketing and Franchise Management
Amy Genkins Senior VP – Business and Legal Affairs
Nairi Gardiner Senior VP – Finance
Jeff Boison VP – Publishing Planning
Mark Chiarello VP – Art Direction and Design
John Cunningham VP – Marketing
Terri Cunningham VP – Editorial Administration
Larry Ganem VP – Talent Relations and Services
Alison Gill Senior VP – Manufacturing and Operations
Jay Kogan VP – Business and Legal Affairs, Publishing
Jack Mahan VP – Business Affairs, Talent
Nick Napolitano VP – Manufacturing Administration
Fred Ruiz VP – Manufacturing Operations
Courtney Simmons Senior VP – Publicity
Bob Wayne Senior VP – Sales

BATMAN: ARKHAM UNHINGED VOLUME 3

Published by DC Comics. Copyright © 2013 DC Comics. All Rights Reserved.
Originally published in single magazine form as BATMAN: ARKHAM UNHINGED Chapters 29-43,
BATMAN – ARKHAM CITY: END GAME Chapters 1-6 © 2012, 2013 DC Comics. All Rights Reserved.
All characters, their distinctive likenesses and related elements featured in this publication are
trademarks of DC Comics. The stories, characters and incidents featured in this publication are
entirely fictional. DC Comics does not read or accept unsolicited ideas, stories or artwork.

DC Comics, 1700 Broadway, New York, NY 10019
A Warner Bros. Entertainment Company.
Printed by RR Donnelley, Owensville, MO, USA. 7/18/14. First Printing.
ISBN: 978-1-4012-4680-8

Library of Congress Cataloging-in-Publication Data

Fridolfs, Derek, author.
  Batman : Arkham Unhinged. Volume 3 / Derek Fridolfs ; [illustrated by] Jason Shawn Alexander.
    pages cm
  ISBN 978-1-4012-4680-8
  1. Graphic novels. I. Alexander, Jason Shawn, illustrator. II. Title.
  PN6728.B36F77 2014
  741.5'973—dc23
                    2013035967

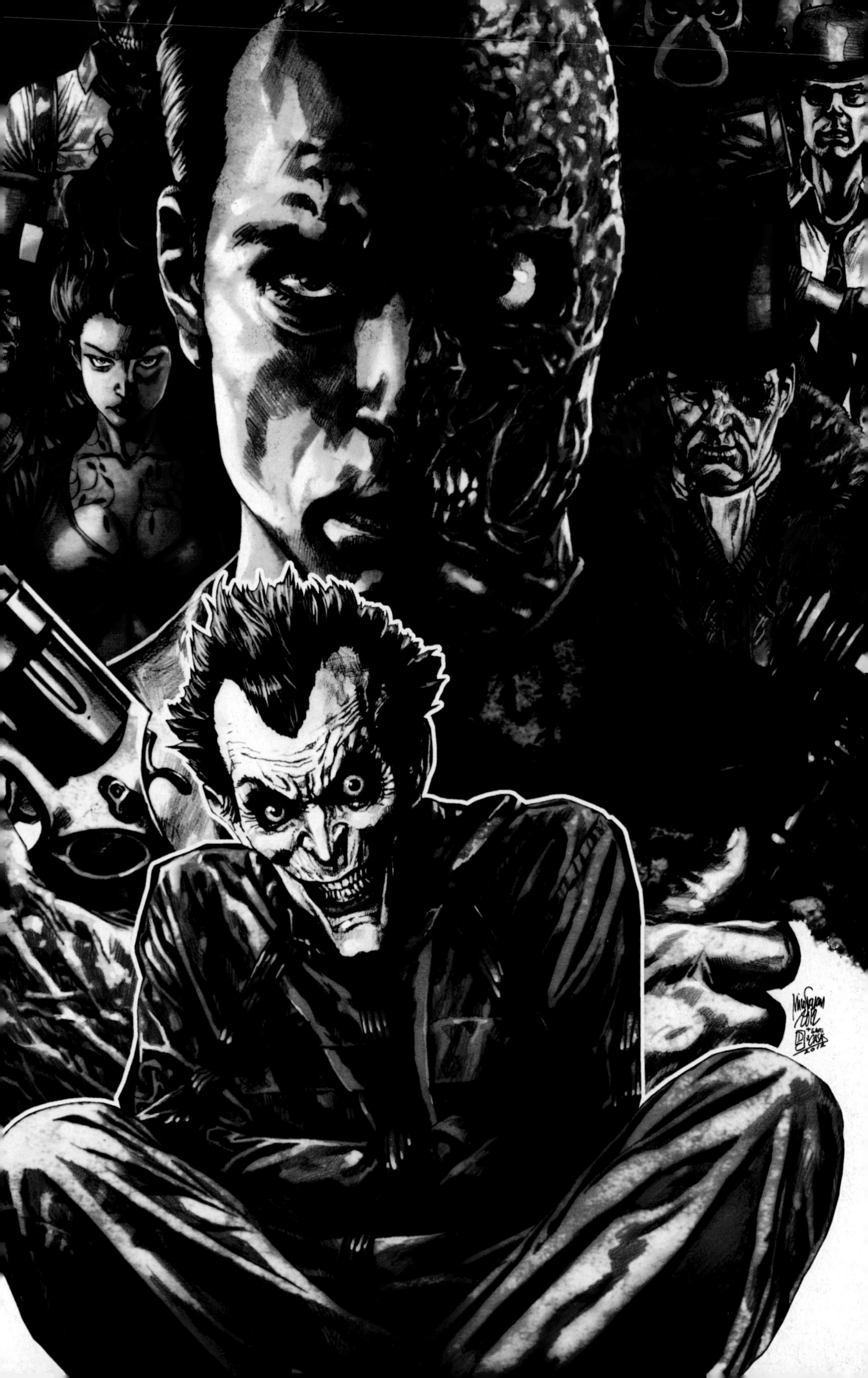

CLOWN COURT

WRITTEN BY: DEREK FRIDOLFS

ART AND COVER BY: MICO SUAYAN

INTERIOR AND COVER COLORS BY:
DAVID LOPEZ & SANTI CASAS OF IKARI STUDIO

LETTERS BY: TRAVIS LANHAM

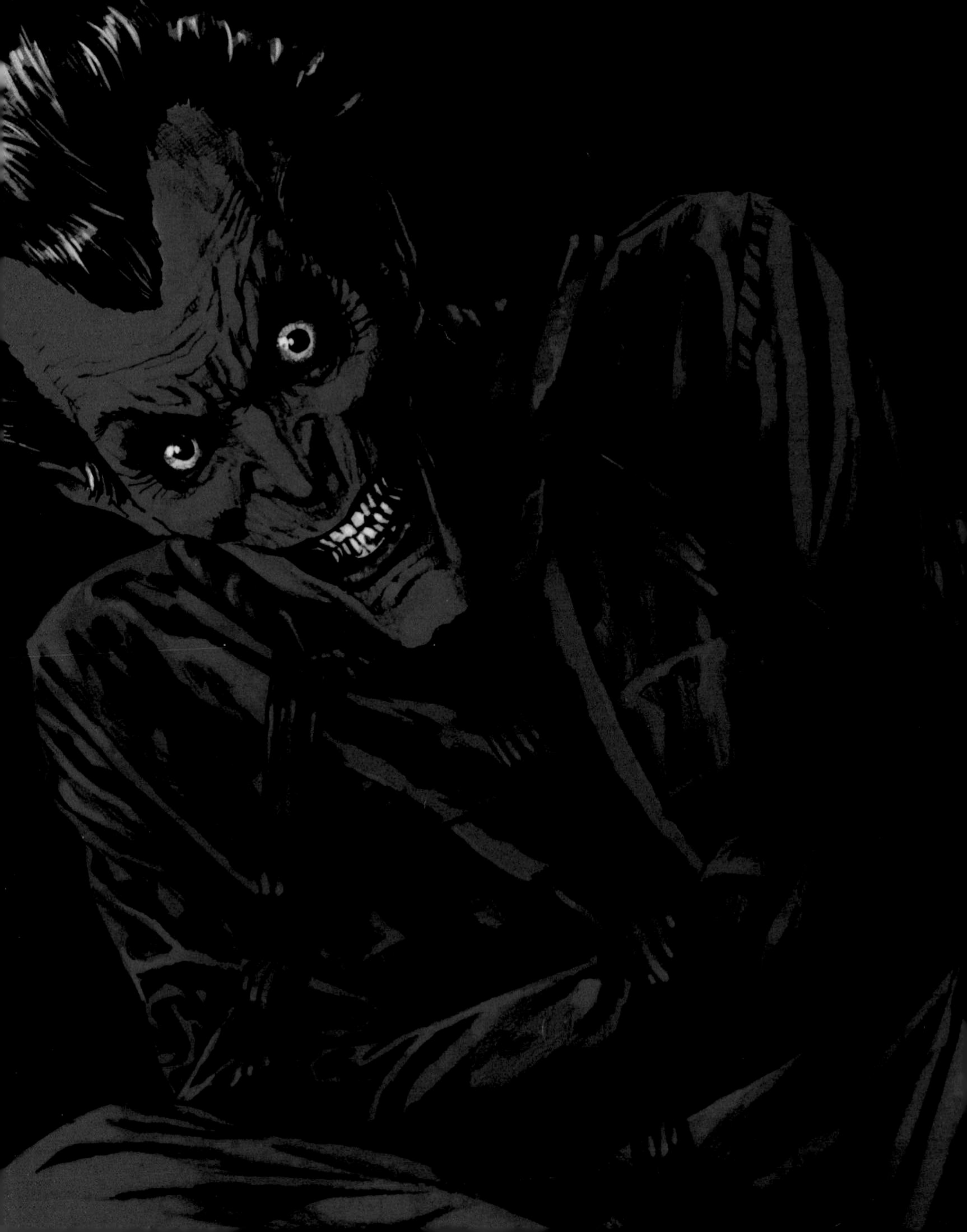

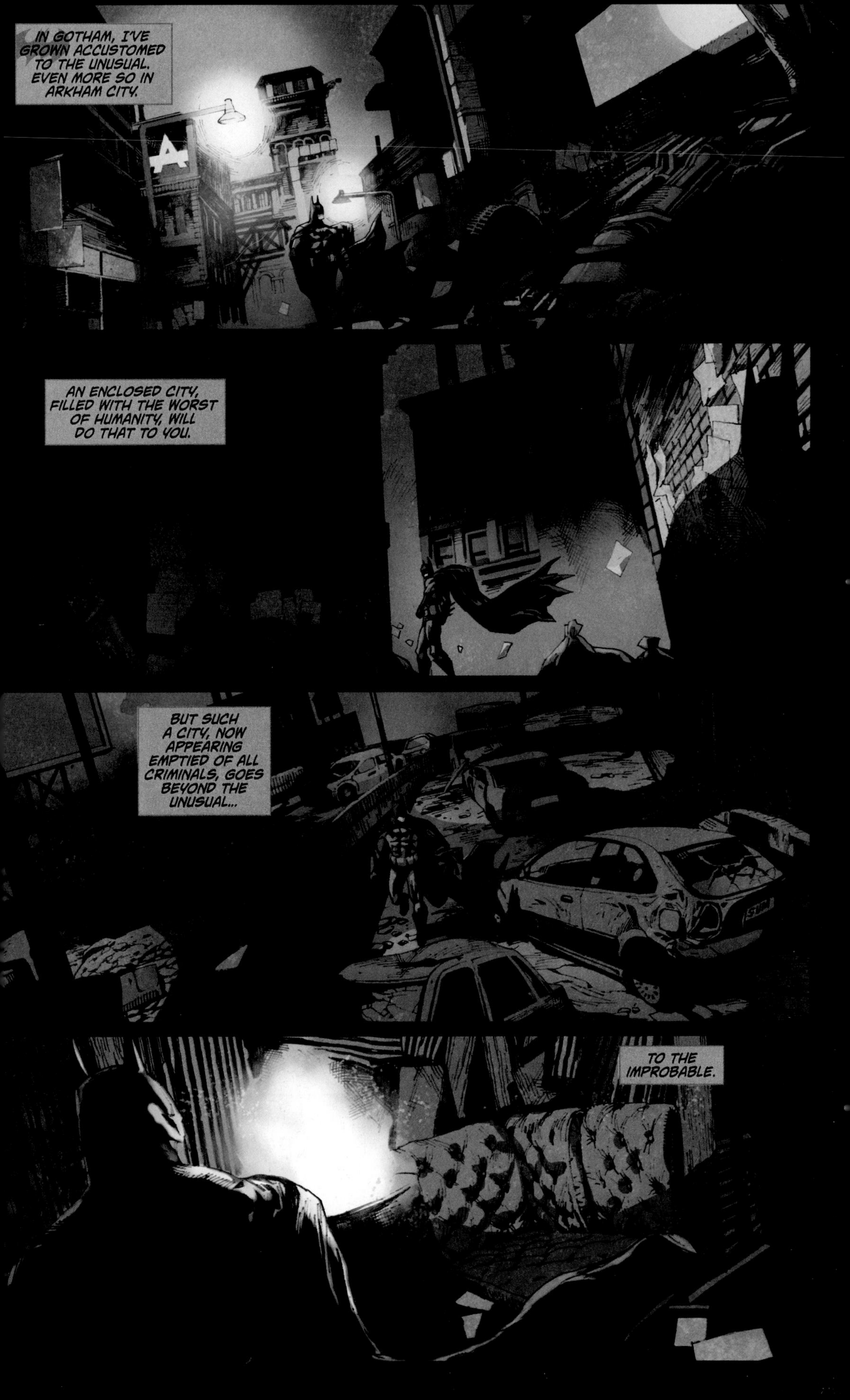
IN GOTHAM, I'VE GROWN ACCUSTOMED TO THE UNUSUAL. EVEN MORE SO IN ARKHAM CITY.
AN ENCLOSED CITY, FILLED WITH THE WORST OF HUMANITY, WILL DO THAT TO YOU.
BUT SUCH A CITY, NOW APPEARING EMPTIED OF ALL CRIMINALS, GOES BEYOND THE UNUSUAL...
TO THE IMPROBABLE.

THE SEQUENCER ISN'T PICKING UP ANYTHING. NO INMATE CHATTER ON ANY OF THE FREQUENCIES.

WHUPP

WHUPP

WHUPP

TYGER AIR SUPPORT HAVE INCREASED THEIR PATROLS.

NO DOUBT THEY'RE ALSO CONCERNED AT THE LACK OF ACTIVITY.

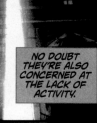

BUT THAT'S ABOUT TO CHANGE.

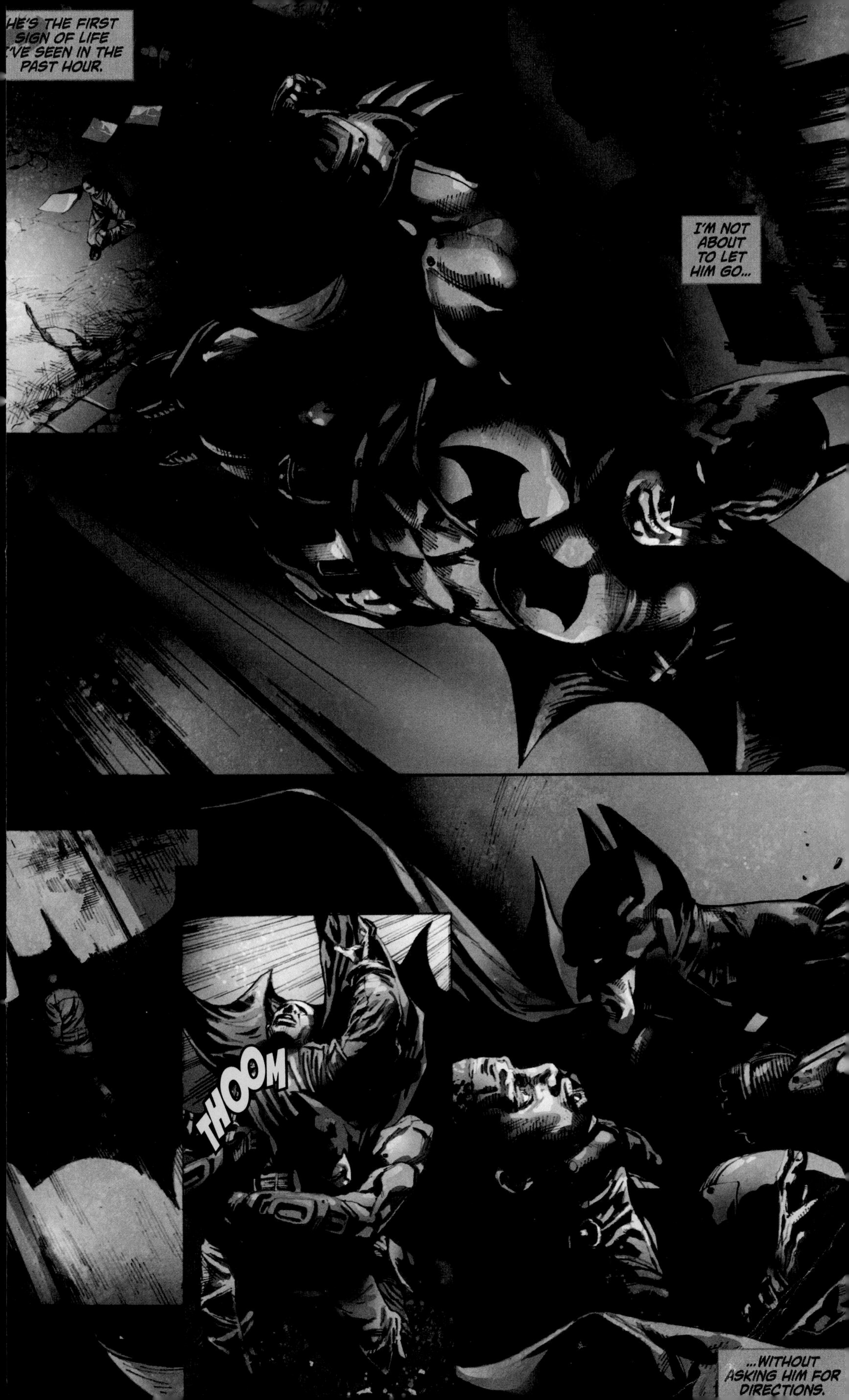
HE'S THE FIRST SIGN OF LIFE I'VE SEEN IN THE PAST HOUR.
I'M NOT ABOUT TO LET HIM GO...
THOOM
...WITHOUT ASKING HIM FOR DIRECTIONS.

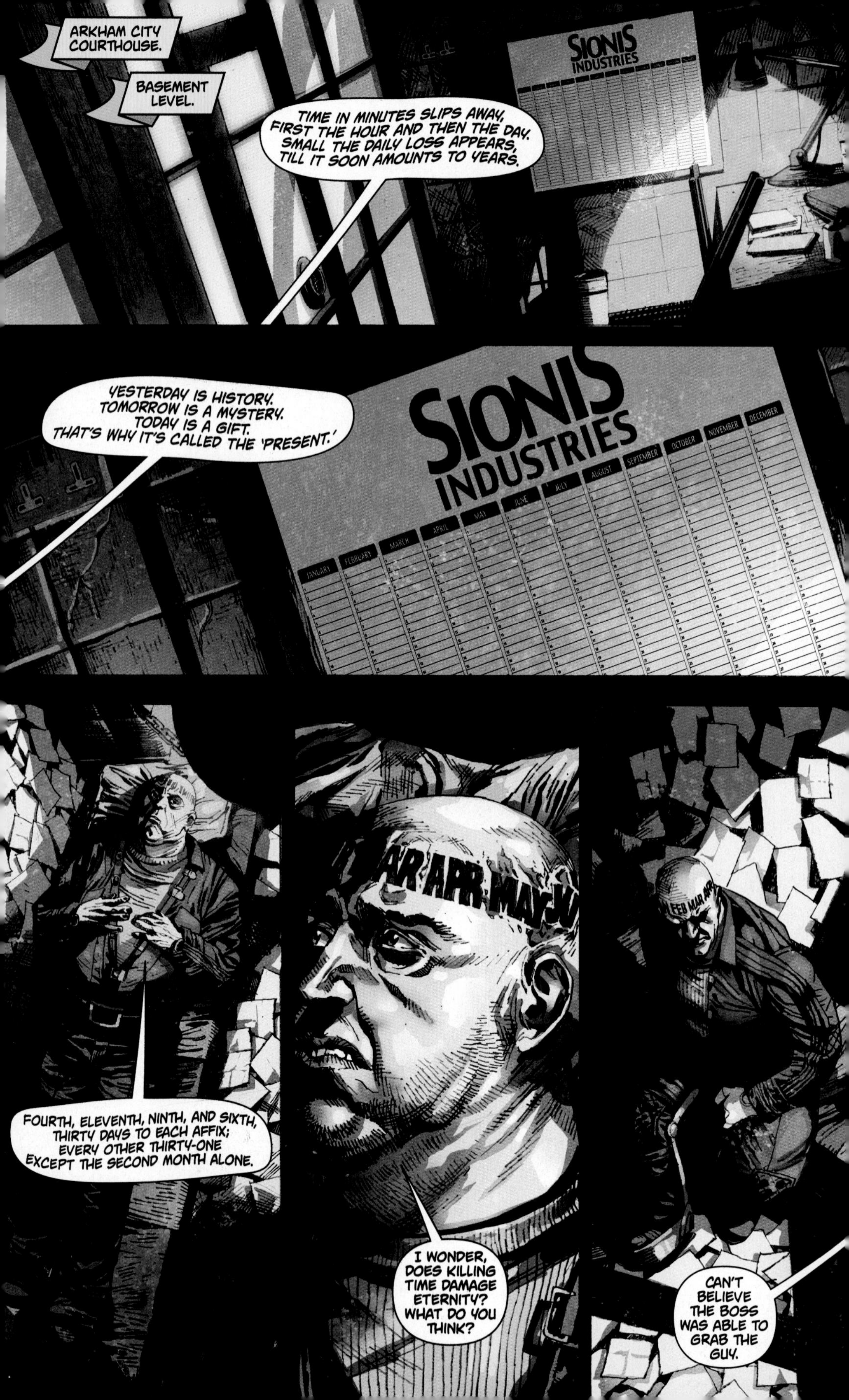
ARKHAM CITY COURTHOUSE.
BASEMENT LEVEL.
SIONIS INDUSTRIES
TIME IN MINUTES SLIPS AWAY, FIRST THE HOUR AND THEN THE DAY. SMALL THE DAILY LOSS APPEARS, TILL IT SOON AMOUNTS TO YEARS.
YESTERDAY IS HISTORY. TOMORROW IS A MYSTERY. TODAY IS A GIFT. THAT'S WHY IT'S CALLED THE 'PRESENT.'
SIONIS INDUSTRIES
JANUARY FEBRUARY MARCH APRIL MAY JUNE JULY AUGUST SEPTEMBER OCTOBER NOVEMBER DECEMBER
FOURTH, ELEVENTH, NINTH, AND SIXTH, THIRTY DAYS TO EACH AFFIX; EVERY OTHER THIRTY-ONE EXCEPT THE SECOND MONTH ALONE.
I WONDER, DOES KILLING TIME DAMAGE ETERNITY? WHAT DO YOU THINK?
CAN'T BELIEVE THE BOSS WAS ABLE TO GRAB THE GUY.

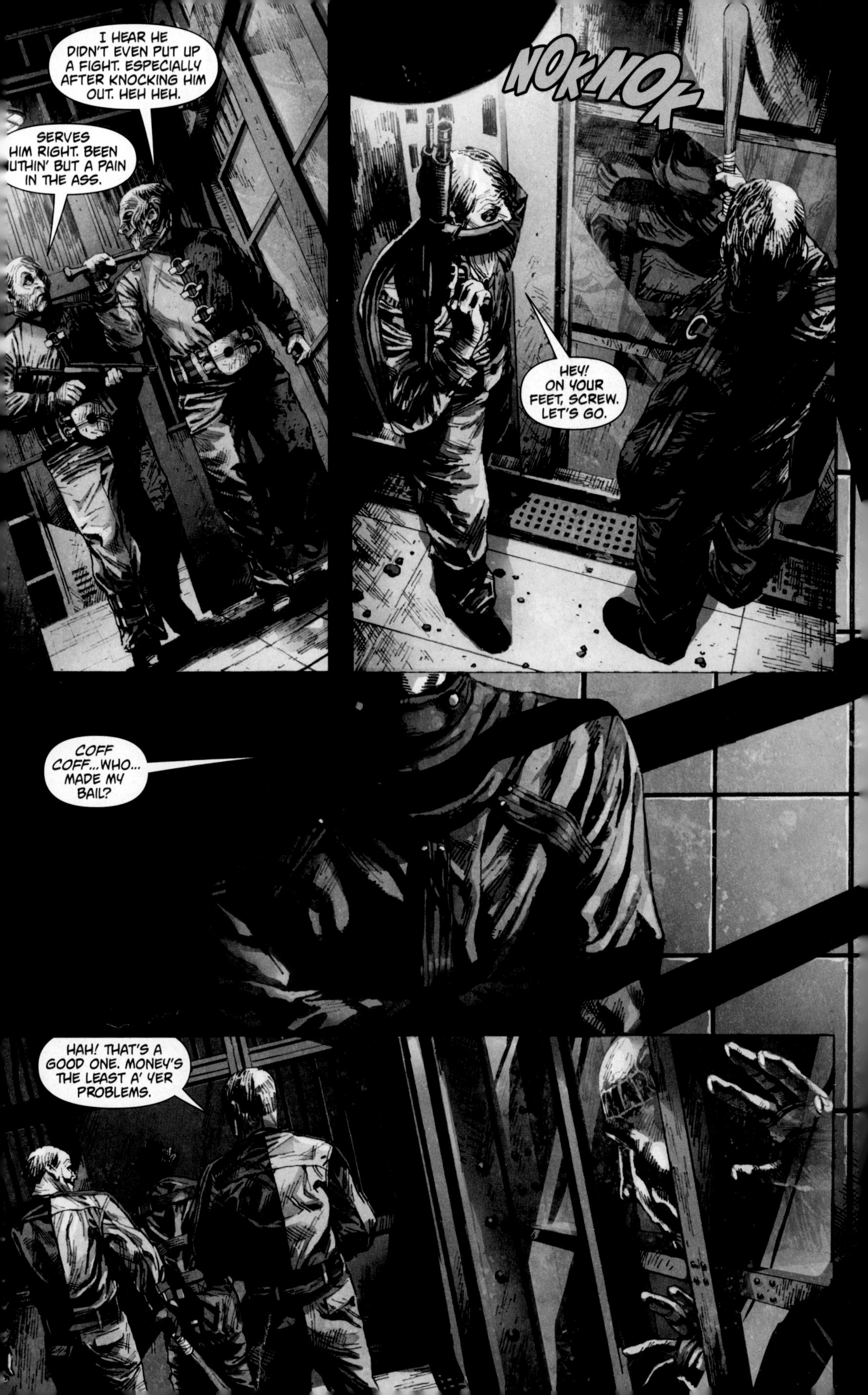
I HEAR HE DIDN'T EVEN PUT UP A FIGHT. ESPECIALLY AFTER KNOCKING HIM OUT. HEH HEH.
SERVES HIM RIGHT. BEEN NUTHIN' BUT A PAIN IN THE ASS.
NOKNOK
HEY! ON YOUR FEET, SCREW. LET'S GO.
COFF COFF...WHO... MADE MY BAIL?
HAH! THAT'S A GOOD ONE. MONEY'S THE LEAST A' YER PROBLEMS.

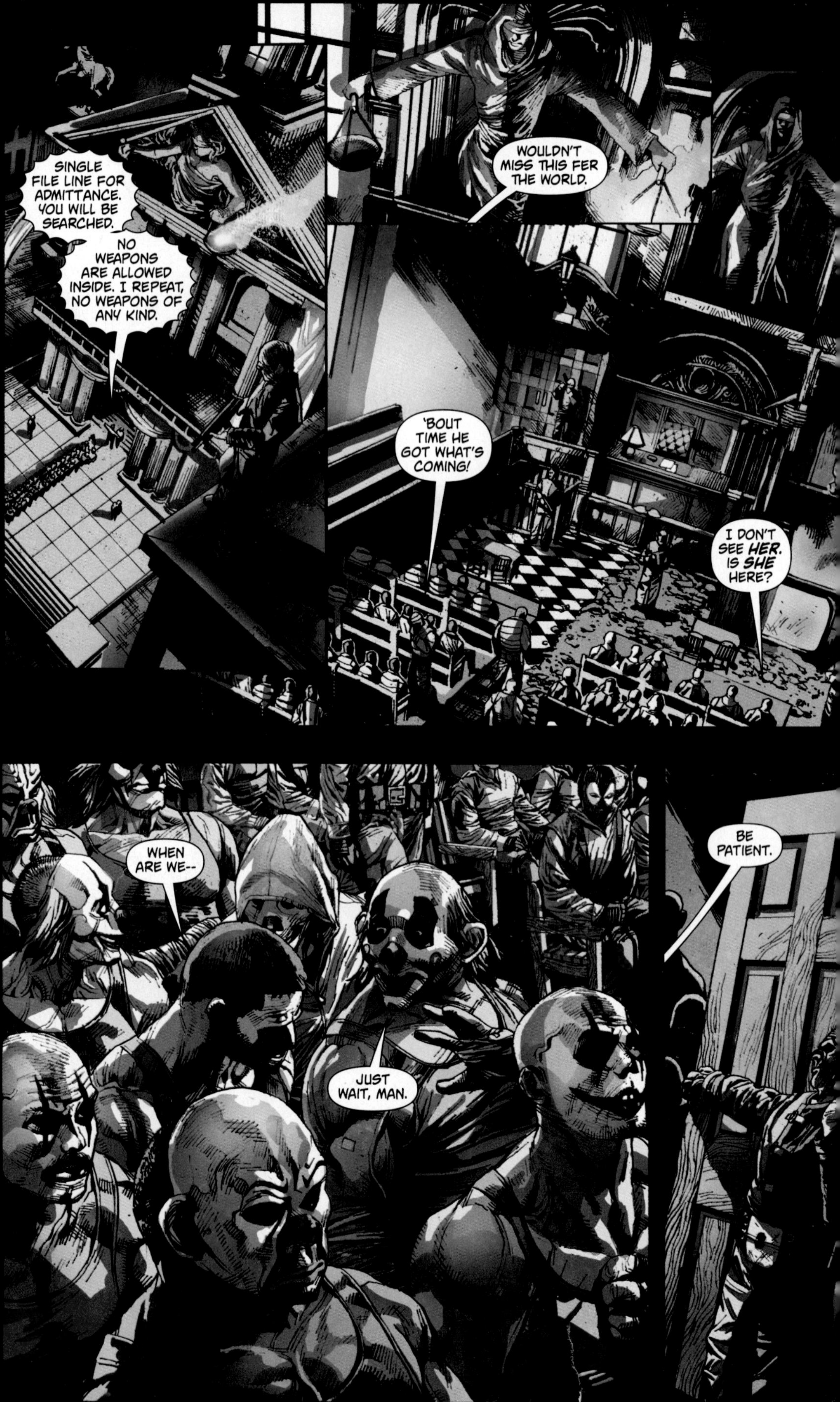
SINGLE FILE LINE FOR ADMITTANCE. YOU WILL BE SEARCHED.
NO WEAPONS ARE ALLOWED INSIDE. I REPEAT, NO WEAPONS OF ANY KIND.
WOULDN'T MISS THIS FER THE WORLD.
'BOUT TIME HE GOT WHAT'S COMING!
I DON'T SEE HER. IS SHE HERE?
WHEN ARE WE--
JUST WAIT, MAN.
BE PATIENT.

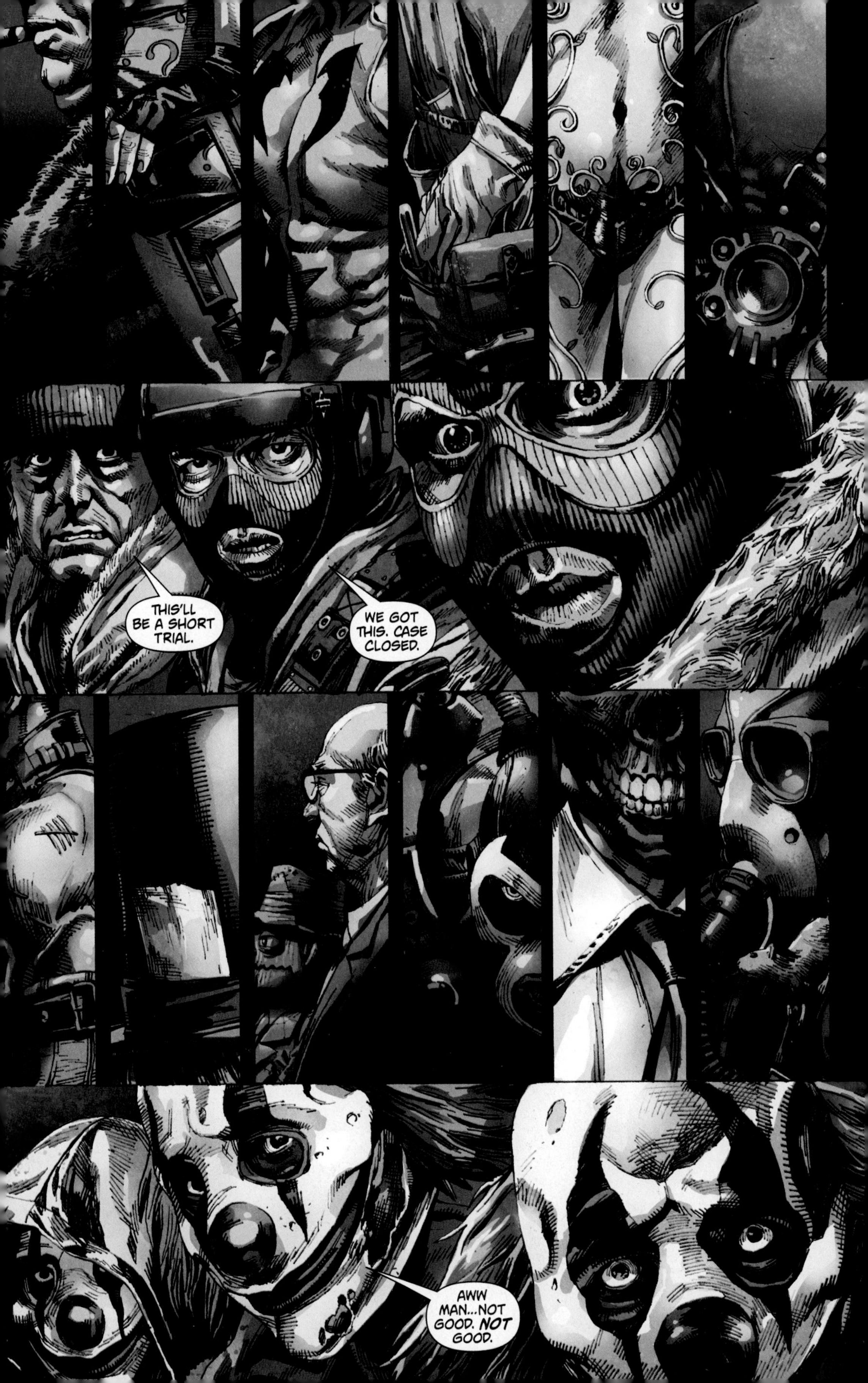
THIS'LL BE A SHORT TRIAL.
WE GOT THIS. CASE CLOSED.
AWW MAN...NOT GOOD. NOT GOOD.

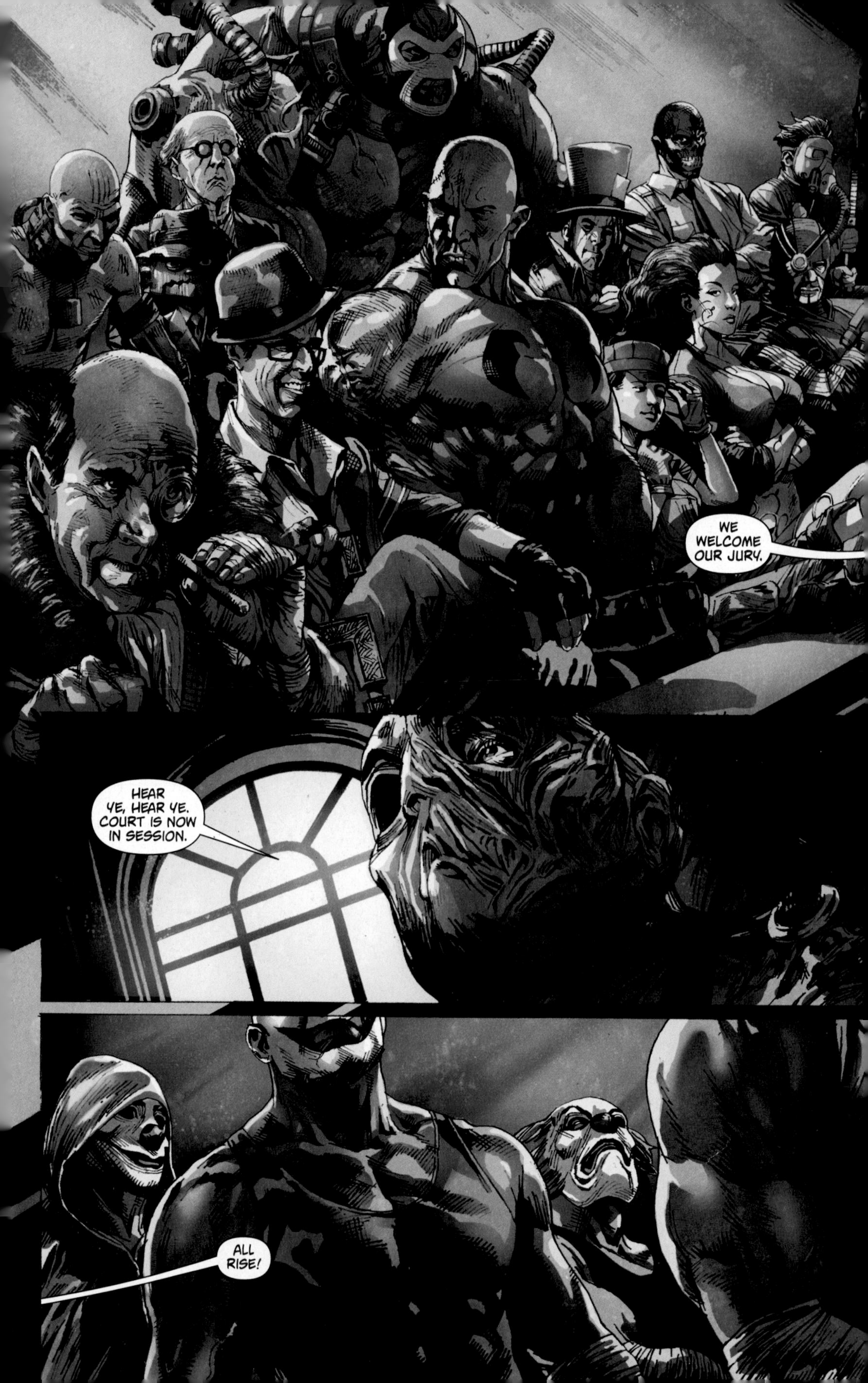
WE WELCOME OUR JURY.
HEAR YE, HEAR YE. COURT IS NOW IN SESSION.
ALL RISE!

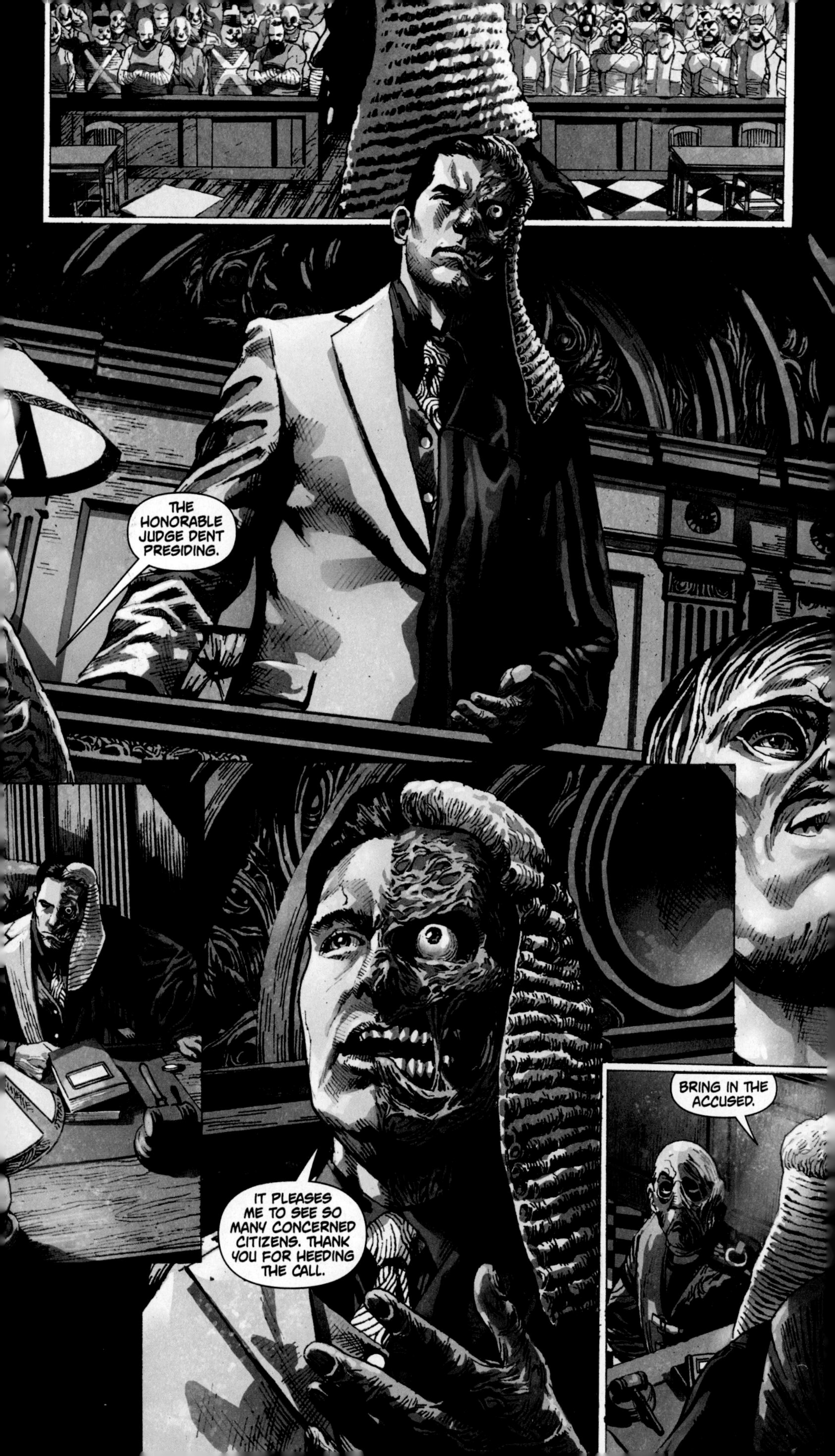
THE HONORABLE JUDGE DENT PRESIDING.
IT PLEASES ME TO SEE SO MANY CONCERNED CITIZENS. THANK YOU FOR HEEDING THE CALL.
BRING IN THE ACCUSED.

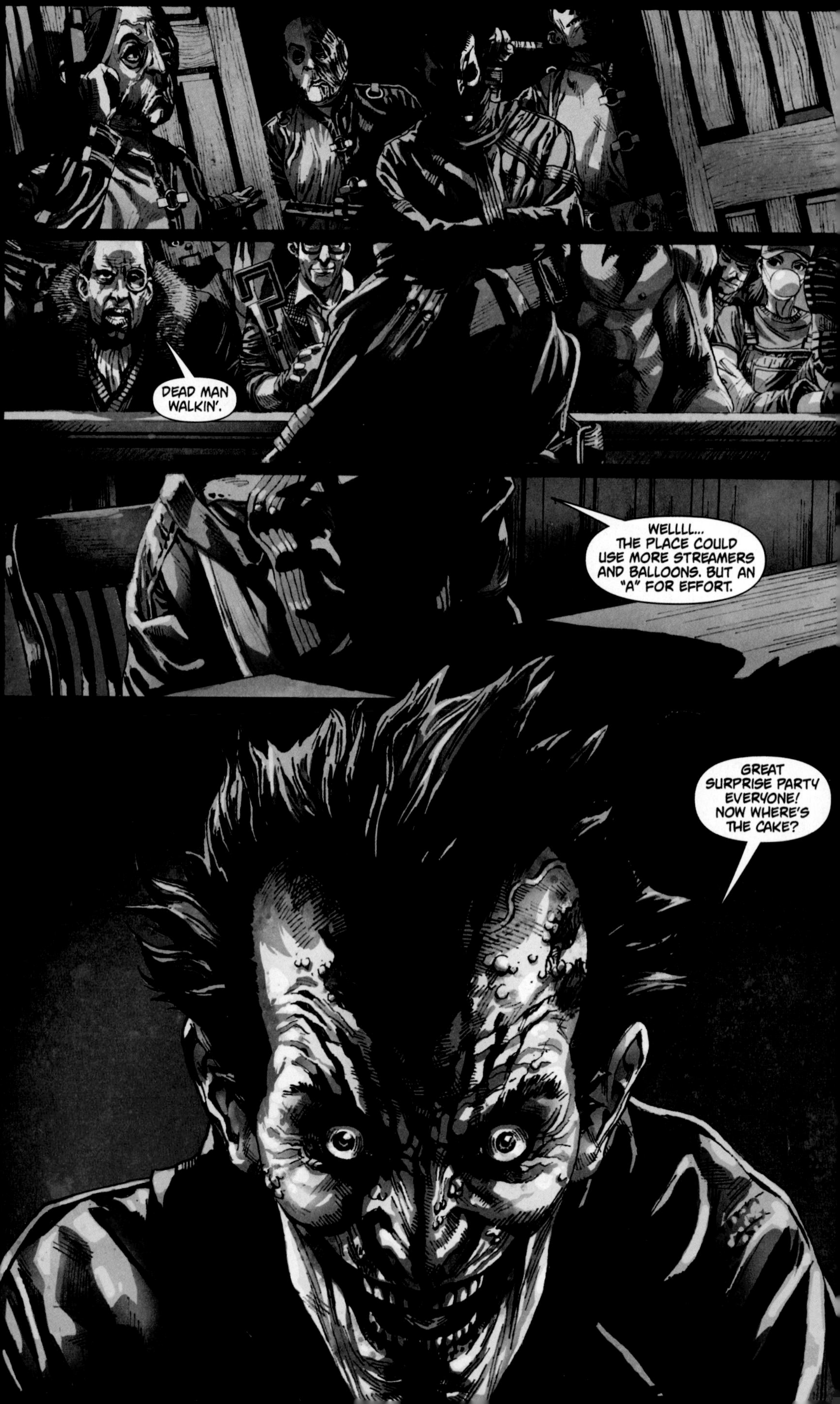
DEAD MAN WALKIN'.
WELLLL... THE PLACE COULD USE MORE STREAMERS AND BALLOONS. BUT AN "A" FOR EFFORT.
GREAT SURPRISE PARTY EVERYONE! NOW WHERE'S THE CAKE?

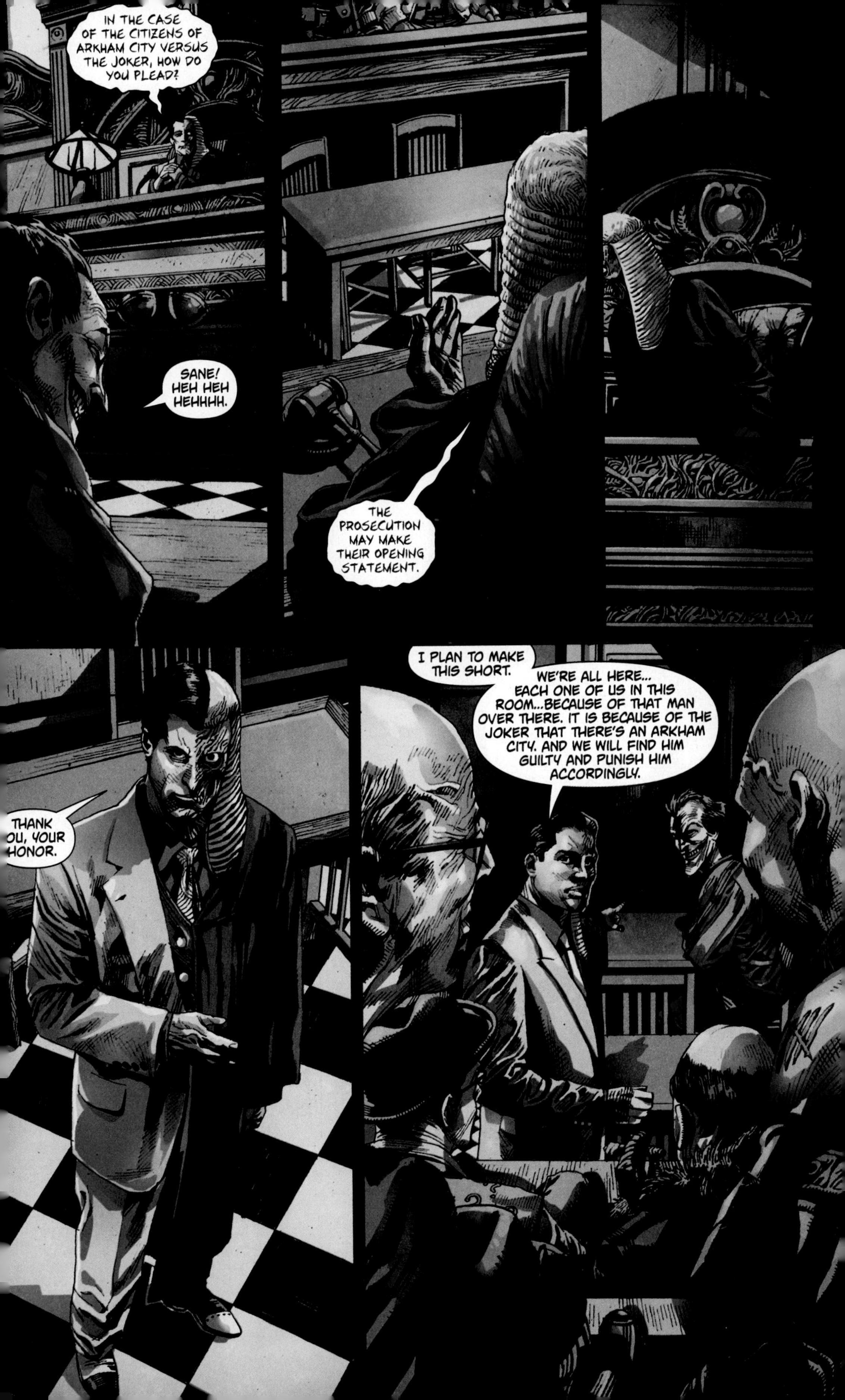
IN THE CASE OF THE CITIZENS OF ARKHAM CITY VERSUS THE JOKER, HOW DO YOU PLEAD?
SANE! HEH HEH HEHHHH.
THE PROSECUTION MAY MAKE THEIR OPENING STATEMENT.
THANK OU, YOUR HONOR.
I PLAN TO MAKE THIS SHORT.
WE'RE ALL HERE... EACH ONE OF US IN THIS ROOM...BECAUSE OF THAT MAN OVER THERE. IT IS BECAUSE OF THE JOKER THAT THERE'S AN ARKHAM CITY. AND WE WILL FIND HIM GUILTY AND PUNISH HIM ACCORDINGLY.

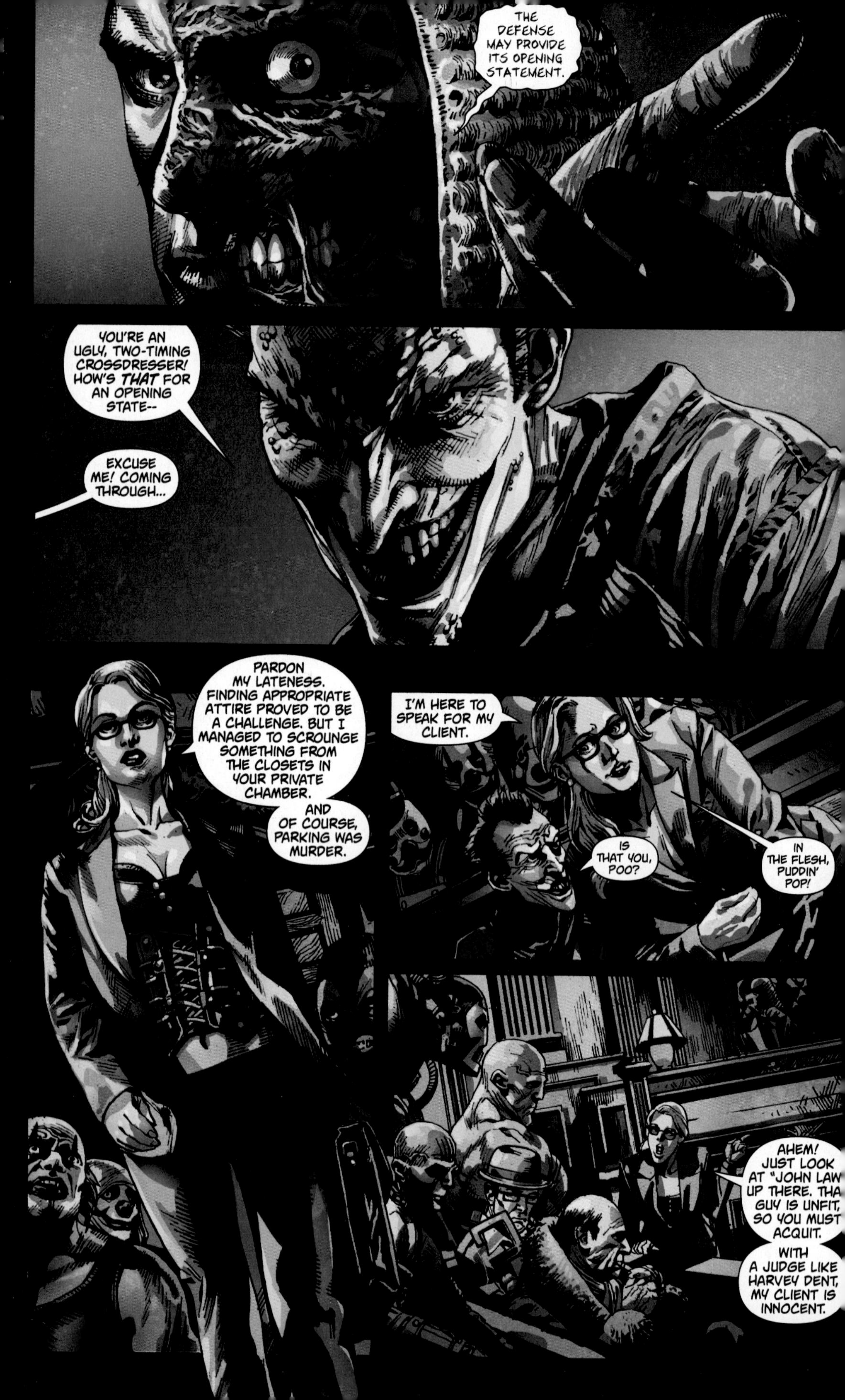
THE DEFENSE MAY PROVIDE ITS OPENING STATEMENT.
YOU'RE AN UGLY, TWO-TIMING CROSSDRESSER! HOW'S *THAT* FOR AN OPENING STATE--
EXCUSE ME! COMING THROUGH...
PARDON MY LATENESS. FINDING APPROPRIATE ATTIRE PROVED TO BE A CHALLENGE. BUT I MANAGED TO SCROUNGE SOMETHING FROM THE CLOSETS IN YOUR PRIVATE CHAMBER.
AND OF COURSE, PARKING WAS MURDER.
I'M HERE TO SPEAK FOR MY CLIENT.
IS THAT YOU, POO?
IN THE FLESH, PUDDIN' POP!
AHEM! JUST LOOK AT "JOHN LAW UP THERE. THA GUY IS UNFIT, SO YOU MUST ACQUIT.
WITH A JUDGE LIKE HARVEY DENT, MY CLIENT IS INNOCENT.

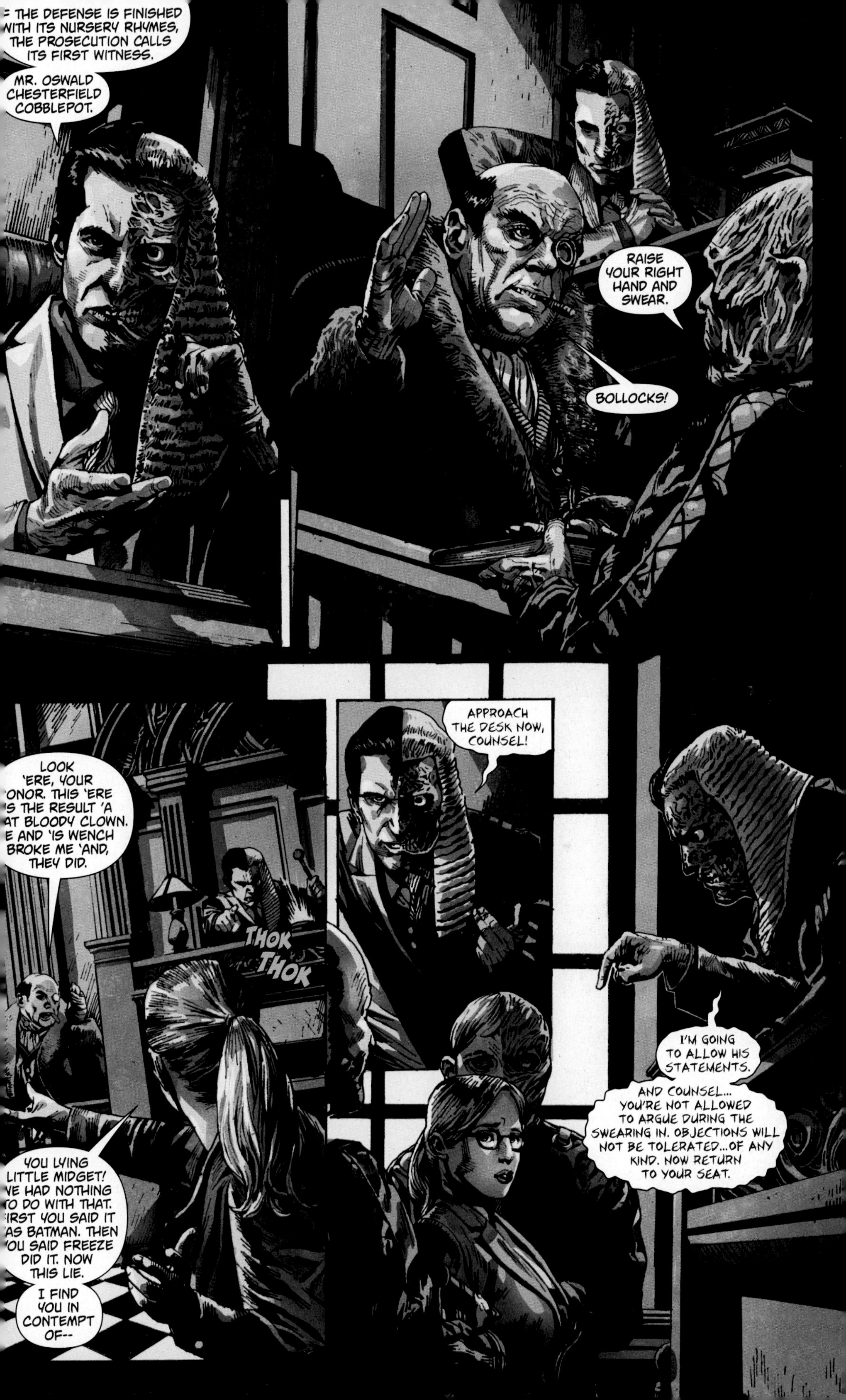

= THE DEFENSE IS FINISHED WITH ITS NURSERY RHYMES, THE PROSECUTION CALLS ITS FIRST WITNESS.
MR. OSWALD CHESTERFIELD COBBLEPOT.
RAISE YOUR RIGHT HAND AND SWEAR.
BOLLOCKS!
LOOK 'ERE, YOUR 'ONOR. THIS 'ERE 'S THE RESULT 'A AT BLOODY CLOWN. E AND 'IS WENCH BROKE ME 'AND, THEY DID.
YOU LYING LITTLE MIDGET! VE HAD NOTHING TO DO WITH THAT. IRST YOU SAID IT AS BATMAN. THEN OU SAID FREEZE DID IT. NOW THIS LIE.
I FIND YOU IN CONTEMPT OF--
THOK
THOK
APPROACH THE DESK NOW, COUNSEL!
I'M GOING TO ALLOW HIS STATEMENTS.
AND COUNSEL... YOU'RE NOT ALLOWED TO ARGUE DURING THE SWEARING IN. OBJECTIONS WILL NOT BE TOLERATED...OF ANY KIND. NOW RETURN TO YOUR SEAT.

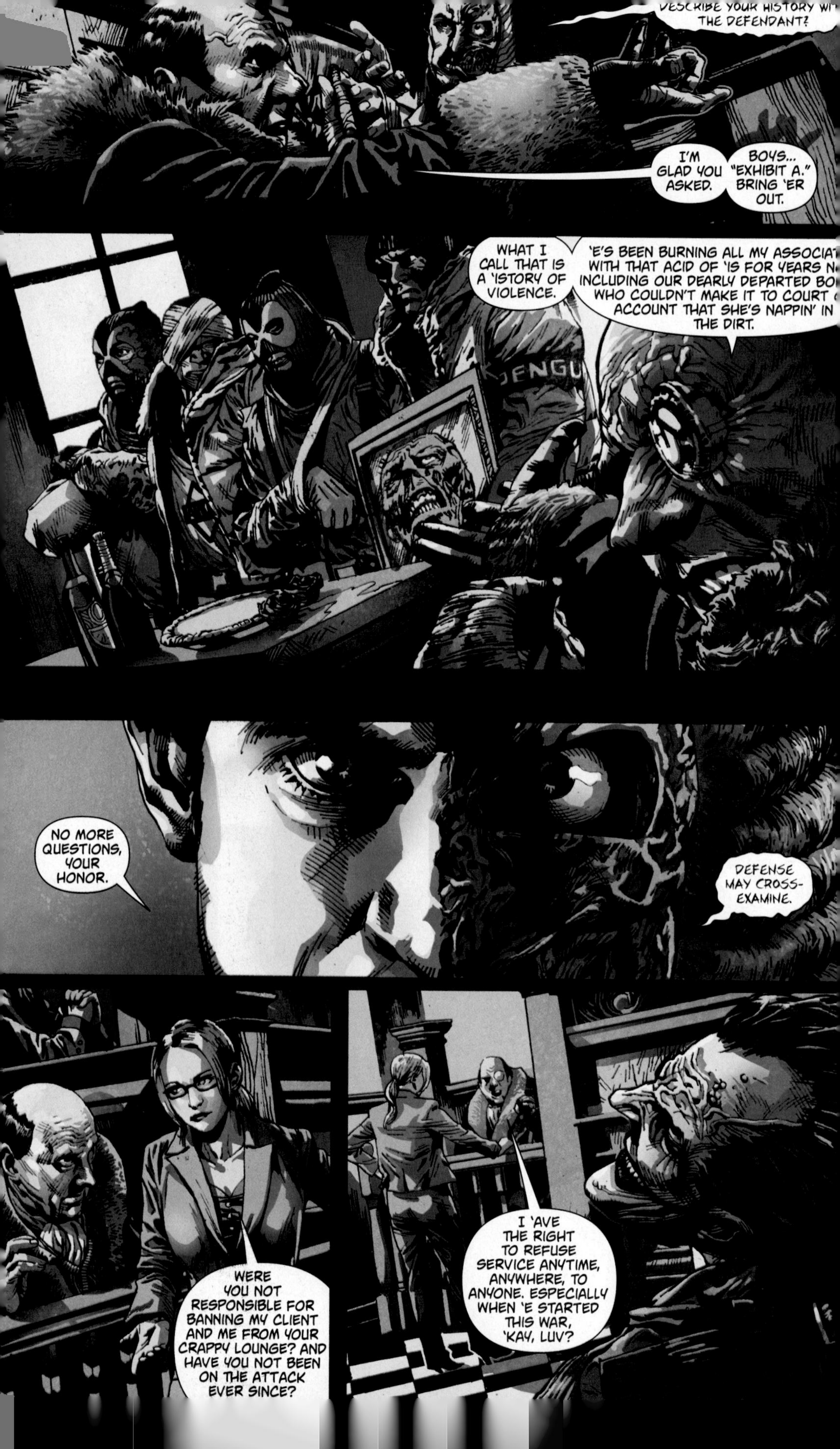
DESCRIBE YOUR HISTORY WI THE DEFENDANT?
I'M GLAD YOU ASKED.
BOYS... "EXHIBIT A." BRING 'ER OUT.
WHAT I CALL THAT IS A 'ISTORY OF VIOLENCE.
'E'S BEEN BURNING ALL MY ASSOCIAT WITH THAT ACID OF 'IS FOR YEARS N INCLUDING OUR DEARLY DEPARTED BO WHO COULDN'T MAKE IT TO COURT ACCOUNT THAT SHE'S NAPPIN' IN THE DIRT.
NO MORE QUESTIONS, YOUR HONOR.
DEFENSE MAY CROSS-EXAMINE.
WERE YOU NOT RESPONSIBLE FOR BANNING MY CLIENT AND ME FROM YOUR CRAPPY LOUNGE? AND HAVE YOU NOT BEEN ON THE ATTACK EVER SINCE?
I 'AVE THE RIGHT TO REFUSE SERVICE ANYTIME, ANYWHERE, TO ANYONE. ESPECIALLY WHEN 'E STARTED THIS WAR, 'KAY, LUV?

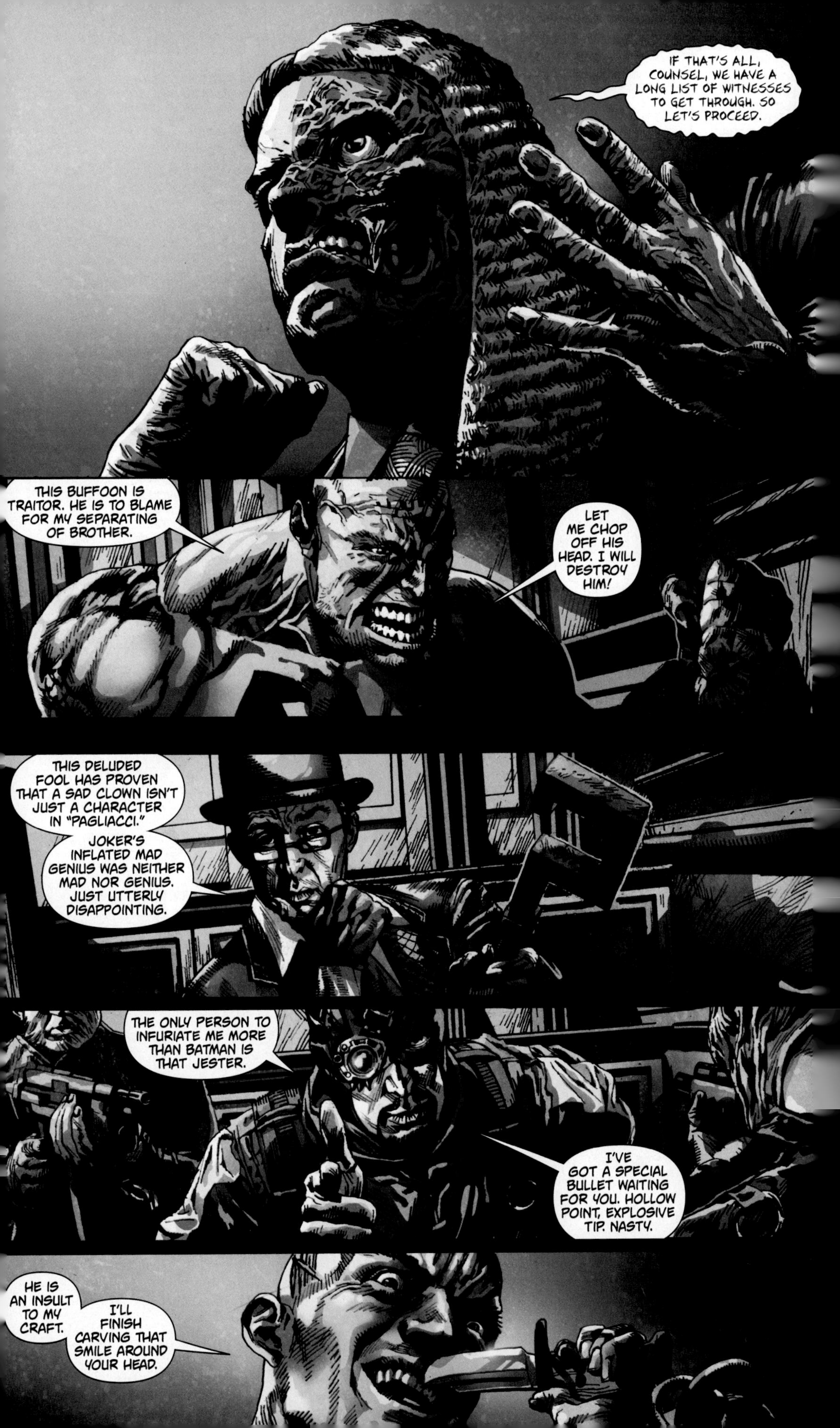
IF THAT'S ALL, COUNSEL, WE HAVE A LONG LIST OF WITNESSES TO GET THROUGH. SO LET'S PROCEED.
THIS BUFFOON IS TRAITOR. HE IS TO BLAME FOR MY SEPARATING OF BROTHER.
LET ME CHOP OFF HIS HEAD. I WILL DESTROY HIM!
THIS DELUDED FOOL HAS PROVEN THAT A SAD CLOWN ISN'T JUST A CHARACTER IN "PAGLIACCI."
JOKER'S INFLATED MAD GENIUS WAS NEITHER MAD NOR GENIUS. JUST UTTERLY DISAPPOINTING.
THE ONLY PERSON TO INFURIATE ME MORE THAN BATMAN IS THAT JESTER.
I'VE GOT A SPECIAL BULLET WAITING FOR YOU. HOLLOW POINT, EXPLOSIVE TIP. NASTY.
HE IS AN INSULT TO MY CRAFT.
I'LL FINISH CARVING THAT SMILE AROUND YOUR HEAD.

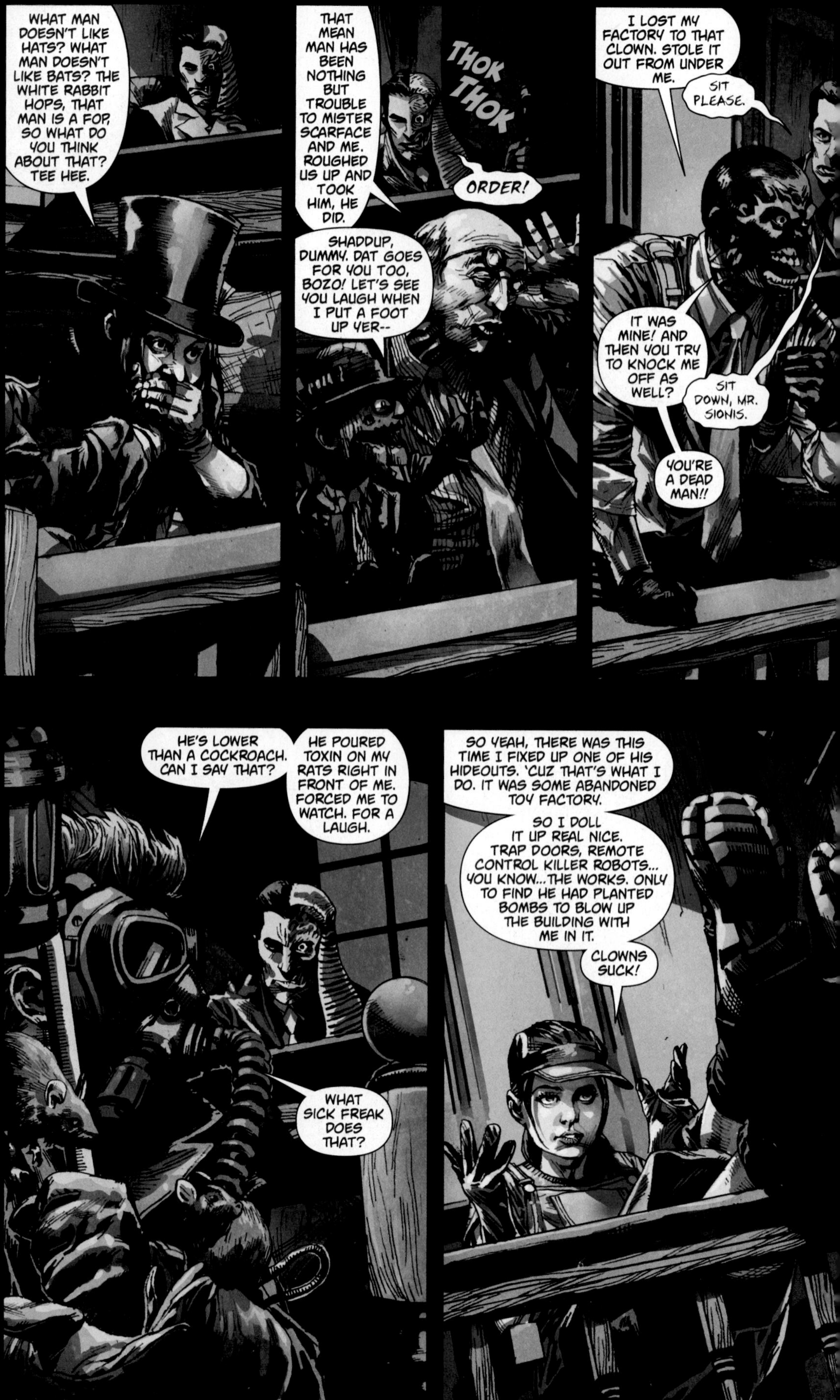
WHAT MAN DOESN'T LIKE HATS? WHAT MAN DOESN'T LIKE BATS? THE WHITE RABBIT HOPS, THAT MAN IS A FOP, SO WHAT DO YOU THINK ABOUT THAT? TEE HEE.
THAT MEAN MAN HAS BEEN NOTHING BUT TROUBLE TO MISTER SCARFACE AND ME. ROUGHED US UP AND TOOK HIM, HE DID.
THOK THOK
ORDER!
SHADDUP, DUMMY. DAT GOES FOR YOU TOO, BOZO! LET'S SEE YOU LAUGH WHEN I PUT A FOOT UP YER--
I LOST MY FACTORY TO THAT CLOWN. STOLE IT OUT FROM UNDER ME.
SIT PLEASE.
IT WAS MINE! AND THEN YOU TRY TO KNOCK ME OFF AS WELL?
SIT DOWN, MR. SIONIS.
YOU'RE A DEAD MAN!!
HE'S LOWER THAN A COCKROACH. CAN I SAY THAT?
HE POURED TOXIN ON MY RATS RIGHT IN FRONT OF ME. FORCED ME TO WATCH. FOR A LAUGH.
WHAT SICK FREAK DOES THAT?
SO YEAH, THERE WAS THIS TIME I FIXED UP ONE OF HIS HIDEOUTS. 'CUZ THAT'S WHAT I DO. IT WAS SOME ABANDONED TOY FACTORY.
SO I DOLL IT UP REAL NICE. TRAP DOORS, REMOTE CONTROL KILLER ROBOTS... YOU KNOW...THE WORKS. ONLY TO FIND HE HAD PLANTED BOMBS TO BLOW UP THE BUILDING WITH ME IN IT.
CLOWNS SUCK!

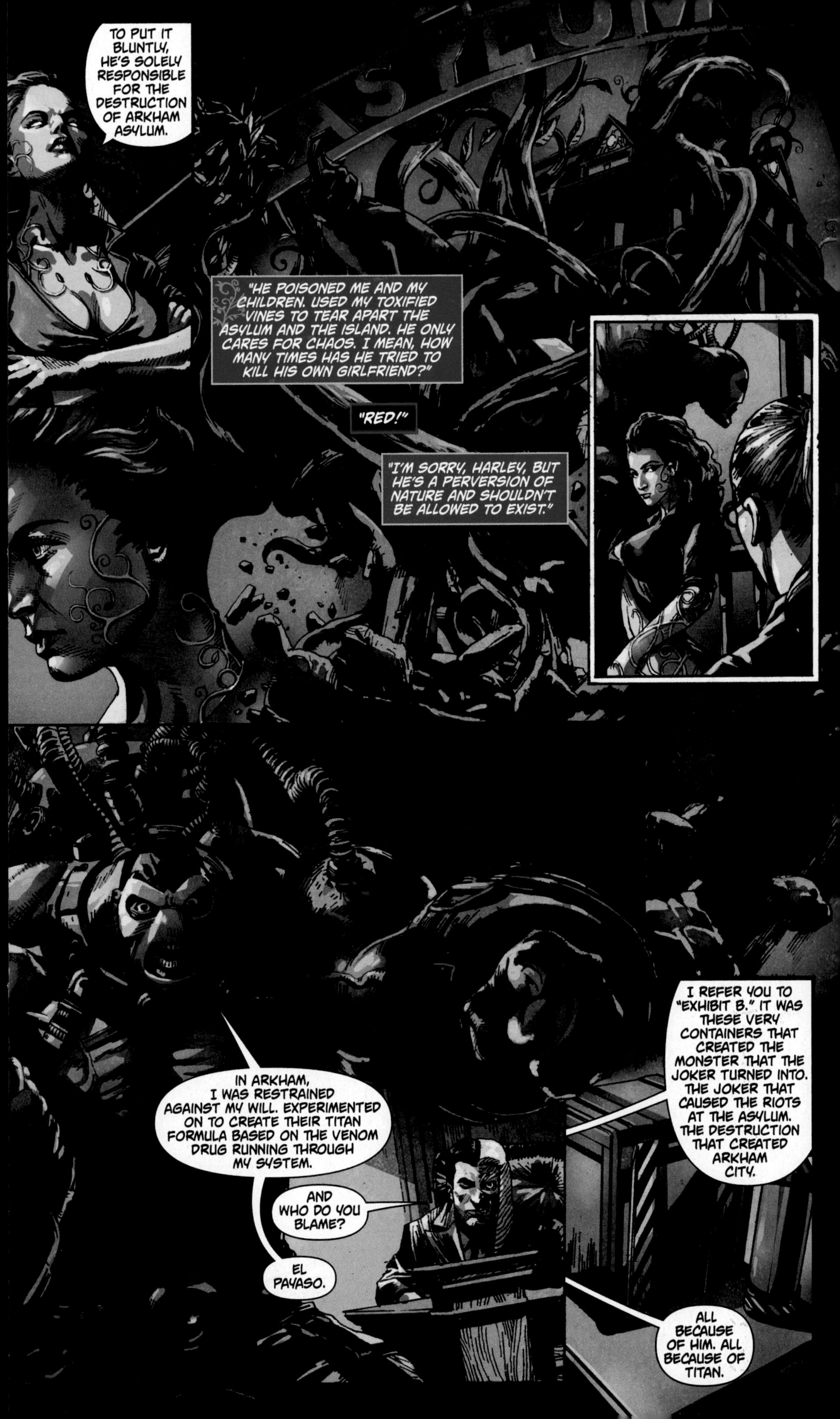
TO PUT IT BLUNTLY, HE'S SOLELY RESPONSIBLE FOR THE DESTRUCTION OF ARKHAM ASYLUM.
"HE POISONED ME AND MY CHILDREN. USED MY TOXIFIED VINES TO TEAR APART THE ASYLUM AND THE ISLAND. HE ONLY CARES FOR CHAOS. I MEAN, HOW MANY TIMES HAS HE TRIED TO KILL HIS OWN GIRLFRIEND?"
"RED!"
"I'M SORRY, HARLEY, BUT HE'S A PERVERSION OF NATURE AND SHOULDN'T BE ALLOWED TO EXIST."
IN ARKHAM, I WAS RESTRAINED AGAINST MY WILL. EXPERIMENTED ON TO CREATE THEIR TITAN FORMULA BASED ON THE VENOM DRUG RUNNING THROUGH MY SYSTEM.
AND WHO DO YOU BLAME?
EL PAYASO.
I REFER YOU TO "EXHIBIT B." IT WAS THESE VERY CONTAINERS THAT CREATED THE MONSTER THAT THE JOKER TURNED INTO. THE JOKER THAT CAUSED THE RIOTS AT THE ASYLUM. THE DESTRUCTION THAT CREATED ARKHAM CITY.
ALL BECAUSE OF HIM. ALL BECAUSE OF TITAN.

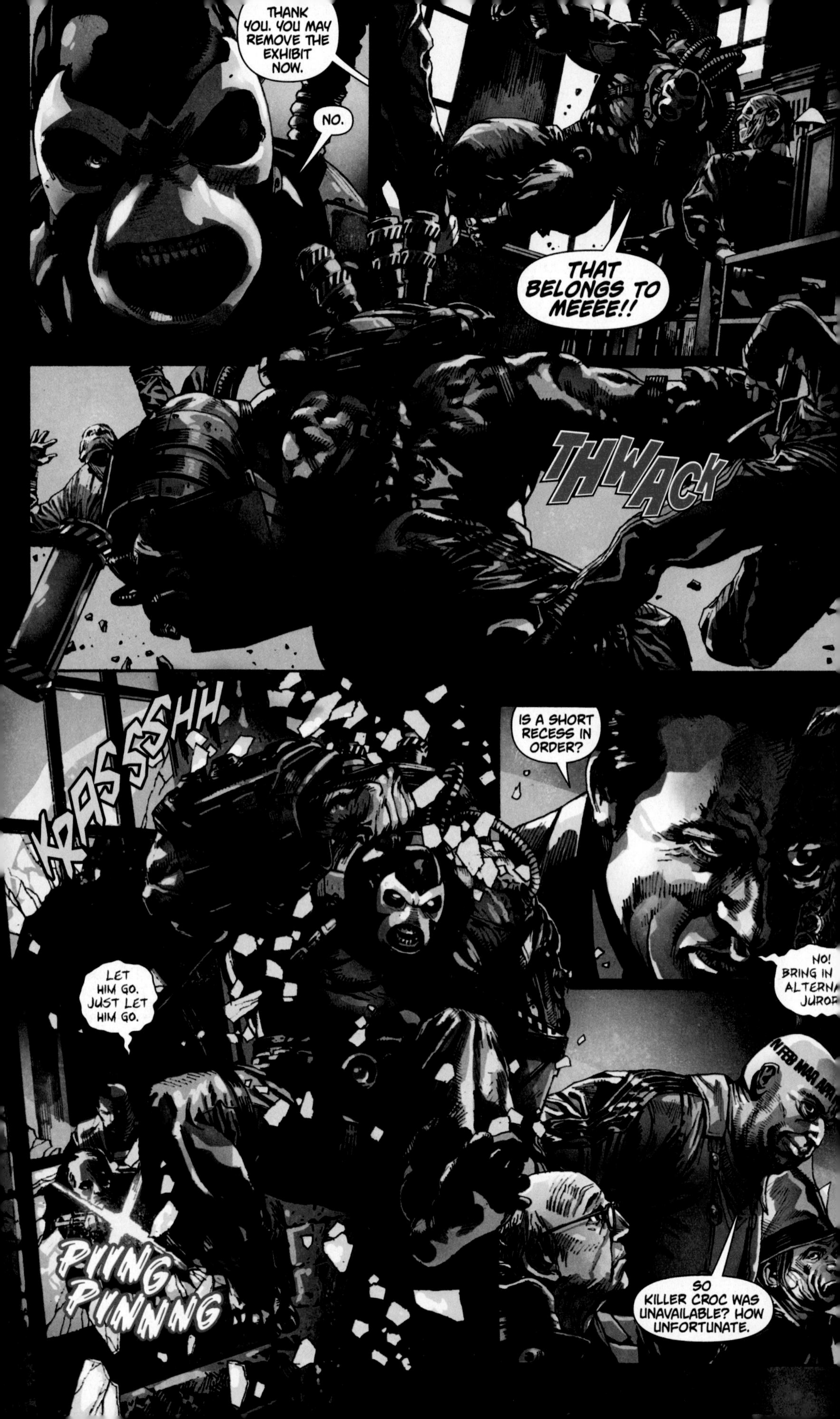
THANK YOU. YOU MAY REMOVE THE EXHIBIT NOW.
NO.
THAT BELONGS TO MEEEE!!
THWACK
KRASSSSHH
IS A SHORT RECESS IN ORDER?
NO! BRING IN ALTERN JUROR
LET HIM GO. JUST LET HIM GO.
PIING PINNNG
SO KILLER CROC WAS UNAVAILABLE? HOW UNFORTUNATE.

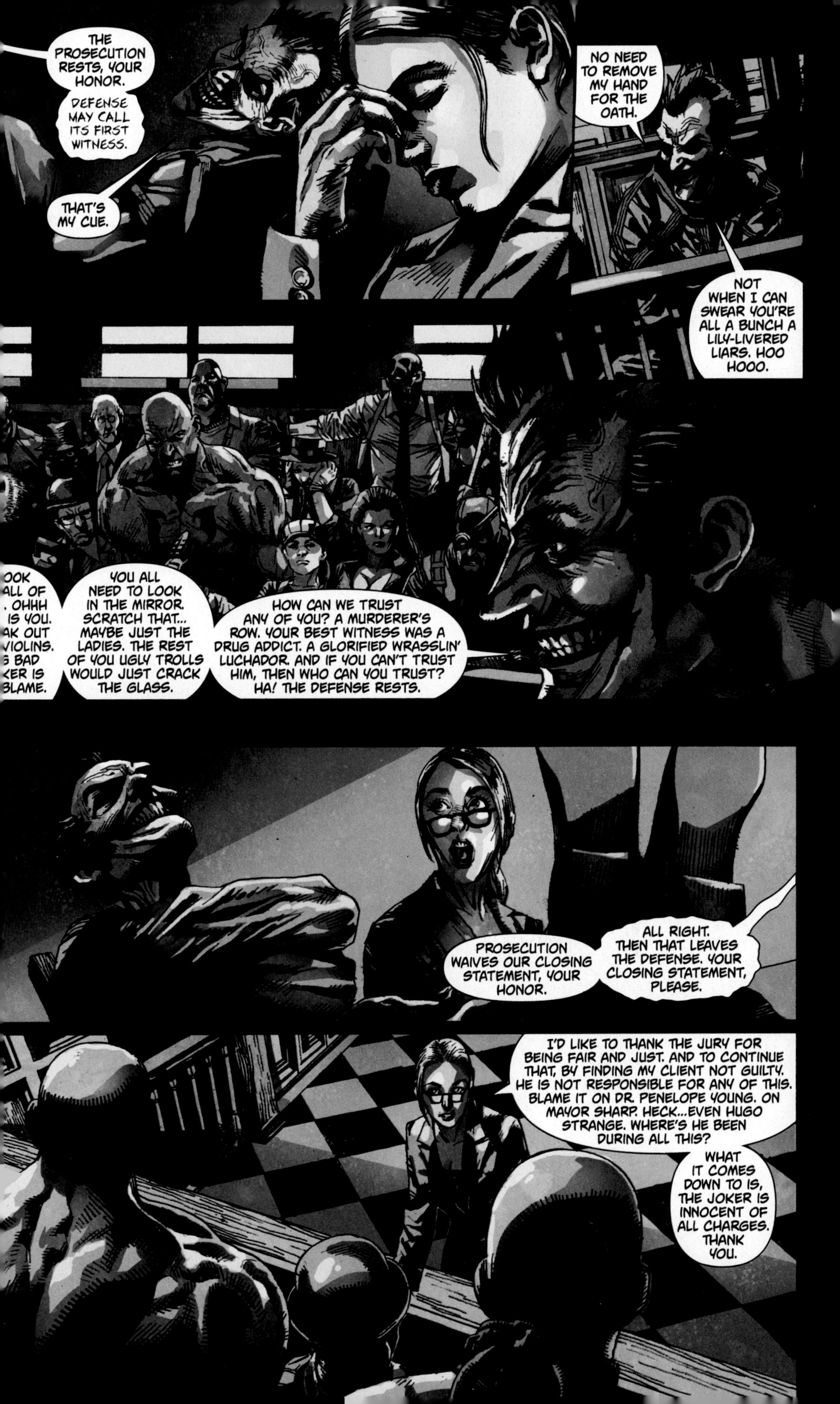
THE PROSECUTION RESTS, YOUR HONOR.
DEFENSE MAY CALL ITS FIRST WITNESS.
THAT'S MY CUE.
NO NEED TO REMOVE MY HAND FOR THE OATH.
NOT WHEN I CAN SWEAR YOU'RE ALL A BUNCH A LILY-LIVERED LIARS. HOO HOOO.
YOU ALL NEED TO LOOK IN THE MIRROR. SCRATCH THAT... MAYBE JUST THE LADIES. THE REST OF YOU UGLY TROLLS WOULD JUST CRACK THE GLASS.
HOW CAN WE TRUST ANY OF YOU? A MURDERER'S ROW. YOUR BEST WITNESS WAS A DRUG ADDICT. A GLORIFIED WRASSLIN' LUCHADOR. AND IF YOU CAN'T TRUST HIM, THEN WHO CAN YOU TRUST? HA! THE DEFENSE RESTS.
PROSECUTION WAIVES OUR CLOSING STATEMENT, YOUR HONOR.
ALL RIGHT. THEN THAT LEAVES THE DEFENSE. YOUR CLOSING STATEMENT, PLEASE.
I'D LIKE TO THANK THE JURY FOR BEING FAIR AND JUST. AND TO CONTINUE THAT, BY FINDING MY CLIENT NOT GUILTY. HE IS NOT RESPONSIBLE FOR ANY OF THIS. BLAME IT ON DR. PENELOPE YOUNG. ON MAYOR SHARP. HECK...EVEN HUGO STRANGE. WHERE'S HE BEEN DURING ALL THIS?
WHAT IT COMES DOWN TO IS, THE JOKER IS INNOCENT OF ALL CHARGES. THANK YOU.

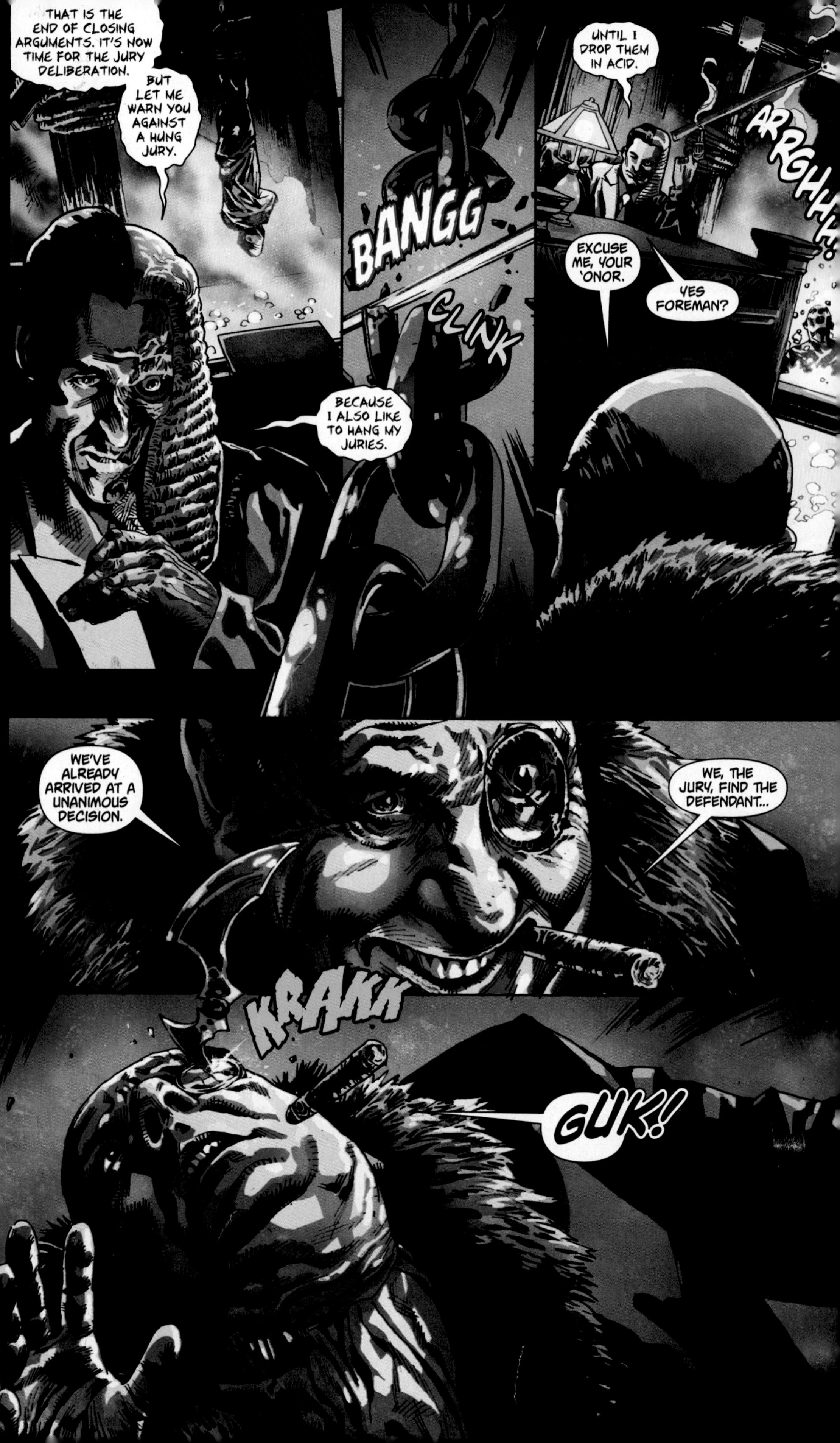
THAT IS THE END OF CLOSING ARGUMENTS. IT'S NOW TIME FOR THE JURY DELIBERATION.
BUT LET ME WARN YOU AGAINST A HUNG JURY.
BANGG
CLINK
BECAUSE I ALSO LIKE TO HANG MY JURIES.
UNTIL I DROP THEM IN ACID.
ARRGHHH!
EXCUSE ME, YOUR 'ONOR.
YES FOREMAN?
WE'VE ALREADY ARRIVED AT A UNANIMOUS DECISION.
WE, THE JURY, FIND THE DEFENDANT...
KRAKK
GUK!

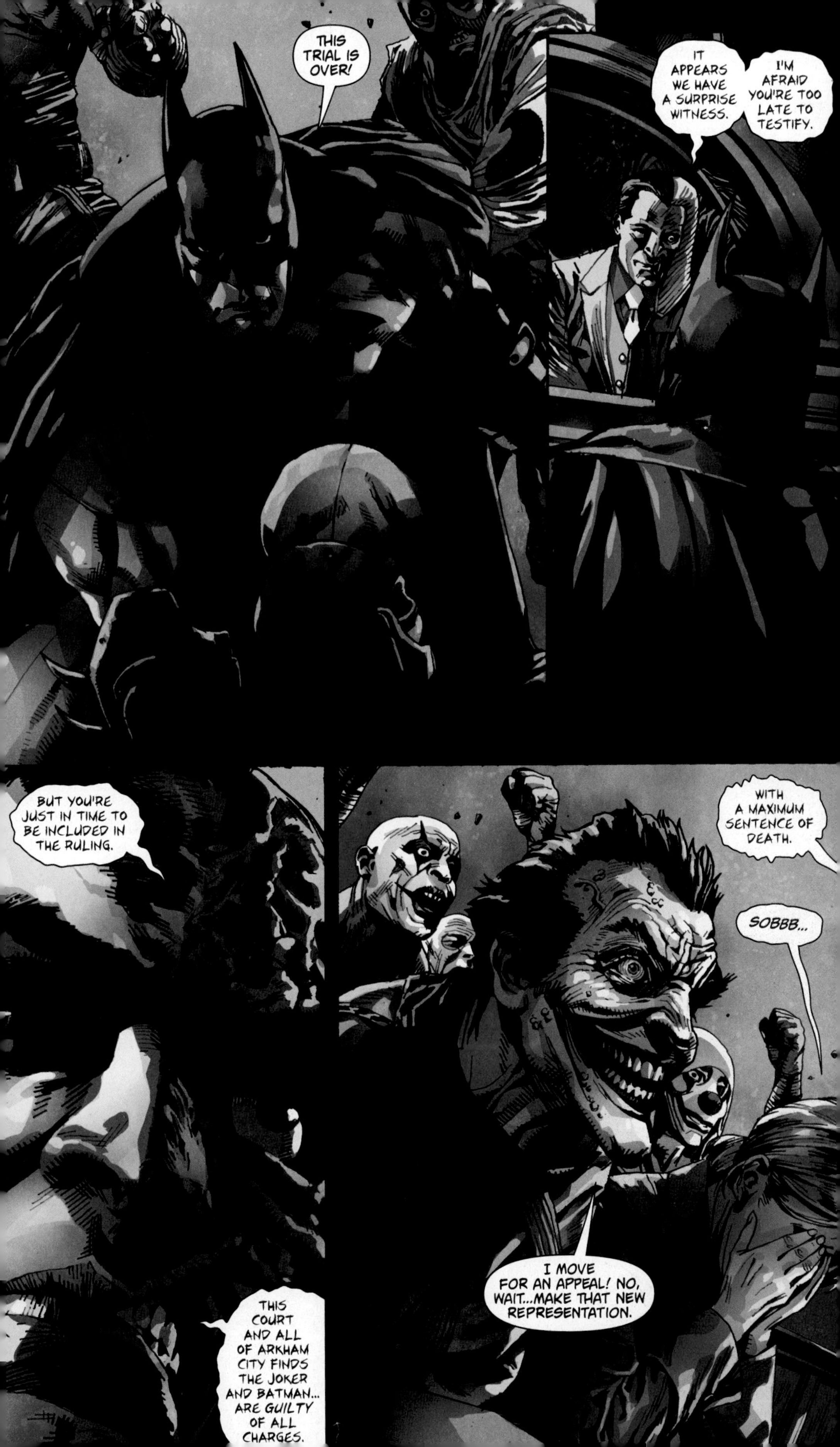
THIS TRIAL IS OVER!
IT APPEARS WE HAVE A SURPRISE WITNESS.
I'M AFRAID YOU'RE TOO LATE TO TESTIFY.
BUT YOU'RE JUST IN TIME TO BE INCLUDED IN THE RULING.
THIS COURT AND ALL OF ARKHAM CITY FINDS THE JOKER AND BATMAN... ARE *GUILTY* OF ALL CHARGES.
WITH A MAXIMUM SENTENCE OF DEATH.
SOBBB...
I MOVE FOR AN APPEAL! NO, WAIT...MAKE THAT NEW REPRESENTATION.

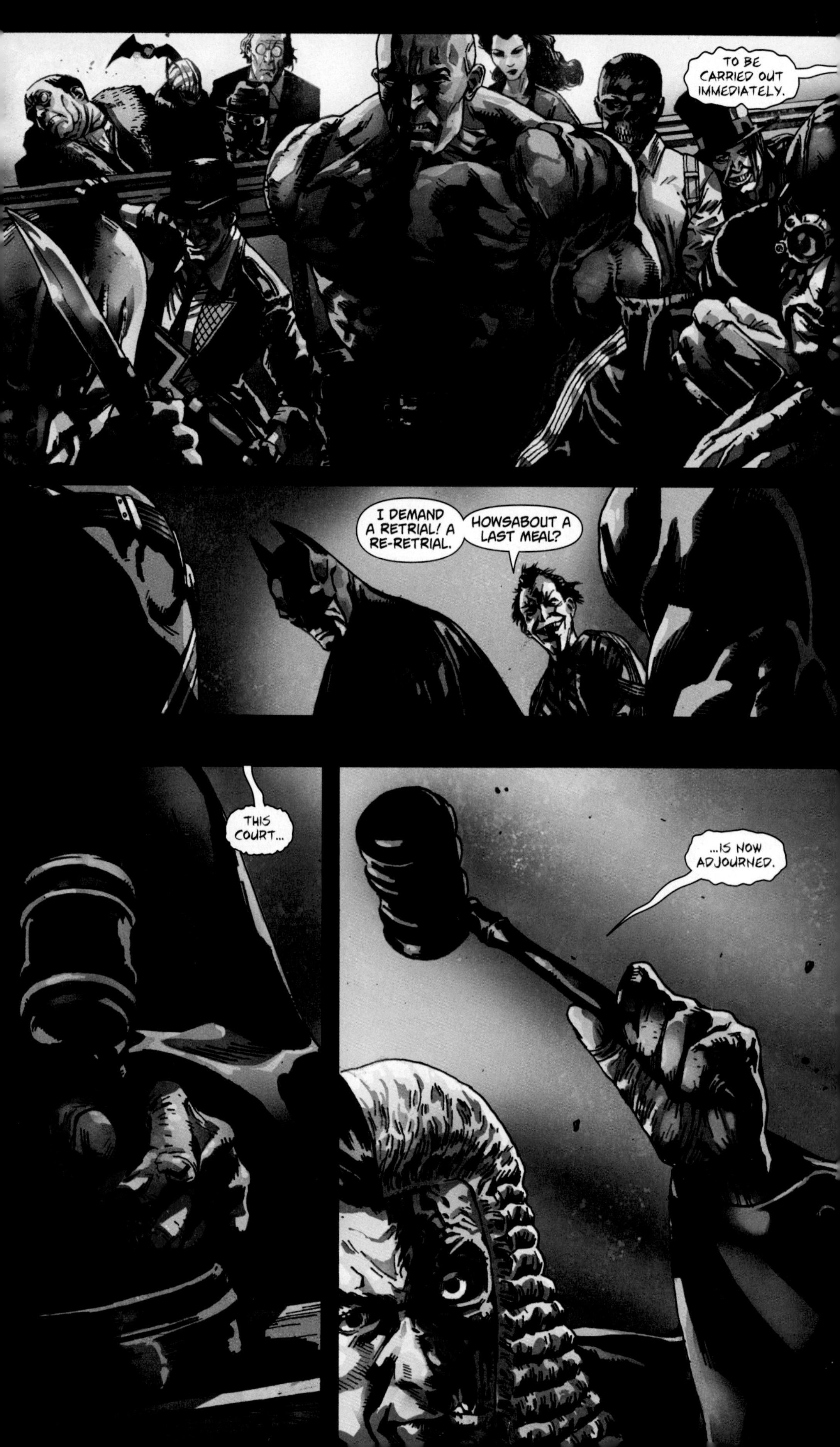
TO BE CARRIED OUT IMMEDIATELY.
I DEMAND A RETRIAL! A RE-RETRIAL.
HOWSABOUT A LAST MEAL?
THIS COURT...
...IS NOW ADJOURNED.

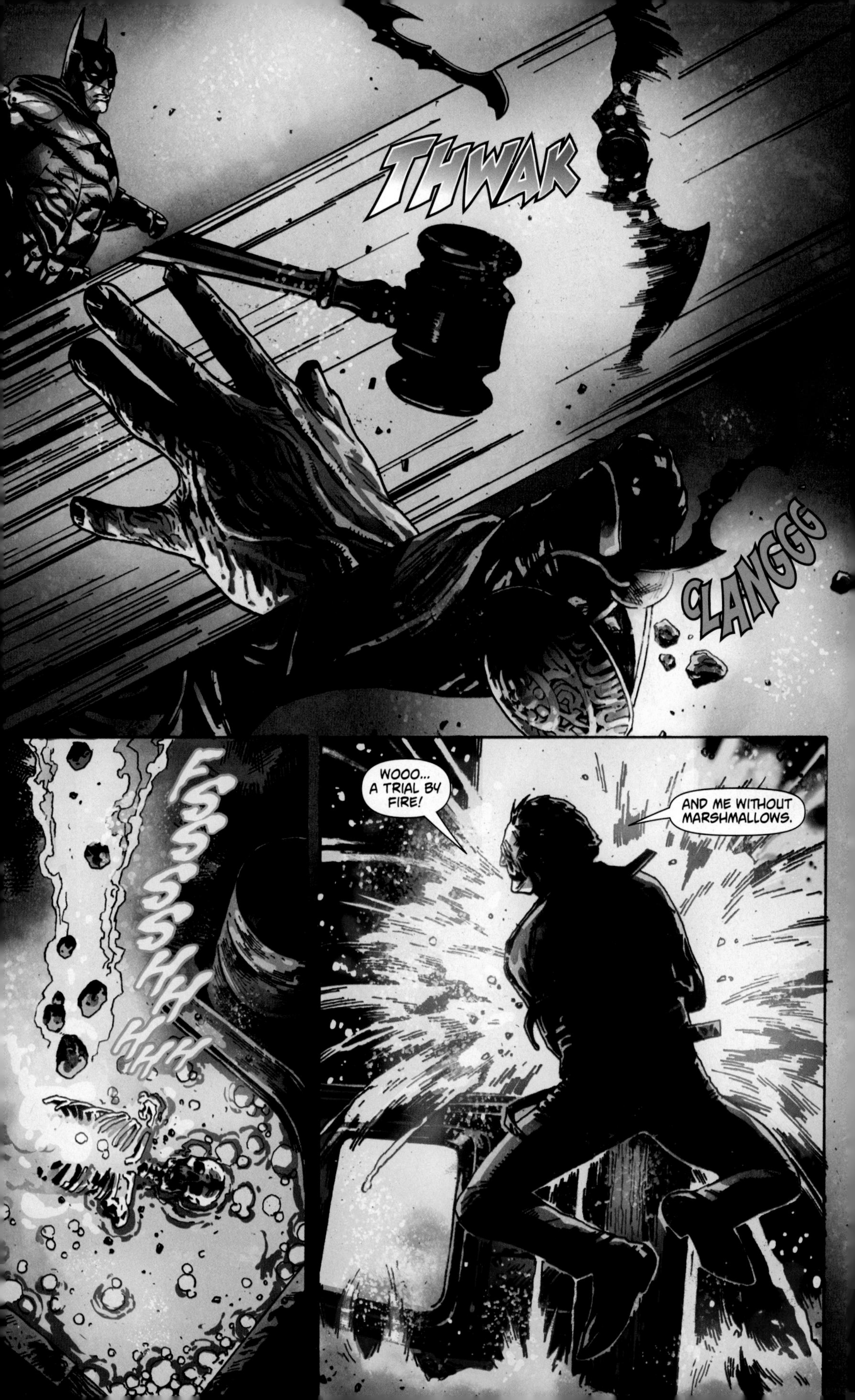
THWAK
CLANGGG
FSSSSSHHHHHH
WOOO... A TRIAL BY FIRE!
AND ME WITHOUT MARSHMALLOWS.

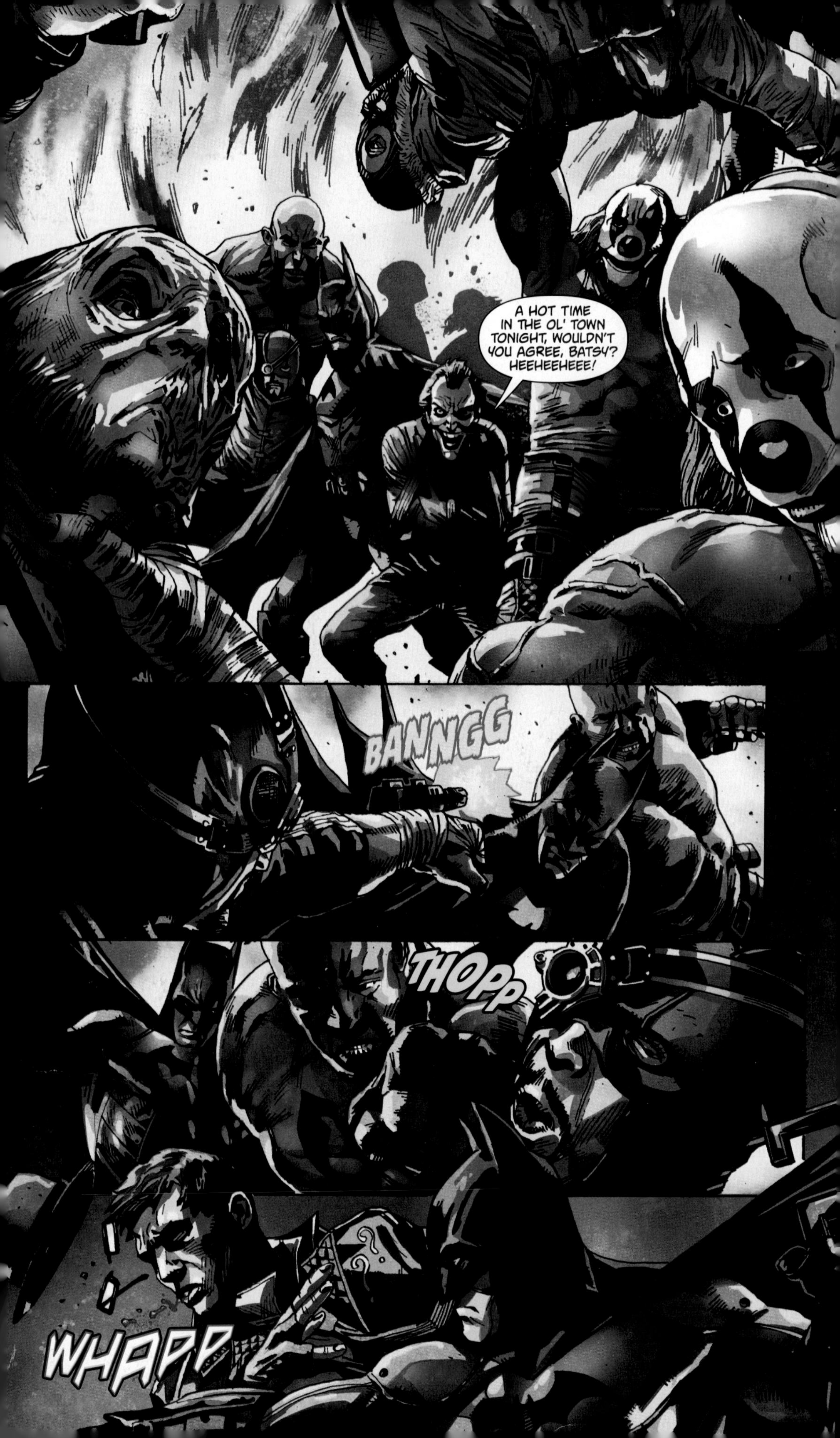
A HOT TIME IN THE OL' TOWN TONIGHT, WOULDN'T YOU AGREE, BATSY? HEEHEEHEEE!
BANNGG
THOPP
WHAPP

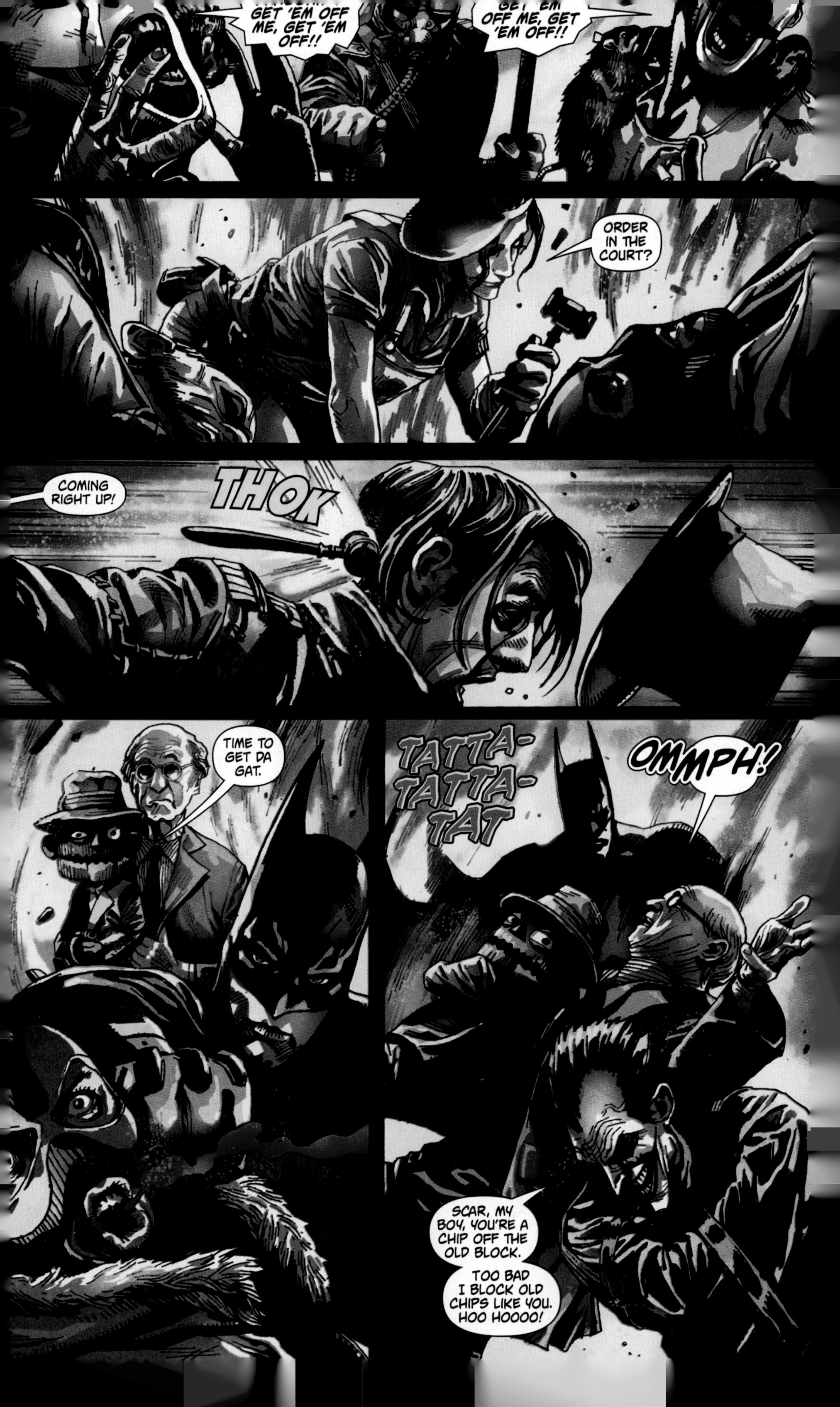
GET 'EM OFF ME, GET 'EM OFF!!
OFF ME, GET 'EM OFF!!
ORDER IN THE COURT?
COMING RIGHT UP!
THOK
TIME TO GET DA GAT.
TATTA-TATTA-TAT
OMMPH!
SCAR, MY BOY, YOU'RE A CHIP OFF THE OLD BLOCK.
TOO BAD I BLOCK OLD CHIPS LIKE YOU. HOO HOOOO!

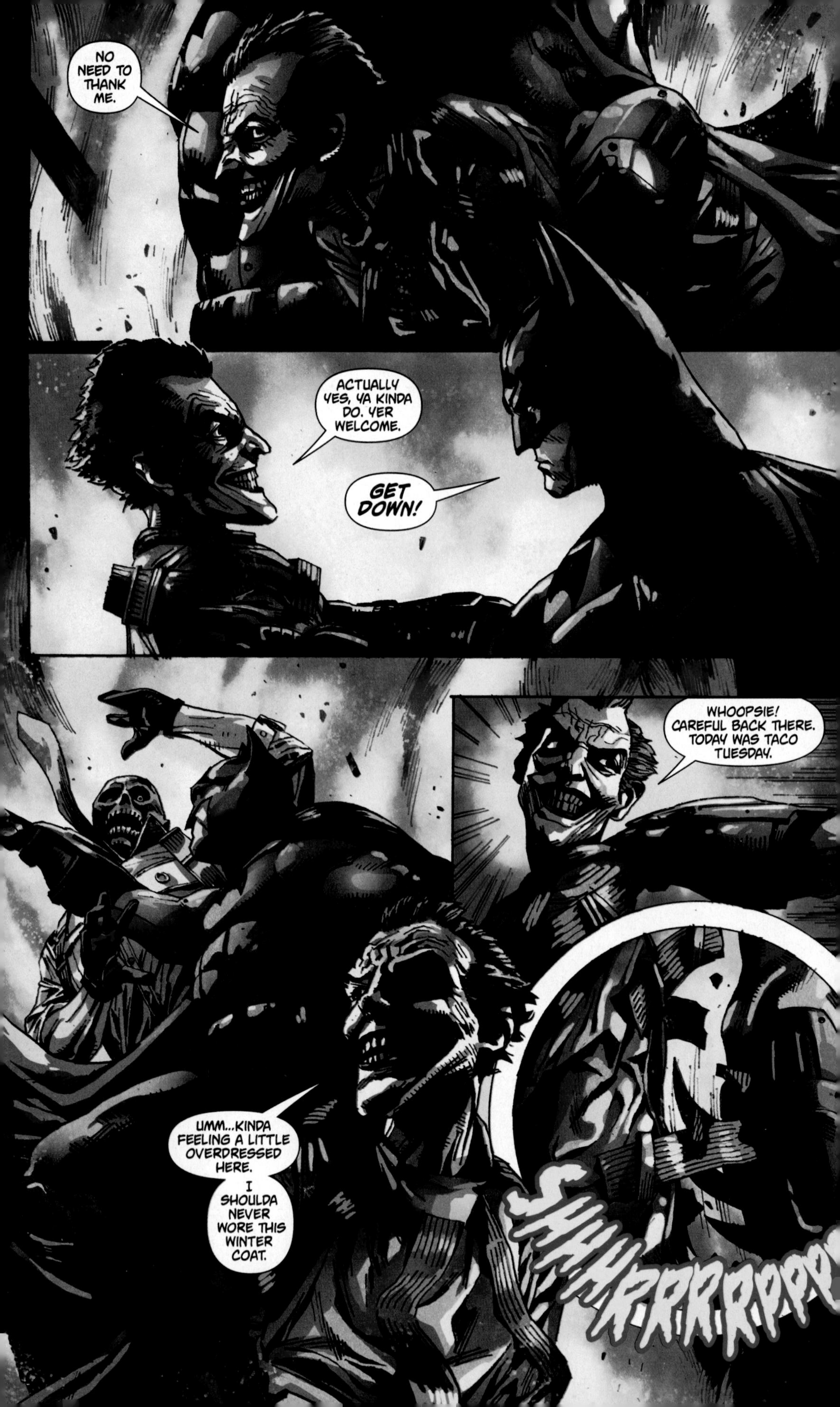
NO NEED TO THANK ME.
ACTUALLY YES, YA KINDA DO. YER WELCOME.
GET DOWN!
WHOOPSIE! CAREFUL BACK THERE. TODAY WAS TACO TUESDAY.
UMM...KINDA FEELING A LITTLE OVERDRESSED HERE.
I SHOULDA NEVER WORE THIS WINTER COAT.
SHHHRRRRPPP

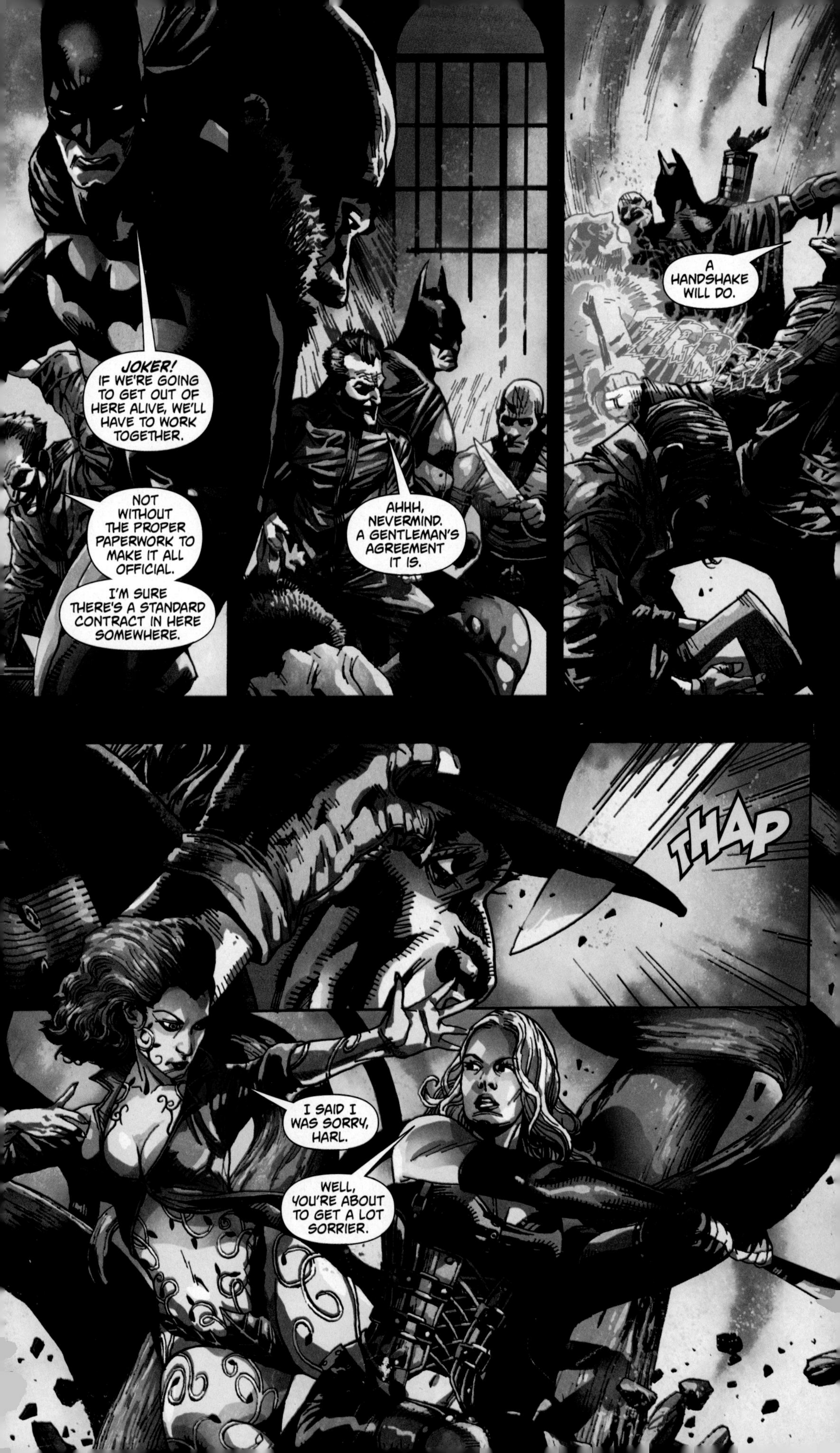
JOKER! IF WE'RE GOING TO GET OUT OF HERE ALIVE, WE'LL HAVE TO WORK TOGETHER.
NOT WITHOUT THE PROPER PAPERWORK TO MAKE IT ALL OFFICIAL.
I'M SURE THERE'S A STANDARD CONTRACT IN HERE SOMEWHERE.
AHHH, NEVERMIND. A GENTLEMAN'S AGREEMENT IT IS.
A HANDSHAKE WILL DO.
THAP
I SAID I WAS SORRY, HARL.
WELL, YOU'RE ABOUT TO GET A LOT SORRIER.

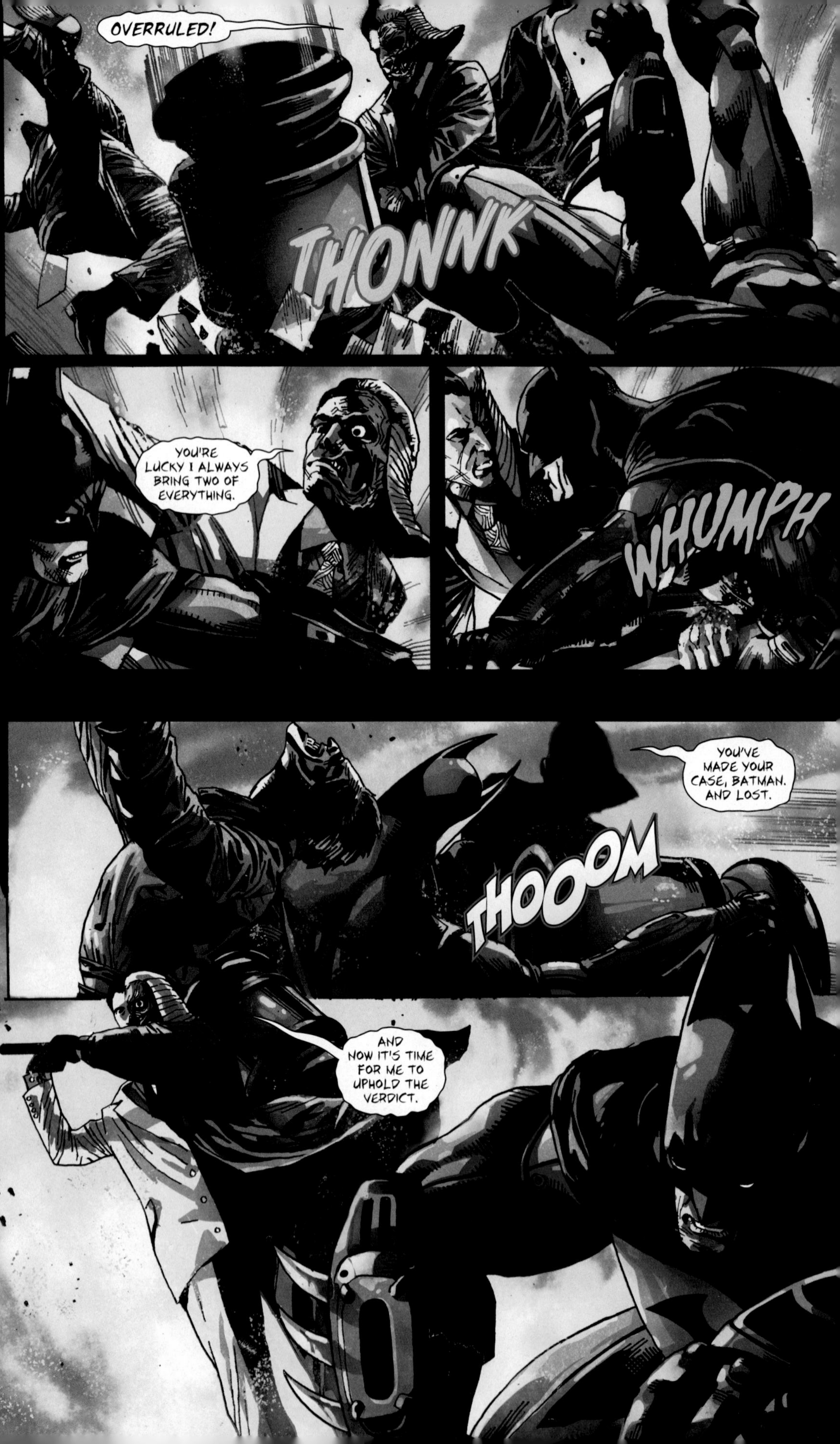
OVERRULED!
THONNK
YOU'RE LUCKY I ALWAYS BRING TWO OF EVERYTHING.
WHUMPH
YOU'VE MADE YOUR CASE, BATMAN. AND LOST.
THOOOM
AND NOW IT'S TIME FOR ME TO UPHOLD THE VERDICT.

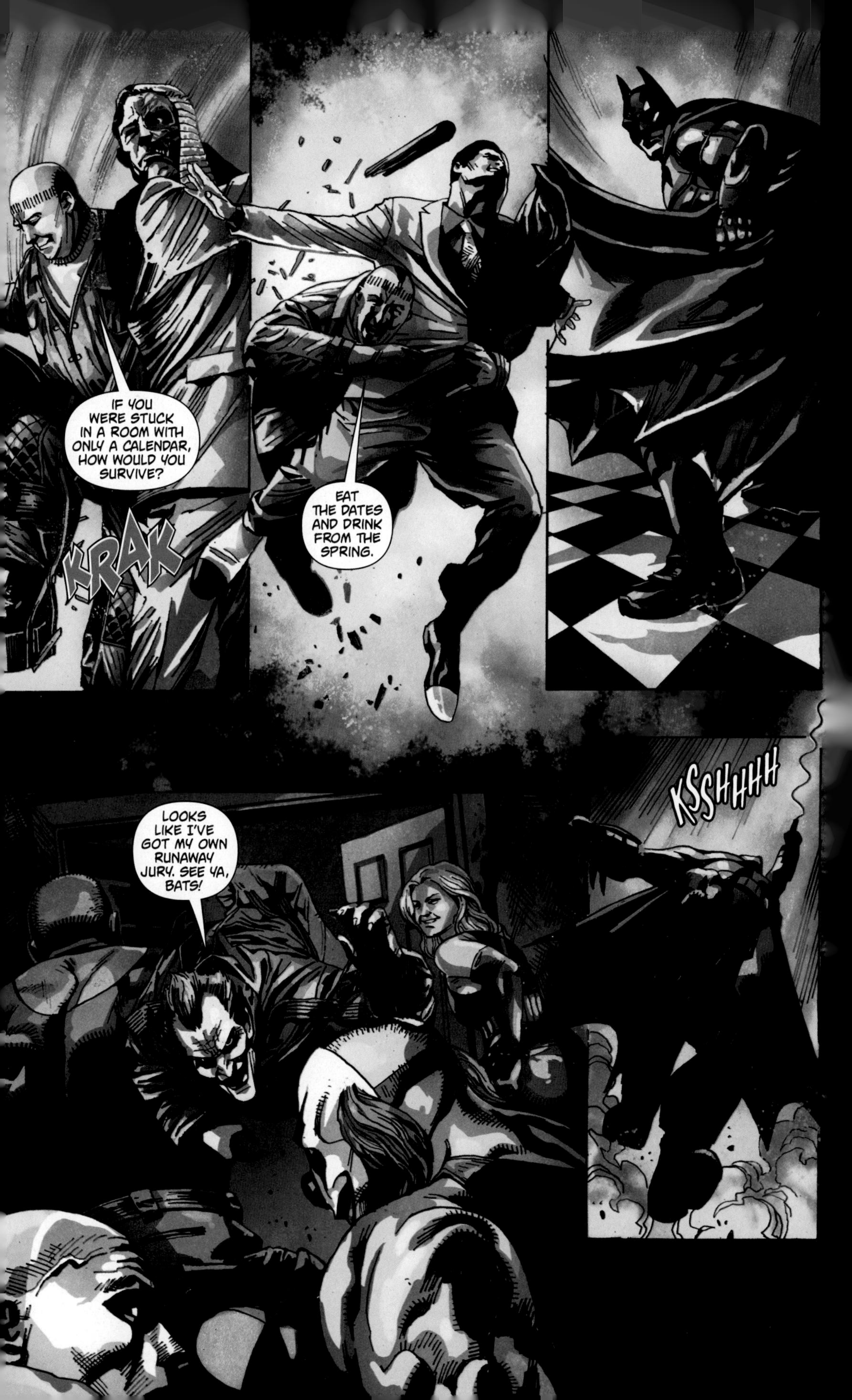
IF YOU WERE STUCK IN A ROOM WITH ONLY A CALENDAR, HOW WOULD YOU SURVIVE?
KRAK
EAT THE DATES AND DRINK FROM THE SPRING.
KSSHHHH
LOOKS LIKE I'VE GOT MY OWN RUNAWAY JURY. SEE YA, BATS!

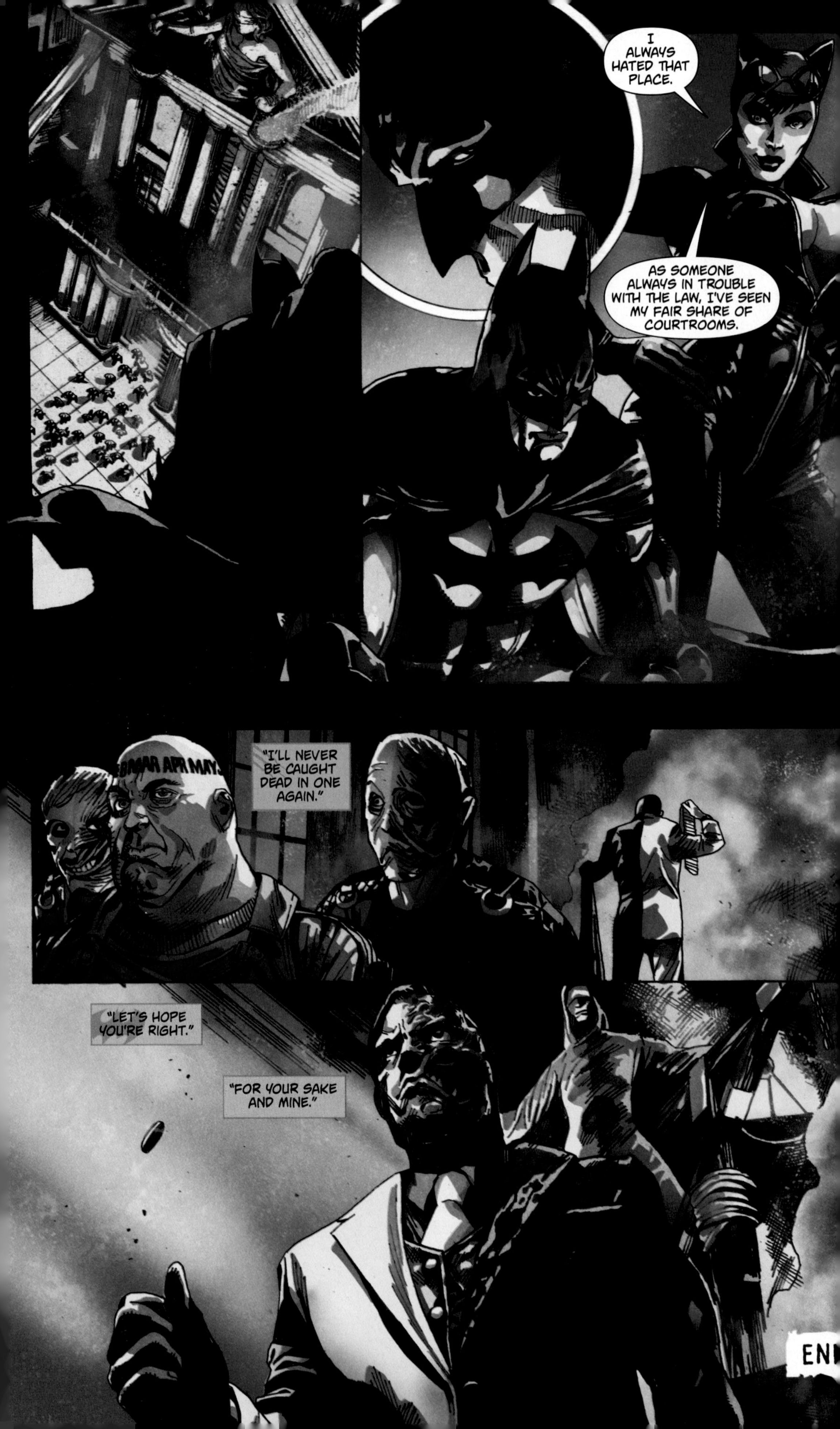
I ALWAYS HATED THAT PLACE.
AS SOMEONE ALWAYS IN TROUBLE WITH THE LAW, I'VE SEEN MY FAIR SHARE OF COURTROOMS.
"I'LL NEVER BE CAUGHT DEAD IN ONE AGAIN."
"LET'S HOPE YOU'RE RIGHT."
"FOR YOUR SAKE AND MINE."

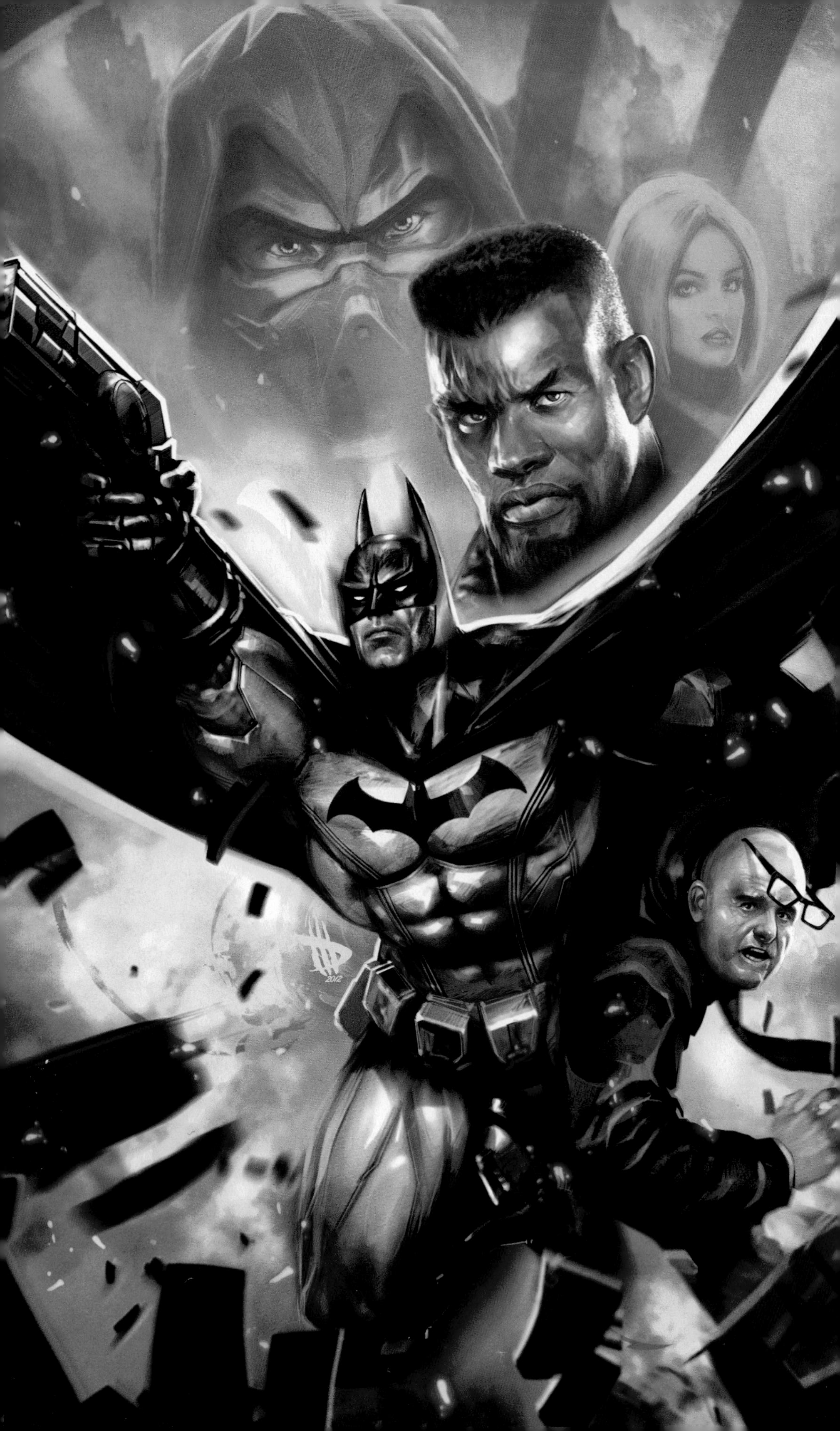

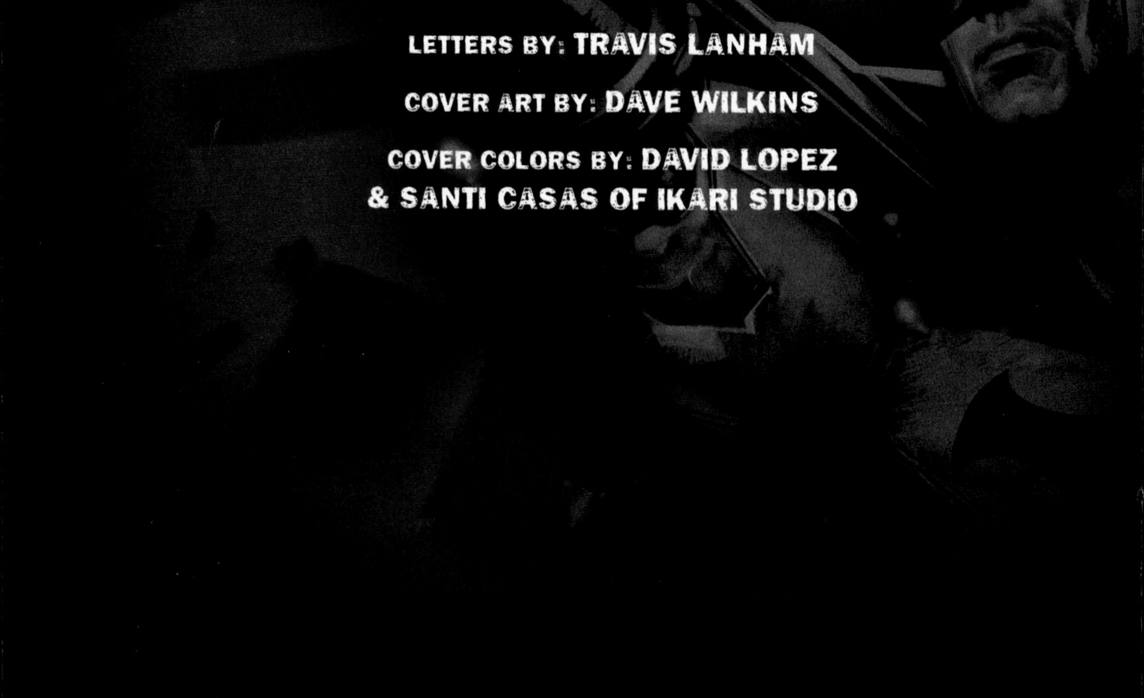

LETTERS BY: TRAVIS LANHAM

COVER ART BY: DAVE WILKINS

COVER COLORS BY: DAVID LOPEZ
& SANTI CASAS OF IKARI STUDIO

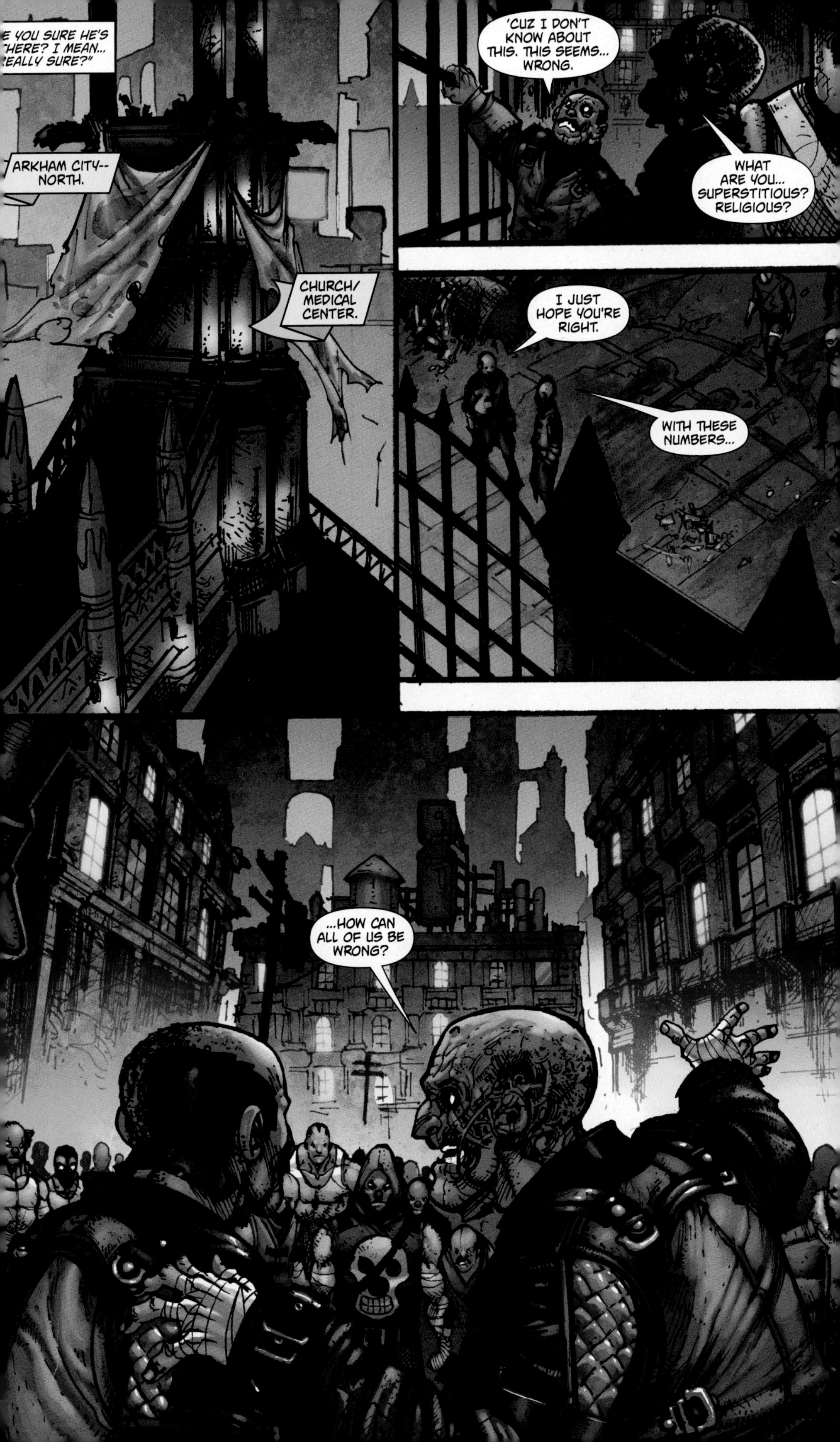
E YOU SURE HE'S
THERE? I MEAN...
REALLY SURE?"
ARKHAM CITY--
NORTH.
CHURCH/
MEDICAL
CENTER.
'CUZ I DON'T KNOW ABOUT THIS. THIS SEEMS... WRONG.
WHAT ARE YOU... SUPERSTITIOUS? RELIGIOUS?
I JUST HOPE YOU'RE RIGHT.
WITH THESE NUMBERS...
...HOW CAN ALL OF US BE WRONG?

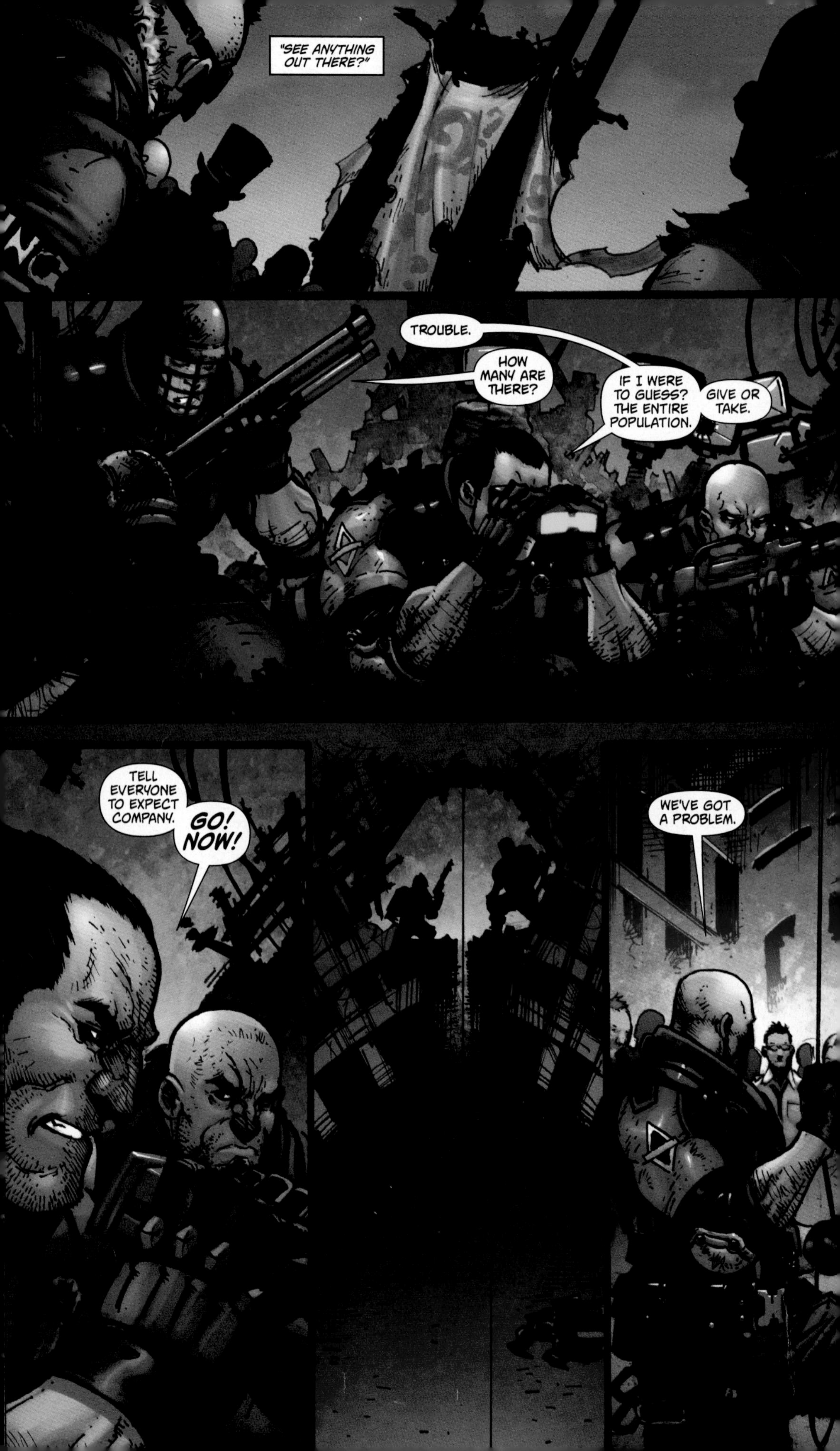
"SEE ANYTHING OUT THERE?"
TROUBLE.
HOW MANY ARE THERE?
IF I WERE TO GUESS? THE ENTIRE POPULATION.
GIVE OR TAKE.
TELL EVERYONE TO EXPECT COMPANY.
GO! NOW!
WE'VE GOT A PROBLEM.

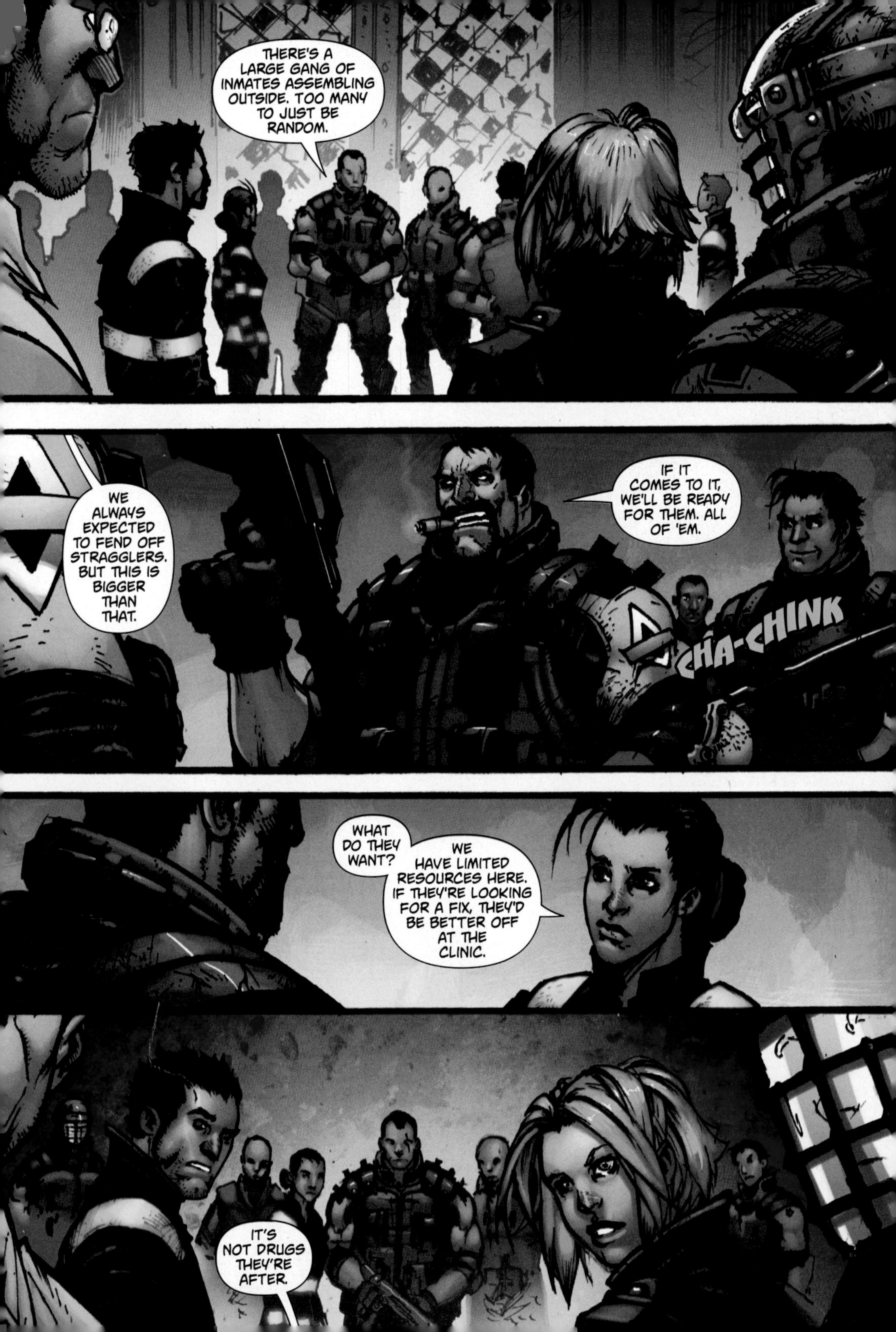
THERE'S A LARGE GANG OF INMATES ASSEMBLING OUTSIDE. TOO MANY TO JUST BE RANDOM.
WE ALWAYS EXPECTED TO FEND OFF STRAGGLERS. BUT THIS IS BIGGER THAN THAT.
IF IT COMES TO IT, WE'LL BE READY FOR THEM. ALL OF 'EM.
CHA-CHINK
WHAT DO THEY WANT?
WE HAVE LIMITED RESOURCES HERE. IF THEY'RE LOOKING FOR A FIX, THEY'D BE BETTER OFF AT THE CLINIC.
IT'S NOT DRUGS THEY'RE AFTER.

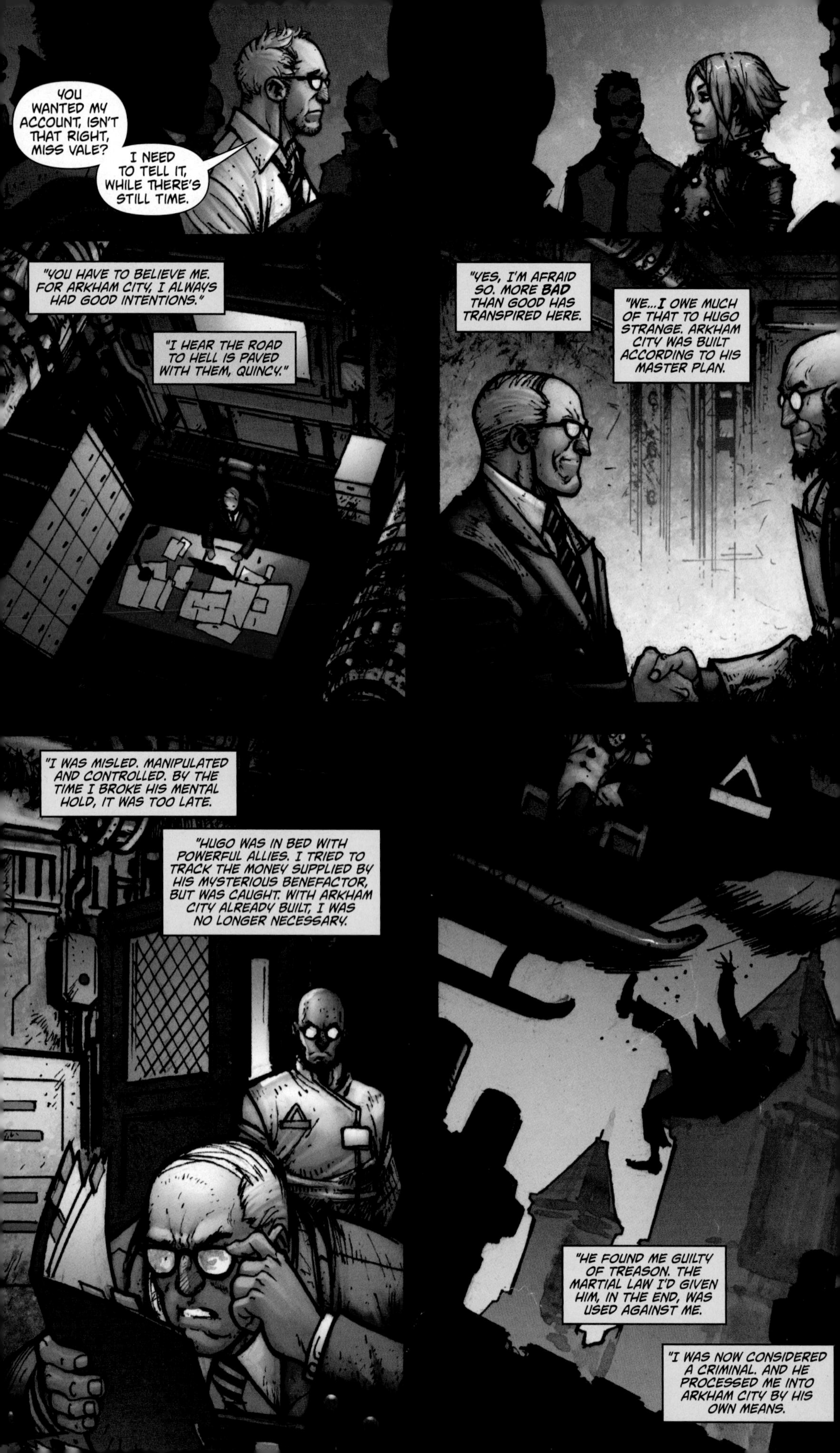
YOU WANTED MY ACCOUNT, ISN'T THAT RIGHT, MISS VALE?
I NEED TO TELL IT, WHILE THERE'S STILL TIME.
"YOU HAVE TO BELIEVE ME. FOR ARKHAM CITY, I ALWAYS HAD GOOD INTENTIONS."
"I HEAR THE ROAD TO HELL IS PAVED WITH THEM, QUINCY."
"YES, I'M AFRAID SO. MORE BAD THAN GOOD HAS TRANSPIRED HERE.
"WE...I OWE MUCH OF THAT TO HUGO STRANGE. ARKHAM CITY WAS BUILT ACCORDING TO HIS MASTER PLAN.
"I WAS MISLED. MANIPULATED AND CONTROLLED. BY THE TIME I BROKE HIS MENTAL HOLD, IT WAS TOO LATE.
"HUGO WAS IN BED WITH POWERFUL ALLIES. I TRIED TO TRACK THE MONEY SUPPLIED BY HIS MYSTERIOUS BENEFACTOR, BUT WAS CAUGHT. WITH ARKHAM CITY ALREADY BUILT, I WAS NO LONGER NECESSARY.
"HE FOUND ME GUILTY OF TREASON. THE MARTIAL LAW I'D GIVEN HIM, IN THE END, WAS USED AGAINST ME.
"I WAS NOW CONSIDERED A CRIMINAL. AND HE PROCESSED ME INTO ARKHAM CITY BY HIS OWN MEANS.

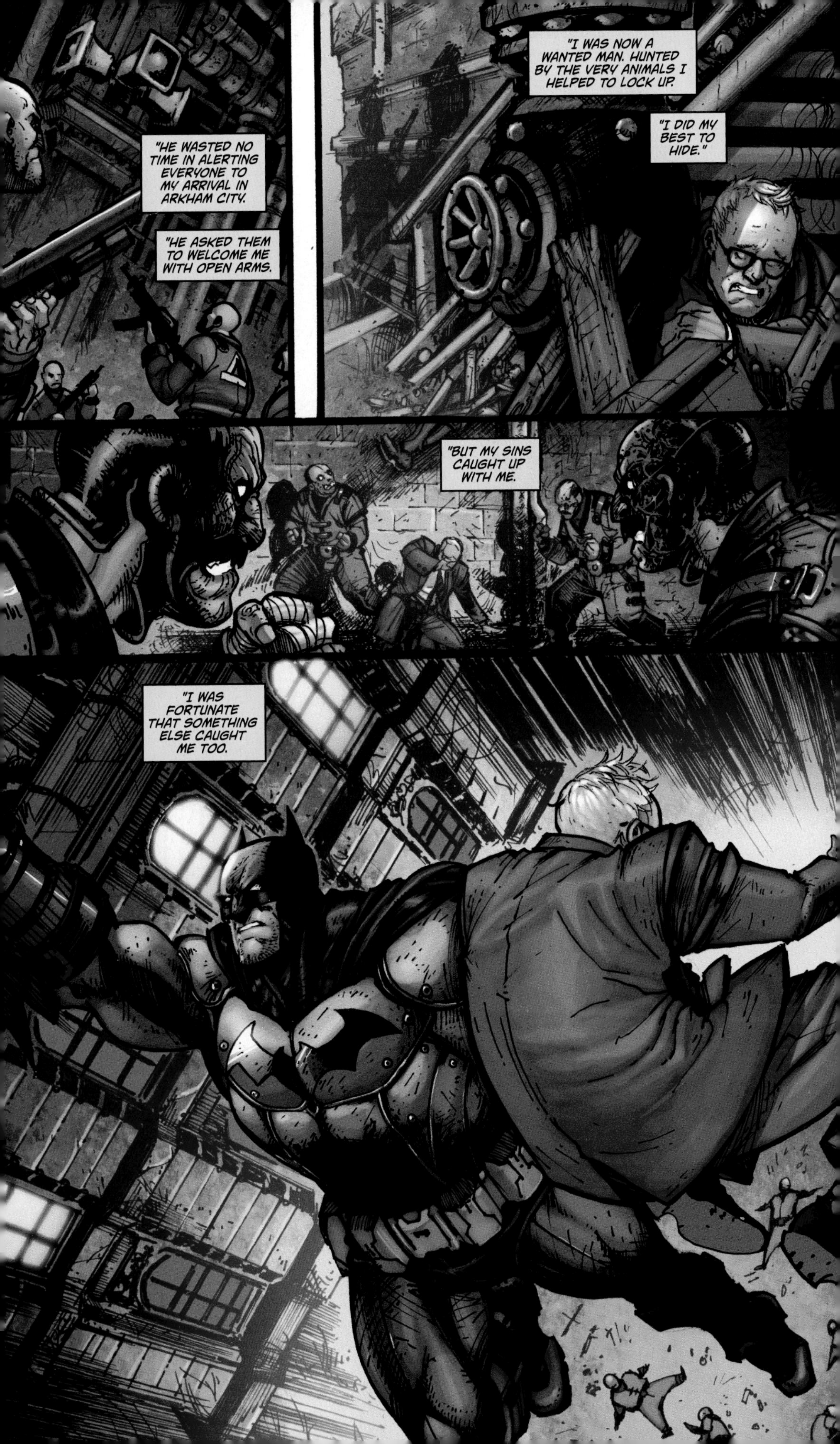
"HE WASTED NO TIME IN ALERTING EVERYONE TO MY ARRIVAL IN ARKHAM CITY.
"HE ASKED THEM TO WELCOME ME WITH OPEN ARMS.
"I WAS NOW A WANTED MAN. HUNTED BY THE VERY ANIMALS I HELPED TO LOCK UP.
"I DID MY BEST TO HIDE."
"BUT MY SINS CAUGHT UP WITH ME.
"I WAS FORTUNATE THAT SOMETHING ELSE CAUGHT ME TOO.

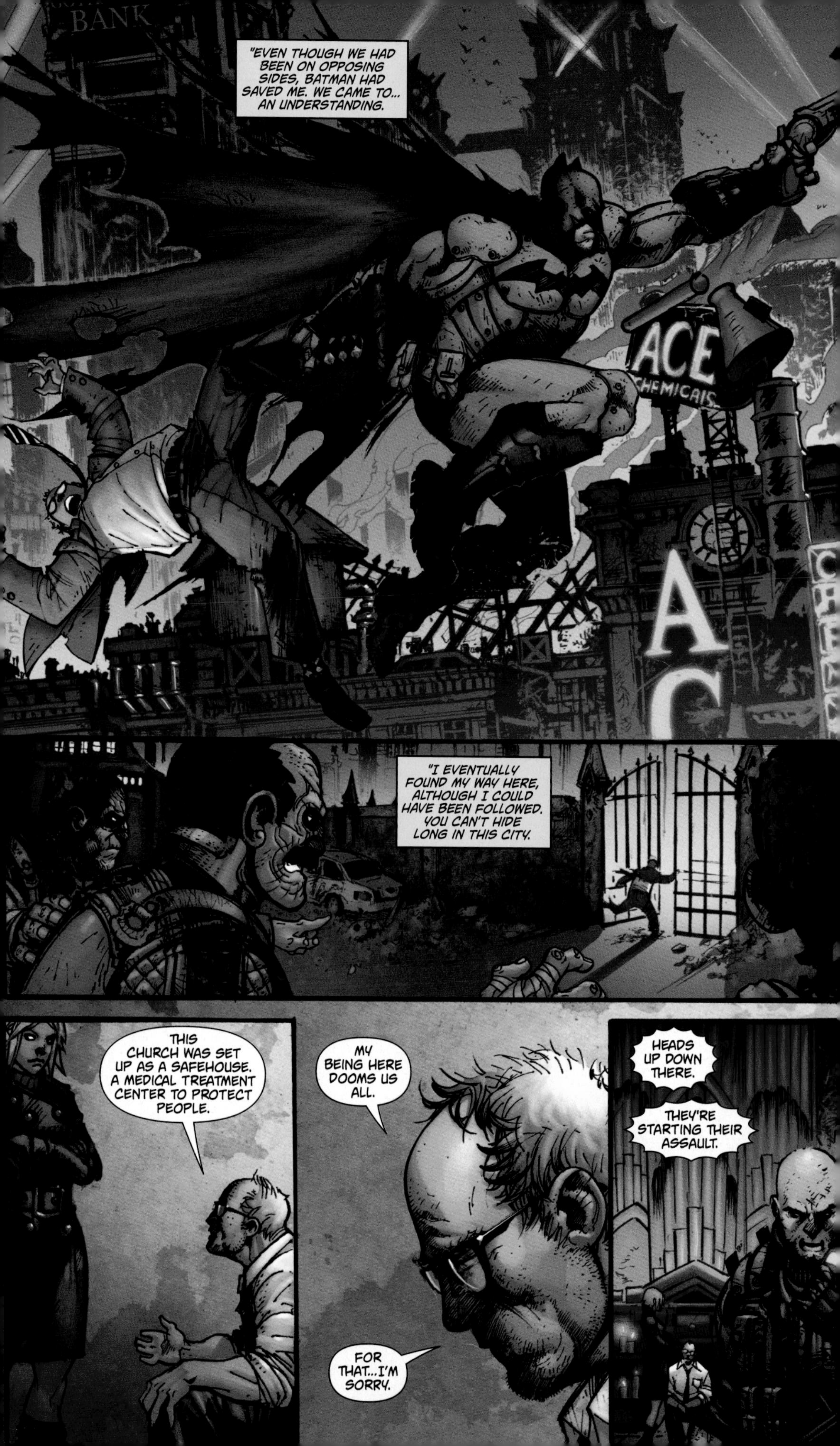
BANK
"EVEN THOUGH WE HAD BEEN ON OPPOSING SIDES, BATMAN HAD SAVED ME. WE CAME TO... AN UNDERSTANDING.
ACE CHEMICALS
"I EVENTUALLY FOUND MY WAY HERE, ALTHOUGH I COULD HAVE BEEN FOLLOWED. YOU CAN'T HIDE LONG IN THIS CITY.
THIS CHURCH WAS SET UP AS A SAFEHOUSE. A MEDICAL TREATMENT CENTER TO PROTECT PEOPLE.
MY BEING HERE DOOMS US ALL.
FOR THAT...I'M SORRY.
HEADS UP DOWN THERE.
THEY'RE STARTING THEIR ASSAULT.

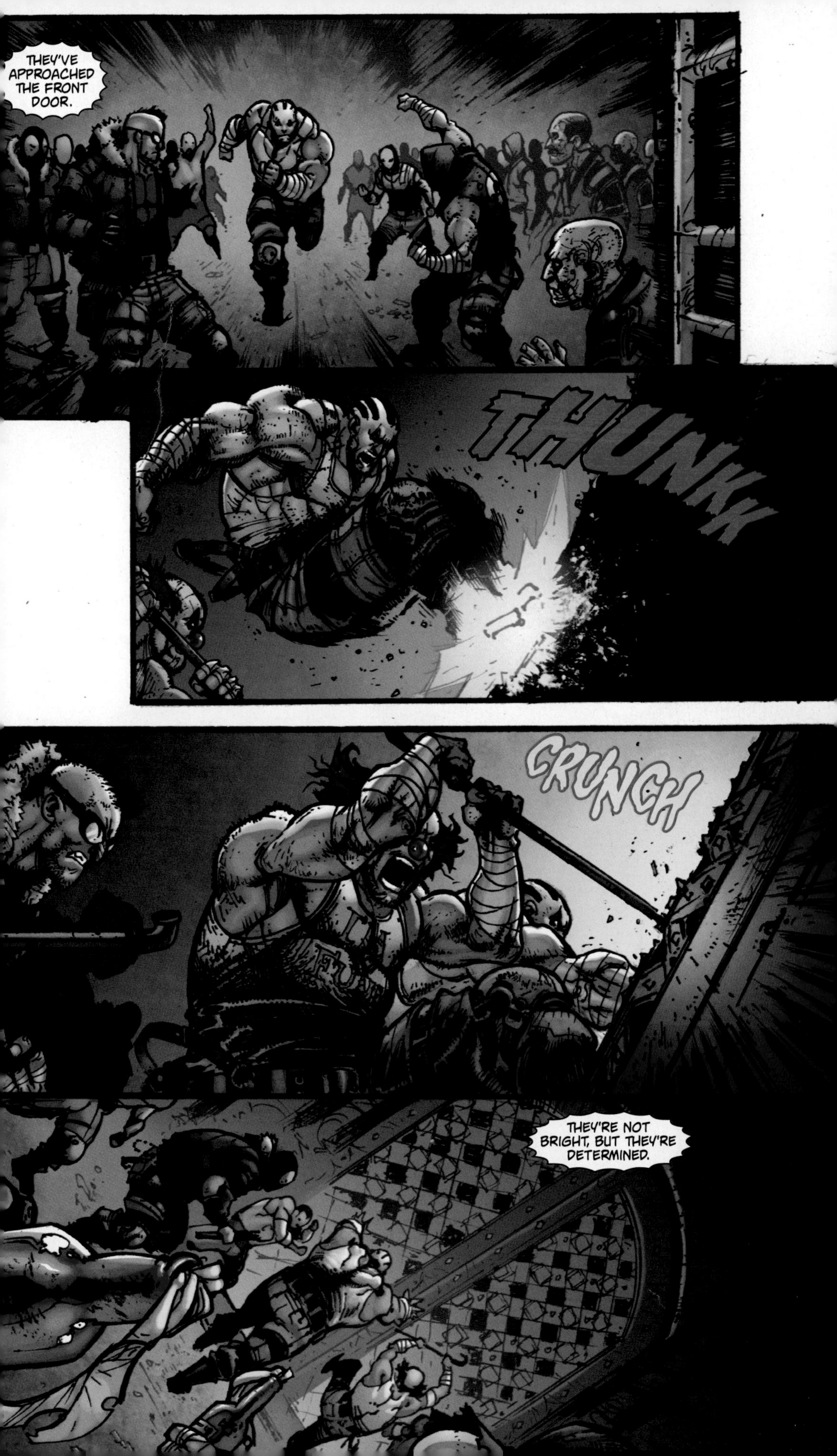
THEY'VE APPROACHED THE FRONT DOOR.
THUNKK
CRUNCH
THEY'RE NOT BRIGHT, BUT THEY'RE DETERMINED.

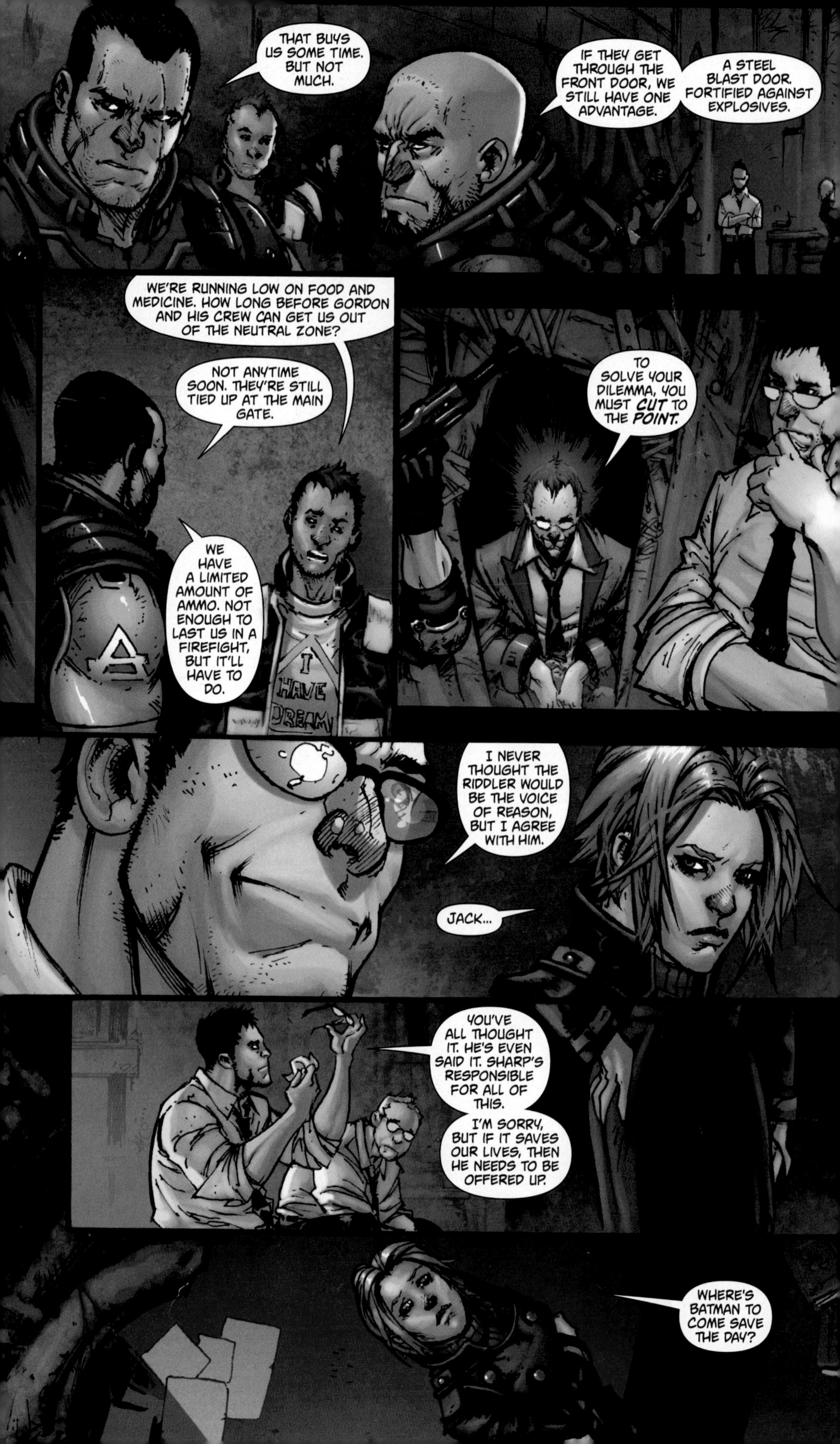
THAT BUYS US SOME TIME. BUT NOT MUCH.
IF THEY GET THROUGH THE FRONT DOOR, WE STILL HAVE ONE ADVANTAGE.
A STEEL BLAST DOOR. FORTIFIED AGAINST EXPLOSIVES.
WE'RE RUNNING LOW ON FOOD AND MEDICINE. HOW LONG BEFORE GORDON AND HIS CREW CAN GET US OUT OF THE NEUTRAL ZONE?
NOT ANYTIME SOON. THEY'RE STILL TIED UP AT THE MAIN GATE.
WE HAVE A LIMITED AMOUNT OF AMMO. NOT ENOUGH TO LAST US IN A FIREFIGHT, BUT IT'LL HAVE TO DO.
I HAVE DREAM
TO SOLVE YOUR DILEMMA, YOU MUST CUT TO THE POINT.
I NEVER THOUGHT THE RIDDLER WOULD BE THE VOICE OF REASON, BUT I AGREE WITH HIM.
JACK...
YOU'VE ALL THOUGHT IT. HE'S EVEN SAID IT. SHARP'S RESPONSIBLE FOR ALL OF THIS.
I'M SORRY, BUT IF IT SAVES OUR LIVES, THEN HE NEEDS TO BE OFFERED UP.
WHERE'S BATMAN TO COME SAVE THE DAY?

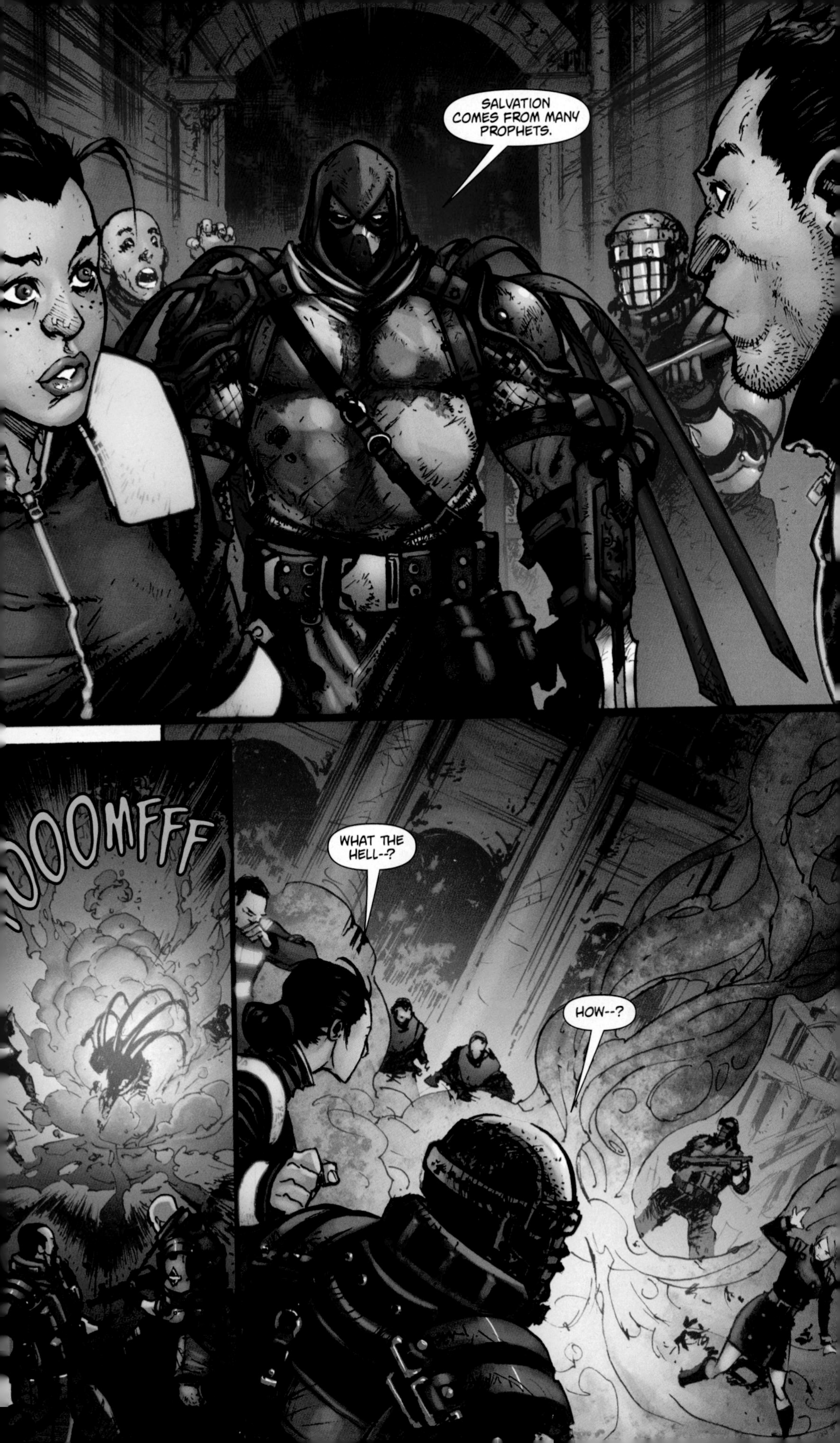
SALVATION COMES FROM MANY PROPHETS.
OOOMFFF
WHAT THE HELL--?
HOW--?

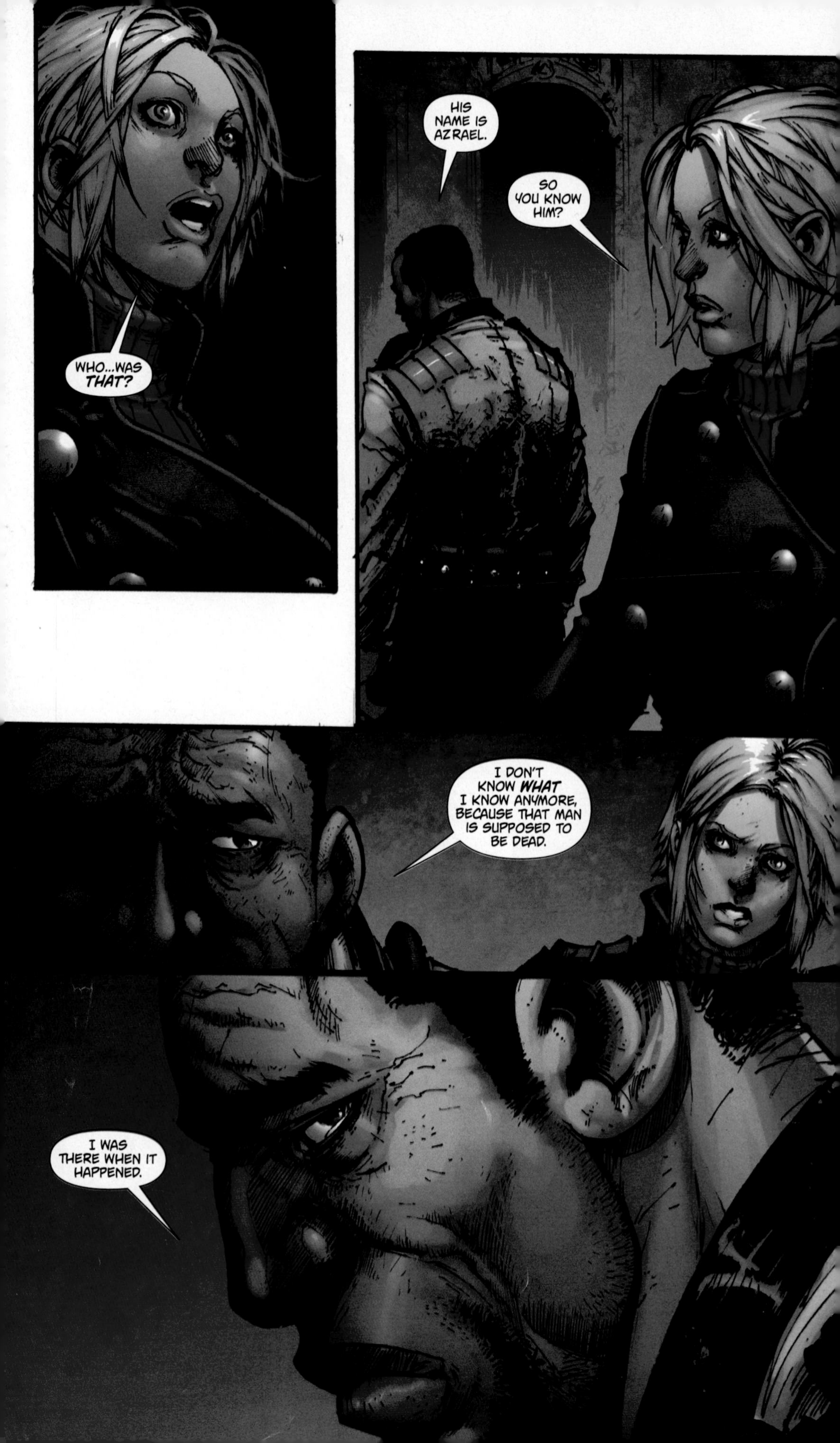
WHO...WAS THAT?
HIS NAME IS AZRAEL.
SO YOU KNOW HIM?
I DON'T KNOW WHAT I KNOW ANYMORE, BECAUSE THAT MAN IS SUPPOSED TO BE DEAD.
I WAS THERE WHEN IT HAPPENED.

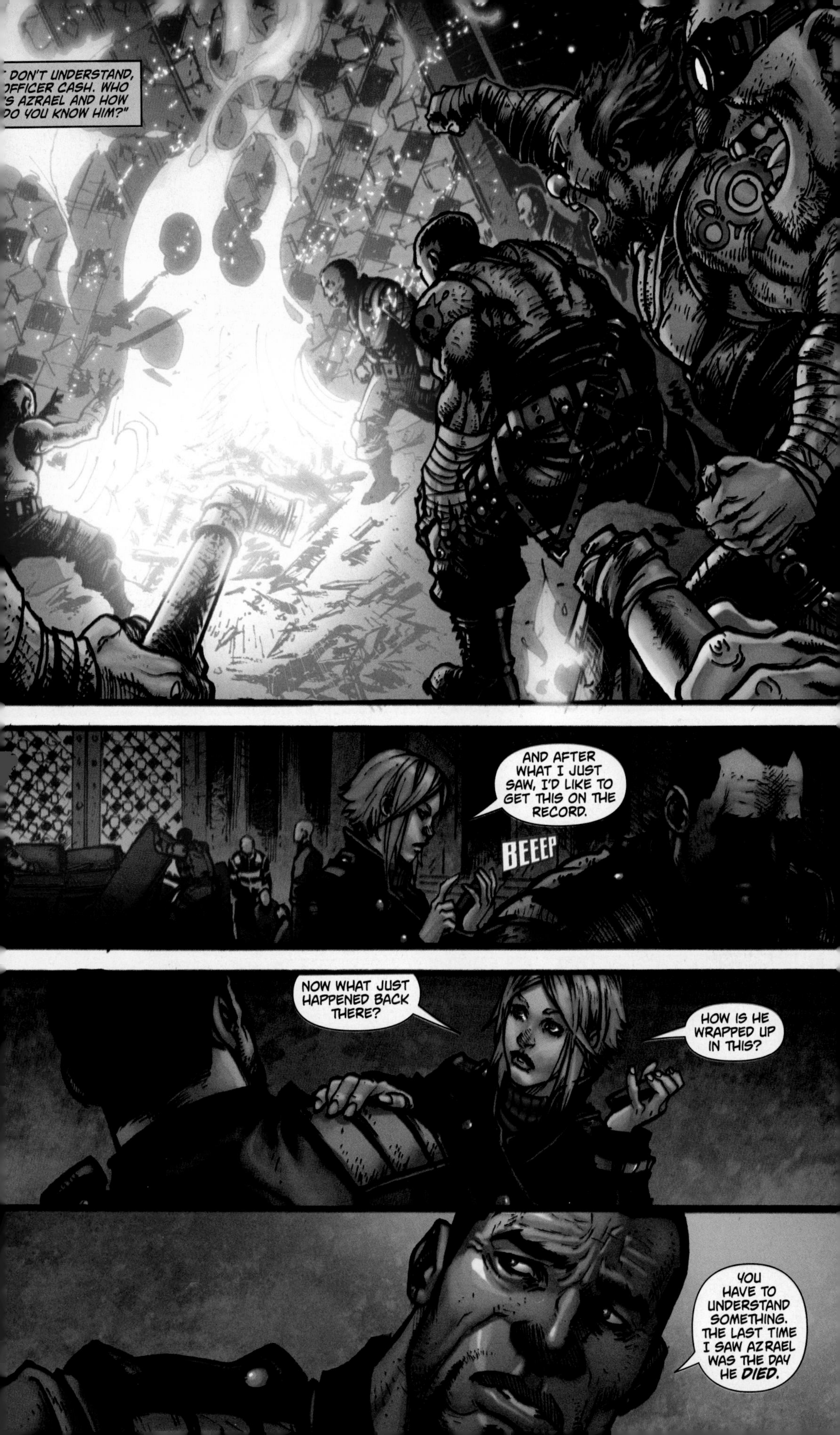
"I DON'T UNDERSTAND, OFFICER CASH. WHO IS AZRAEL AND HOW DO YOU KNOW HIM?"
AND AFTER WHAT I JUST SAW, I'D LIKE TO GET THIS ON THE RECORD.
BEEEP
NOW WHAT JUST HAPPENED BACK THERE?
HOW IS HE WRAPPED UP IN THIS?
YOU HAVE TO UNDERSTAND SOMETHING. THE LAST TIME I SAW AZRAEL WAS THE DAY HE DIED.

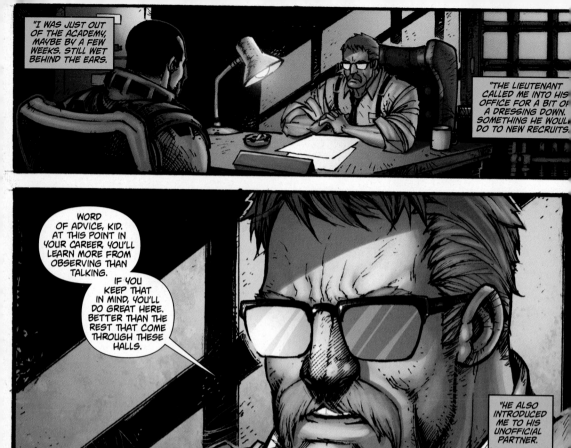

"I WAS JUST OUT OF THE ACADEMY, MAYBE BY A FEW WEEKS. STILL WET BEHIND THE EARS.

"THE LIEUTENANT CALLED ME INTO HIS OFFICE FOR A BIT OF A DRESSING DOWN. SOMETHING HE WOUL[D] DO TO NEW RECRUITS.

WORD OF ADVICE, KID. AT THIS POINT IN YOUR CAREER, YOU'LL LEARN MORE FROM OBSERVING THAN TALKING.

IF YOU KEEP THAT IN MIND, YOU'LL DO GREAT HERE. BETTER THAN THE REST THAT COME THROUGH THESE HALLS.

"HE ALSO INTRODUCED ME TO HIS UNOFFICIAL PARTNER.

WHA--?

IT'S OKAY, KID. STA[Y] AND LEARN SOMETHING.

"FROM THAT POINT ON, I WAS ALLOWED INTO THEIR INNER CIRCLE. NOT ALL THE TIME, MIND YOU. BUT ENOUGH TO OBSERVE.

"THE GCPD HAD AN OPEN CASE FILE ON A SECRET SOCIETY RESPONSIBLE FOR MANY KILLINGS. THE ORDER OF ST. DUMAS.

"SOLDIER-MONKS TRACING BACK TO THE CRUSADES. KNIGHTS TEMPLAR FORMED TO PROTECT PILGRIMS JOURNEYING TO THE HOLY LAND.

"SINCE THEN, THEY'VE SPLINTERED INTO FACTIONS WHOSE SOLE PURPOSE IS EXTINGUISHING EVIL AS THEY SEE FIT.

AT ONE TIME, BATMAN EVEN ACQUIRED THEIR MYSTICAL ARMOR TO COMBAT THEM. A SUIT OF SORROWS.

BUT IT PROVE[D] TOO DAR[K] AN INFLUE[NCE] AND HE W[AS] FORCED [TO] ABANDO[N] IT.

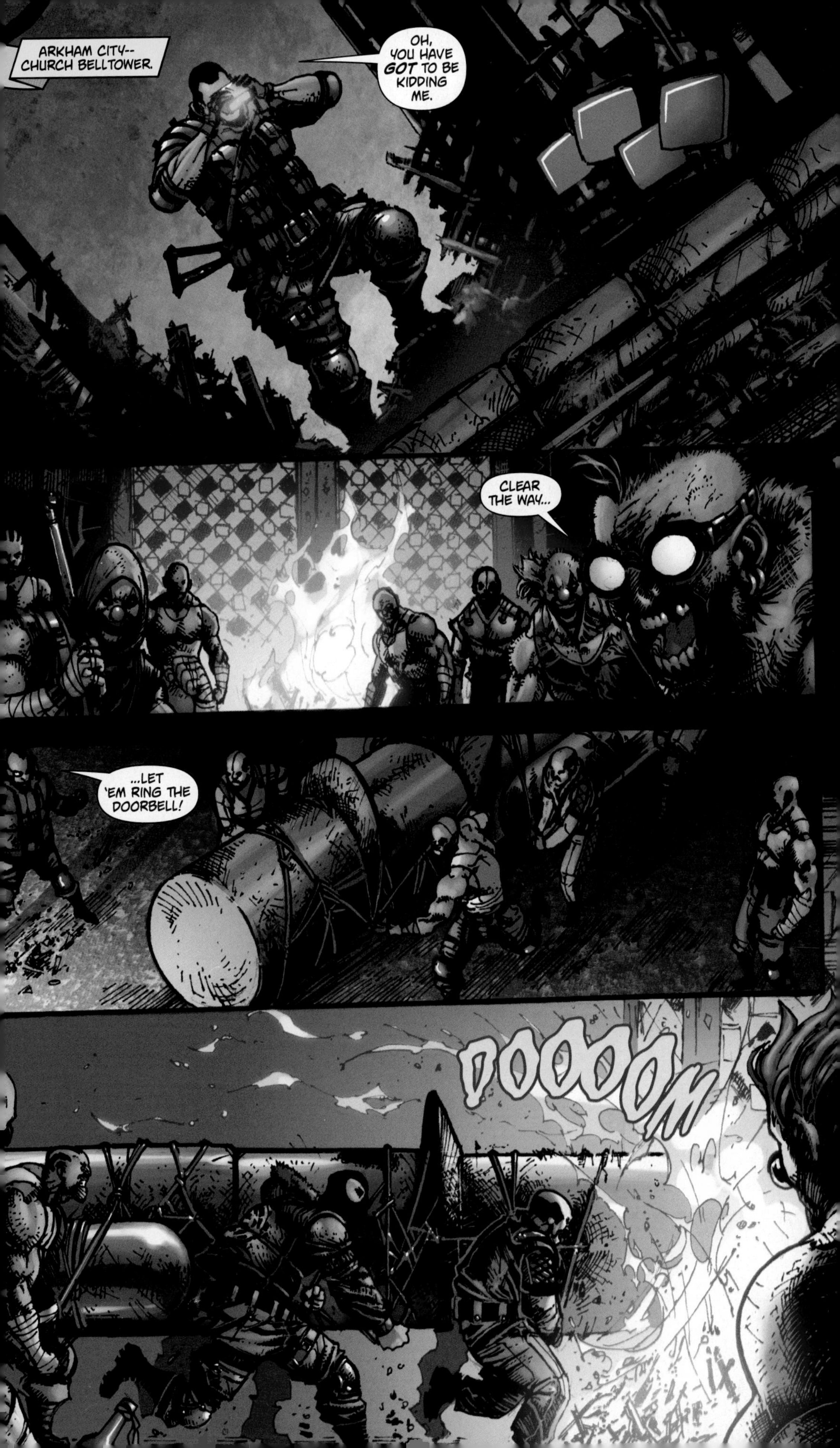
ARKHAM CITY-- CHURCH BELLTOWER.
OH, YOU HAVE GOT TO BE KIDDING ME.
CLEAR THE WAY...
...LET 'EM RING THE DOORBELL!
DOOOOOM

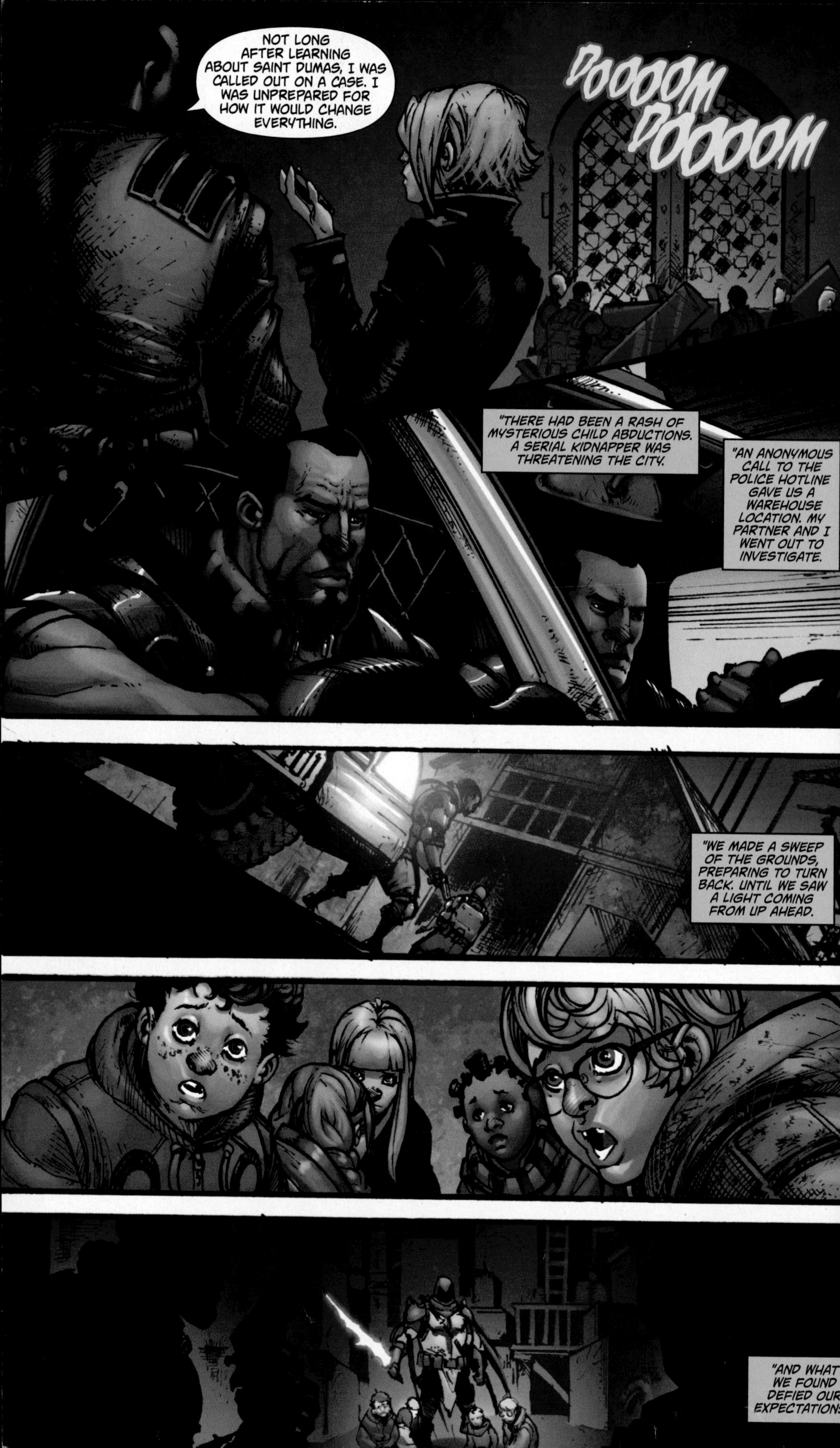
NOT LONG AFTER LEARNING ABOUT SAINT DUMAS, I WAS CALLED OUT ON A CASE. I WAS UNPREPARED FOR HOW IT WOULD CHANGE EVERYTHING.
DOOOOM DOOOOM
"THERE HAD BEEN A RASH OF MYSTERIOUS CHILD ABDUCTIONS. A SERIAL KIDNAPPER WAS THREATENING THE CITY.
"AN ANONYMOUS CALL TO THE POLICE HOTLINE GAVE US A WAREHOUSE LOCATION. MY PARTNER AND I WENT OUT TO INVESTIGATE.
"WE MADE A SWEEP OF THE GROUNDS, PREPARING TO TURN BACK. UNTIL WE SAW A LIGHT COMING FROM UP AHEAD.
"AND WHAT WE FOUND DEFIED OUR EXPECTATIONS

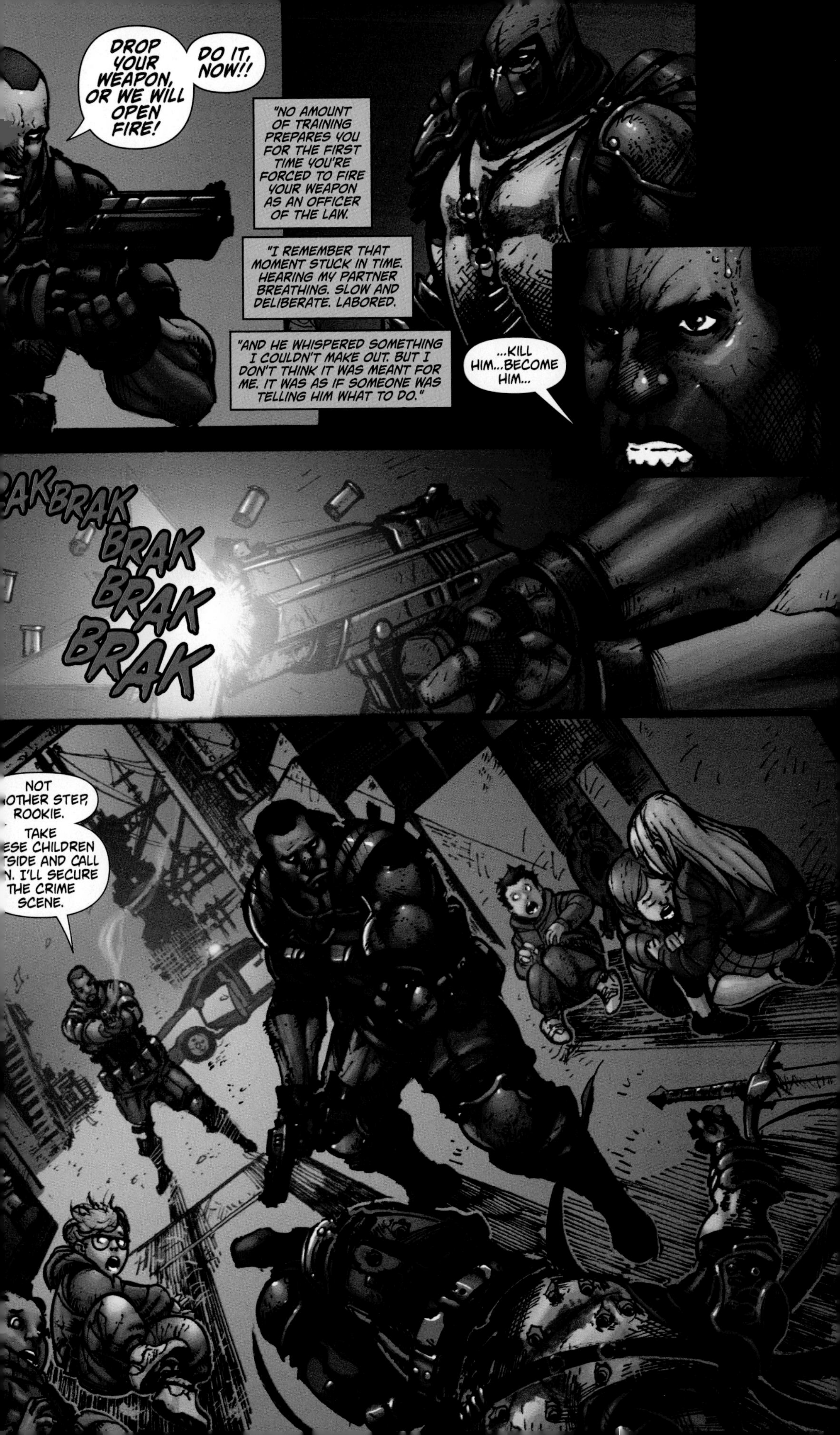
DROP YOUR WEAPON, OR WE WILL OPEN FIRE!
DO IT, NOW!!
"NO AMOUNT OF TRAINING PREPARES YOU FOR THE FIRST TIME YOU'RE FORCED TO FIRE YOUR WEAPON AS AN OFFICER OF THE LAW.
"I REMEMBER THAT MOMENT STUCK IN TIME. HEARING MY PARTNER BREATHING. SLOW AND DELIBERATE. LABORED.
"AND HE WHISPERED SOMETHING I COULDN'T MAKE OUT. BUT I DON'T THINK IT WAS MEANT FOR ME. IT WAS AS IF SOMEONE WAS TELLING HIM WHAT TO DO."
...KILL HIM...BECOME HIM...
BRAK BRAK BRAK BRAK
NOT
OTHER STEP, ROOKIE.
TAKE
ESE CHILDREN
TSIDE AND CALL
N. I'LL SECURE THE CRIME SCENE.

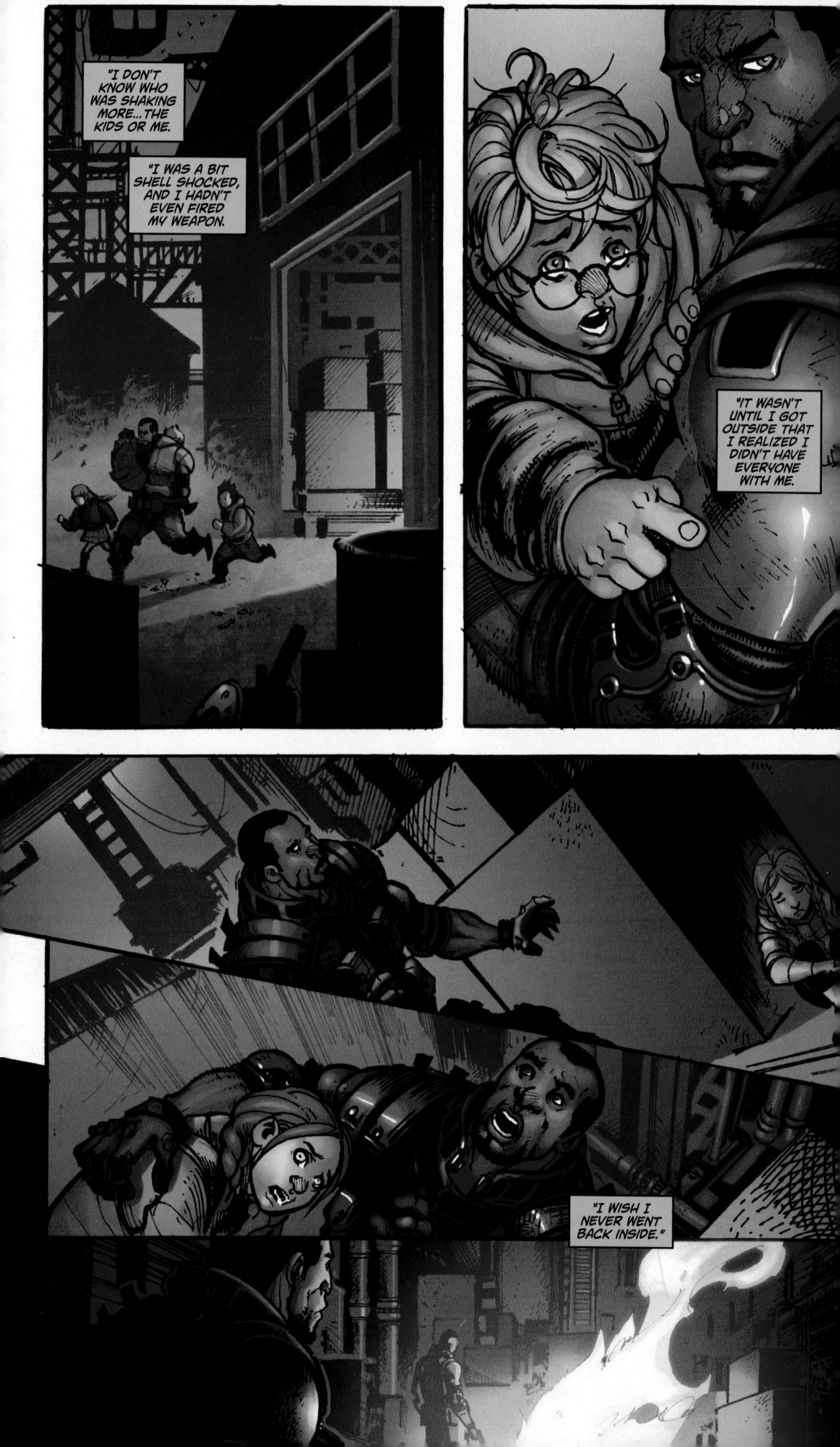
"I DON'T KNOW WHO WAS SHAKING MORE...THE KIDS OR ME.
"I WAS A BIT SHELL SHOCKED, AND I HADN'T EVEN FIRED MY WEAPON.
"IT WASN'T UNTIL I GOT OUTSIDE THAT I REALIZED I DIDN'T HAVE EVERYONE WITH ME.
"I WISH I NEVER WENT BACK INSIDE."

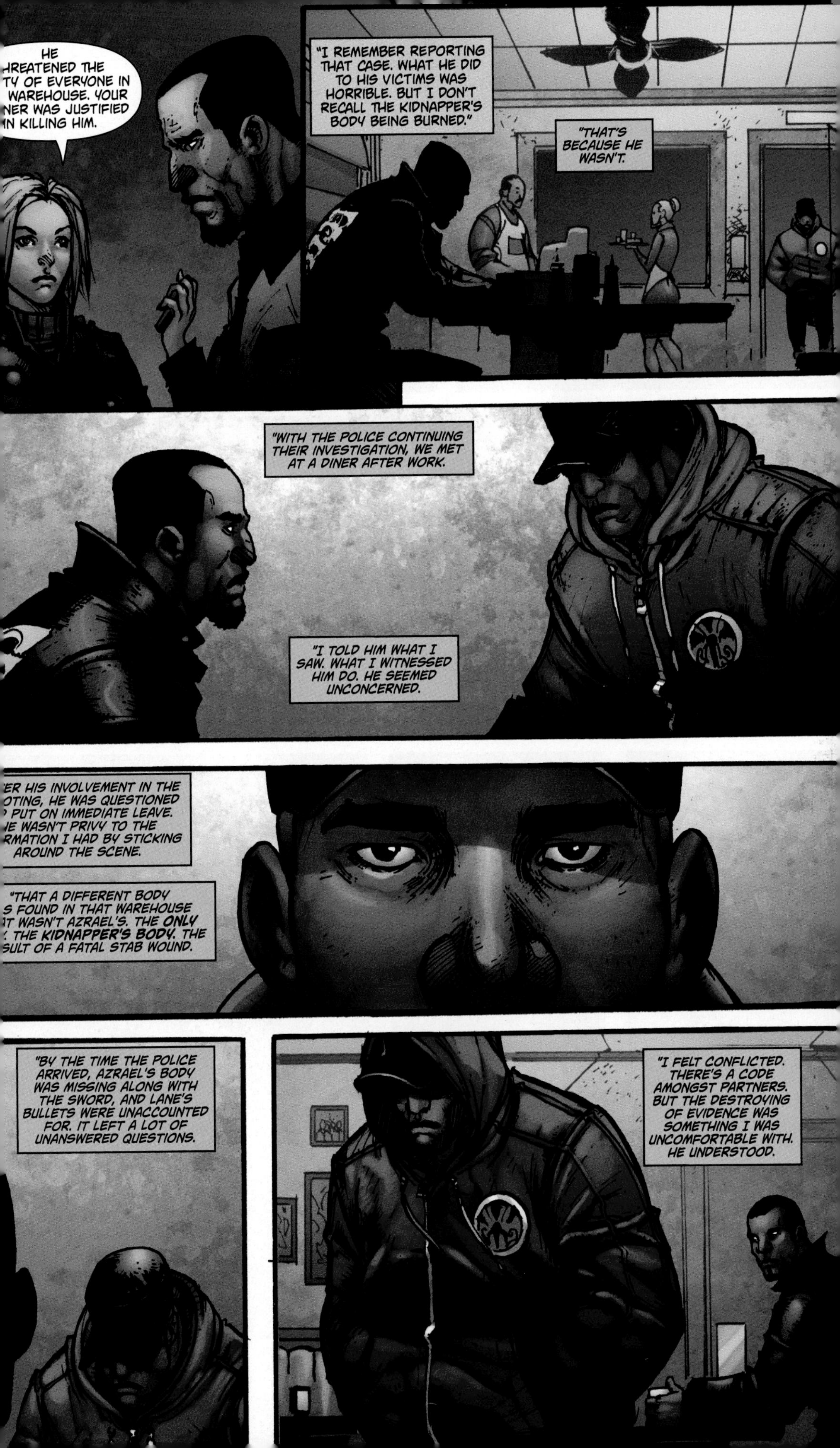

HE
HREATENED THE
TY OF EVERYONE IN
WAREHOUSE. YOUR
NER WAS JUSTIFIED
IN KILLING HIM.
"I REMEMBER REPORTING THAT CASE. WHAT HE DID TO HIS VICTIMS WAS HORRIBLE. BUT I DON'T RECALL THE KIDNAPPER'S BODY BEING BURNED."
"THAT'S BECAUSE HE WASN'T.
"WITH THE POLICE CONTINUING THEIR INVESTIGATION, WE MET AT A DINER AFTER WORK.
"I TOLD HIM WHAT I SAW. WHAT I WITNESSED HIM DO. HE SEEMED UNCONCERNED.
ER HIS INVOLVEMENT IN THE
OTING, HE WAS QUESTIONED
PUT ON IMMEDIATE LEAVE.
IE WASN'T PRIVY TO THE
RMATION I HAD BY STICKING
AROUND THE SCENE.
"THAT A DIFFERENT BODY
S FOUND IN THAT WAREHOUSE
T WASN'T AZRAEL'S. THE ONLY
THE KIDNAPPER'S BODY. THE
SULT OF A FATAL STAB WOUND.
"BY THE TIME THE POLICE ARRIVED, AZRAEL'S BODY WAS MISSING ALONG WITH THE SWORD, AND LANE'S BULLETS WERE UNACCOUNTED FOR. IT LEFT A LOT OF UNANSWERED QUESTIONS.
"I FELT CONFLICTED. THERE'S A CODE AMONGST PARTNERS. BUT THE DESTROYING OF EVIDENCE WAS SOMETHING I WAS UNCOMFORTABLE WITH. HE UNDERSTOOD.

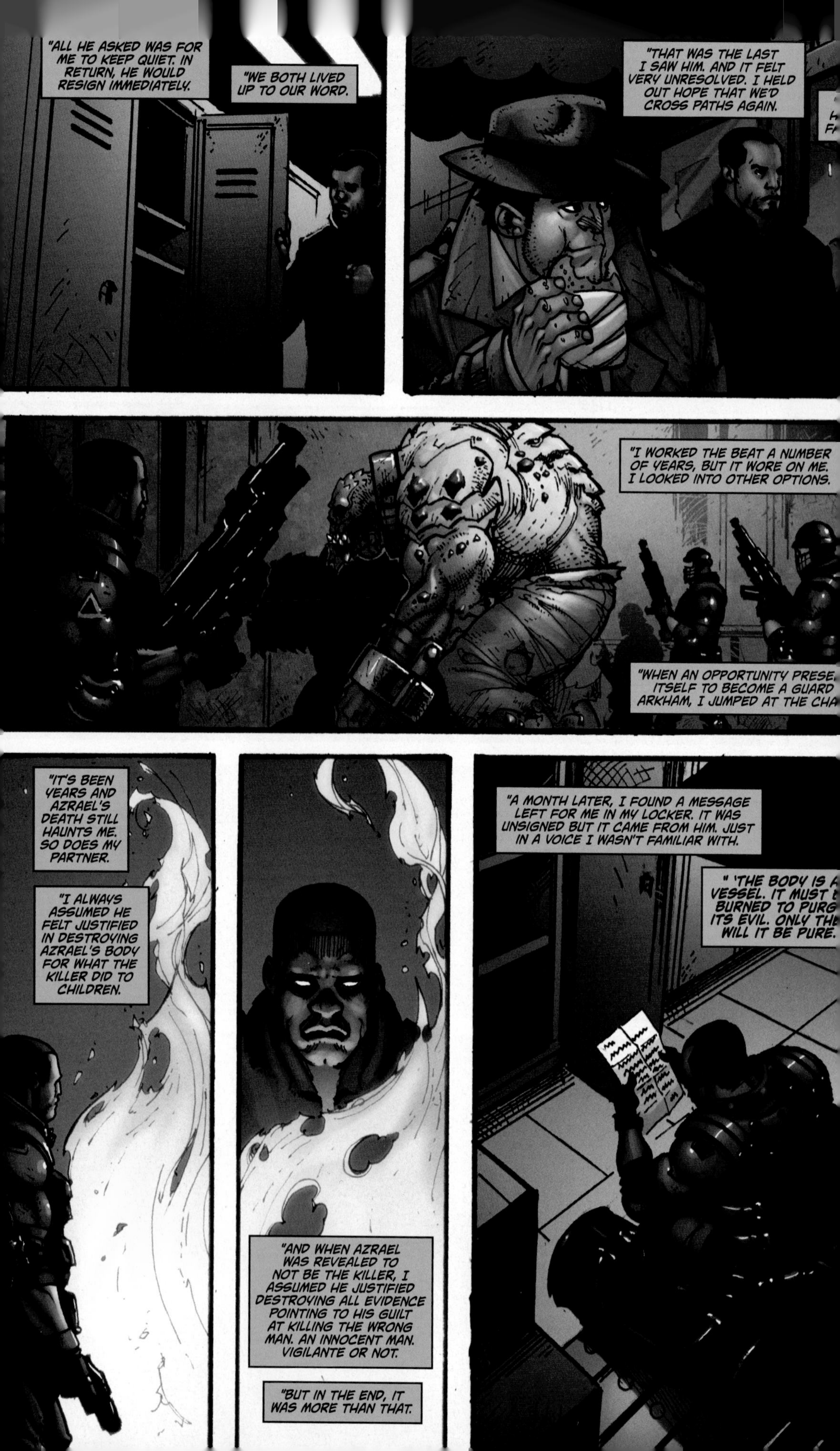
"ALL HE ASKED WAS FOR ME TO KEEP QUIET. IN RETURN, HE WOULD RESIGN IMMEDIATELY.
"WE BOTH LIVED UP TO OUR WORD.
"THAT WAS THE LAST I SAW HIM. AND IT FELT VERY UNRESOLVED. I HELD OUT HOPE THAT WE'D CROSS PATHS AGAIN.
"I WORKED THE BEAT A NUMBER OF YEARS, BUT IT WORE ON ME. I LOOKED INTO OTHER OPTIONS.
"WHEN AN OPPORTUNITY PRESE ITSELF TO BECOME A GUARD ARKHAM, I JUMPED AT THE CHA
"IT'S BEEN YEARS AND AZRAEL'S DEATH STILL HAUNTS ME. SO DOES MY PARTNER.
"I ALWAYS ASSUMED HE FELT JUSTIFIED IN DESTROYING AZRAEL'S BODY FOR WHAT THE KILLER DID TO CHILDREN.
"AND WHEN AZRAEL WAS REVEALED TO NOT BE THE KILLER, I ASSUMED HE JUSTIFIED DESTROYING ALL EVIDENCE POINTING TO HIS GUILT AT KILLING THE WRONG MAN. AN INNOCENT MAN. VIGILANTE OR NOT.
"BUT IN THE END, IT WAS MORE THAN THAT.
"A MONTH LATER, I FOUND A MESSAGE LEFT FOR ME IN MY LOCKER. IT WAS UNSIGNED BUT IT CAME FROM HIM. JUST IN A VOICE I WASN'T FAMILIAR WITH.
" 'THE BODY IS A VESSEL. IT MUST B BURNED TO PURG ITS EVIL. ONLY TH WILL IT BE PURE.

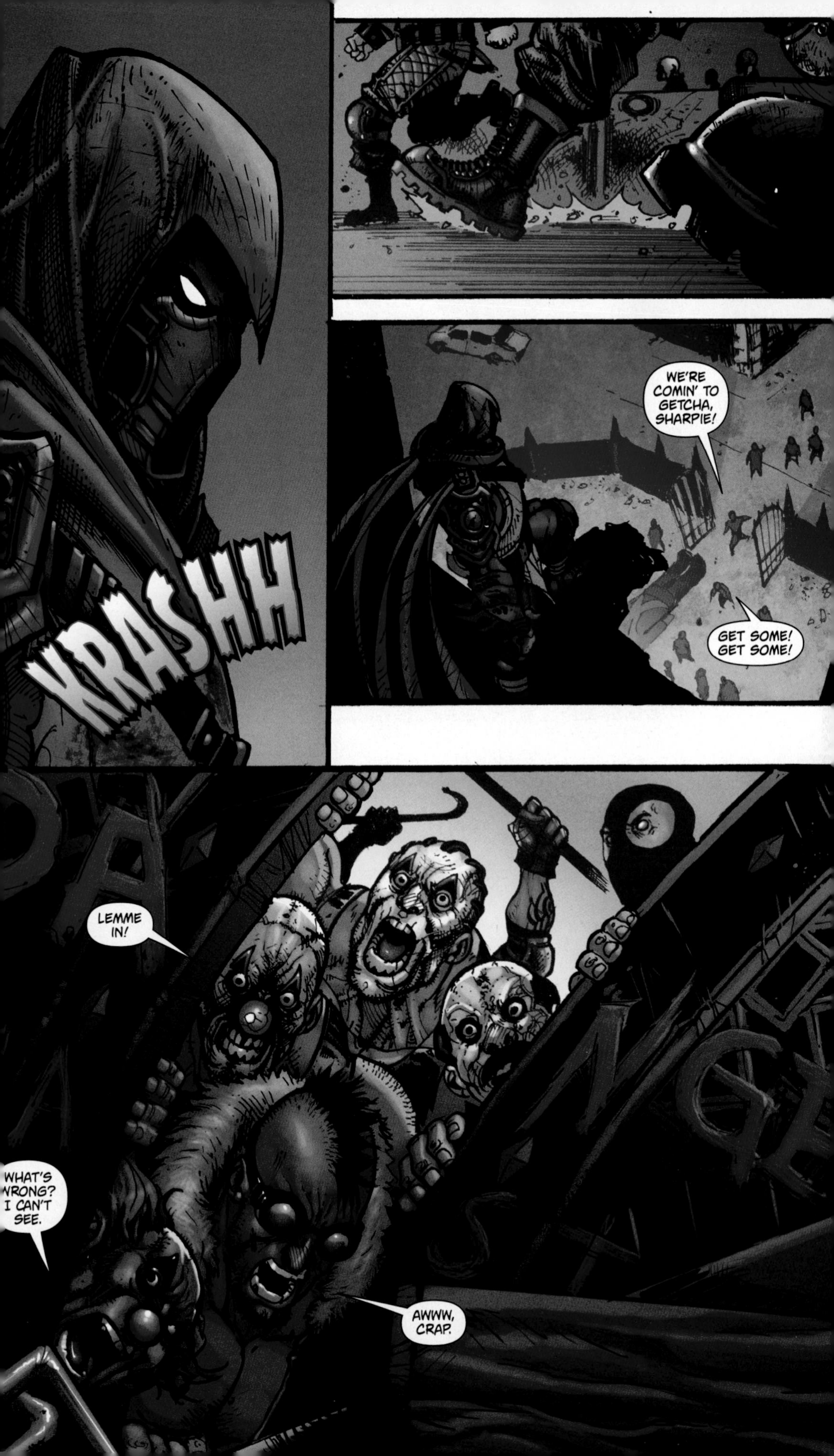
KRASHH
WE'RE COMIN' TO GETCHA, SHARPIE!
GET SOME! GET SOME!
LEMME IN!
WHAT'S WRONG? I CAN'T SEE.
AWWW, CRAP.

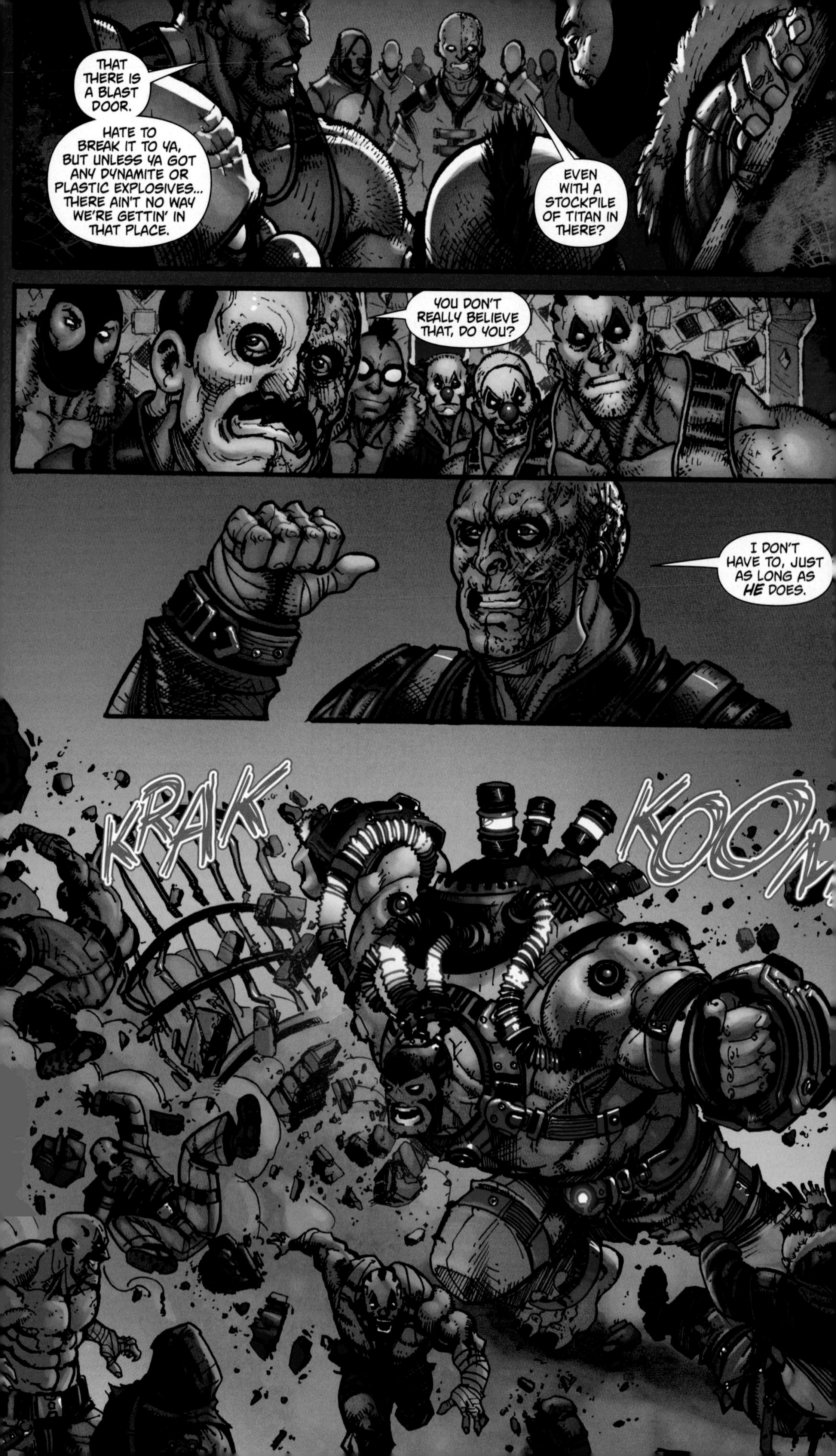
THAT THERE IS A BLAST DOOR.
HATE TO BREAK IT TO YA, BUT UNLESS YA GOT ANY DYNAMITE OR PLASTIC EXPLOSIVES... THERE AIN'T NO WAY WE'RE GETTIN' IN THAT PLACE.
EVEN WITH A STOCKPILE OF TITAN IN THERE?
YOU DON'T REALLY BELIEVE THAT, DO YOU?
I DON'T HAVE TO, JUST AS LONG AS *HE* DOES.
KRAK
KOOM

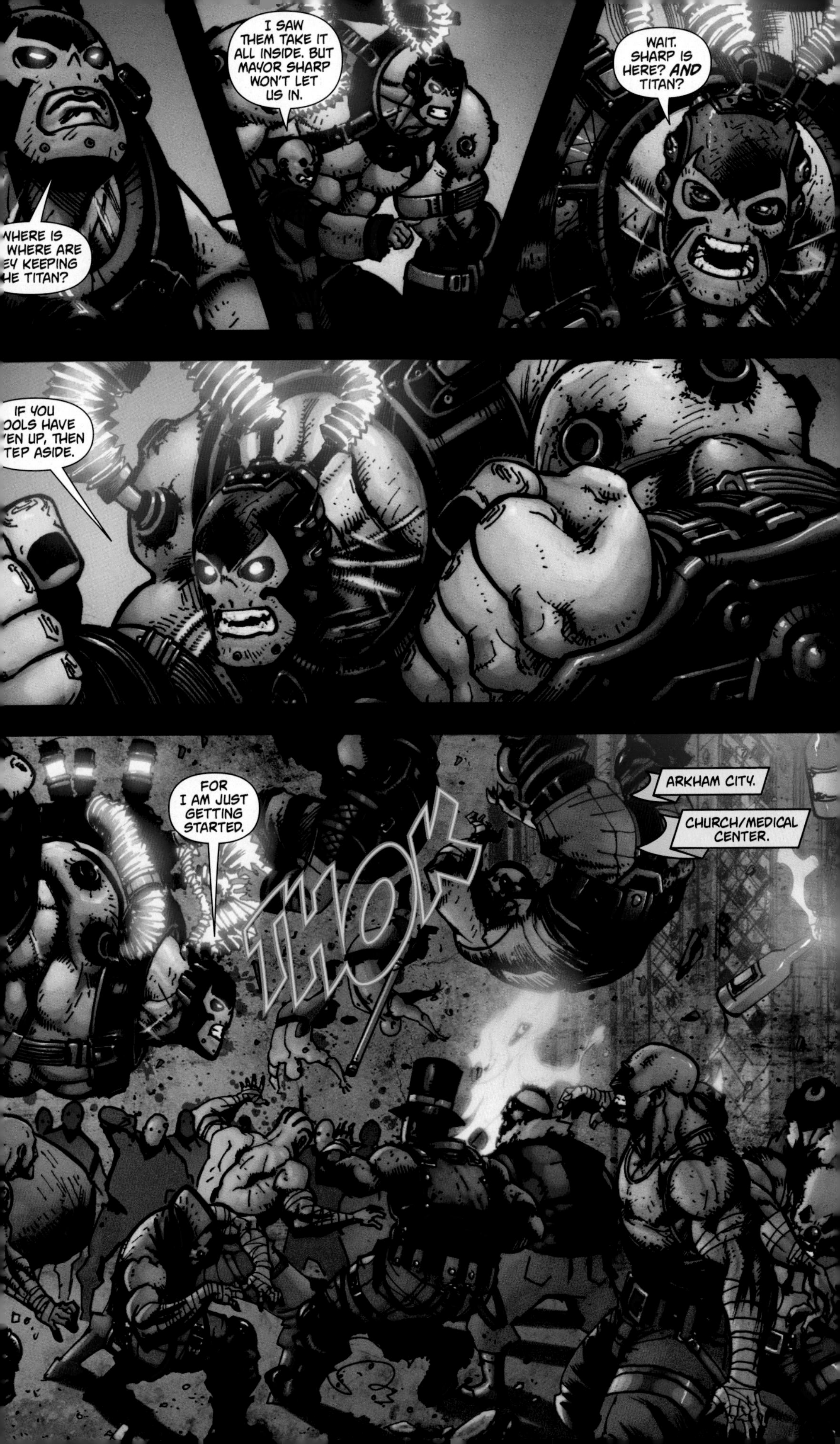
WHERE IS
WHERE ARE
EY KEEPING
HE TITAN?
I SAW THEM TAKE IT ALL INSIDE. BUT MAYOR SHARP WON'T LET US IN.
WAIT. SHARP IS HERE? AND TITAN?
IF YOU
OOLS HAVE
'EN UP, THEN
TEP ASIDE.
FOR I AM JUST GETTING STARTED.
ARKHAM CITY.
CHURCH/MEDICAL CENTER.
THOK

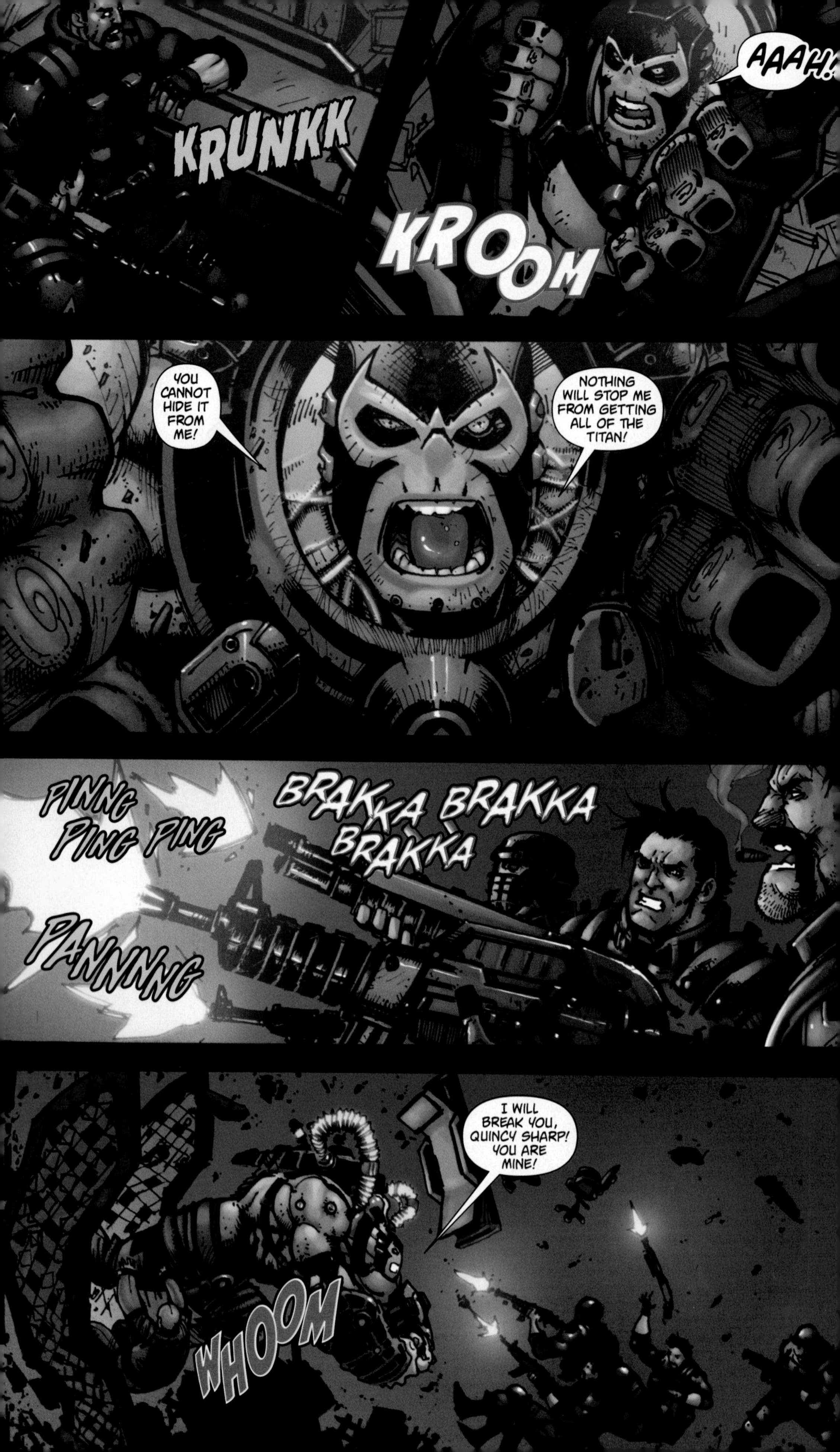
KRUNKK
AAAH!
KROOM
YOU CANNOT HIDE IT FROM ME!
NOTHING WILL STOP ME FROM GETTING ALL OF THE TITAN!
PINNG PING PING
BRAKKA BRAKKA BRAKKA
PANNNNG
I WILL BREAK YOU, QUINCY SHARP! YOU ARE MINE!
WHOOM

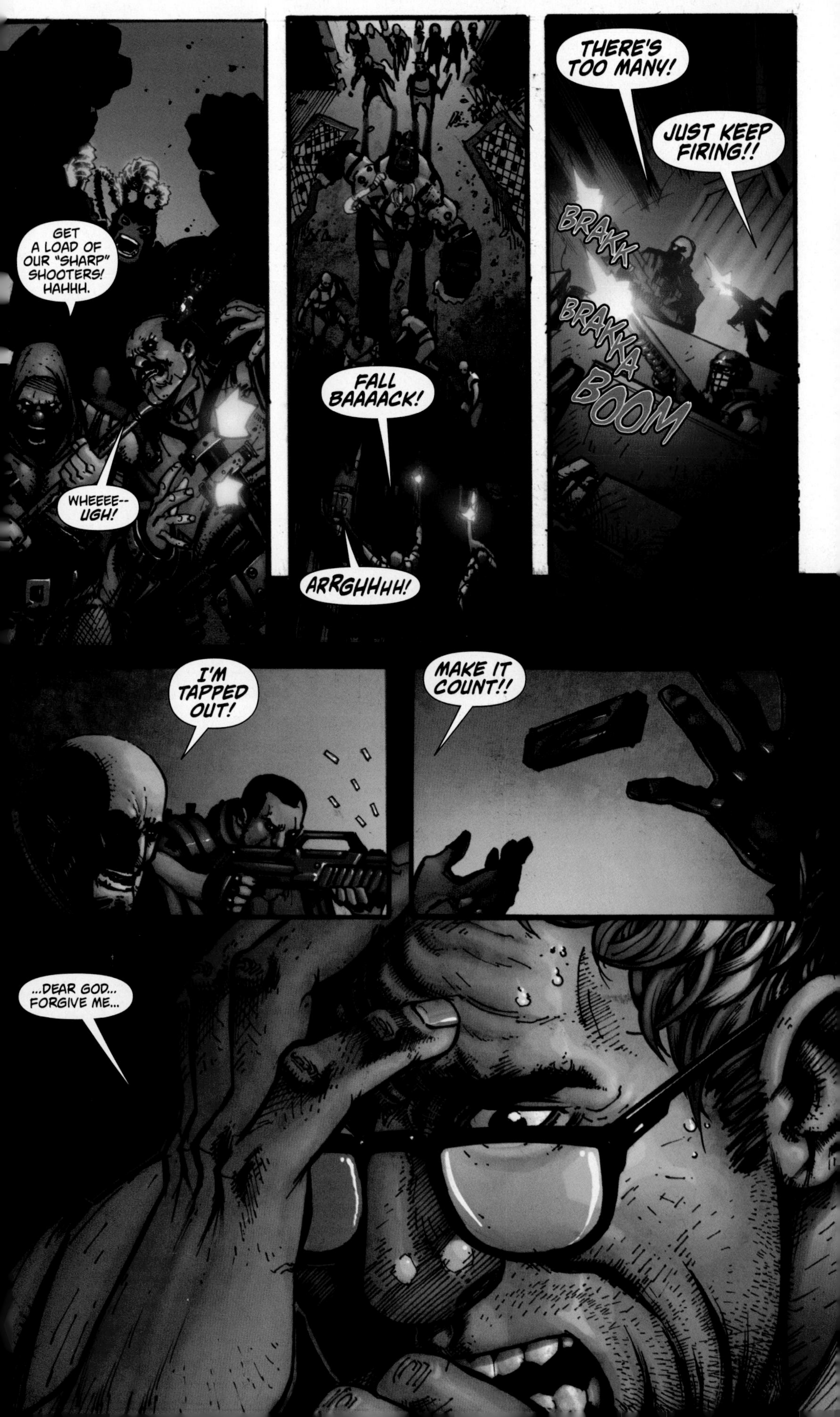
GET A LOAD OF OUR "SHARP" SHOOTERS! HAHHH.
WHEEEE-- UGH!
FALL BAAAACK!
ARRGHHHH!
THERE'S TOO MANY!
JUST KEEP FIRING!!
BRAKK
BRAKKA
BOOM
I'M TAPPED OUT!
MAKE IT COUNT!!
...DEAR GOD... FORGIVE ME...

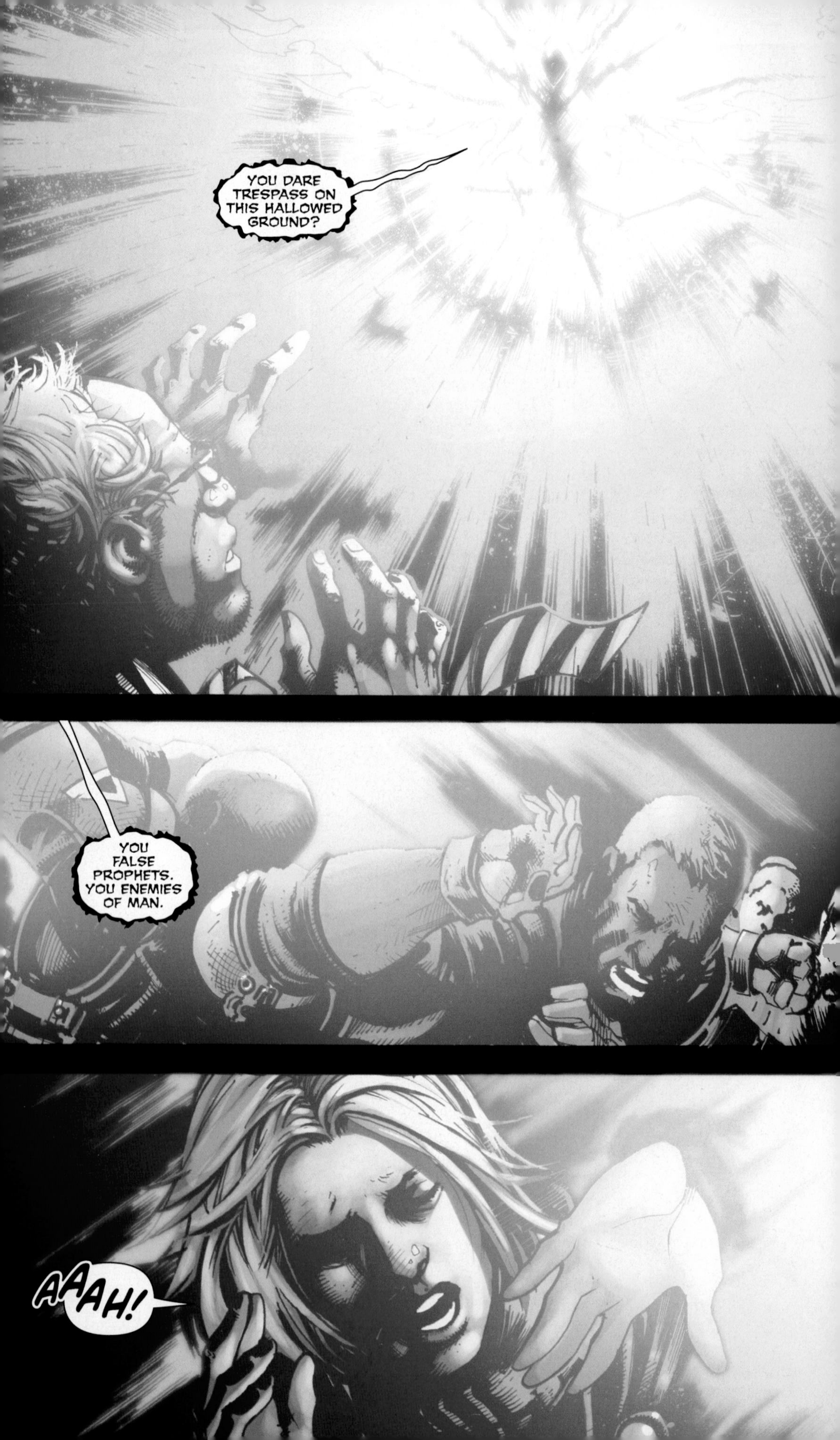
YOU DARE TRESPASS ON THIS HALLOWED GROUND?
YOU FALSE PROPHETS. YOU ENEMIES OF MAN.
AAAAH!

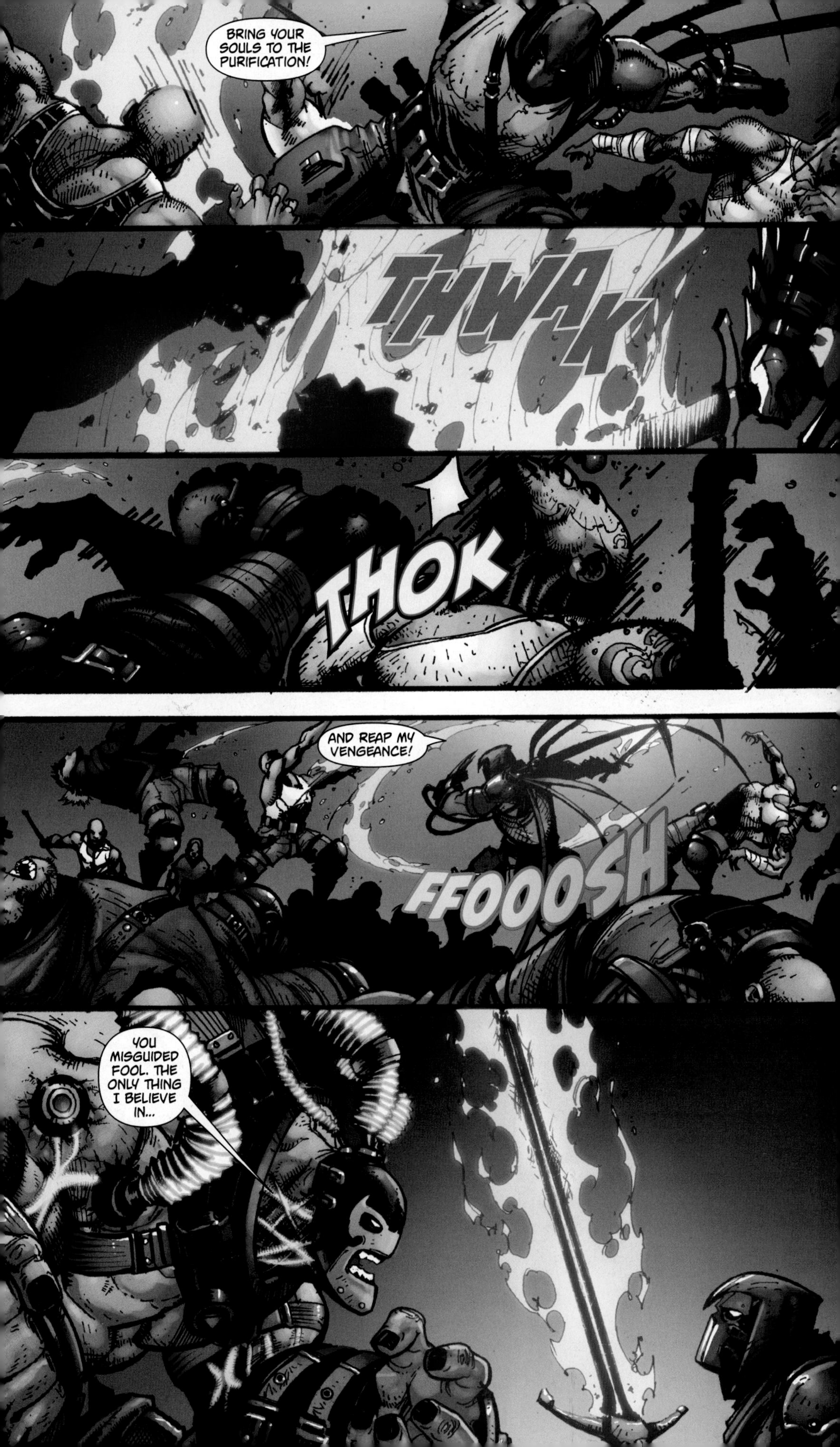
BRING YOUR SOULS TO THE PURIFICATION!
THWAK
THOK
AND REAP MY VENGEANCE!
FFOOOSH
YOU MISGUIDED FOOL. THE ONLY THING I BELIEVE IN...

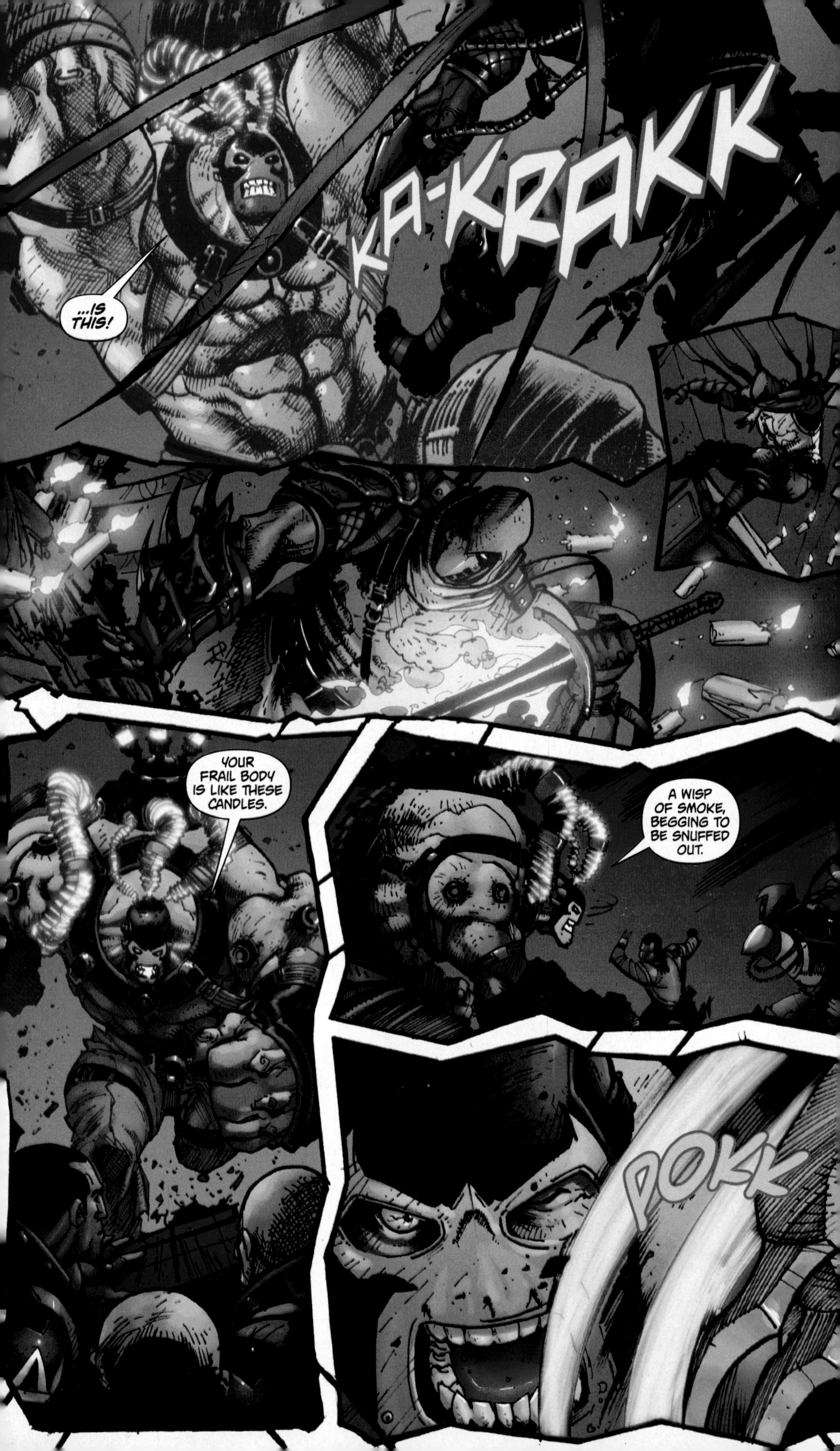
...IS THIS!
KA-KRAKK
YOUR FRAIL BODY IS LIKE THESE CANDLES.
A WISP OF SMOKE, BEGGING TO BE SNUFFED OUT.
POKK

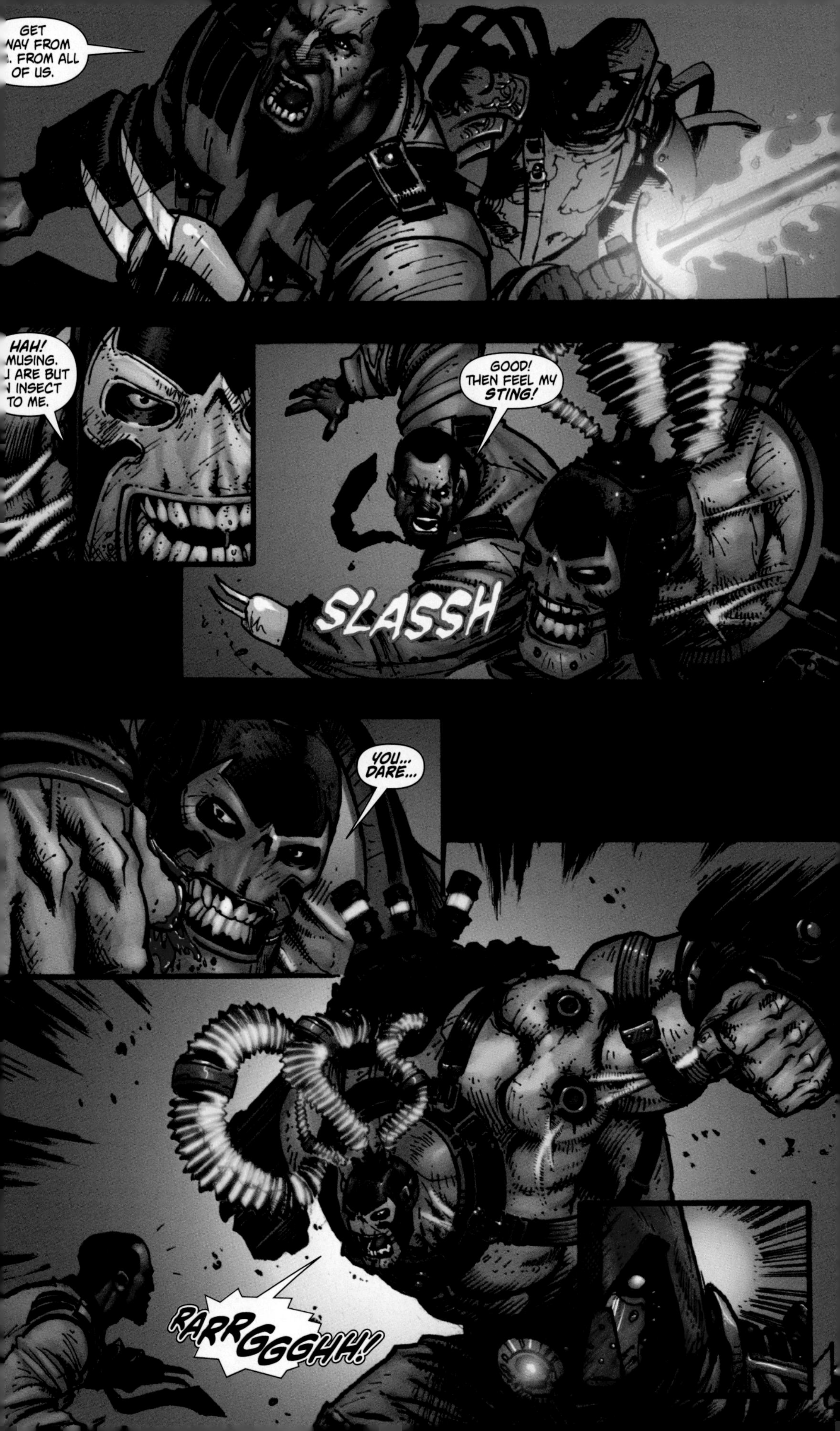
GET ...AY FROM ... FROM ALL OF US.
HAH! ...MUSING. ...ARE BUT ...INSECT TO ME.
GOOD! THEN FEEL MY STING!
SLASSH
YOU... DARE...
RARRGGGHH!

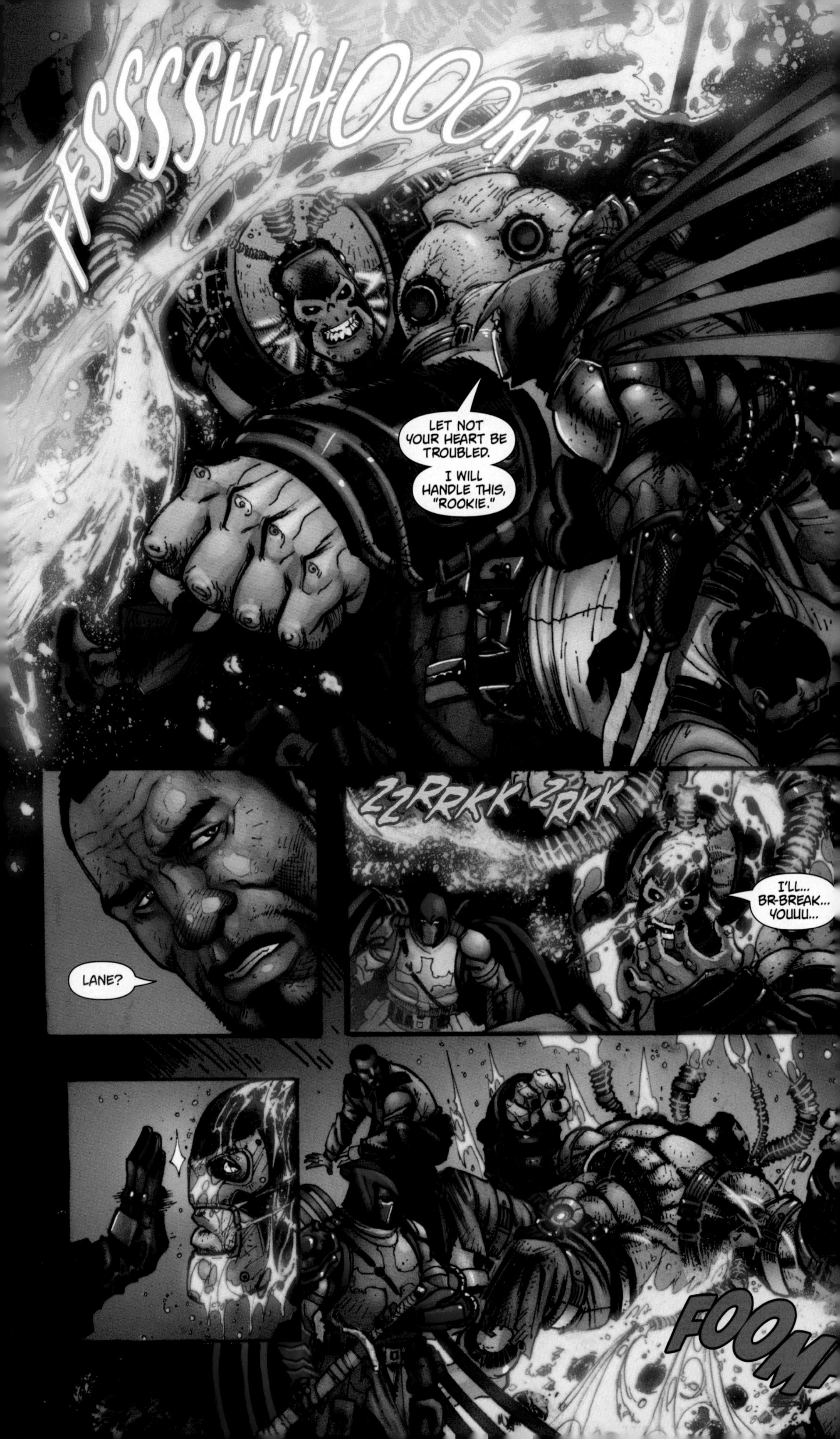
FFSSSSHHHOOOM
LET NOT YOUR HEART BE TROUBLED.
I WILL HANDLE THIS, "ROOKIE."
LANE?
ZZRRKK ZRKK
I'LL... BR-BREAK... YOUUU...
FOOM

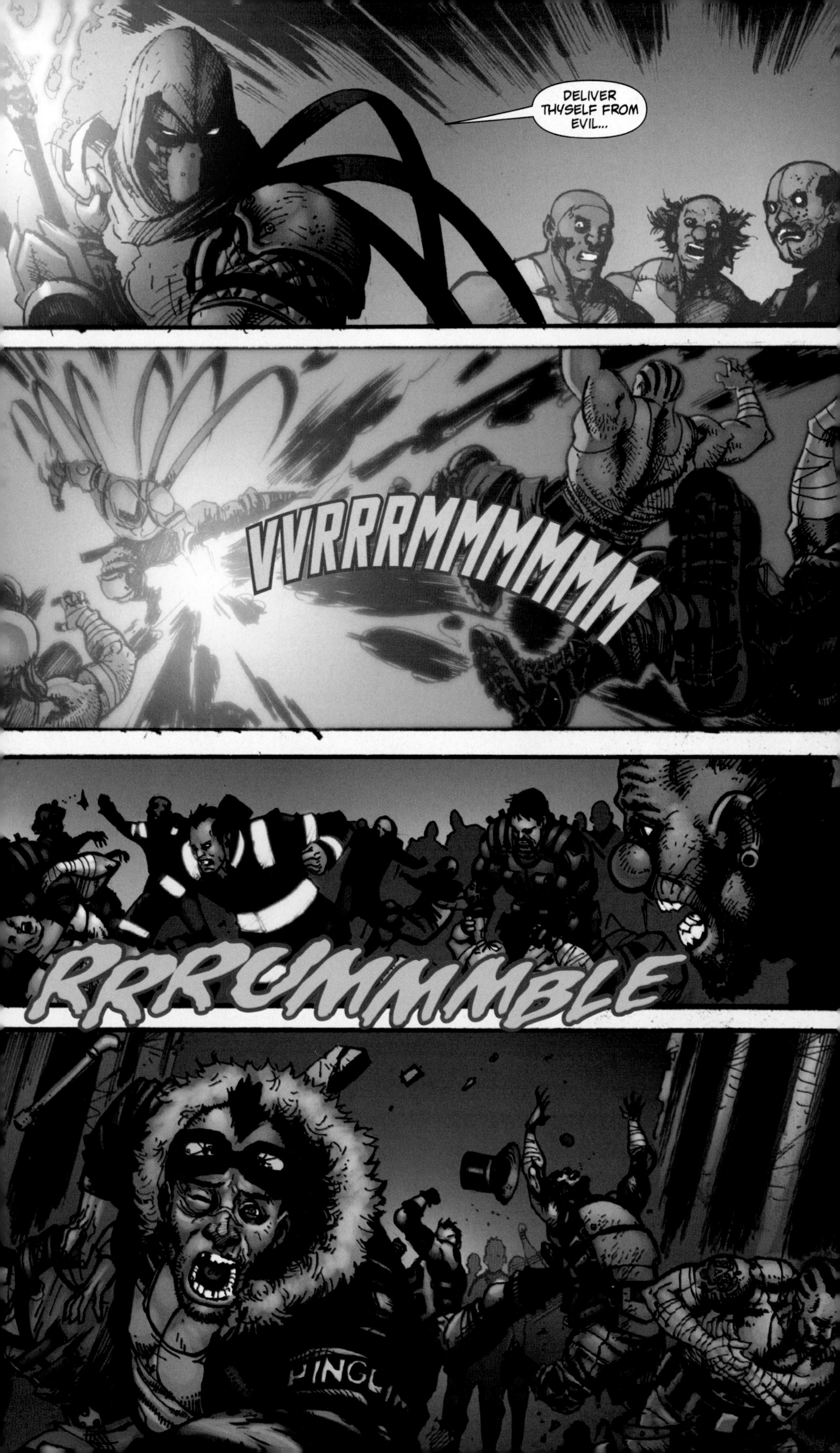
DELIVER THYSELF FROM EVIL...
VVRRRMMMMMMM
RRRUMMMBLE

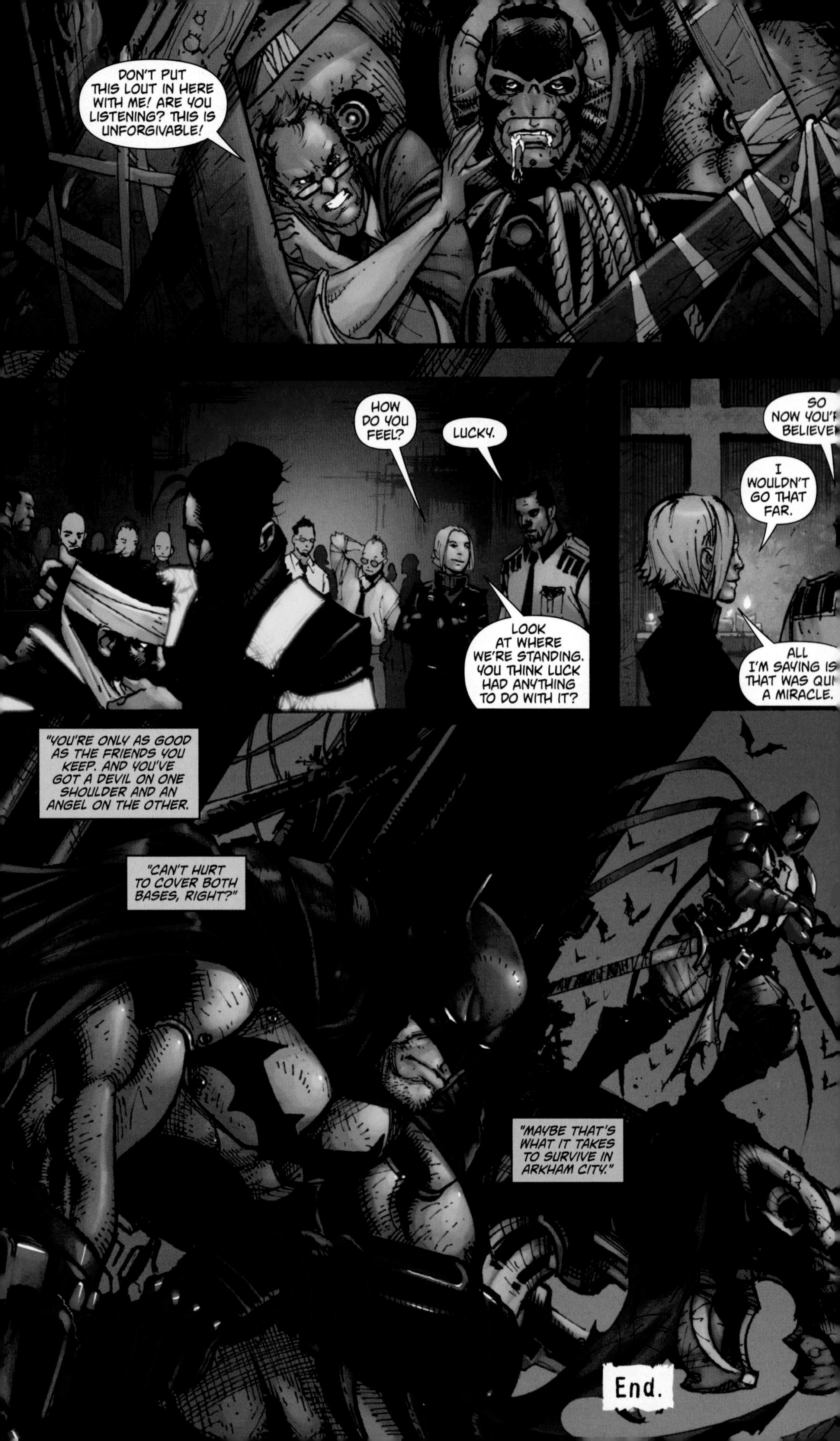
DON'T PUT THIS LOUT IN HERE WITH ME! ARE YOU LISTENING? THIS IS UNFORGIVABLE!
HOW DO YOU FEEL?
LUCKY.
LOOK AT WHERE WE'RE STANDING. YOU THINK LUCK HAD ANYTHING TO DO WITH IT?
I WOULDN'T GO THAT FAR.
"YOU'RE ONLY AS GOOD AS THE FRIENDS YOU KEEP. AND YOU'VE GOT A DEVIL ON ONE SHOULDER AND AN ANGEL ON THE OTHER.
"CAN'T HURT TO COVER BOTH BASES, RIGHT?"
"MAYBE THAT'S WHAT IT TAKES TO SURVIVE IN ARKHAM CITY."
End.

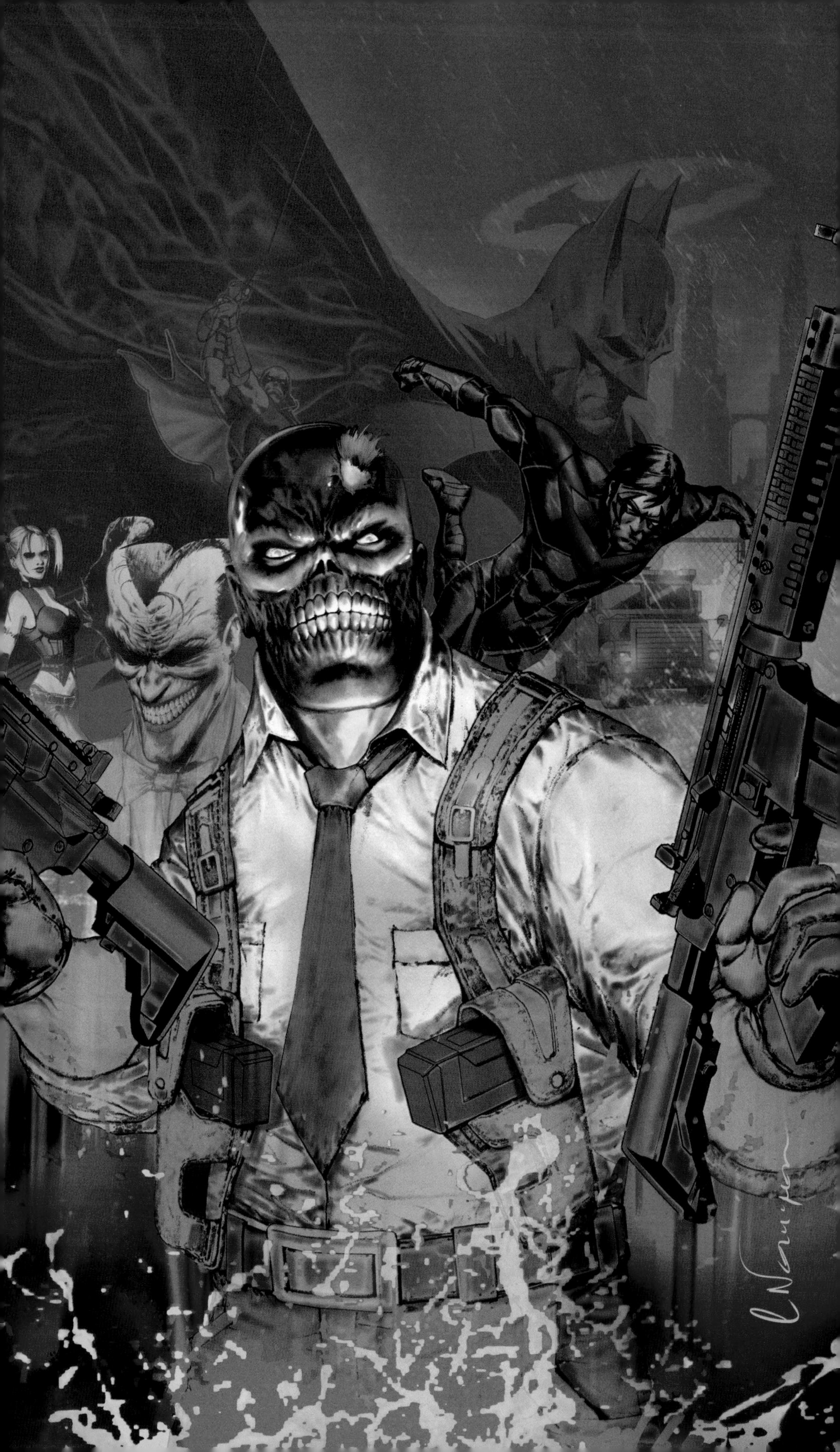

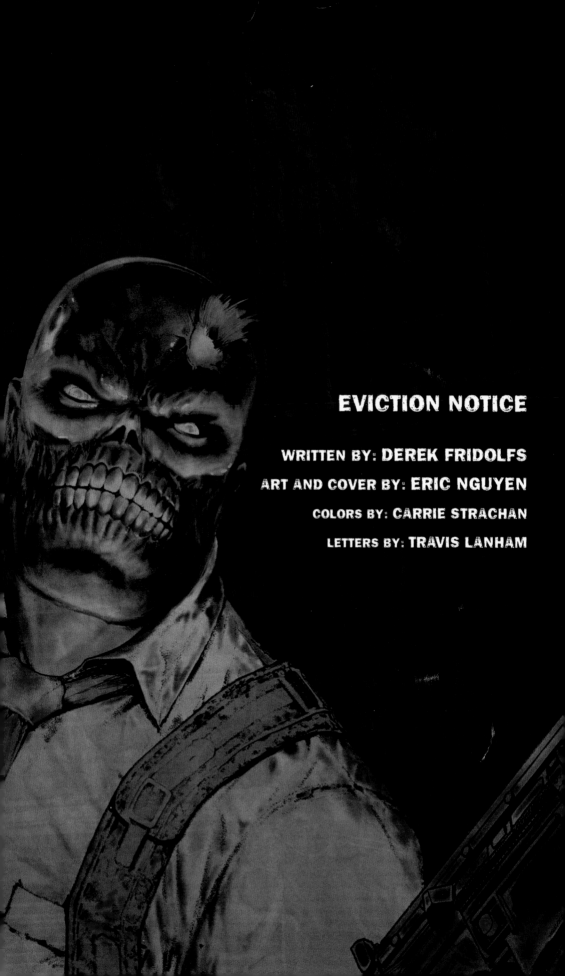

EVICTION NOTICE

WRITTEN BY: DEREK FRIDOLFS

ART AND COVER BY: ERIC NGUYEN

COLORS BY: CARRIE STRACHAN

LETTERS BY: TRAVIS LANHAM

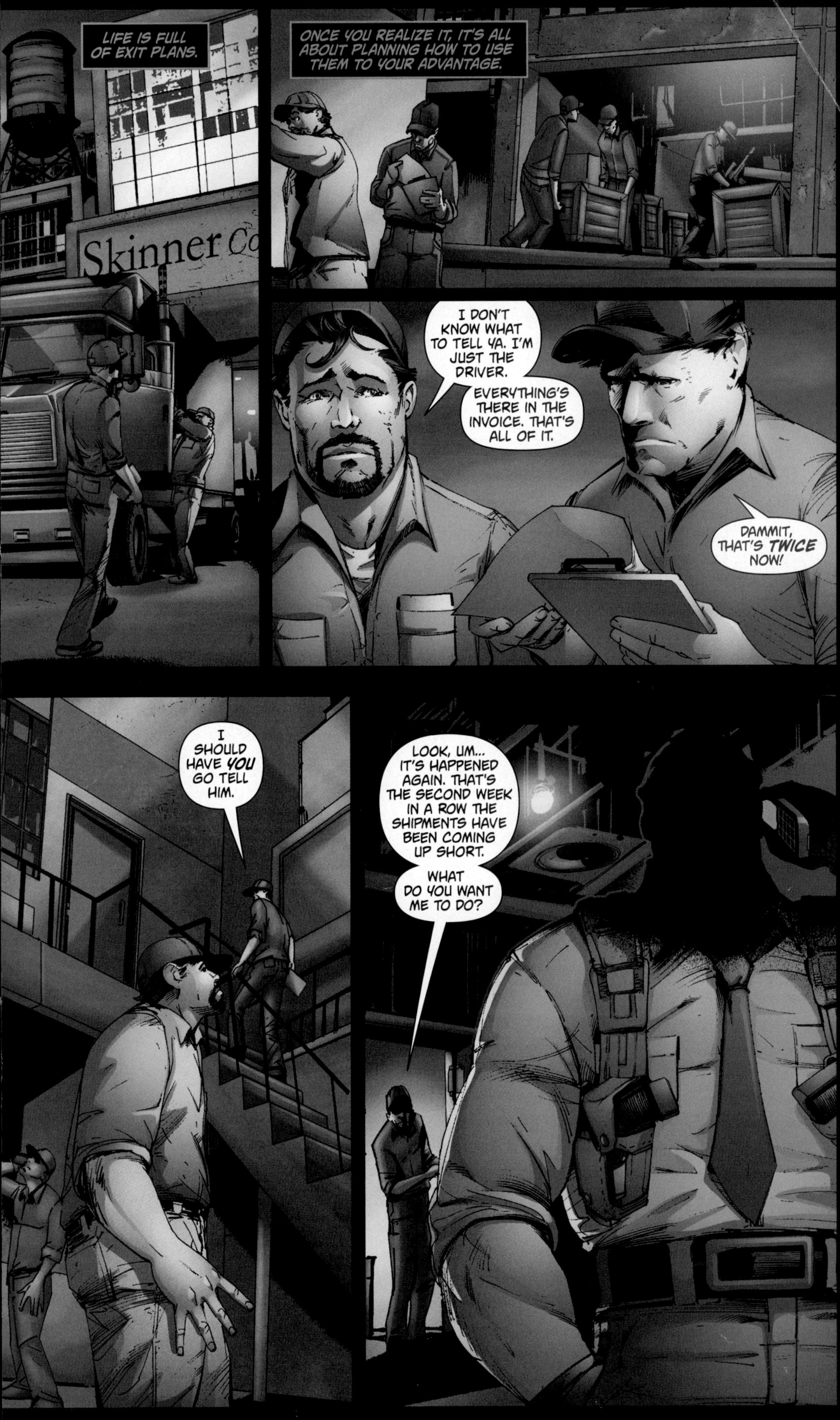
LIFE IS FULL OF EXIT PLANS.
Skinner Co
ONCE YOU REALIZE IT, IT'S ALL ABOUT PLANNING HOW TO USE THEM TO YOUR ADVANTAGE.
I DON'T KNOW WHAT TO TELL YA. I'M JUST THE DRIVER.
EVERYTHING'S THERE IN THE INVOICE. THAT'S ALL OF IT.
DAMMIT, THAT'S TWICE NOW!
I SHOULD HAVE YOU GO TELL HIM.
LOOK, UM... IT'S HAPPENED AGAIN. THAT'S THE SECOND WEEK IN A ROW THE SHIPMENTS HAVE BEEN COMING UP SHORT.
WHAT DO YOU WANT ME TO DO?

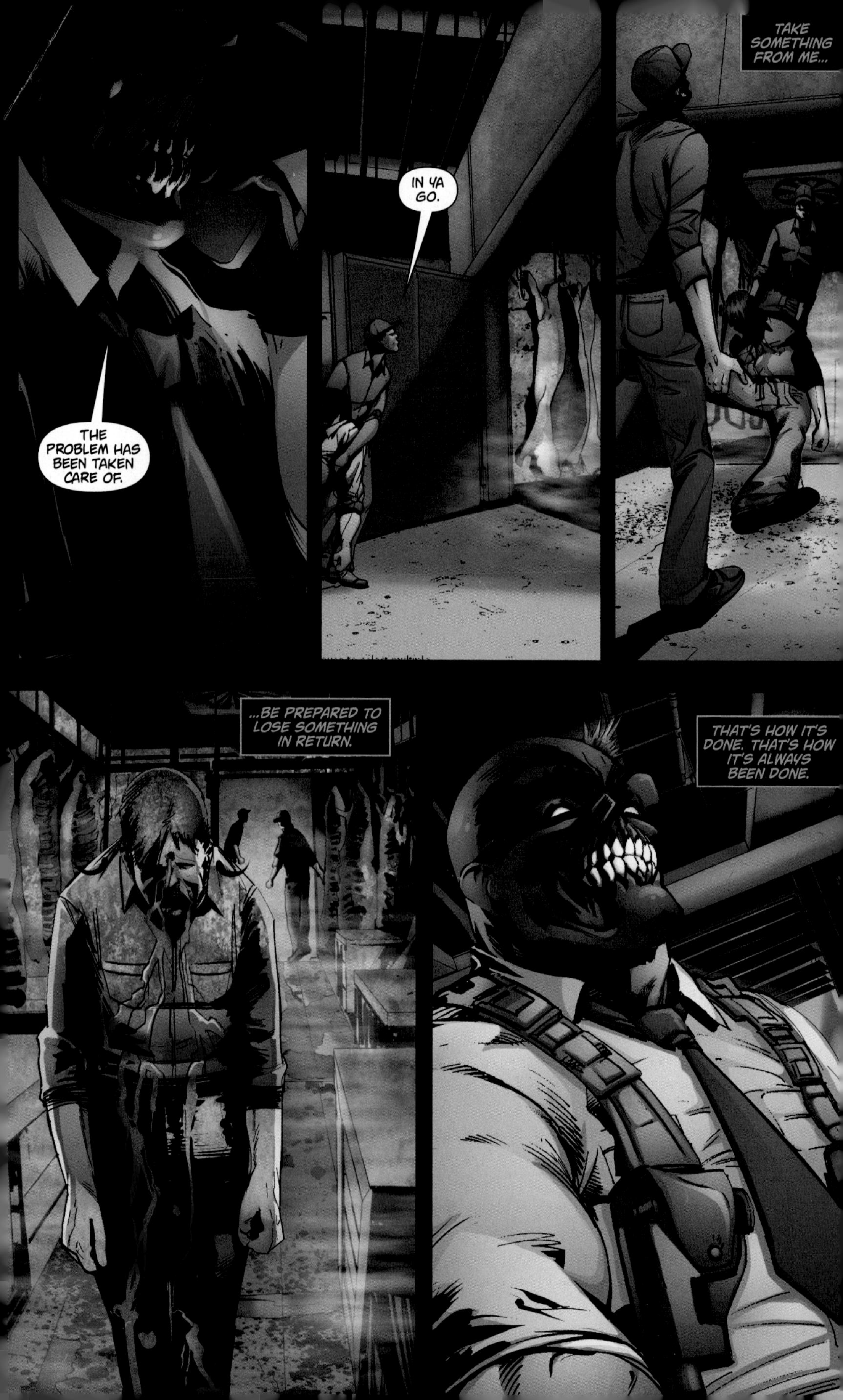
THE PROBLEM HAS BEEN TAKEN CARE OF.
IN YA GO.
TAKE SOMETHING FROM ME...
...BE PREPARED TO LOSE SOMETHING IN RETURN.
THAT'S HOW IT'S DONE. THAT'S HOW IT'S ALWAYS BEEN DONE.

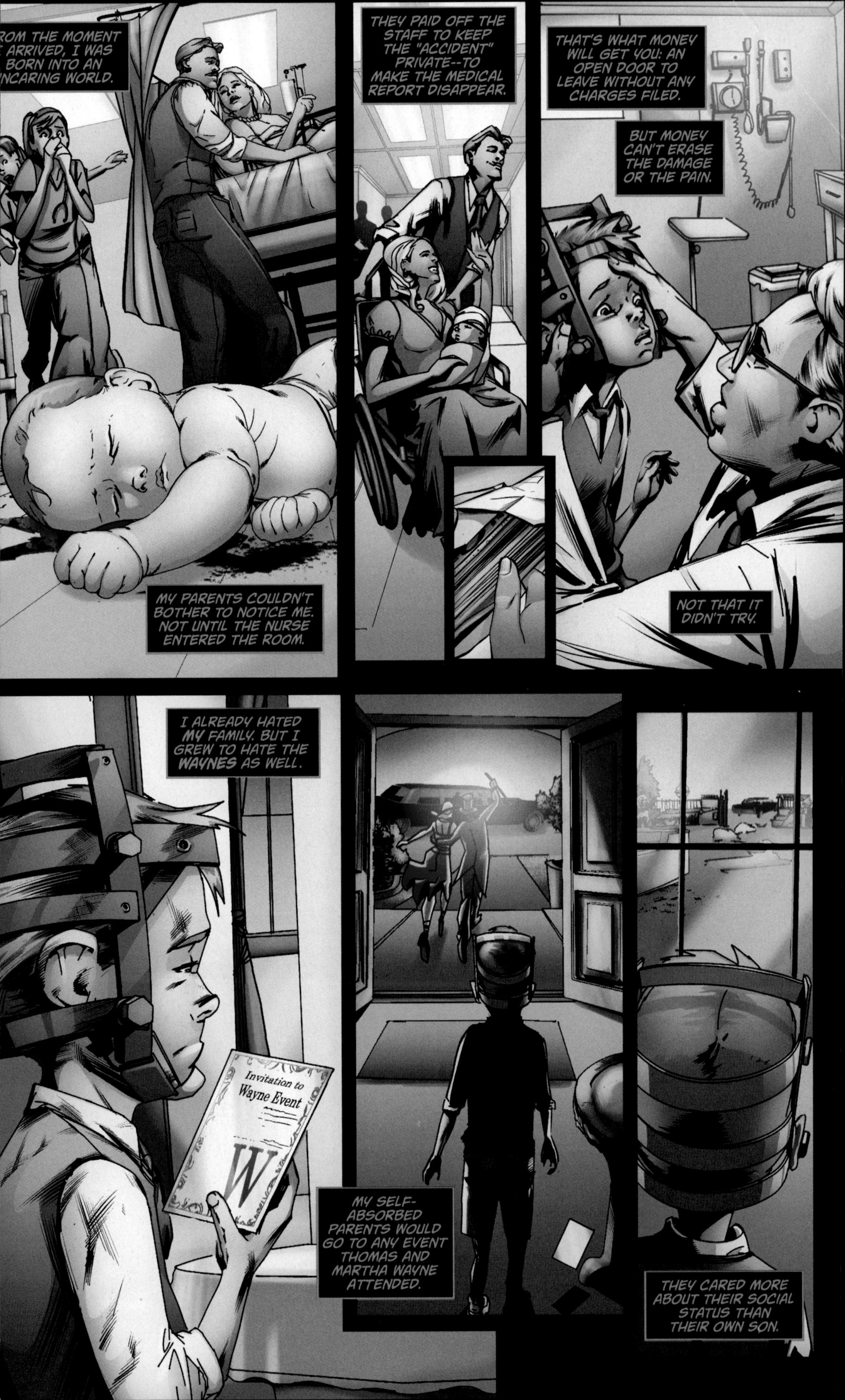
FROM THE MOMENT I ARRIVED, I WAS BORN INTO AN UNCARING WORLD.
MY PARENTS COULDN'T BOTHER TO NOTICE ME. NOT UNTIL THE NURSE ENTERED THE ROOM.
THEY PAID OFF THE STAFF TO KEEP THE "ACCIDENT" PRIVATE--TO MAKE THE MEDICAL REPORT DISAPPEAR.
THAT'S WHAT MONEY WILL GET YOU: AN OPEN DOOR TO LEAVE WITHOUT ANY CHARGES FILED.
BUT MONEY CAN'T ERASE THE DAMAGE OR THE PAIN.
NOT THAT IT DIDN'T TRY.
I ALREADY HATED MY FAMILY. BUT I GREW TO HATE THE WAYNES AS WELL.
Invitation to Wayne Event
W
MY SELF-ABSORBED PARENTS WOULD GO TO ANY EVENT THOMAS AND MARTHA WAYNE ATTENDED.
THEY CARED MORE ABOUT THEIR SOCIAL STATUS THAN THEIR OWN SON.

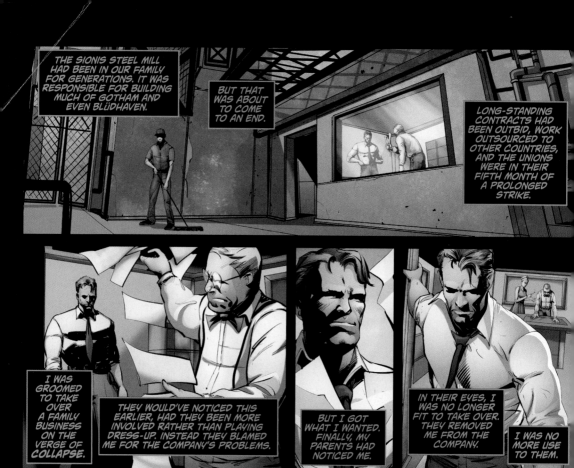

THE SIONIS STEEL MILL HAD BEEN IN OUR FAMILY FOR GENERATIONS. IT WAS RESPONSIBLE FOR BUILDING MUCH OF GOTHAM AND EVEN BLÜDHAVEN.

BUT THAT WAS ABOUT TO COME TO AN END.

LONG-STANDING CONTRACTS HAD BEEN OUTBID, WORK OUTSOURCED TO OTHER COUNTRIES, AND THE UNIONS WERE IN THEIR FIFTH MONTH OF A PROLONGED STRIKE.

I WAS GROOMED TO TAKE OVER A FAMILY BUSINESS ON THE VERGE OF COLLAPSE.

THEY WOULD'VE NOTICED THIS EARLIER, HAD THEY BEEN MORE INVOLVED RATHER THAN PLAYING DRESS-UP. INSTEAD THEY BLAMED ME FOR THE COMPANY'S PROBLEMS.

BUT I GOT WHAT I WANTED. FINALLY, MY PARENTS HAD NOTICED ME.

IN THEIR EYES, I WAS NO LONGER FIT TO TAKE OVER. THEY REMOVED ME FROM THE COMPANY.

I WAS NO MORE USE TO THEM.

THE FEELING WAS MUTUAL.

WITH MY NAME REMOVED FROM THE FAMILY TRUST, I WAS LEFT WITH NOTHING. THE FINAL INSULT CAME WHEN BRUCE WAYNE PURCHASED THE SIONIS FACTORY, SAVING IT FROM COLLAPSE.

THOMAS AND MARTHA'S OWN SON HAD EVERYTHING I WAS SUPPOSED TO HAVE...WEALTH AND OWNERSHIP.

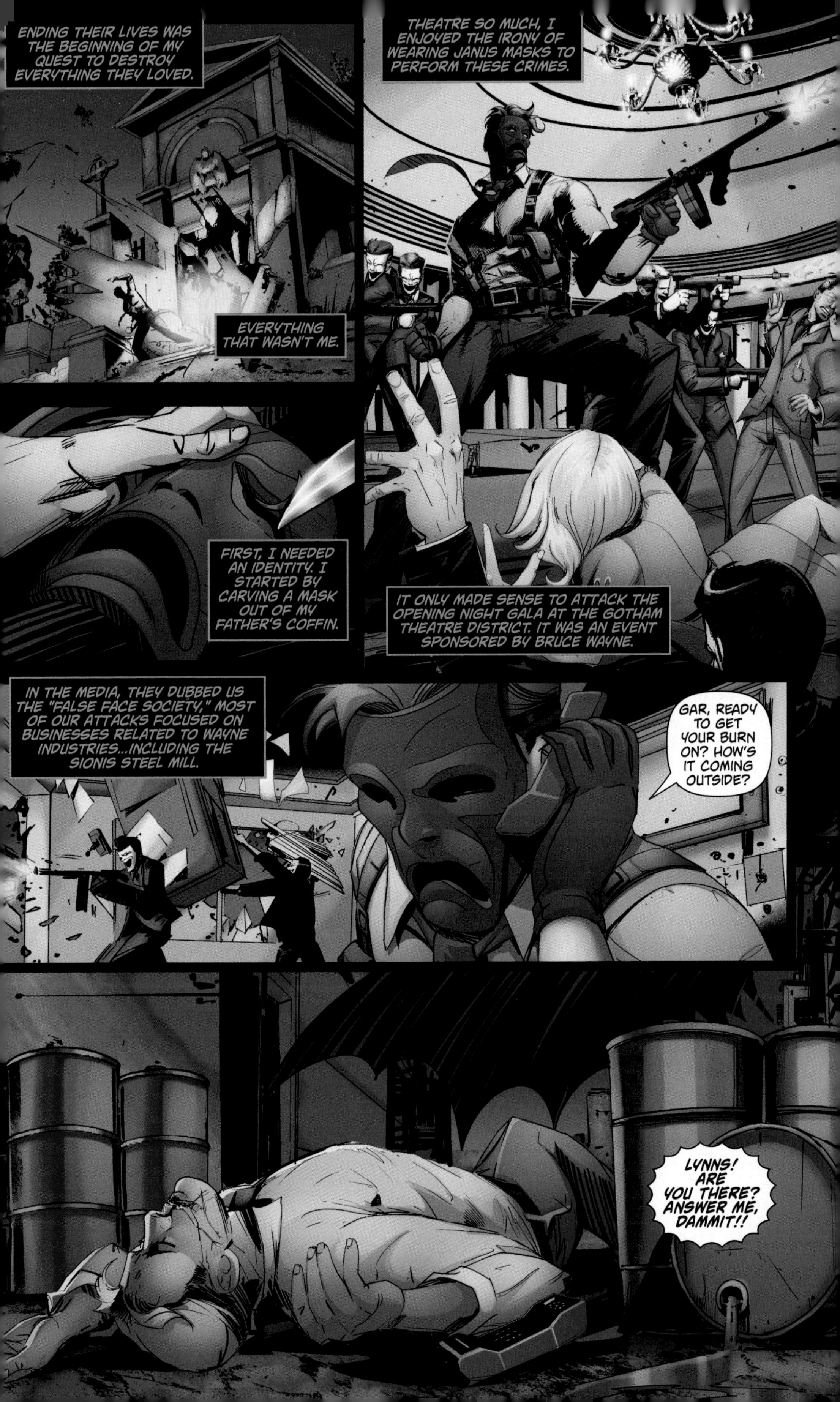
ENDING THEIR LIVES WAS THE BEGINNING OF MY QUEST TO DESTROY EVERYTHING THEY LOVED.
EVERYTHING THAT WASN'T ME.
FIRST, I NEEDED AN IDENTITY. I STARTED BY CARVING A MASK OUT OF MY FATHER'S COFFIN.
THEATRE SO MUCH, I ENJOYED THE IRONY OF WEARING JANUS MASKS TO PERFORM THESE CRIMES.
IT ONLY MADE SENSE TO ATTACK THE OPENING NIGHT GALA AT THE GOTHAM THEATRE DISTRICT. IT WAS AN EVENT SPONSORED BY BRUCE WAYNE.
IN THE MEDIA, THEY DUBBED US THE "FALSE FACE SOCIETY," MOST OF OUR ATTACKS FOCUSED ON BUSINESSES RELATED TO WAYNE INDUSTRIES...INCLUDING THE SIONIS STEEL MILL.
GAR, READY TO GET YOUR BURN ON? HOW'S IT COMING OUTSIDE?
LYNNS! ARE YOU THERE? ANSWER ME, DAMMIT!!

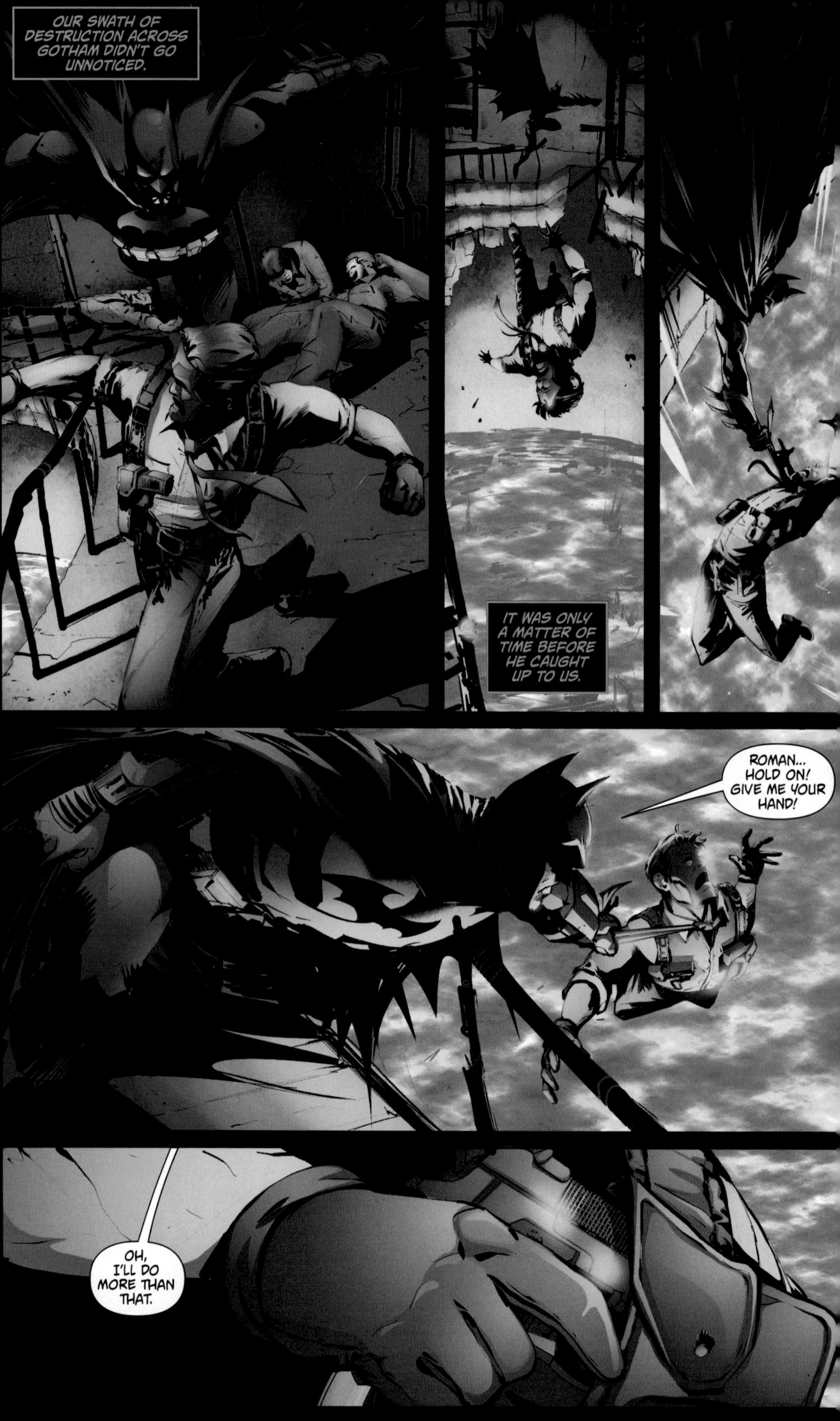
OUR SWATH OF DESTRUCTION ACROSS GOTHAM DIDN'T GO UNNOTICED.
IT WAS ONLY A MATTER OF TIME BEFORE HE CAUGHT UP TO US.
ROMAN... HOLD ON! GIVE ME YOUR HAND!
OH, I'LL DO MORE THAN THAT.

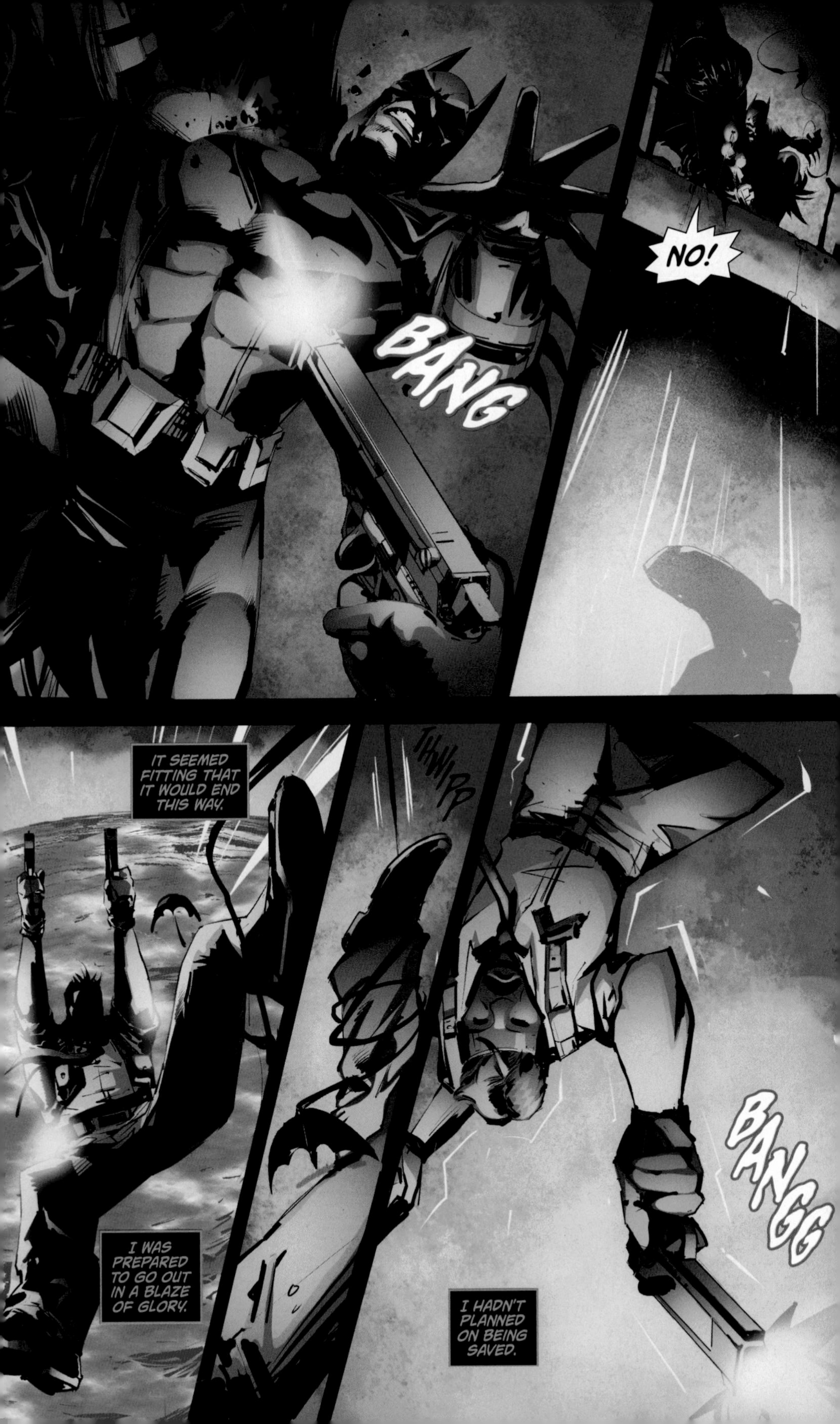
BANG
NO!
IT SEEMED FITTING THAT IT WOULD END THIS WAY.
I WAS PREPARED TO GO OUT IN A BLAZE OF GLORY.
THWIPP
I HADN'T PLANNED ON BEING SAVED.
BANGG

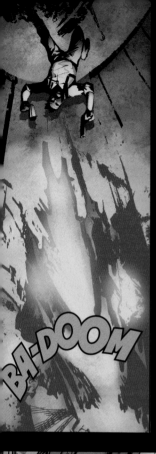

BA-DOOM

YAAAARGHH!

BUT YOU KNOW WHAT THEY SAY ABOUT MAKING PLANS.

GOD LAUGHS.

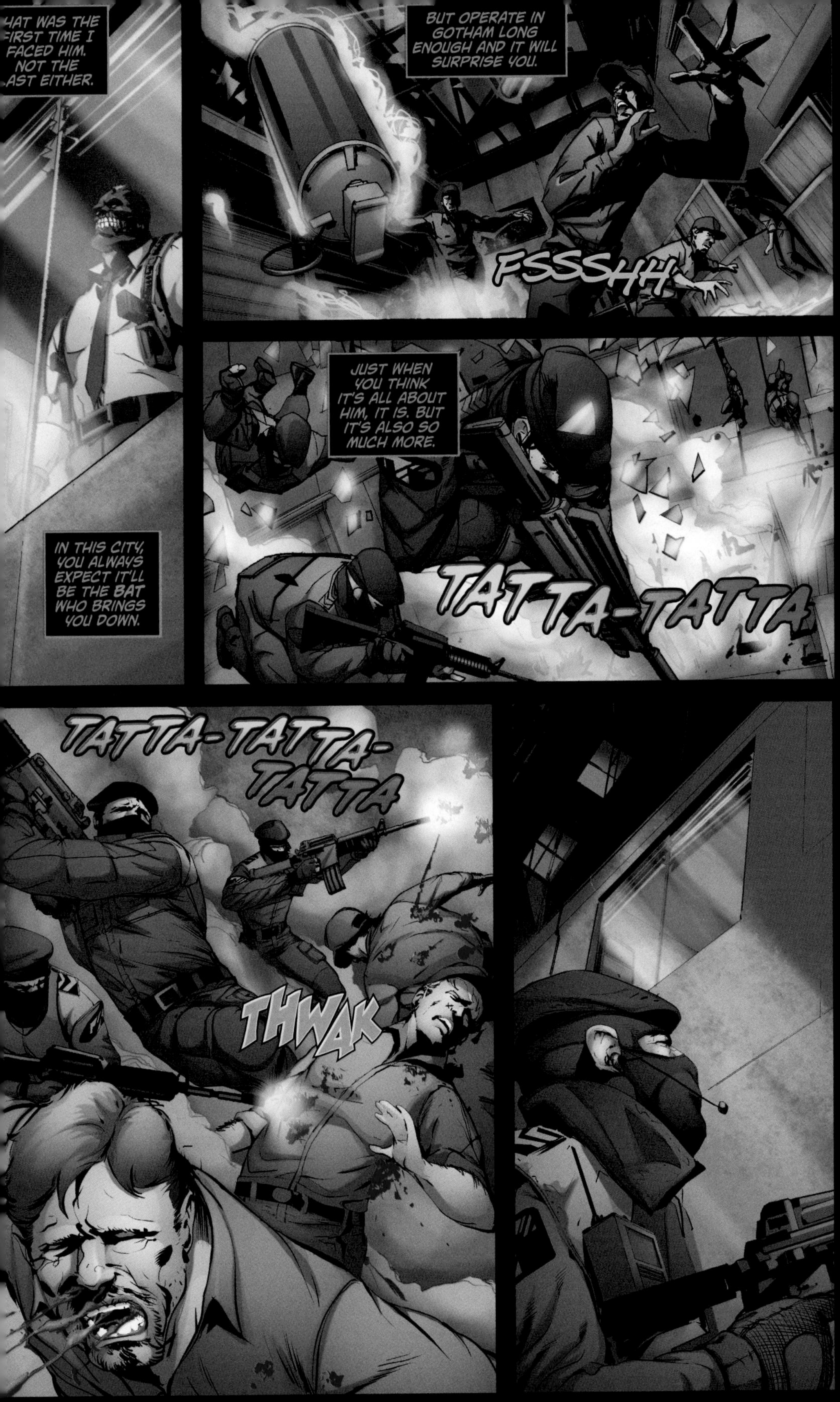
HAT WAS THE FIRST TIME I FACED HIM. NOT THE AST EITHER.
BUT OPERATE IN GOTHAM LONG ENOUGH AND IT WILL SURPRISE YOU.
FSSSHH
IN THIS CITY, YOU ALWAYS EXPECT IT'LL BE THE BAT WHO BRINGS YOU DOWN.
JUST WHEN YOU THINK IT'S ALL ABOUT HIM, IT IS. BUT IT'S ALSO SO MUCH MORE.
TATTA-TATTA
TATTA-TATTA-TATTA
THWAK

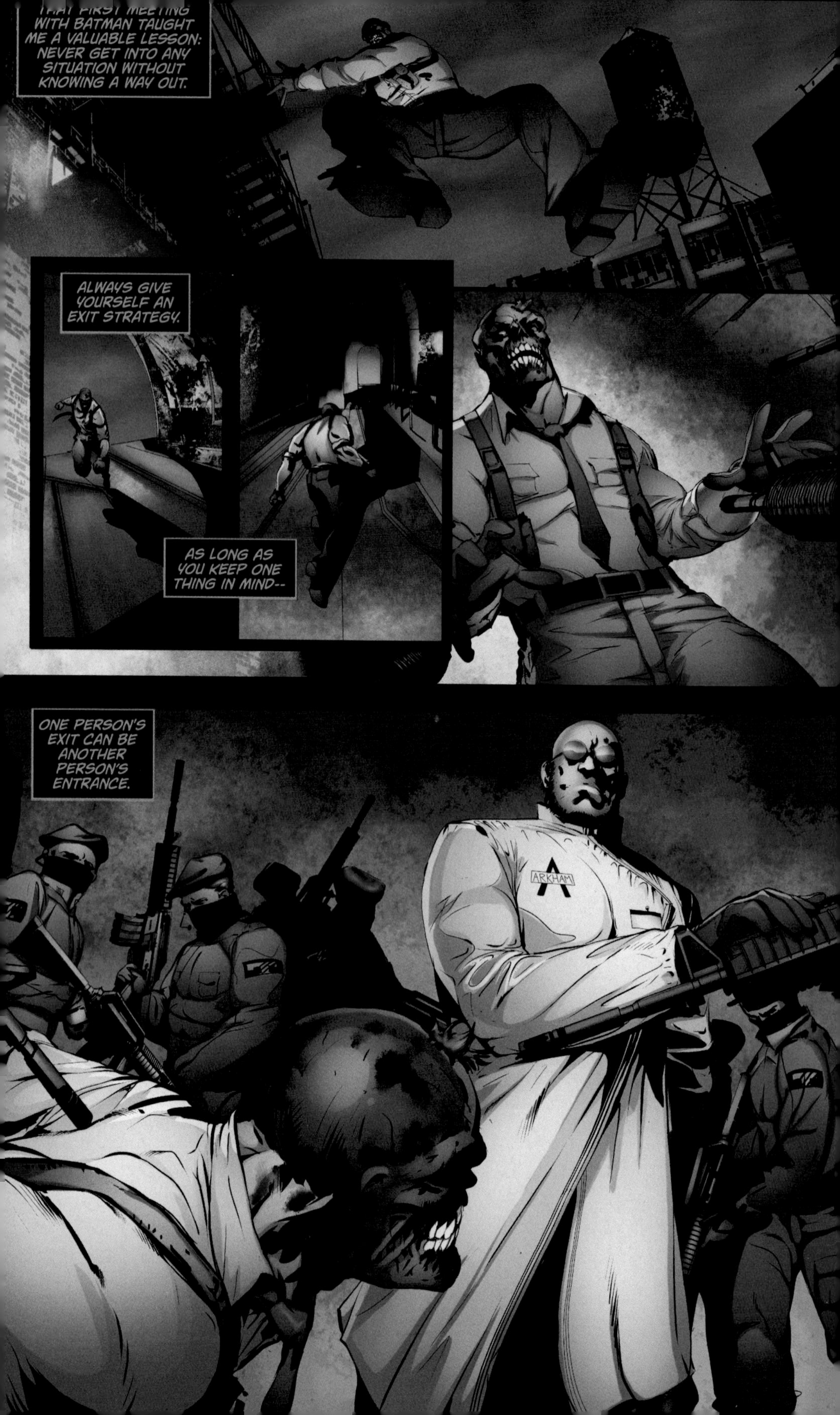
THAT FIRST MEETING WITH BATMAN TAUGHT ME A VALUABLE LESSON: NEVER GET INTO ANY SITUATION WITHOUT KNOWING A WAY OUT.
ALWAYS GIVE YOURSELF AN EXIT STRATEGY.
AS LONG AS YOU KEEP ONE THING IN MIND--
ONE PERSON'S EXIT CAN BE ANOTHER PERSON'S ENTRANCE.
ARKHAM

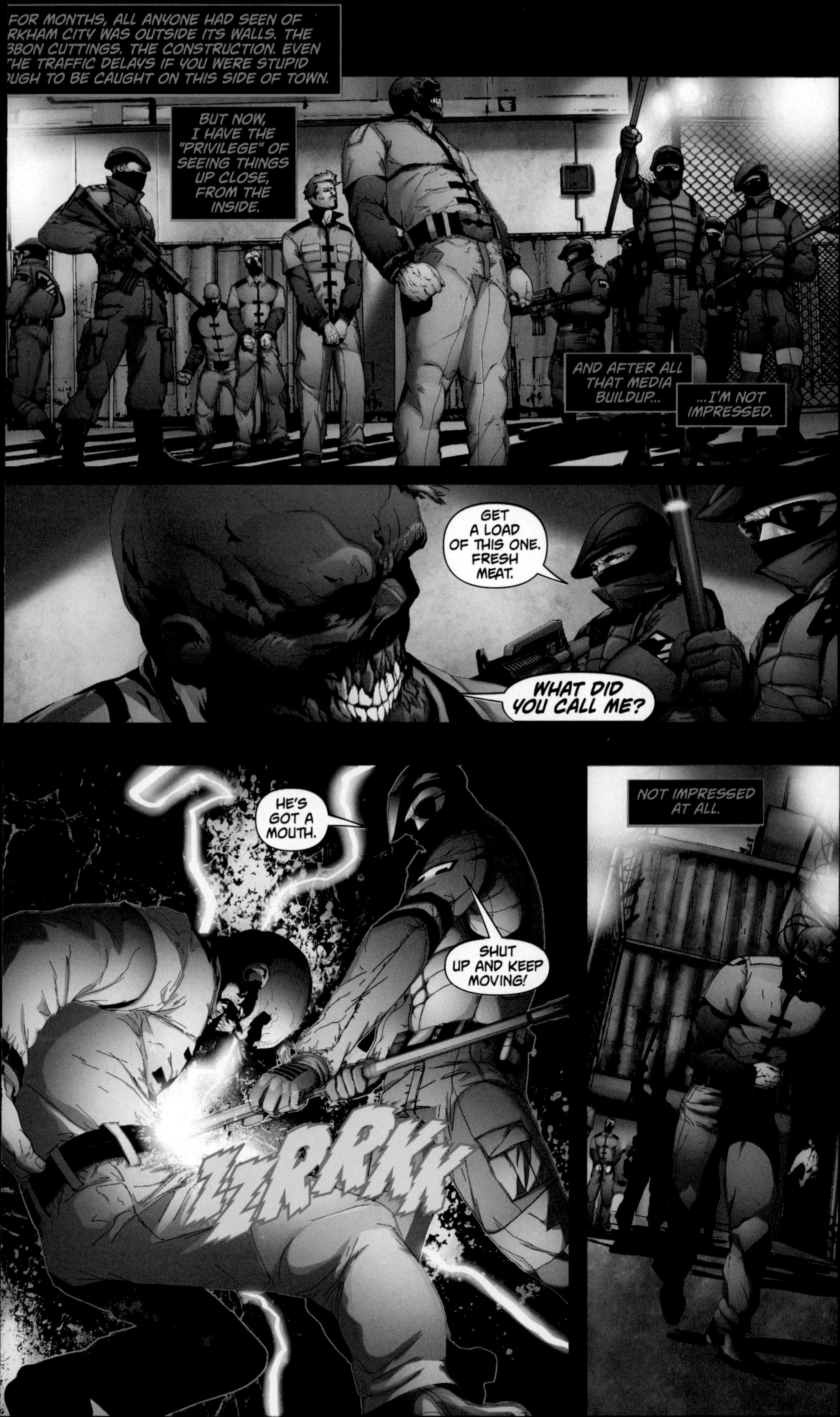

FOR MONTHS, ALL ANYONE HAD SEEN OF RKHAM CITY WAS OUTSIDE ITS WALLS. THE BBON CUTTINGS. THE CONSTRUCTION. EVEN THE TRAFFIC DELAYS IF YOU WERE STUPID OUGH TO BE CAUGHT ON THIS SIDE OF TOWN.
BUT NOW, I HAVE THE "PRIVILEGE" OF SEEING THINGS UP CLOSE, FROM THE INSIDE.
AND AFTER ALL THAT MEDIA BUILDUP...
...I'M NOT IMPRESSED.
GET A LOAD OF THIS ONE. FRESH MEAT.
WHAT DID YOU CALL ME?
HE'S GOT A MOUTH.
SHUT UP AND KEEP MOVING!
ZZRRKK
NOT IMPRESSED AT ALL.

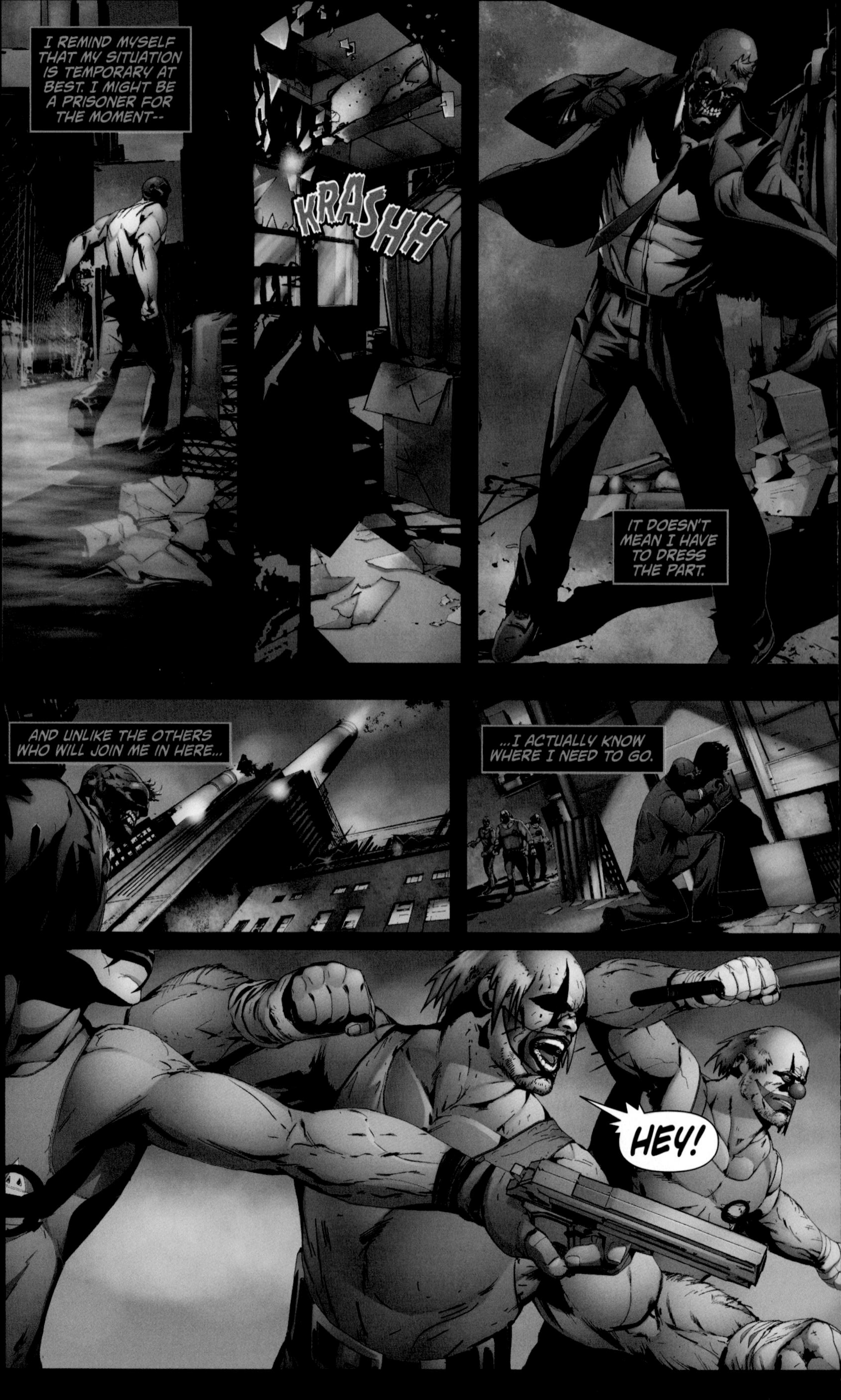
I REMIND MYSELF THAT MY SITUATION IS TEMPORARY AT BEST. I MIGHT BE A PRISONER FOR THE MOMENT--
KRASHH
IT DOESN'T MEAN I HAVE TO DRESS THE PART.
AND UNLIKE THE OTHERS WHO WILL JOIN ME IN HERE...
...I ACTUALLY KNOW WHERE I NEED TO GO.
HEY!

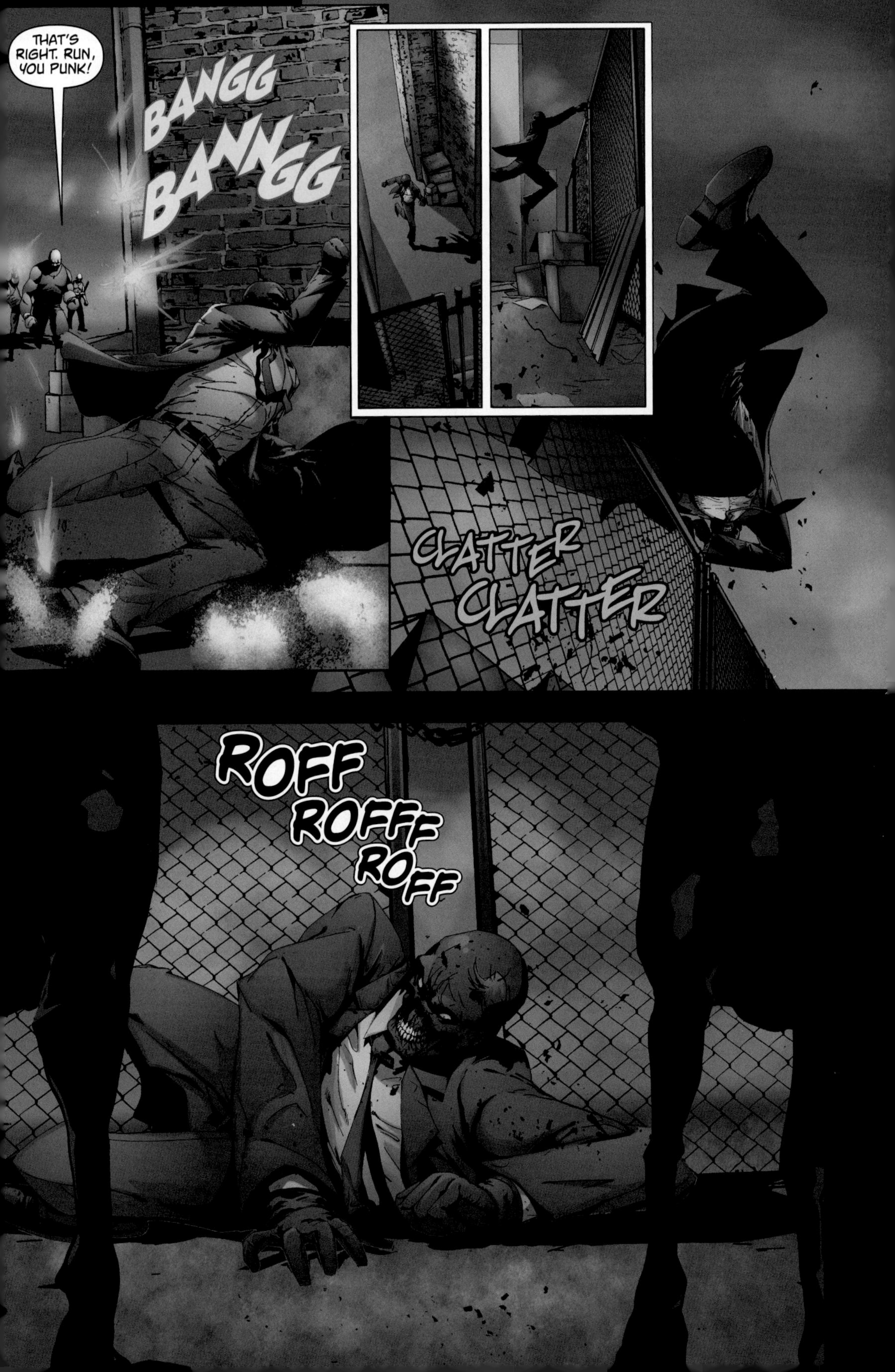
THAT'S RIGHT. RUN, YOU PUNK!
BANGG
BANNGG
CLATTER
CLATTER
ROFF
ROFFF
ROFF

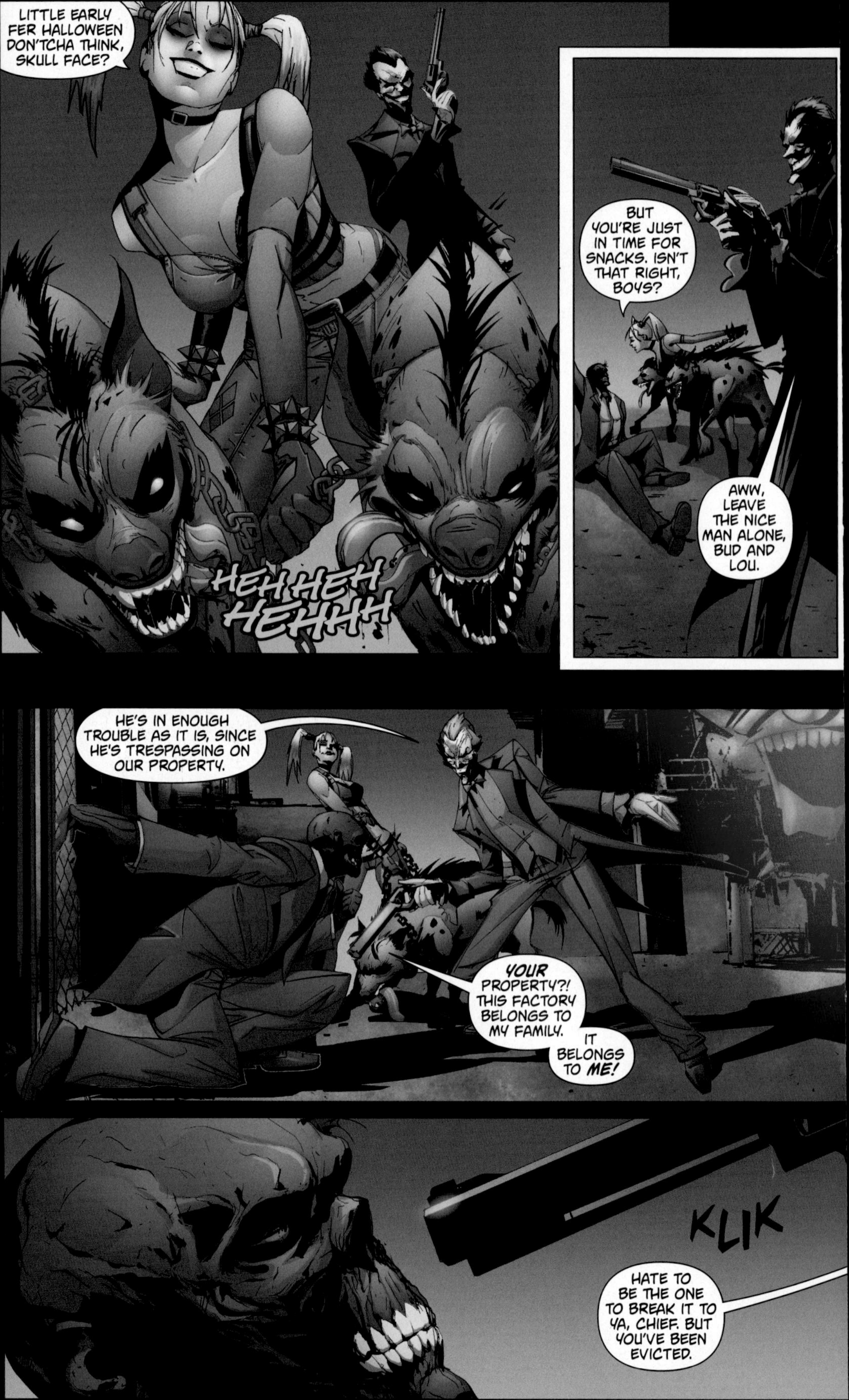
LITTLE EARLY FER HALLOWEEN DON'TCHA THINK, SKULL FACE?
HEH HEH HEHHH
BUT YOU'RE JUST IN TIME FOR SNACKS. ISN'T THAT RIGHT, BOYS?
AWW, LEAVE THE NICE MAN ALONE, BUD AND LOU.
HE'S IN ENOUGH TROUBLE AS IT IS, SINCE HE'S TRESPASSING ON OUR PROPERTY.
YOUR PROPERTY?! THIS FACTORY BELONGS TO MY FAMILY.
IT BELONGS TO ME!
KLIK
HATE TO BE THE ONE TO BREAK IT TO YA, CHIEF. BUT YOU'VE BEEN EVICTED.

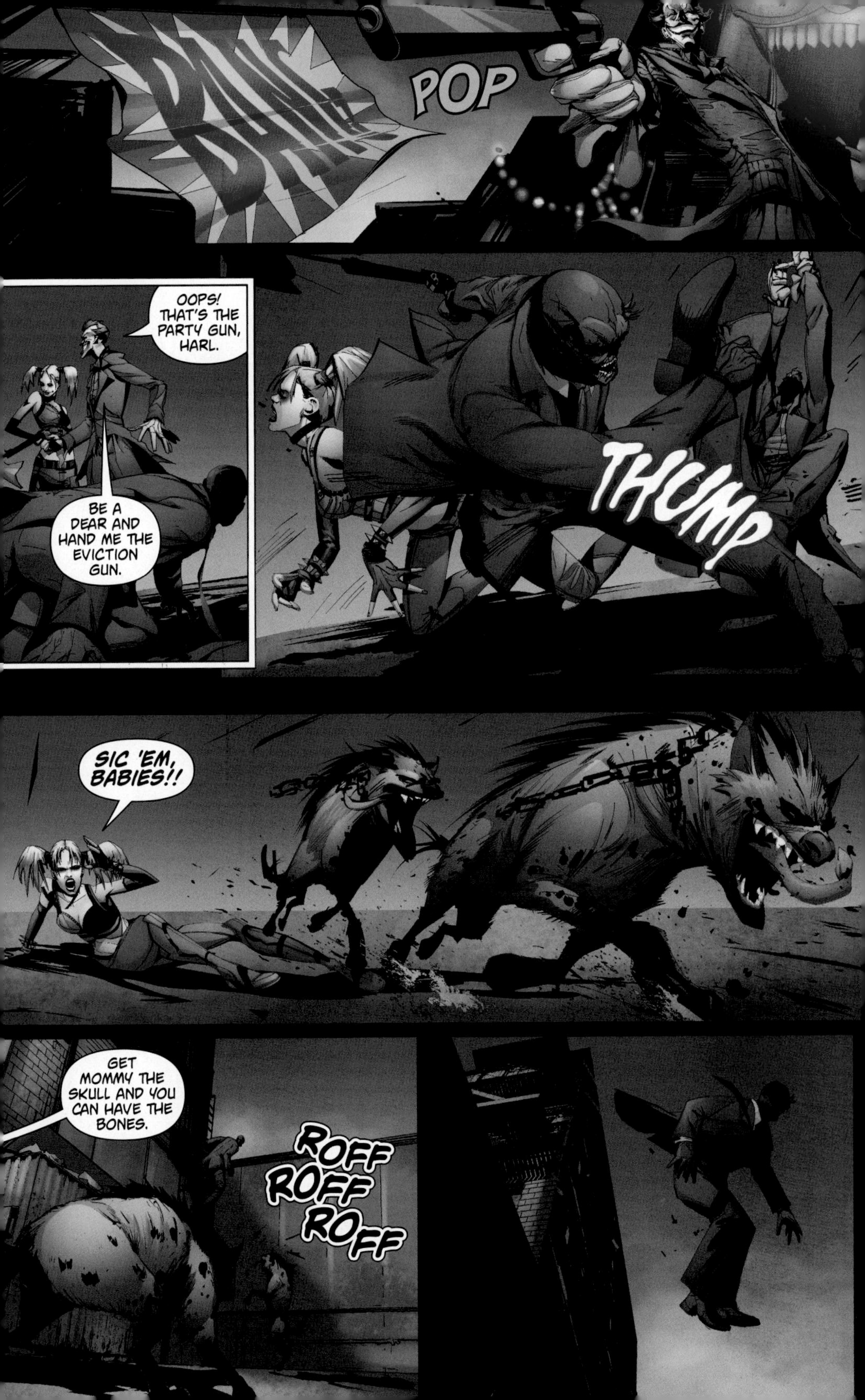
POP
OOPS! THAT'S THE PARTY GUN, HARL.
BE A DEAR AND HAND ME THE EVICTION GUN.
THUMP
SIC 'EM, BABIES!!
GET MOMMY THE SKULL AND YOU CAN HAVE THE BONES.
ROFF ROFF ROFF

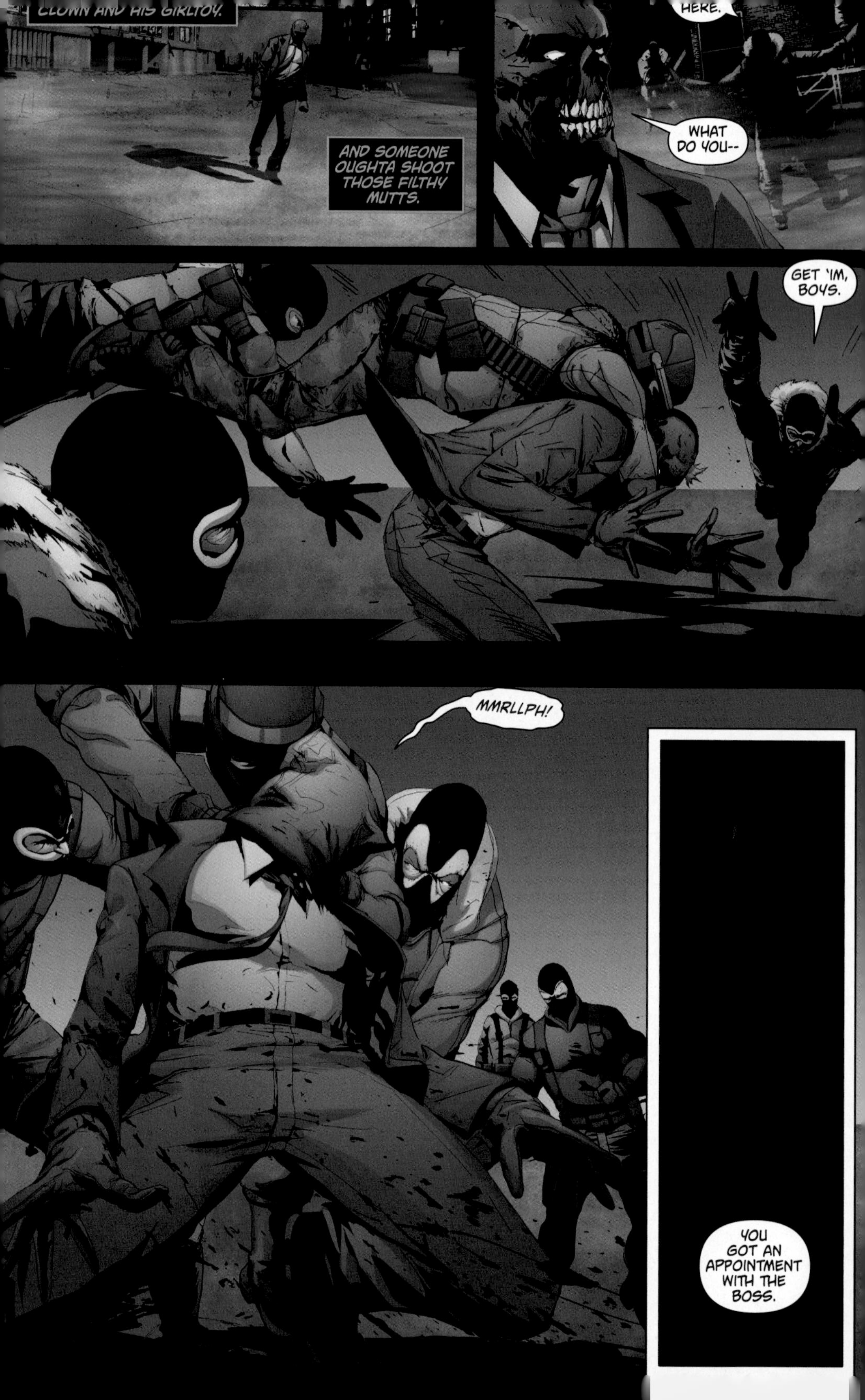
CLOWN AND HIS GIRLTOY.
AND SOMEONE OUGHTA SHOOT THOSE FILTHY MUTTS.
HERE.
WHAT DO YOU--
GET 'IM, BOYS.
MMRLLPH!
YOU GOT AN APPOINTMENT WITH THE BOSS.

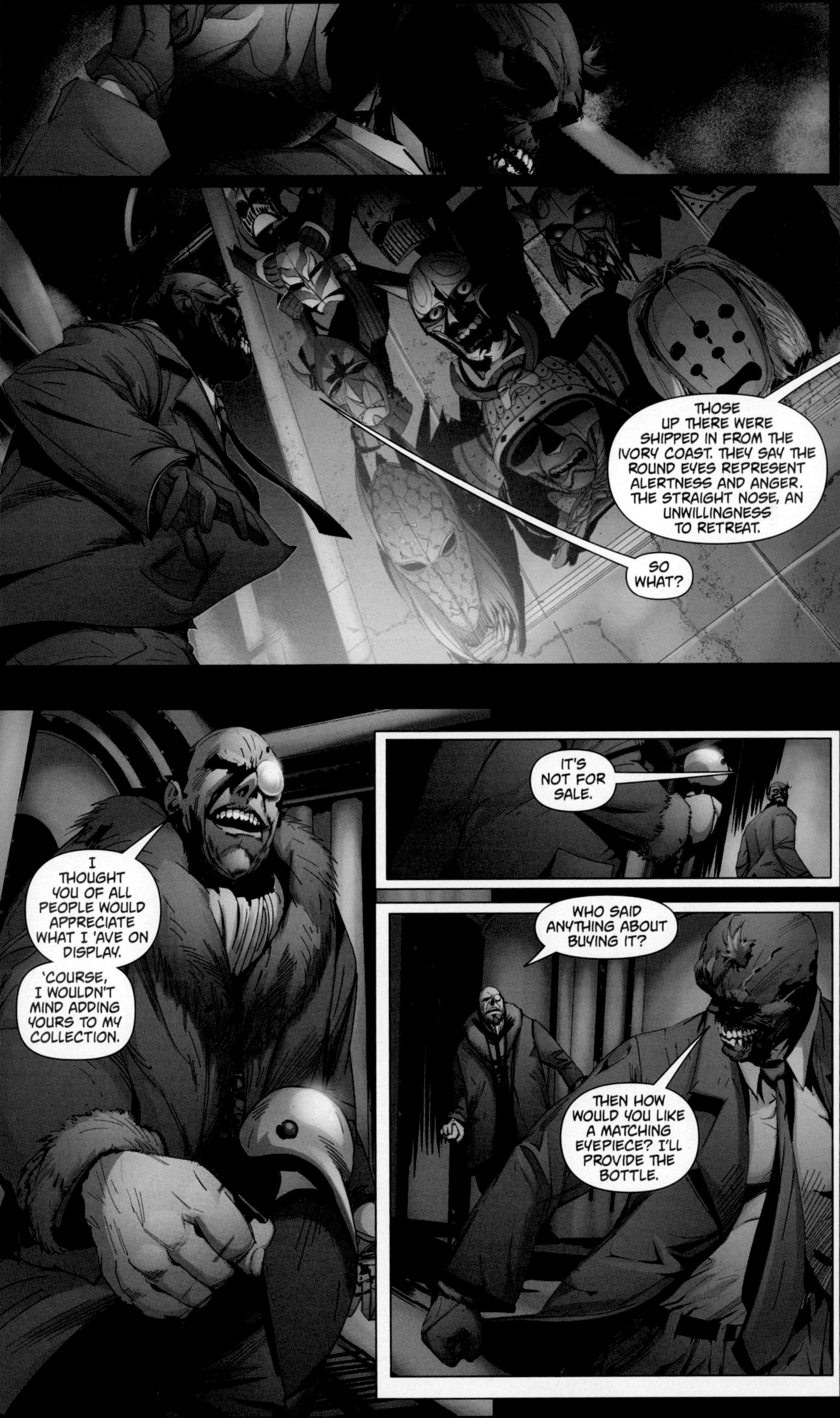
THOSE UP THERE WERE SHIPPED IN FROM THE IVORY COAST. THEY SAY THE ROUND EYES REPRESENT ALERTNESS AND ANGER. THE STRAIGHT NOSE, AN UNWILLINGNESS TO RETREAT.
SO WHAT?
I THOUGHT YOU OF ALL PEOPLE WOULD APPRECIATE WHAT I 'AVE ON DISPLAY.
'COURSE, I WOULDN'T MIND ADDING YOURS TO MY COLLECTION.
IT'S NOT FOR SALE.
WHO SAID ANYTHING ABOUT BUYING IT?
THEN HOW WOULD YOU LIKE A MATCHING EYEPIECE? I'LL PROVIDE THE BOTTLE.

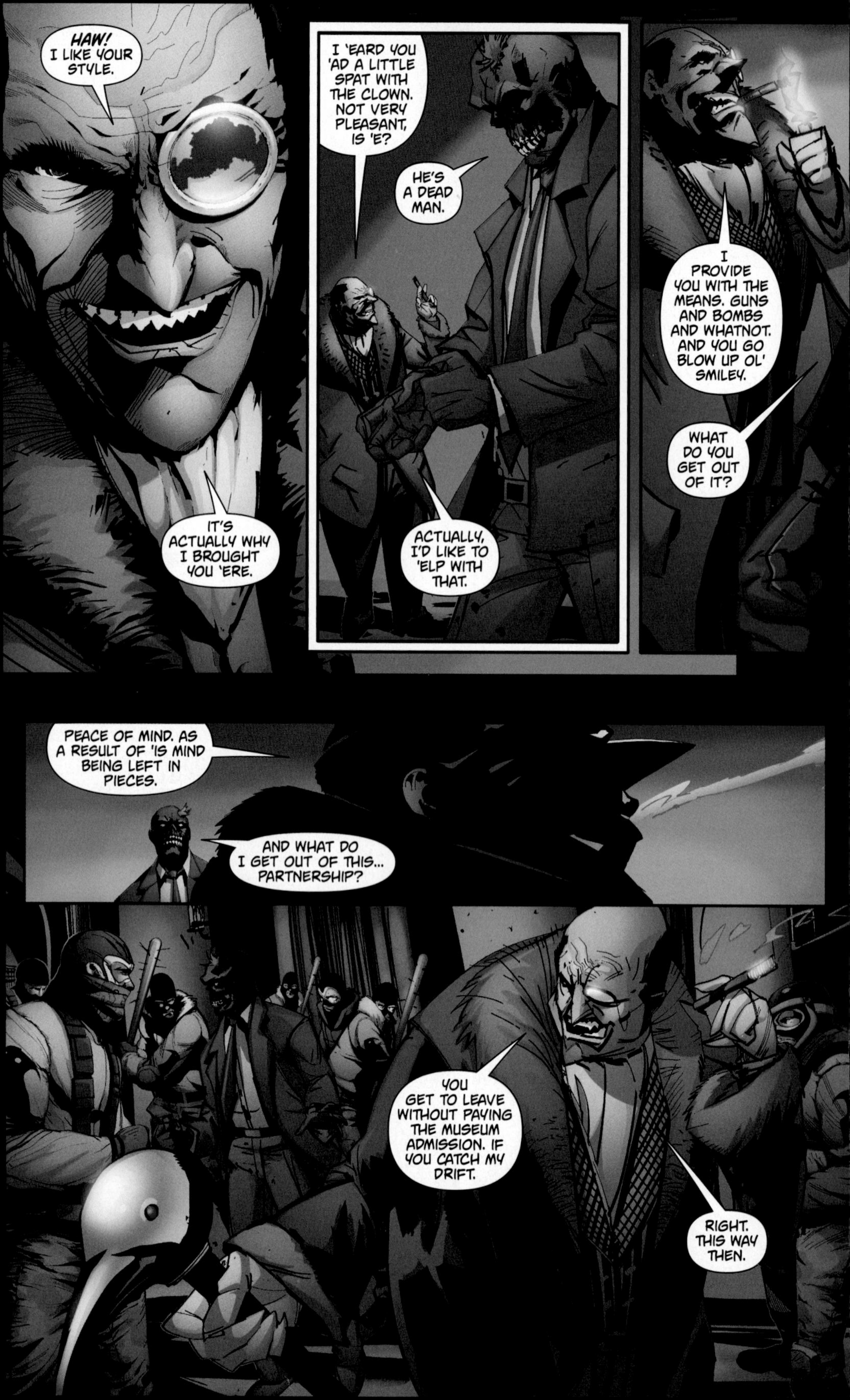
HAW! I LIKE YOUR STYLE.
IT'S ACTUALLY WHY I BROUGHT YOU 'ERE.
I 'EARD YOU 'AD A LITTLE SPAT WITH THE CLOWN. NOT VERY PLEASANT, IS 'E?
HE'S A DEAD MAN.
ACTUALLY, I'D LIKE TO 'ELP WITH THAT.
I PROVIDE YOU WITH THE MEANS. GUNS AND BOMBS AND WHATNOT. AND YOU GO BLOW UP OL' SMILEY.
WHAT DO YOU GET OUT OF IT?
PEACE OF MIND. AS A RESULT OF 'IS MIND BEING LEFT IN PIECES.
AND WHAT DO I GET OUT OF THIS... PARTNERSHIP?
YOU GET TO LEAVE WITHOUT PAYING THE MUSEUM ADMISSION. IF YOU CATCH MY DRIFT.
RIGHT. THIS WAY THEN.

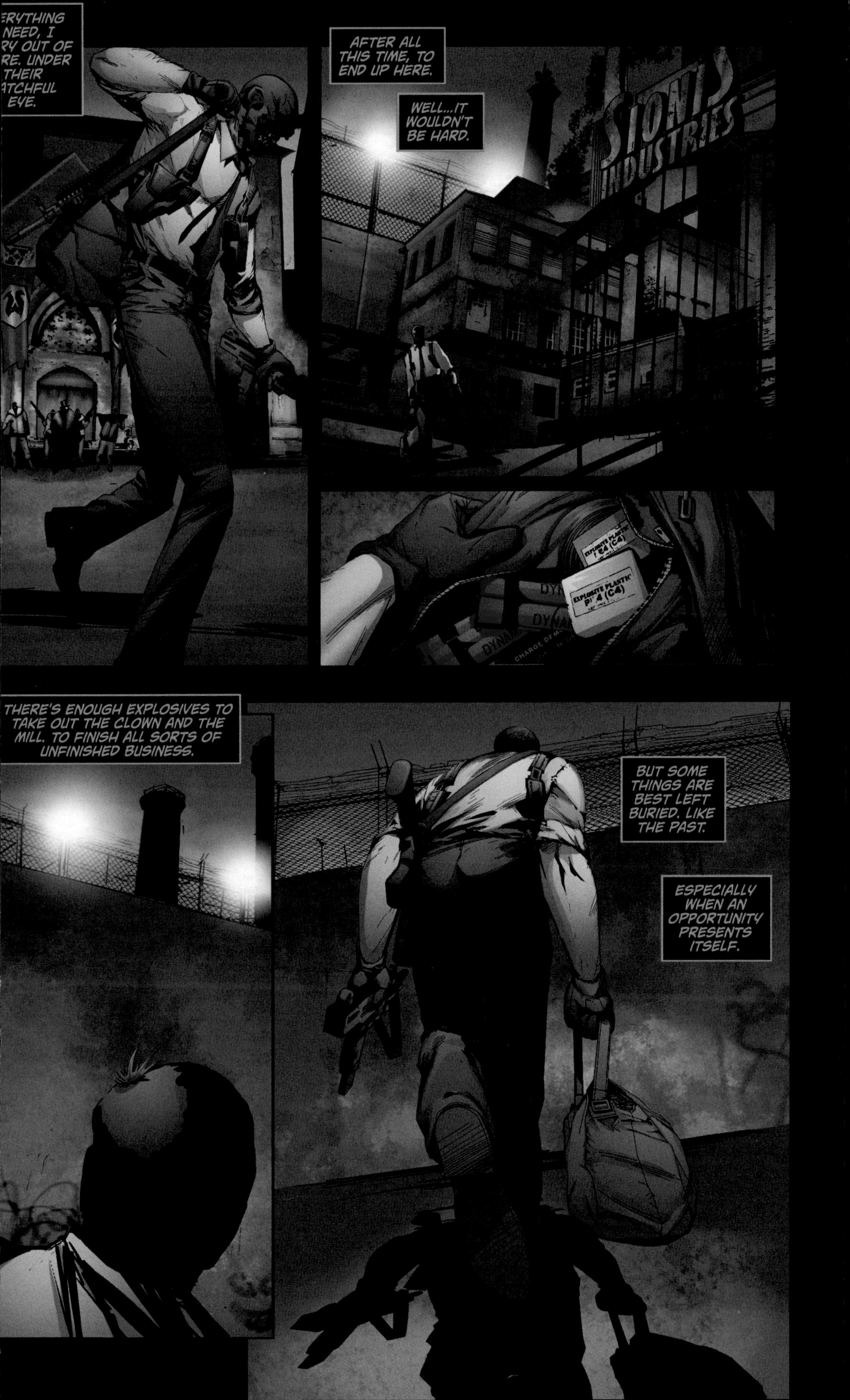

ERYTHING NEED, I RY OUT OF RE. UNDER THEIR ATCHFUL EYE.
AFTER ALL THIS TIME, TO END UP HERE.
WELL...IT WOULDN'T BE HARD.
SIONIS INDUSTRIES
THERE'S ENOUGH EXPLOSIVES TO TAKE OUT THE CLOWN AND THE MILL. TO FINISH ALL SORTS OF UNFINISHED BUSINESS.
BUT SOME THINGS ARE BEST LEFT BURIED. LIKE THE PAST.
ESPECIALLY WHEN AN OPPORTUNITY PRESENTS ITSELF.

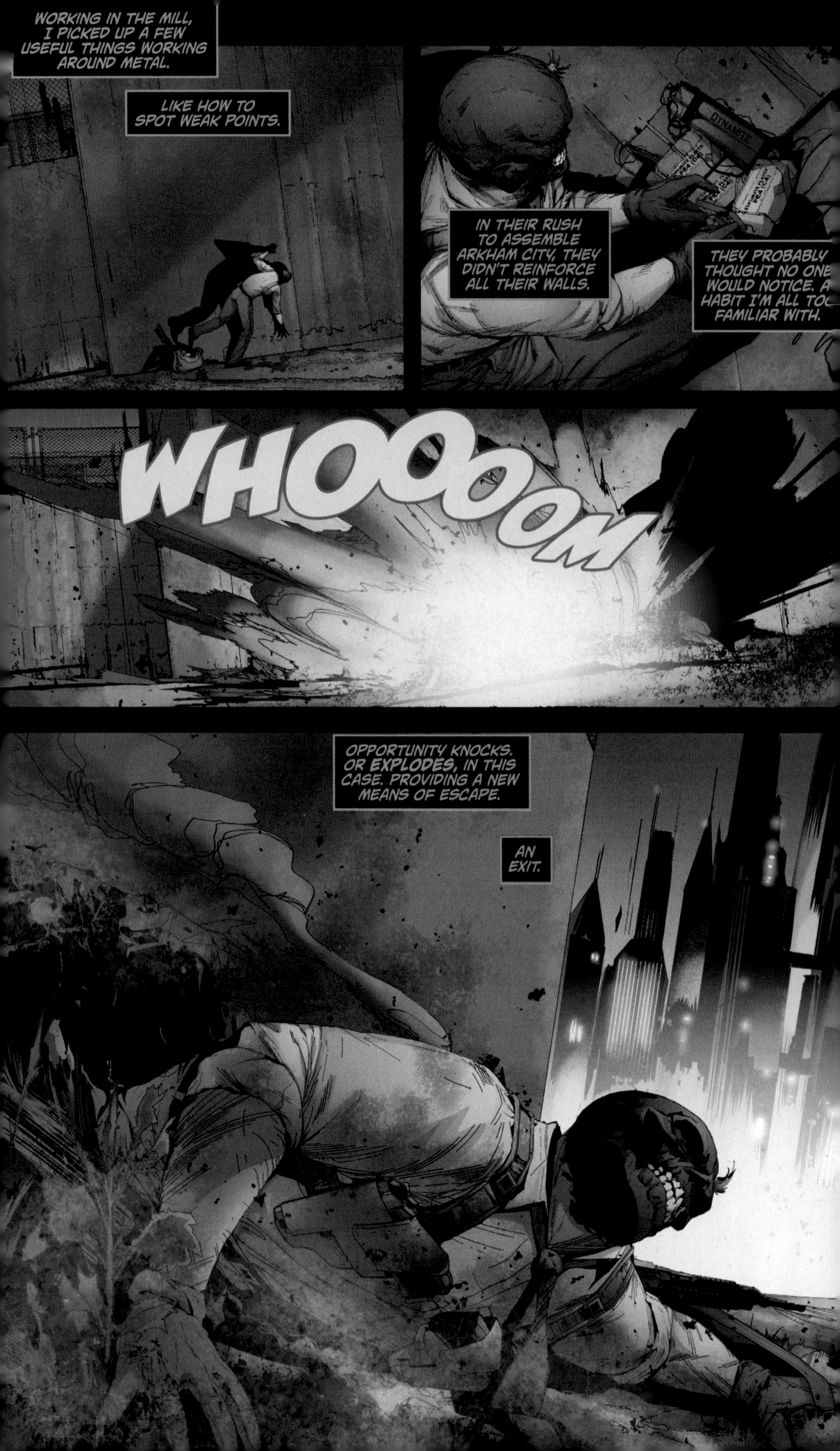
WORKING IN THE MILL, I PICKED UP A FEW USEFUL THINGS WORKING AROUND METAL.
LIKE HOW TO SPOT WEAK POINTS.
DYNAMITE
IN THEIR RUSH TO ASSEMBLE ARKHAM CITY, THEY DIDN'T REINFORCE ALL THEIR WALLS.
THEY PROBABLY THOUGHT NO ONE WOULD NOTICE. A HABIT I'M ALL TOO FAMILIAR WITH.
WHOOOOOM
OPPORTUNITY KNOCKS. OR **EXPLODES,** IN THIS CASE. PROVIDING A NEW MEANS OF ESCAPE.
AN EXIT.

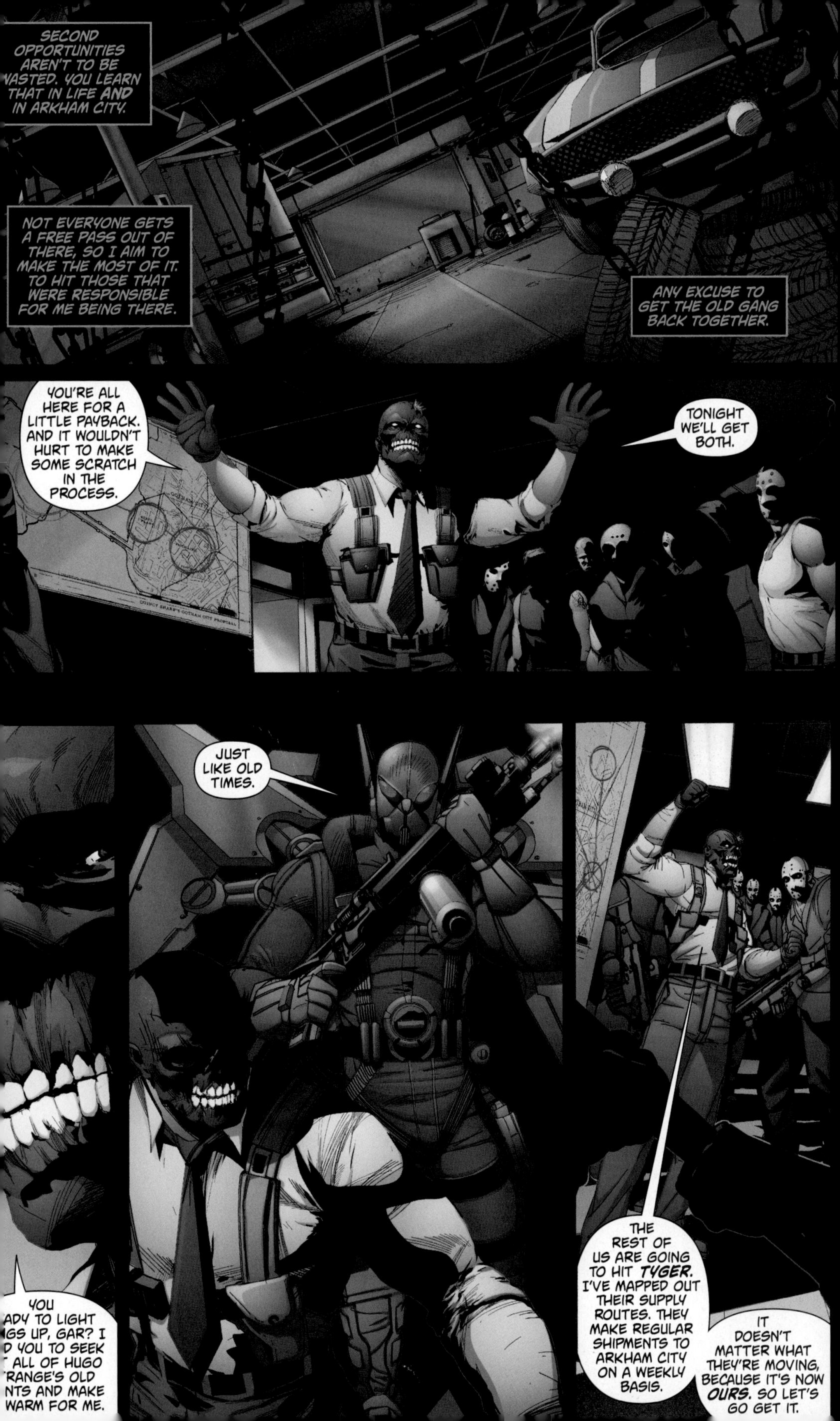

SECOND OPPORTUNITIES AREN'T TO BE WASTED. YOU LEARN THAT IN LIFE AND IN ARKHAM CITY.
NOT EVERYONE GETS A FREE PASS OUT OF THERE, SO I AIM TO MAKE THE MOST OF IT. TO HIT THOSE THAT WERE RESPONSIBLE FOR ME BEING THERE.
ANY EXCUSE TO GET THE OLD GANG BACK TOGETHER.
YOU'RE ALL HERE FOR A LITTLE PAYBACK. AND IT WOULDN'T HURT TO MAKE SOME SCRATCH IN THE PROCESS.
TONIGHT WE'LL GET BOTH.
JUST LIKE OLD TIMES.
YOU ...ADY TO LIGHT ...GS UP, GAR? I ...D YOU TO SEEK ... ALL OF HUGO ...RANGE'S OLD ...NTS AND MAKE ...WARM FOR ME.
THE REST OF US ARE GOING TO HIT TYGER. I'VE MAPPED OUT THEIR SUPPLY ROUTES. THEY MAKE REGULAR SHIPMENTS TO ARKHAM CITY ON A WEEKLY BASIS.
IT DOESN'T MATTER WHAT THEY'RE MOVING, BECAUSE IT'S NOW OURS. SO LET'S GO GET IT.

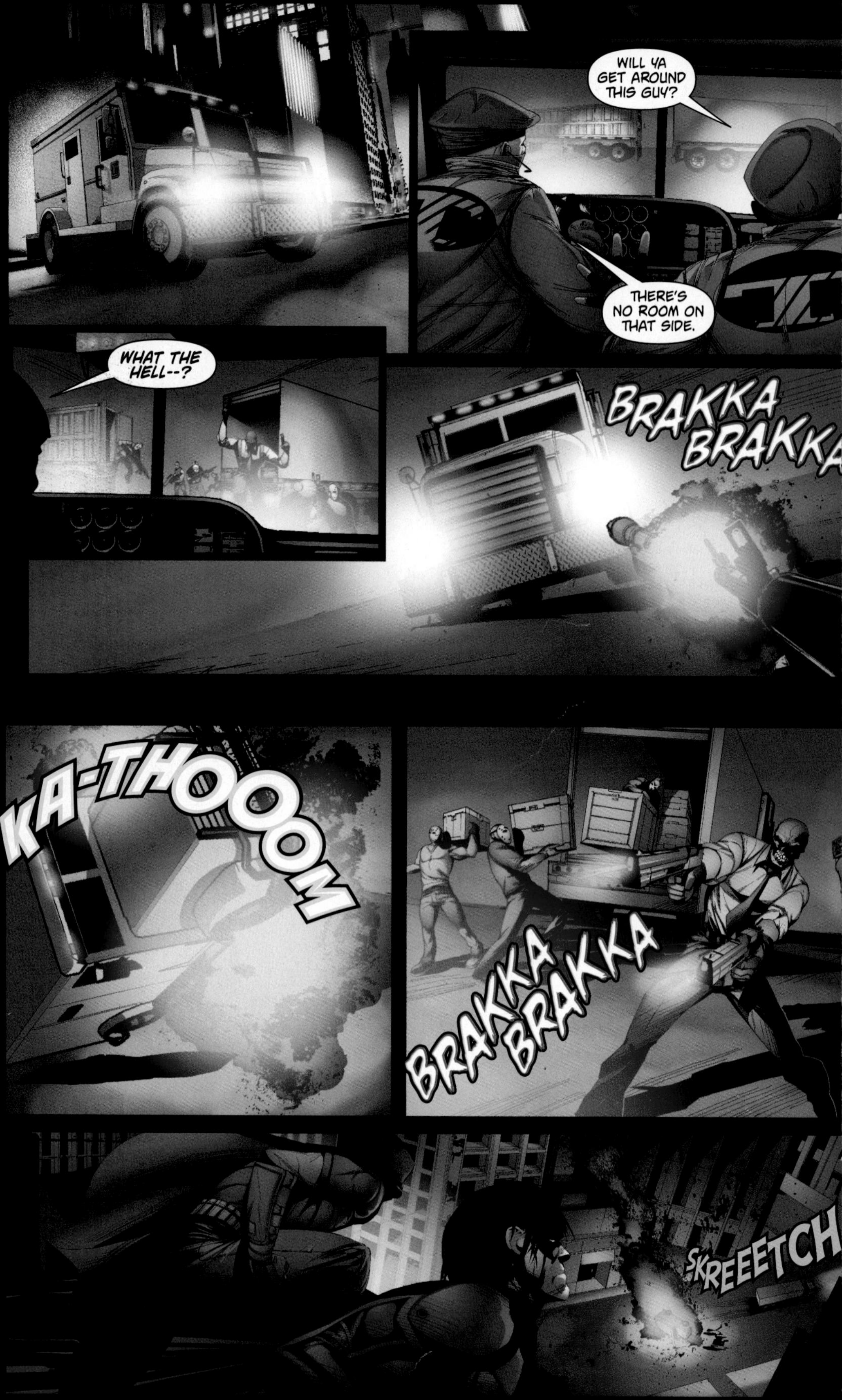

WILL YA GET AROUND THIS GUY?
THERE'S NO ROOM ON THAT SIDE.
WHAT THE HELL--?
BRAKKA BRAKKA
KA-THOOOOM
BRAKKA BRAKKA
SKREEETCH

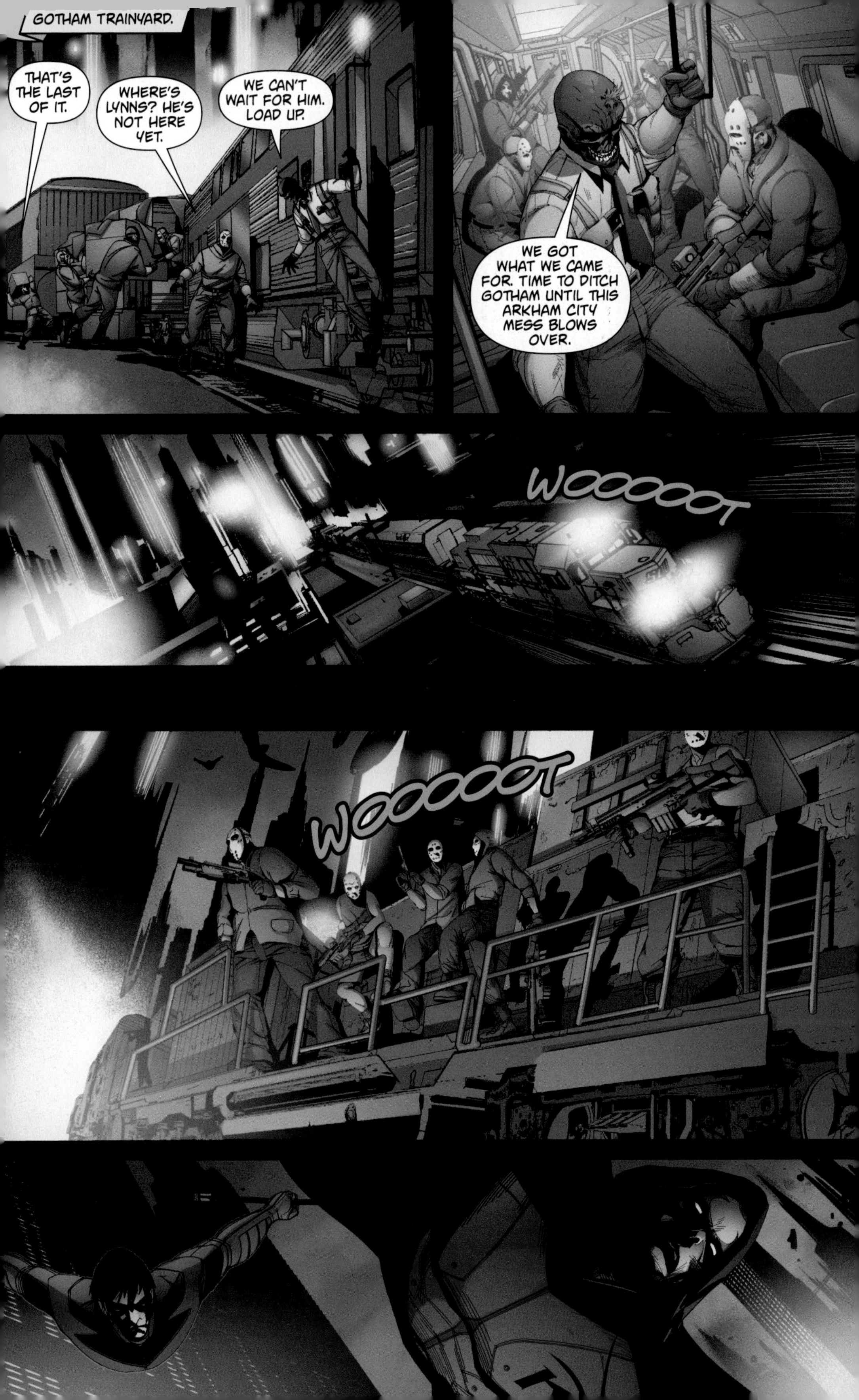
GOTHAM TRAINYARD.
THAT'S THE LAST OF IT.
WHERE'S LYNNS? HE'S NOT HERE YET.
WE CAN'T WAIT FOR HIM. LOAD UP.
WE GOT WHAT WE CAME FOR. TIME TO DITCH GOTHAM UNTIL THIS ARKHAM CITY MESS BLOWS OVER.
WOOOOOT
WOOOOOT

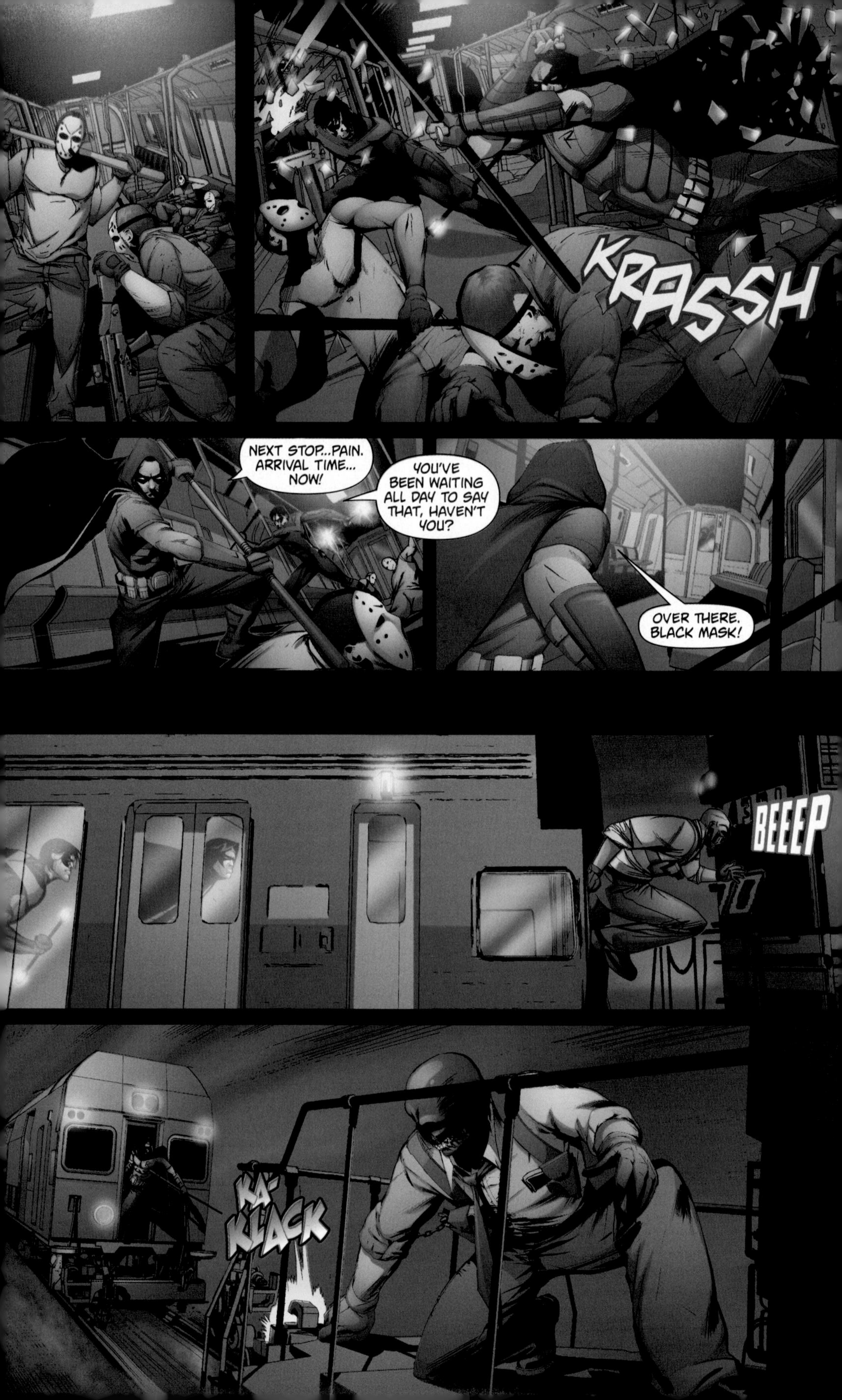
KRASSH
NEXT STOP...PAIN. ARRIVAL TIME... NOW!
YOU'VE BEEN WAITING ALL DAY TO SAY THAT, HAVEN'T YOU?
OVER THERE. BLACK MASK!
BEEEP
KA-KLACK

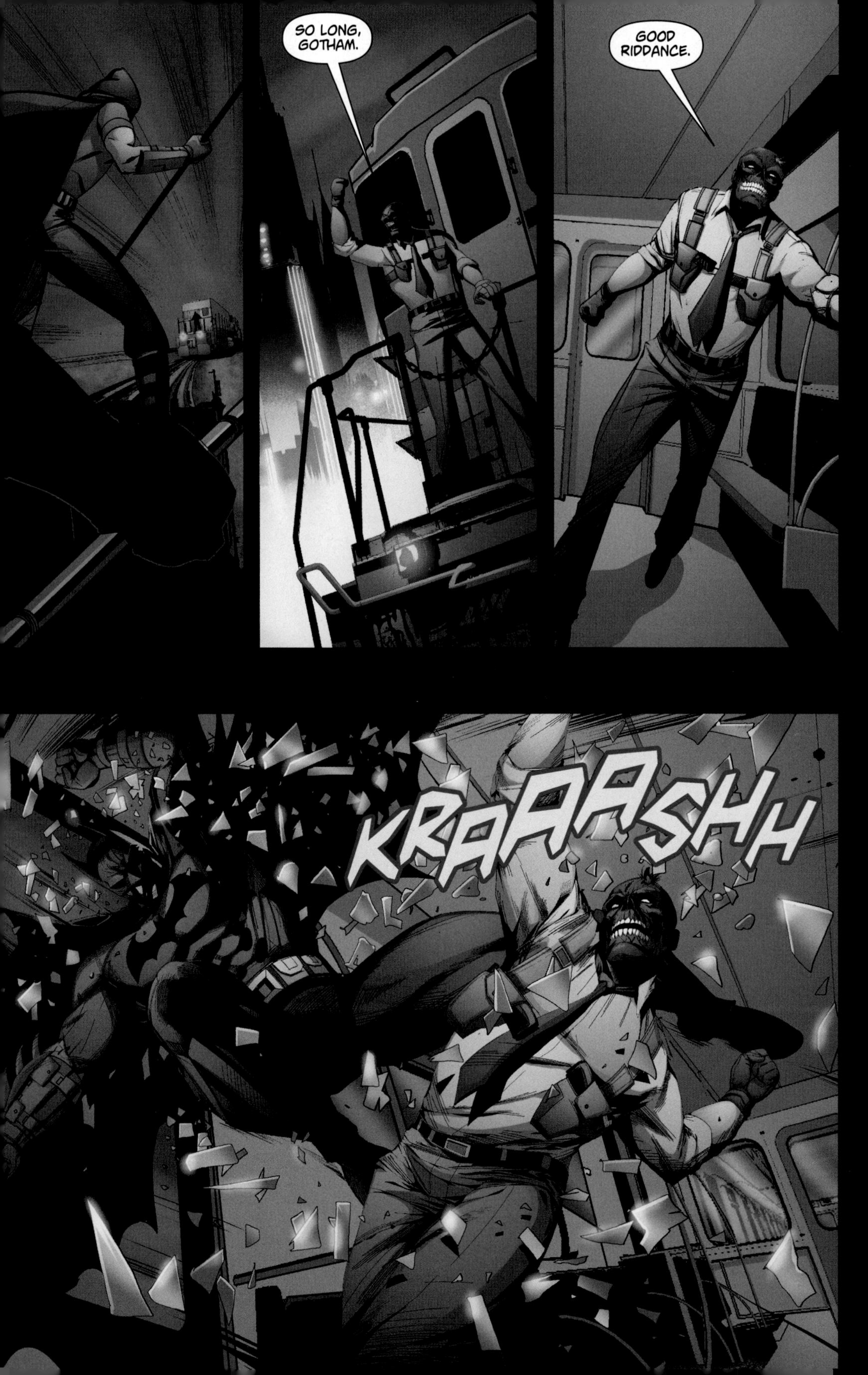
SO LONG, GOTHAM.
GOOD RIDDANCE.
KRAAASHH

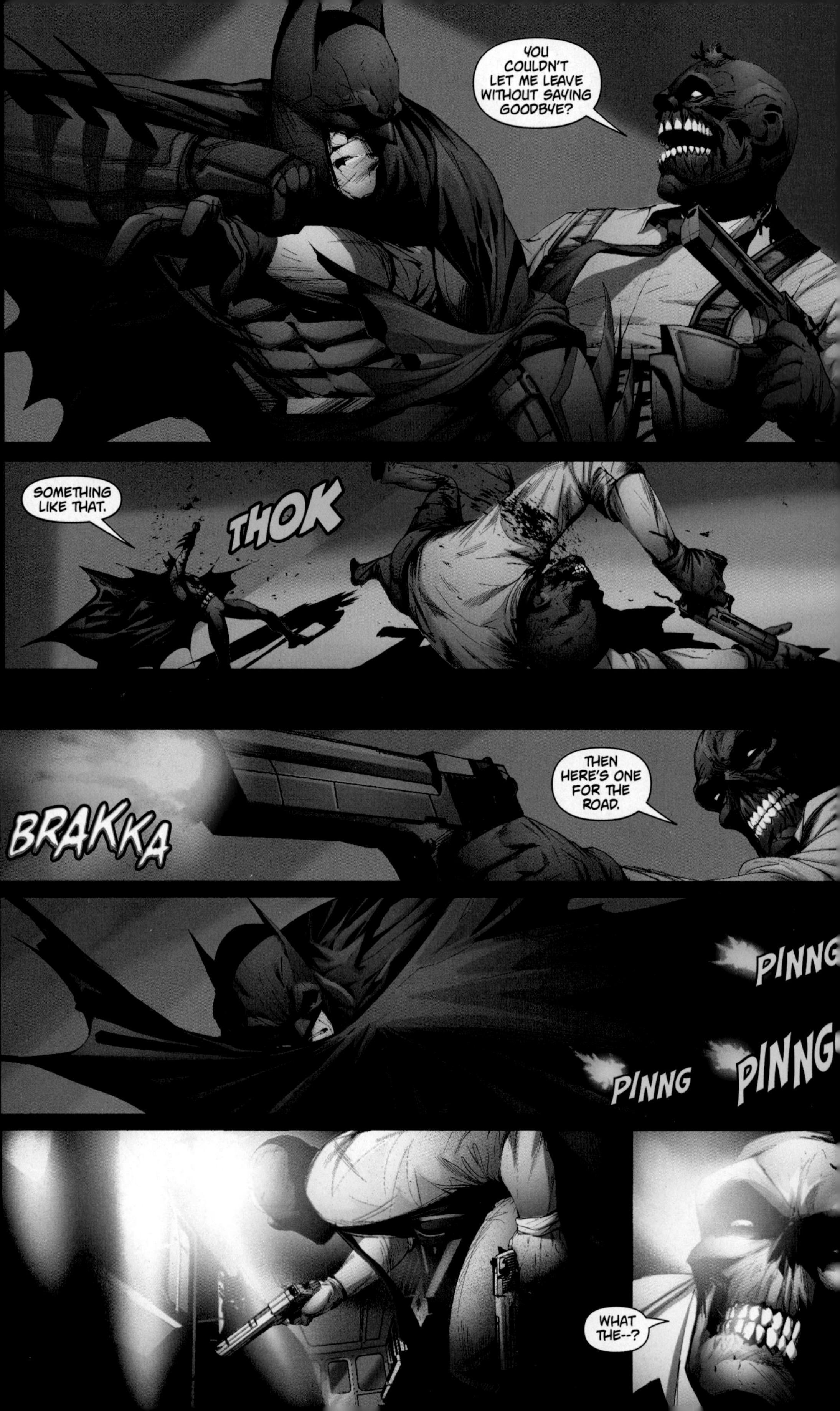
YOU COULDN'T LET ME LEAVE WITHOUT SAYING GOODBYE?
SOMETHING LIKE THAT.
THOK
BRAKKA
THEN HERE'S ONE FOR THE ROAD.
PINNG
PINNG
PINNG
WHAT THE--?

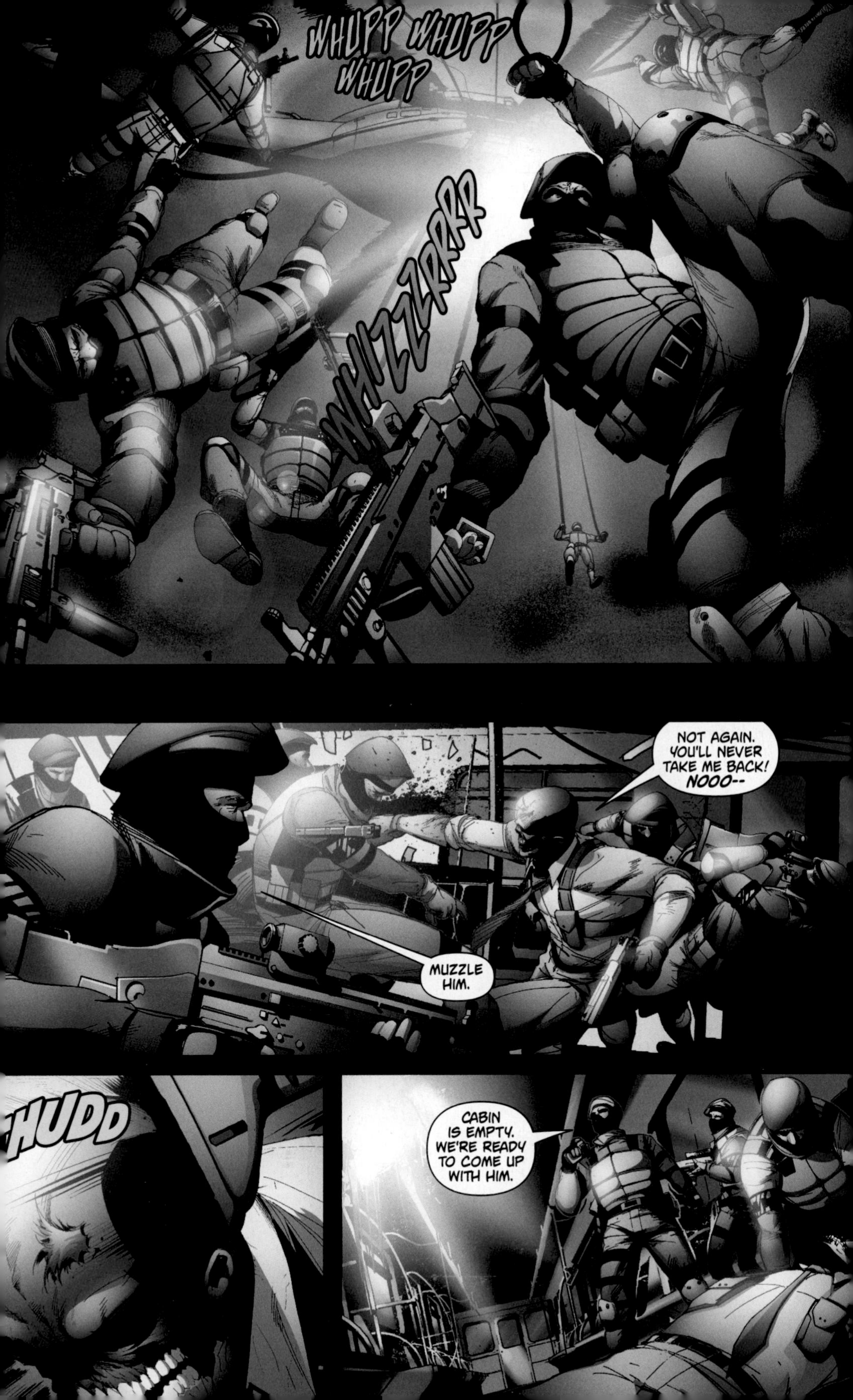
WHUPP WHUPP WHUPP
WHIZZZRRRR
NOT AGAIN. YOU'LL NEVER TAKE ME BACK! NOOO--
MUZZLE HIM.
HUDD
CABIN IS EMPTY. WE'RE READY TO COME UP WITH HIM.

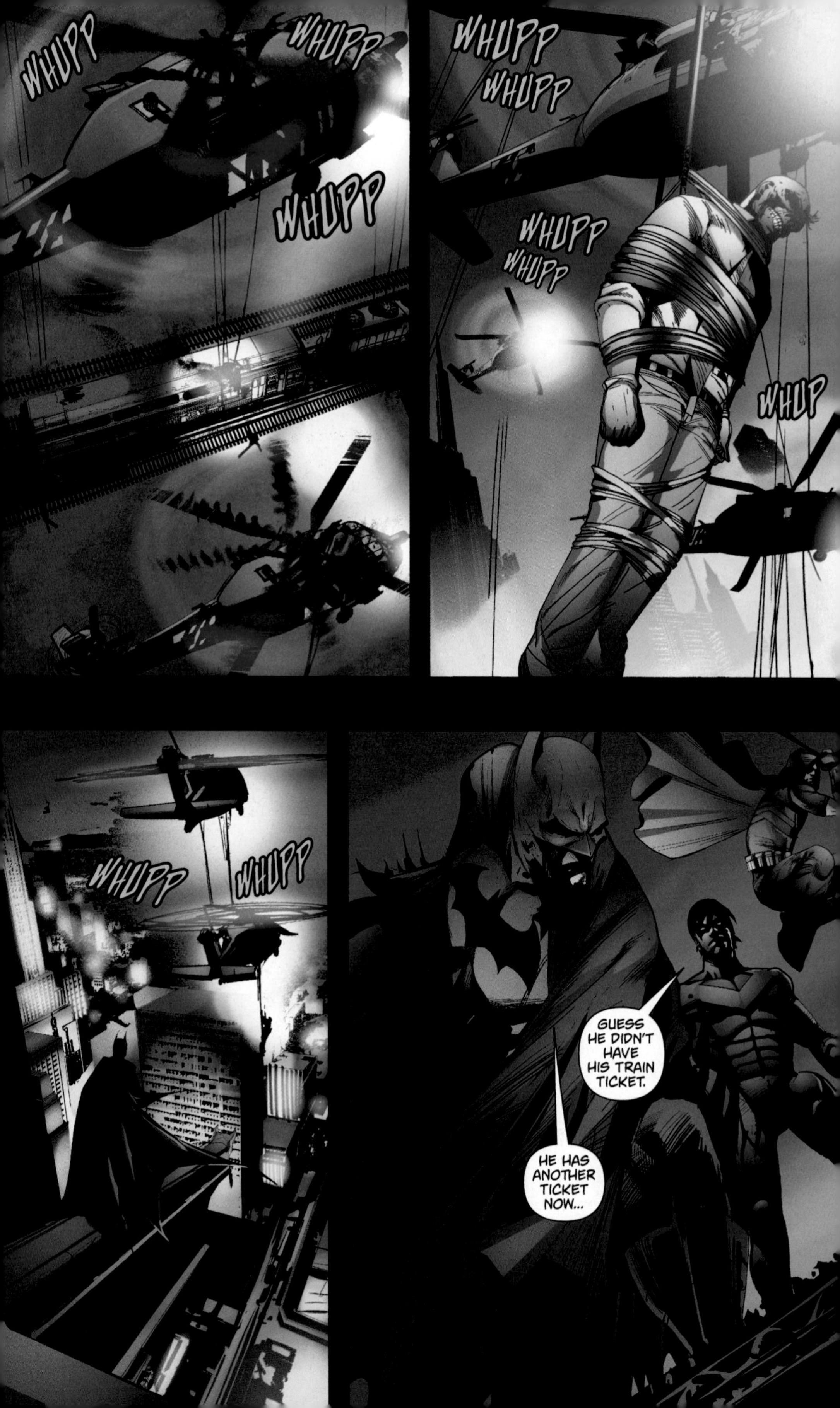
WHUPP
WHUPP
WHUPP
WHUPP
WHUPP
WHUPP
WHUPP
WHUP
WHUPP
WHUPP
GUESS HE DIDN'T HAVE HIS TRAIN TICKET.
HE HAS ANOTHER TICKET NOW...

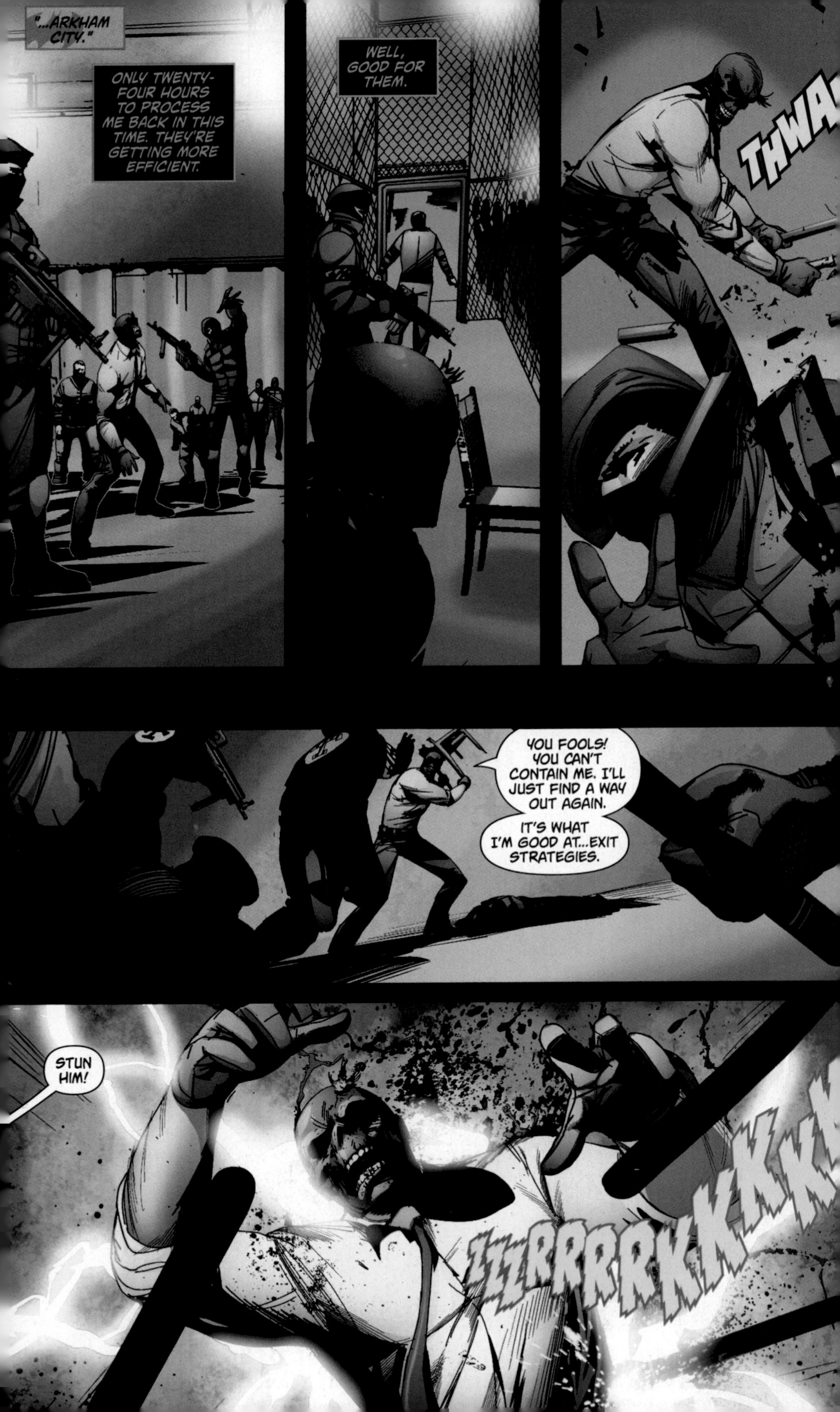
"...ARKHAM CITY."
ONLY TWENTY-FOUR HOURS TO PROCESS ME BACK IN THIS TIME. THEY'RE GETTING MORE EFFICIENT.
WELL, GOOD FOR THEM.
THWA
YOU FOOLS! YOU CAN'T CONTAIN ME. I'LL JUST FIND A WAY OUT AGAIN.
IT'S WHAT I'M GOOD AT...EXIT STRATEGIES.
STUN HIM!
ZZZRRRRKKKKK

...YOU'LL... DIE FOR THIS...

LEAVE HIM. WE'VE GOT THE RICH BOY COMING THROUGH.

I'VE GONE ABOUT THIS ALL WRONG, HAVEN'T I?

NO MORE EXITS.

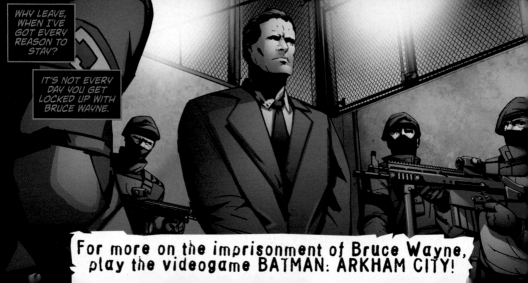

WHY LEAVE, WHEN I'VE GOT EVERY REASON TO STAY?

IT'S NOT EVERY DAY YOU GET LOCKED UP WITH BRUCE WAYNE.

For more on the imprisonment of Bruce Wayne, play the videogame BATMAN: ARKHAM CITY!

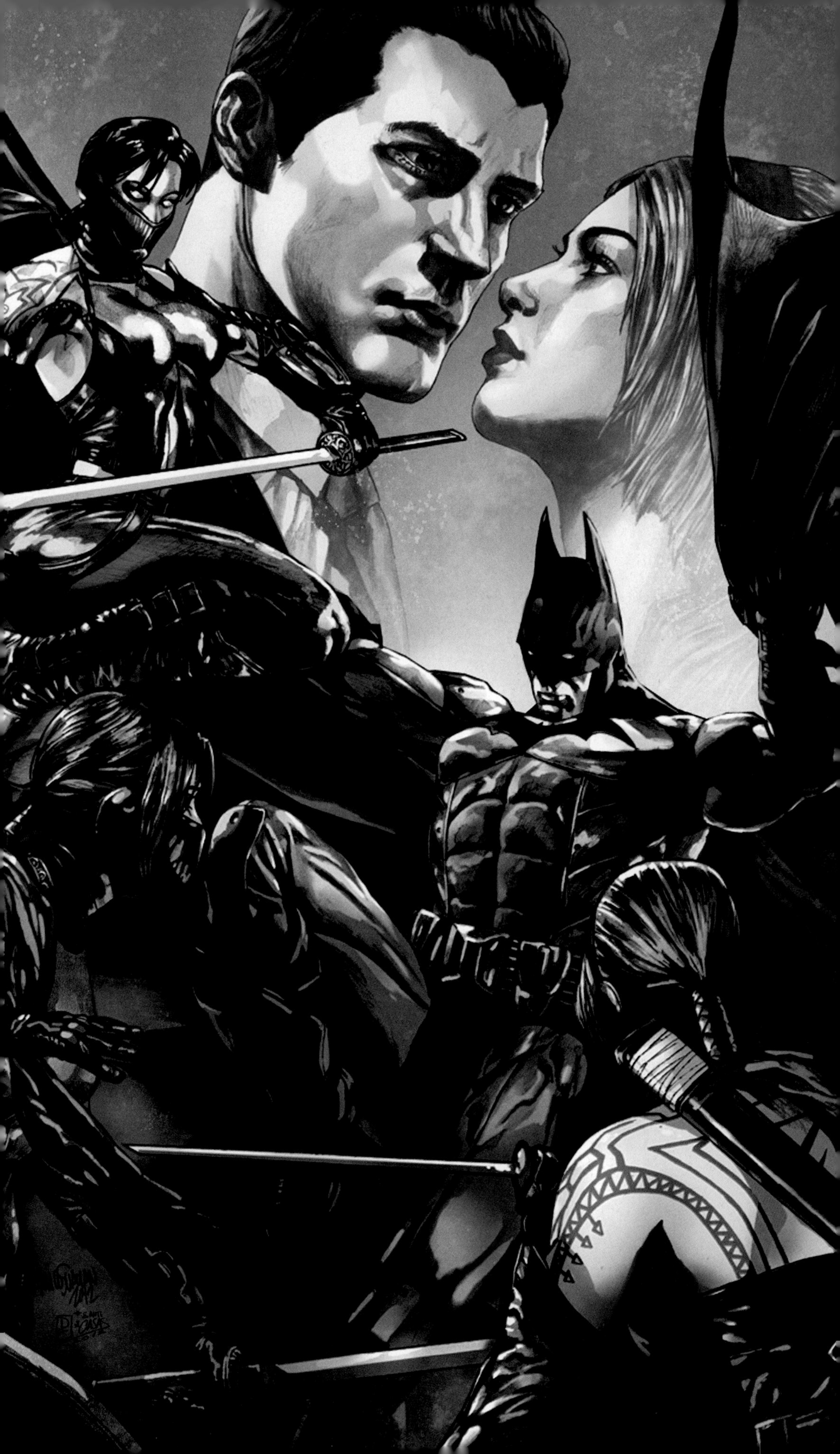

BELOVED

WRITTEN BY: DEREK FRIDOLFS
ART BY: FEDERICO DALLOCCHIO
COLORS BY: CARRIE STRACHAN
LETTERS BY: TRAVIS LANHAM
COVER ART BY: MICO SUAYAN
COVER COLORS BY: DAVID LOPEZ
& SANTI CASAS OF IKARI STUDIO

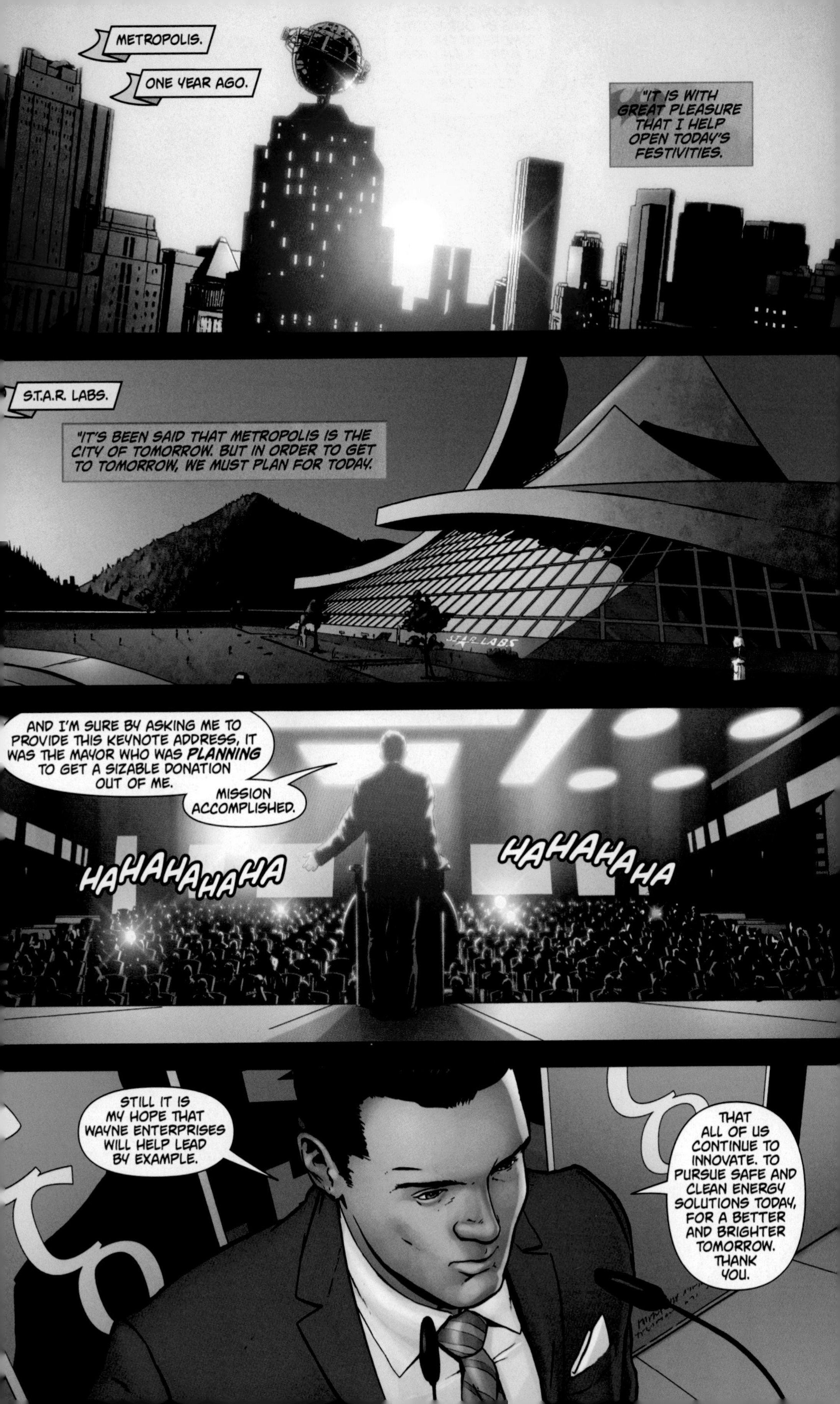
METROPOLIS.
ONE YEAR AGO.
"IT IS WITH GREAT PLEASURE THAT I HELP OPEN TODAY'S FESTIVITIES.
S.T.A.R. LABS.
"IT'S BEEN SAID THAT METROPOLIS IS THE CITY OF TOMORROW. BUT IN ORDER TO GET TO TOMORROW, WE MUST PLAN FOR TODAY.
AND I'M SURE BY ASKING ME TO PROVIDE THIS KEYNOTE ADDRESS, IT WAS THE MAYOR WHO WAS PLANNING TO GET A SIZABLE DONATION OUT OF ME.
MISSION ACCOMPLISHED.
HAHAHAHAHAHA
HAHAHAHAHA
STILL IT IS MY HOPE THAT WAYNE ENTERPRISES WILL HELP LEAD BY EXAMPLE.
THAT ALL OF US CONTINUE TO INNOVATE. TO PURSUE SAFE AND CLEAN ENERGY SOLUTIONS TODAY, FOR A BETTER AND BRIGHTER TOMORROW. THANK YOU.

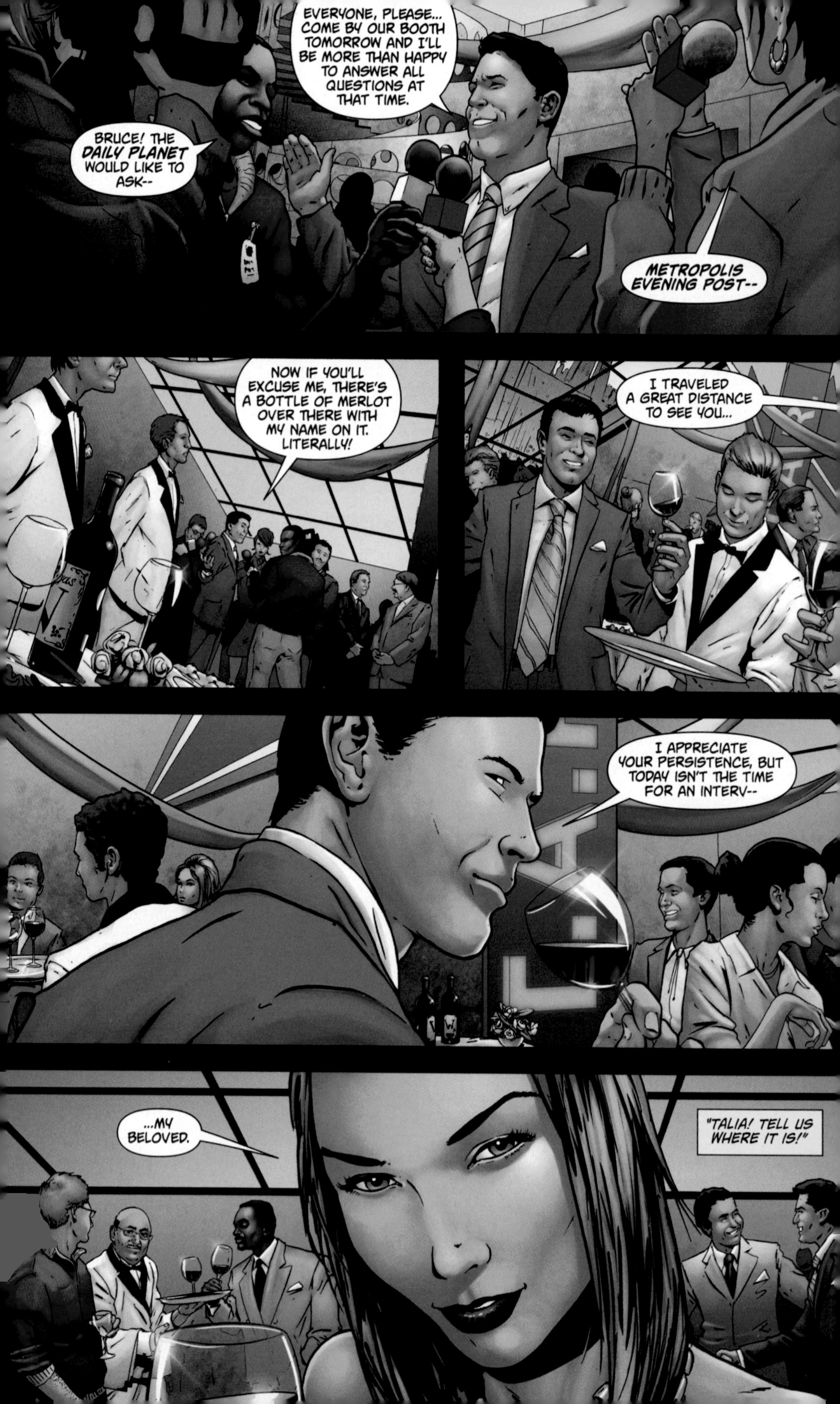
EVERYONE, PLEASE... COME BY OUR BOOTH TOMORROW AND I'LL BE MORE THAN HAPPY TO ANSWER ALL QUESTIONS AT THAT TIME.
BRUCE! THE DAILY PLANET WOULD LIKE TO ASK--
METROPOLIS EVENING POST--
NOW IF YOU'LL EXCUSE ME, THERE'S A BOTTLE OF MERLOT OVER THERE WITH MY NAME ON IT. LITERALLY!
I TRAVELED A GREAT DISTANCE TO SEE YOU...
I APPRECIATE YOUR PERSISTENCE, BUT TODAY ISN'T THE TIME FOR AN INTERV--
...MY BELOVED.
"TALIA! TELL US WHERE IT IS!"

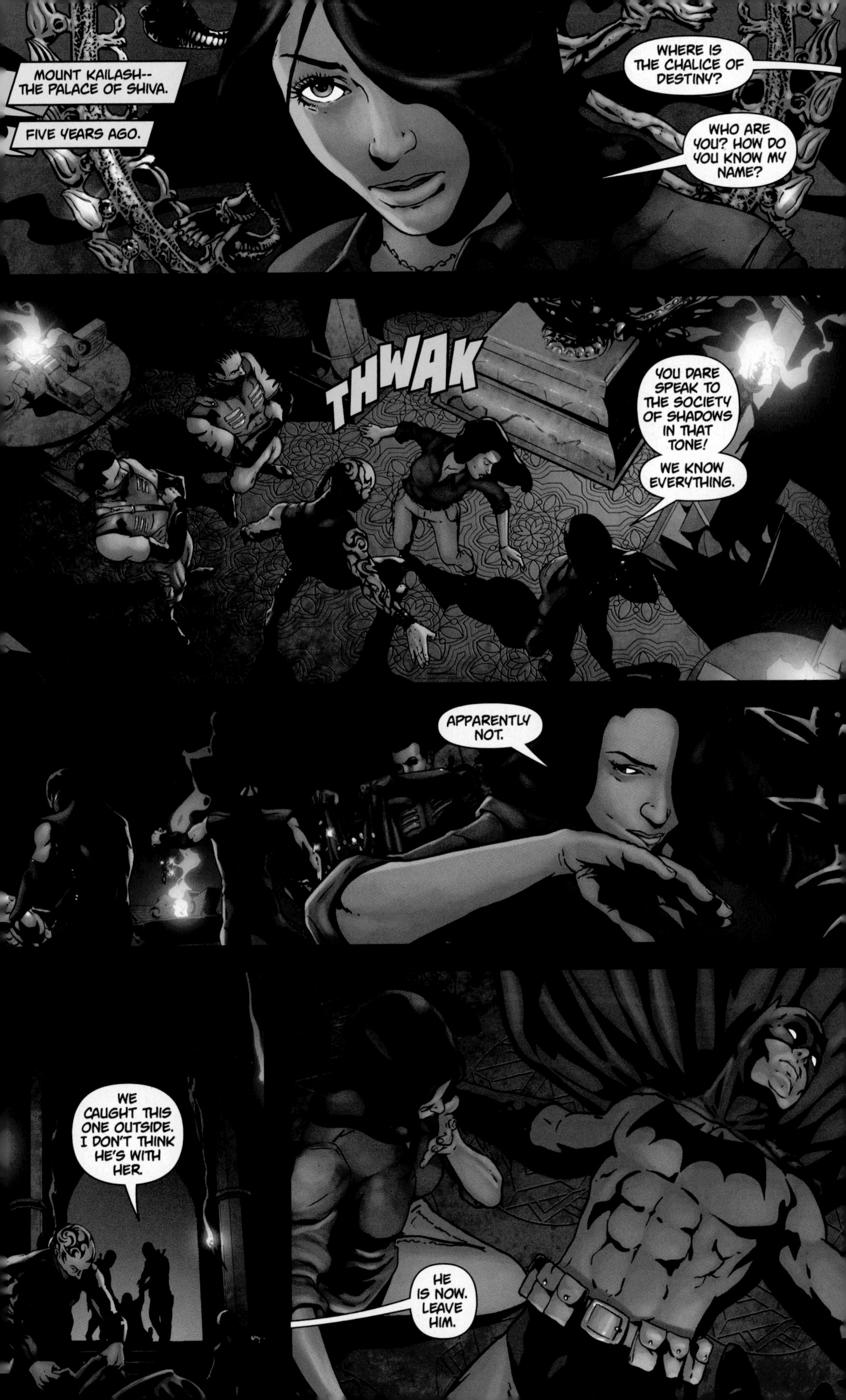
MOUNT KAILASH--
THE PALACE OF SHIVA.
FIVE YEARS AGO.
WHERE IS THE CHALICE OF DESTINY?
WHO ARE YOU? HOW DO YOU KNOW MY NAME?
THWAK
YOU DARE SPEAK TO THE SOCIETY OF SHADOWS IN THAT TONE!
WE KNOW EVERYTHING.
APPARENTLY NOT.
WE CAUGHT THIS ONE OUTSIDE. I DON'T THINK HE'S WITH HER.
HE IS NOW. LEAVE HIM.

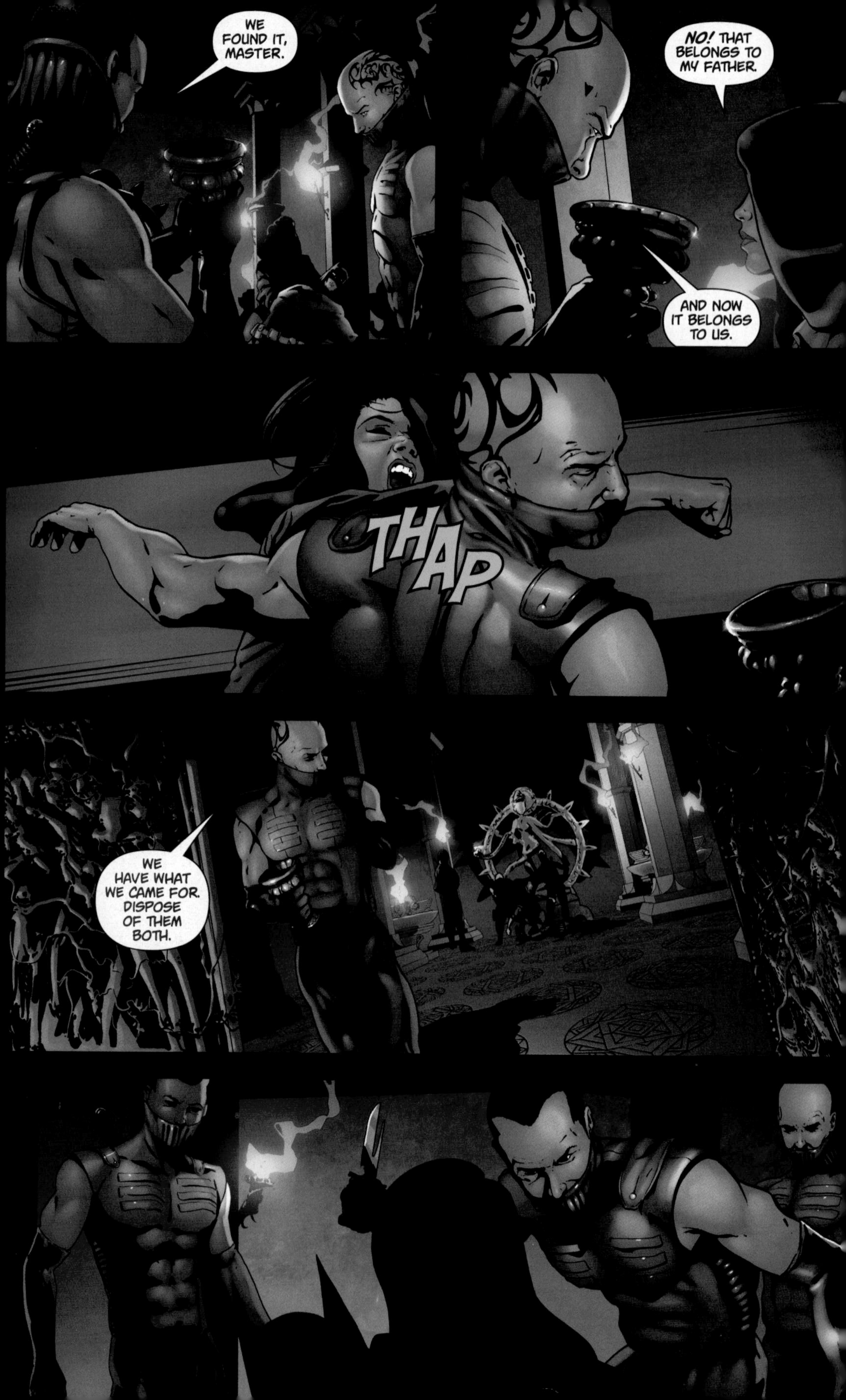
WE FOUND IT, MASTER.
NO! THAT BELONGS TO MY FATHER.
AND NOW IT BELONGS TO US.
THAP
WE HAVE WHAT WE CAME FOR. DISPOSE OF THEM BOTH.

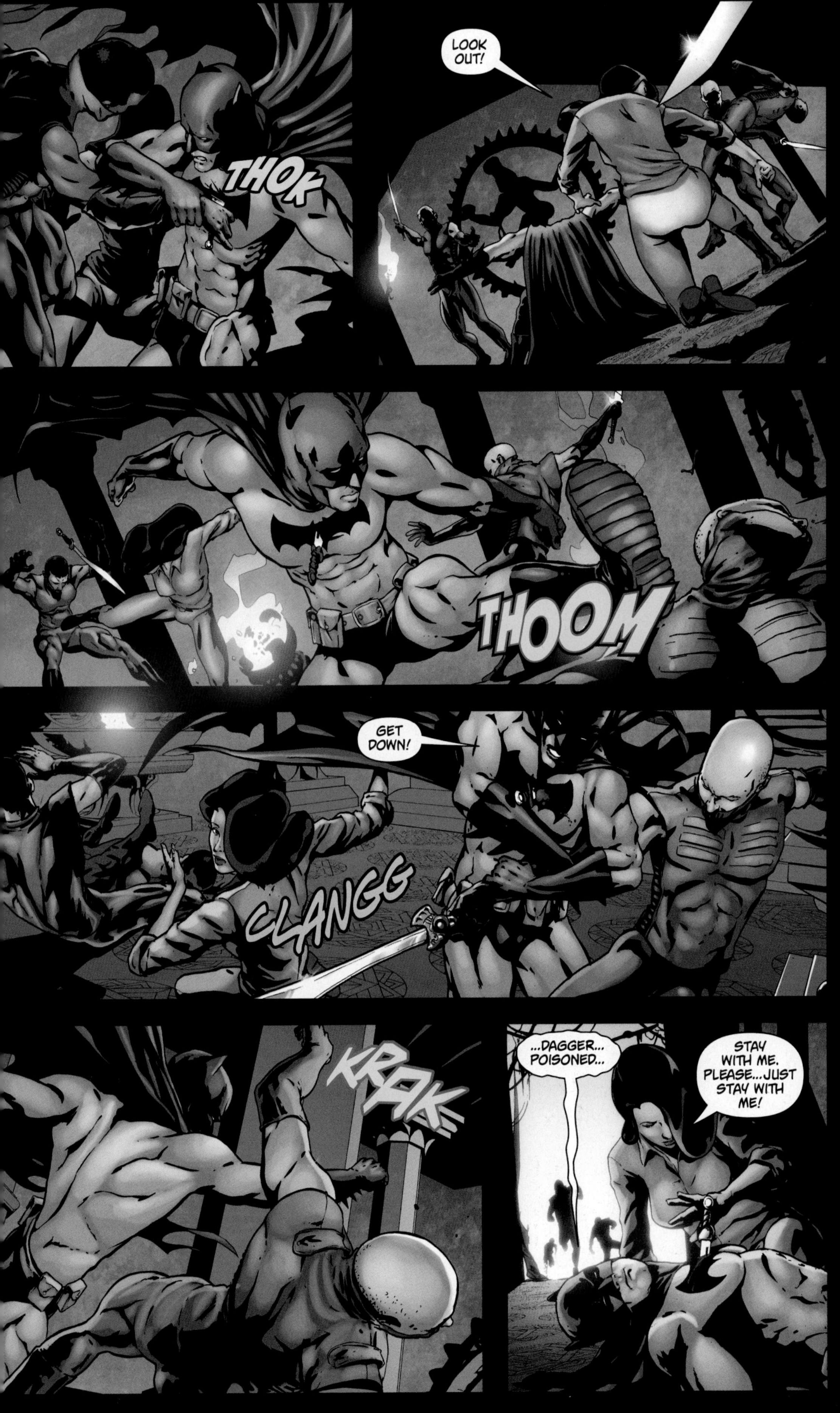
THOK
LOOK OUT!
THOOM
GET DOWN!
CLANGG
KRAK
...DAGGER... POISONED...
STAY WITH ME. PLEASE...JUST STAY WITH ME!

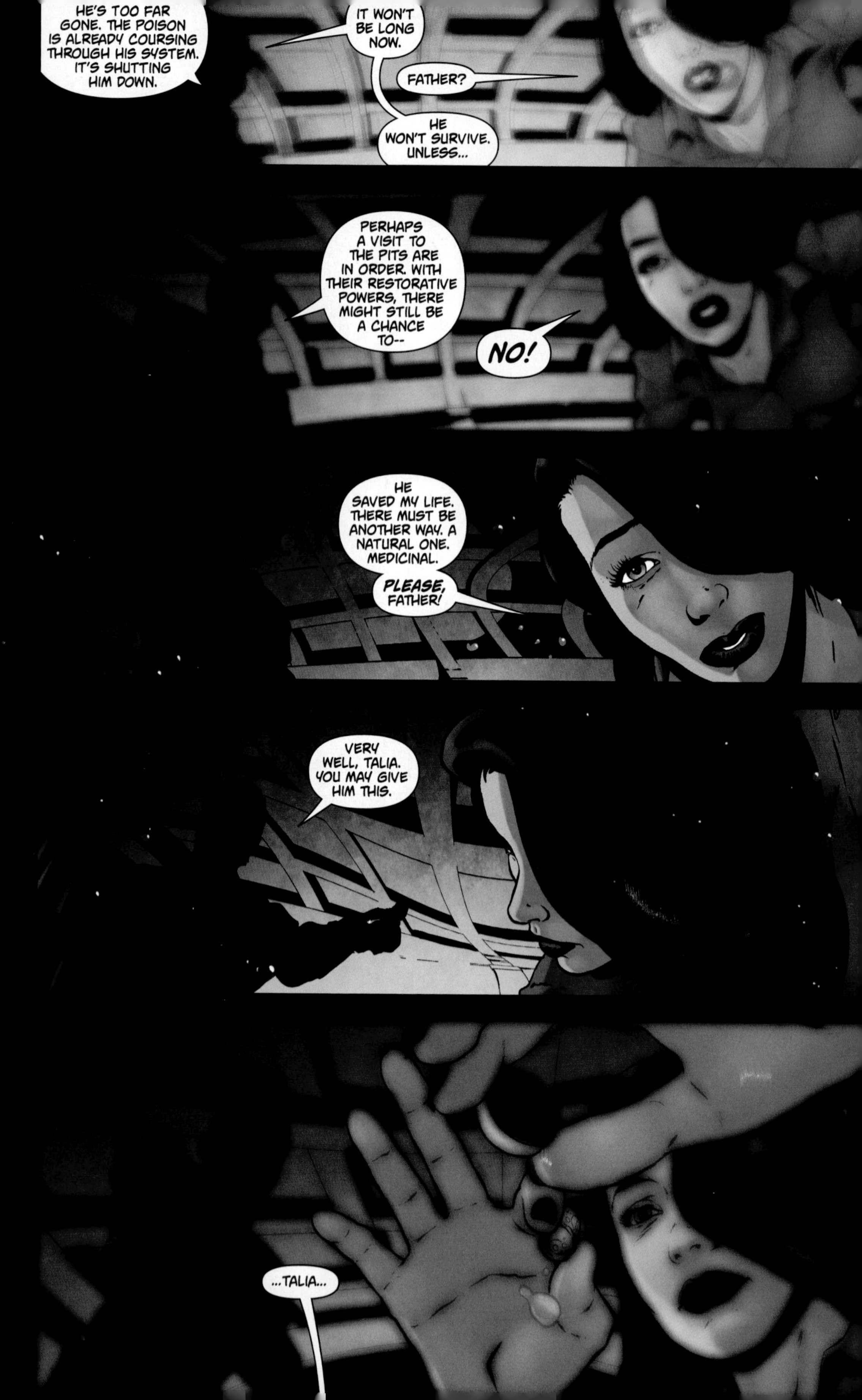
HE'S TOO FAR GONE. THE POISON IS ALREADY COURSING THROUGH HIS SYSTEM. IT'S SHUTTING HIM DOWN.
IT WON'T BE LONG NOW.
FATHER?
HE WON'T SURVIVE. UNLESS...
PERHAPS A VISIT TO THE PITS ARE IN ORDER. WITH THEIR RESTORATIVE POWERS, THERE MIGHT STILL BE A CHANCE TO--
NO!
HE SAVED MY LIFE. THERE MUST BE ANOTHER WAY. A NATURAL ONE. MEDICINAL.
PLEASE, FATHER!
VERY WELL, TALIA. YOU MAY GIVE HIM THIS.
...TALIA...

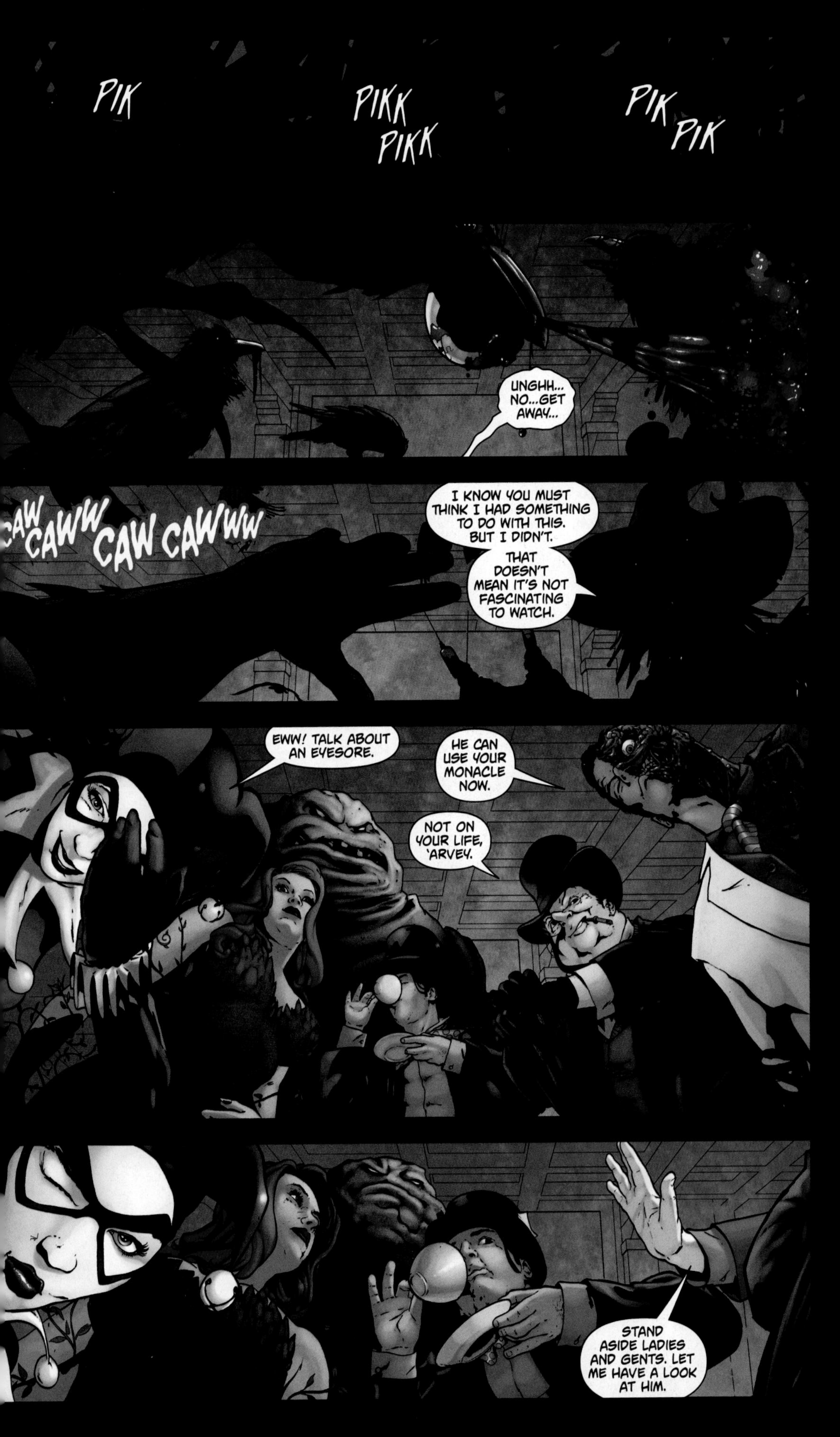
PIK
PIKK PIKK
PIK PIK
UNGHH... NO...GET AWAY...
CAW CAWW CAW CAWWW
I KNOW YOU MUST THINK I HAD SOMETHING TO DO WITH THIS. BUT I DIDN'T.
THAT DOESN'T MEAN IT'S NOT FASCINATING TO WATCH.
EWW! TALK ABOUT AN EYESORE.
HE CAN USE YOUR MONACLE NOW.
NOT ON YOUR LIFE, 'ARVEY.
STAND ASIDE LADIES AND GENTS. LET ME HAVE A LOOK AT HIM.

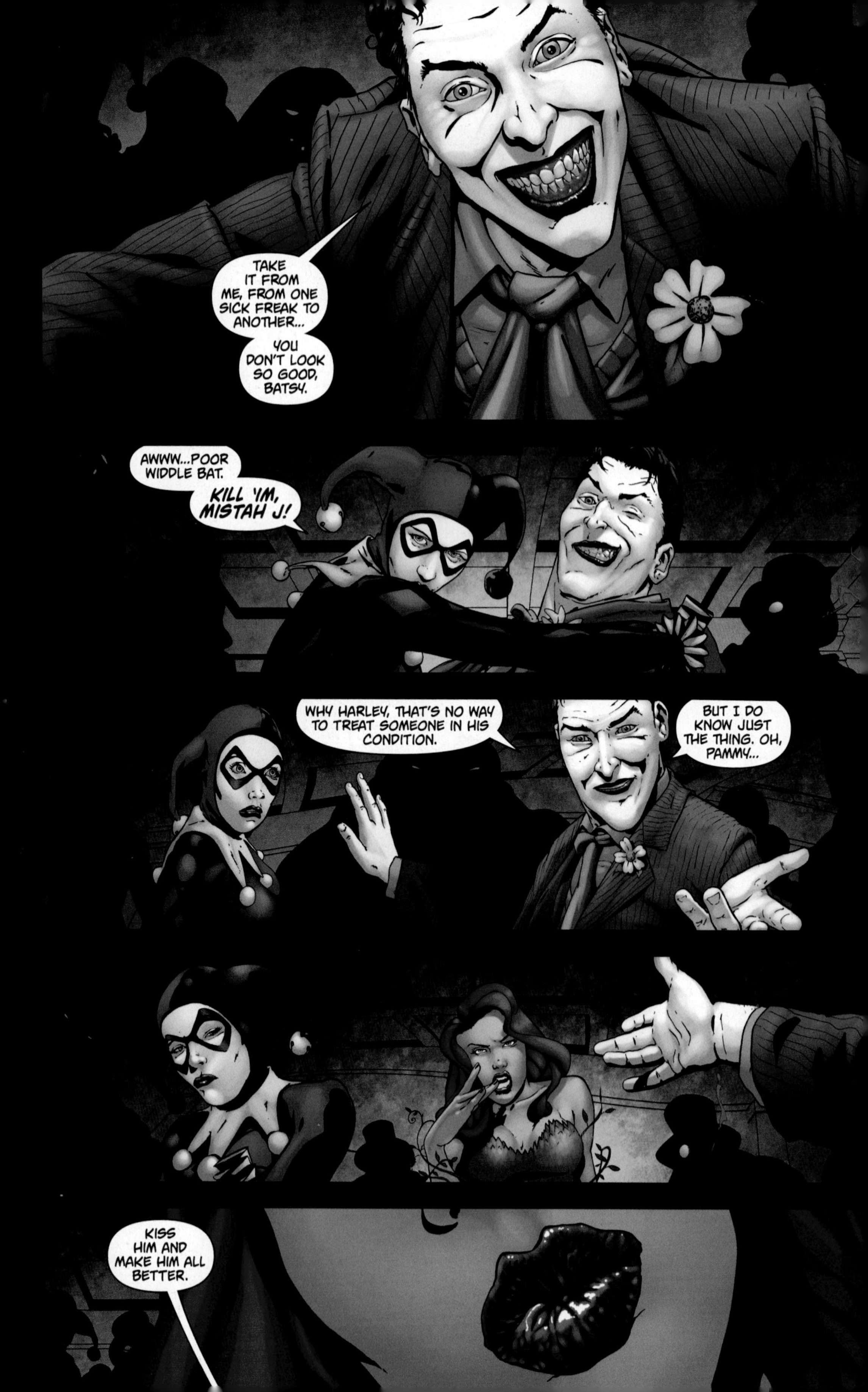
TAKE IT FROM ME, FROM ONE SICK FREAK TO ANOTHER...
YOU DON'T LOOK SO GOOD, BATSY.
AWWW...POOR WIDDLE BAT.
KILL 'IM, MISTAH J!
WHY HARLEY, THAT'S NO WAY TO TREAT SOMEONE IN HIS CONDITION.
BUT I DO KNOW JUST THE THING. OH, PAMMY...
KISS HIM AND MAKE HIM ALL BETTER.

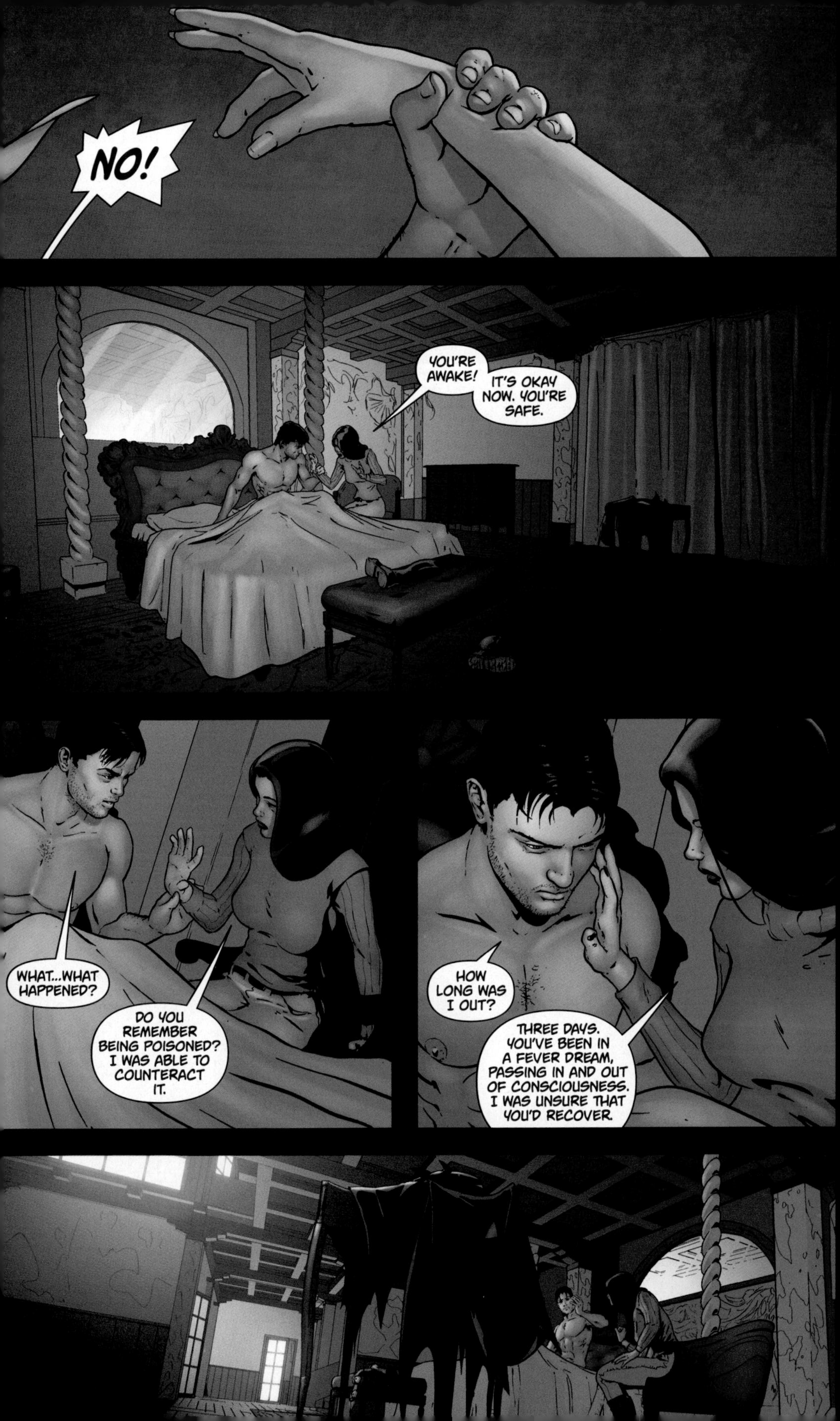
NO!
YOU'RE AWAKE!
IT'S OKAY NOW. YOU'RE SAFE.
WHAT...WHAT HAPPENED?
DO YOU REMEMBER BEING POISONED? I WAS ABLE TO COUNTERACT IT.
HOW LONG WAS I OUT?
THREE DAYS. YOU'VE BEEN IN A FEVER DREAM, PASSING IN AND OUT OF CONSCIOUSNESS. I WAS UNSURE THAT YOU'D RECOVER.

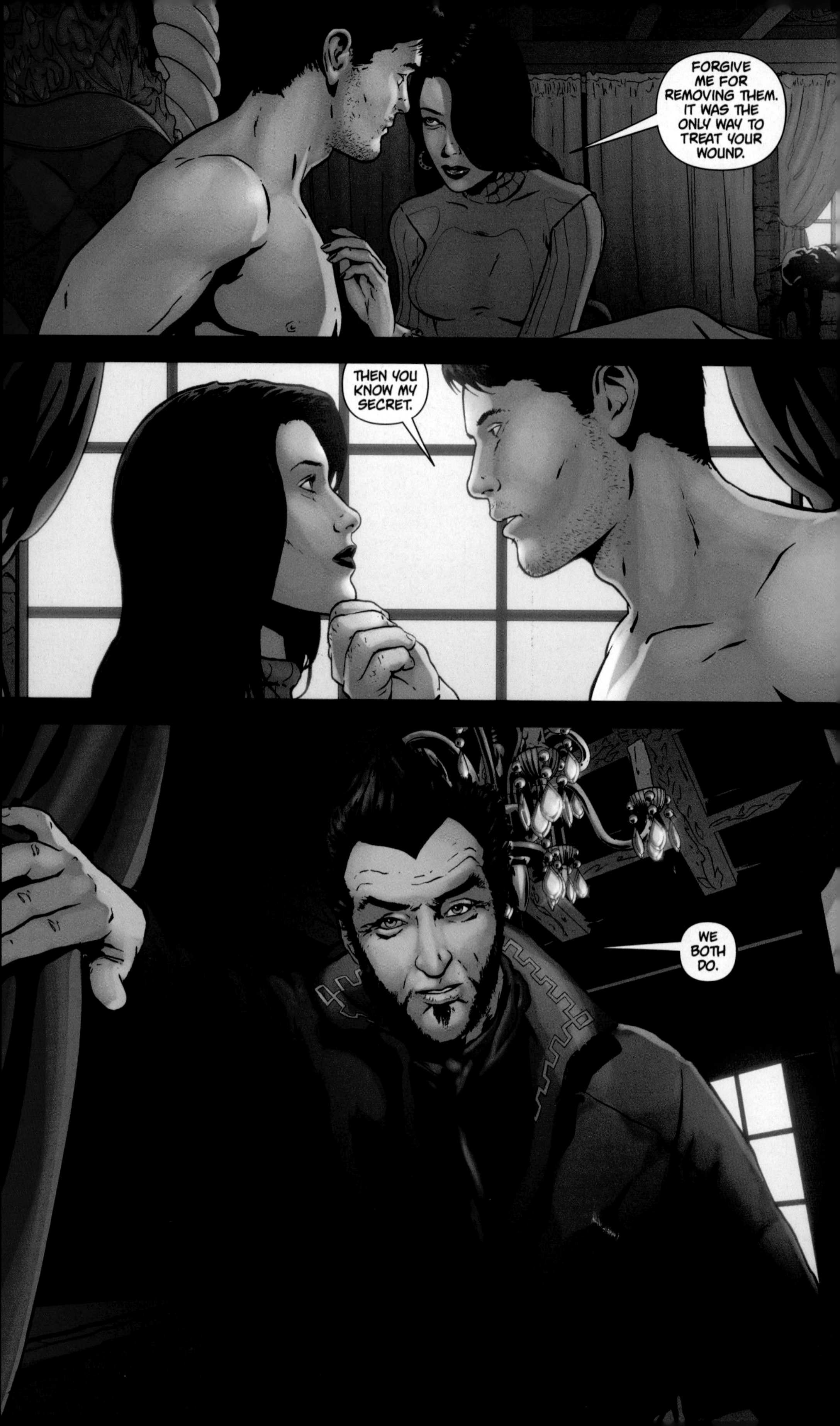
FORGIVE ME FOR REMOVING THEM. IT WAS THE ONLY WAY TO TREAT YOUR WOUND.
THEN YOU KNOW MY SECRET.
WE BOTH DO.

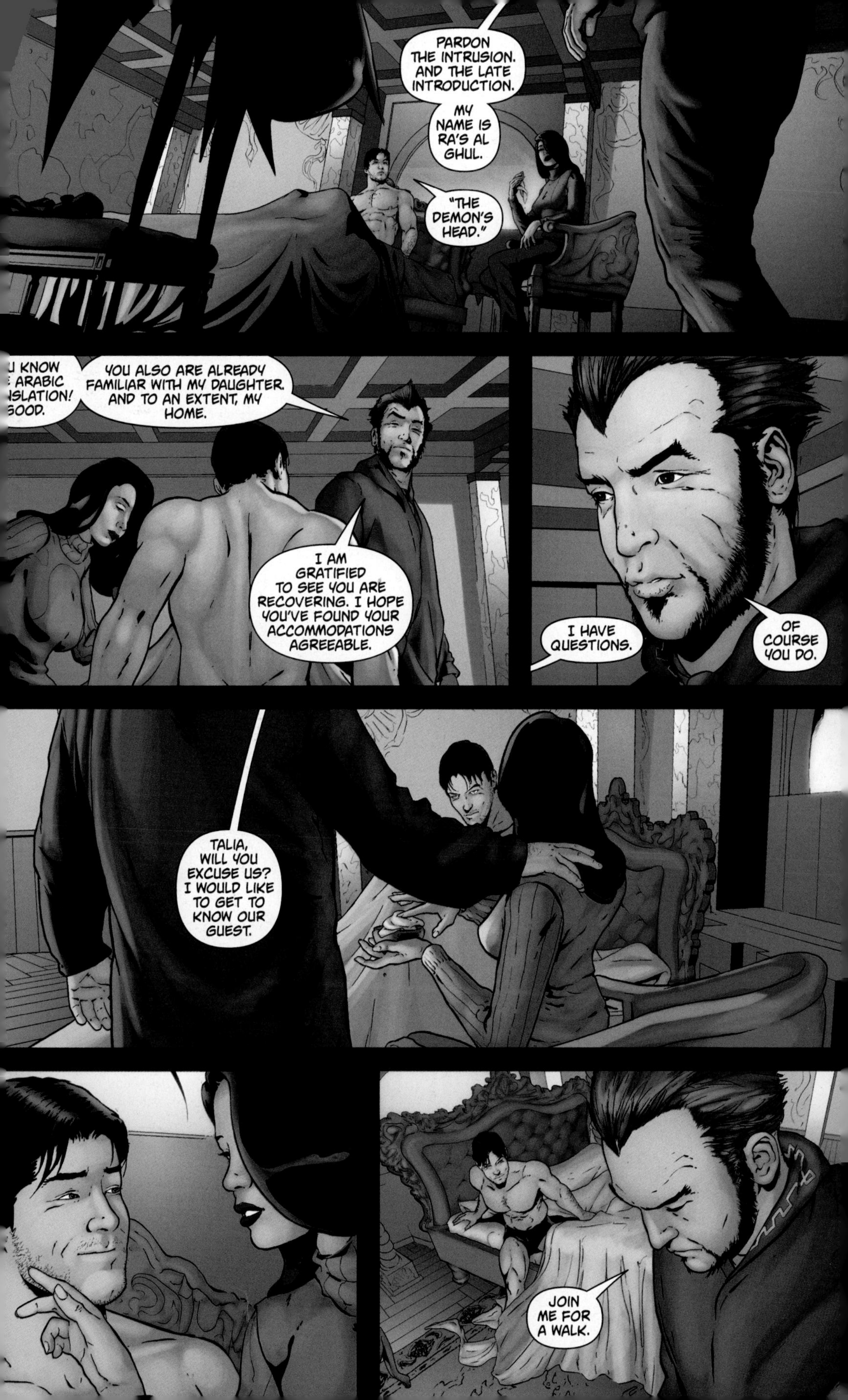
PARDON THE INTRUSION. AND THE LATE INTRODUCTION.
MY NAME IS RA'S AL GHUL.
"THE DEMON'S HEAD."
U KNOW E ARABIC NSLATION! GOOD.
YOU ALSO ARE ALREADY FAMILIAR WITH MY DAUGHTER. AND TO AN EXTENT, MY HOME.
I AM GRATIFIED TO SEE YOU ARE RECOVERING. I HOPE YOU'VE FOUND YOUR ACCOMMODATIONS AGREEABLE.
I HAVE QUESTIONS.
OF COURSE YOU DO.
TALIA, WILL YOU EXCUSE US? I WOULD LIKE TO GET TO KNOW OUR GUEST.
JOIN ME FOR A WALK.

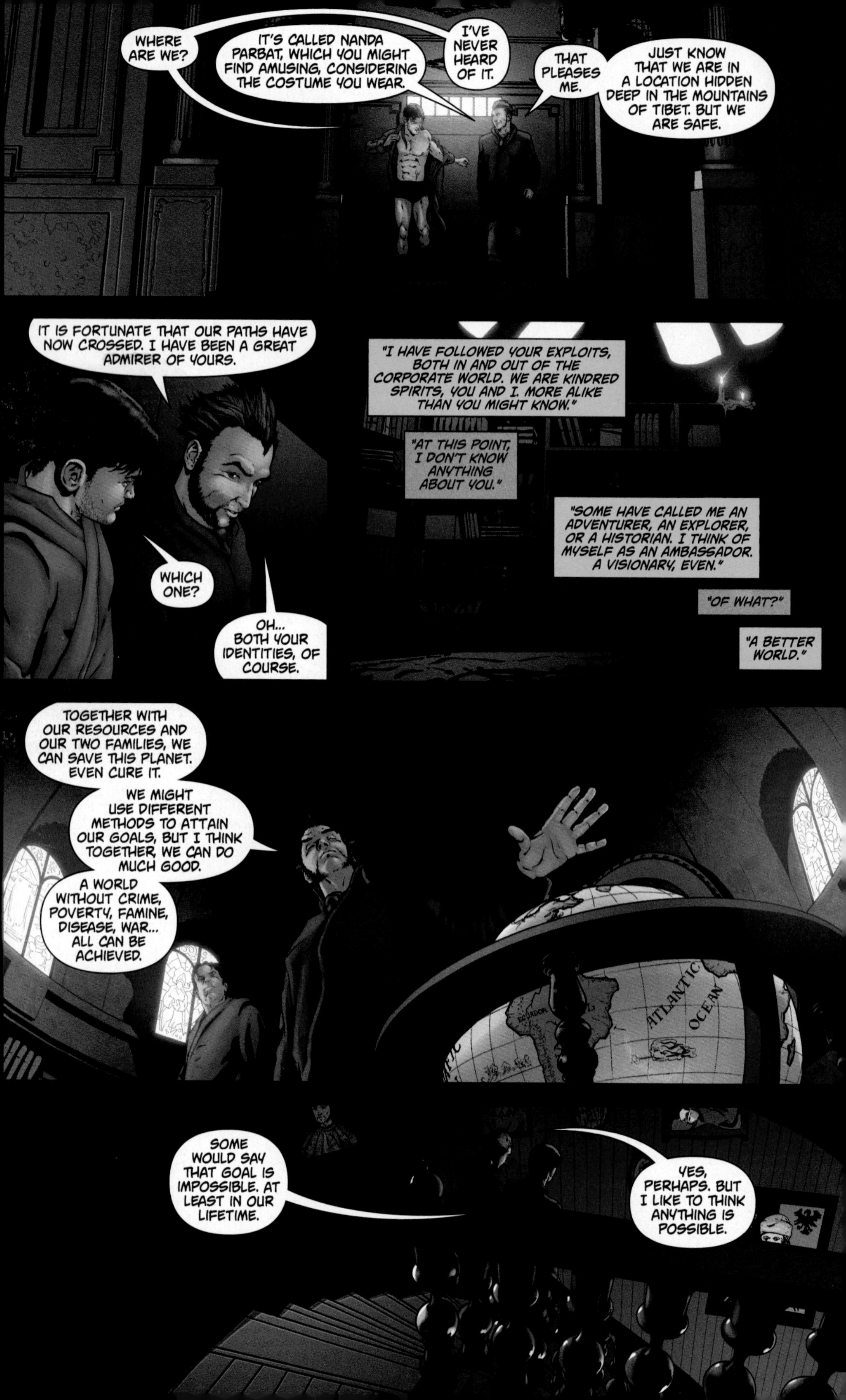
WHERE ARE WE?
IT'S CALLED NANDA PARBAT, WHICH YOU MIGHT FIND AMUSING, CONSIDERING THE COSTUME YOU WEAR.
I'VE NEVER HEARD OF IT.
THAT PLEASES ME.
JUST KNOW THAT WE ARE IN A LOCATION HIDDEN DEEP IN THE MOUNTAINS OF TIBET. BUT WE ARE SAFE.
IT IS FORTUNATE THAT OUR PATHS HAVE NOW CROSSED. I HAVE BEEN A GREAT ADMIRER OF YOURS.
WHICH ONE?
OH... BOTH YOUR IDENTITIES, OF COURSE.
"I HAVE FOLLOWED YOUR EXPLOITS, BOTH IN AND OUT OF THE CORPORATE WORLD. WE ARE KINDRED SPIRITS, YOU AND I. MORE ALIKE THAN YOU MIGHT KNOW."
"AT THIS POINT, I DON'T KNOW ANYTHING ABOUT YOU."
"SOME HAVE CALLED ME AN ADVENTURER, AN EXPLORER, OR A HISTORIAN. I THINK OF MYSELF AS AN AMBASSADOR. A VISIONARY, EVEN."
"OF WHAT?"
"A BETTER WORLD."
TOGETHER WITH OUR RESOURCES AND OUR TWO FAMILIES, WE CAN SAVE THIS PLANET. EVEN CURE IT.
WE MIGHT USE DIFFERENT METHODS TO ATTAIN OUR GOALS, BUT I THINK TOGETHER, WE CAN DO MUCH GOOD.
A WORLD WITHOUT CRIME, POVERTY, FAMINE, DISEASE, WAR... ALL CAN BE ACHIEVED.
ATLANTIC OCEAN
SOME WOULD SAY THAT GOAL IS IMPOSSIBLE. AT LEAST IN OUR LIFETIME.
YES, PERHAPS. BUT I LIKE TO THINK ANYTHING IS POSSIBLE.

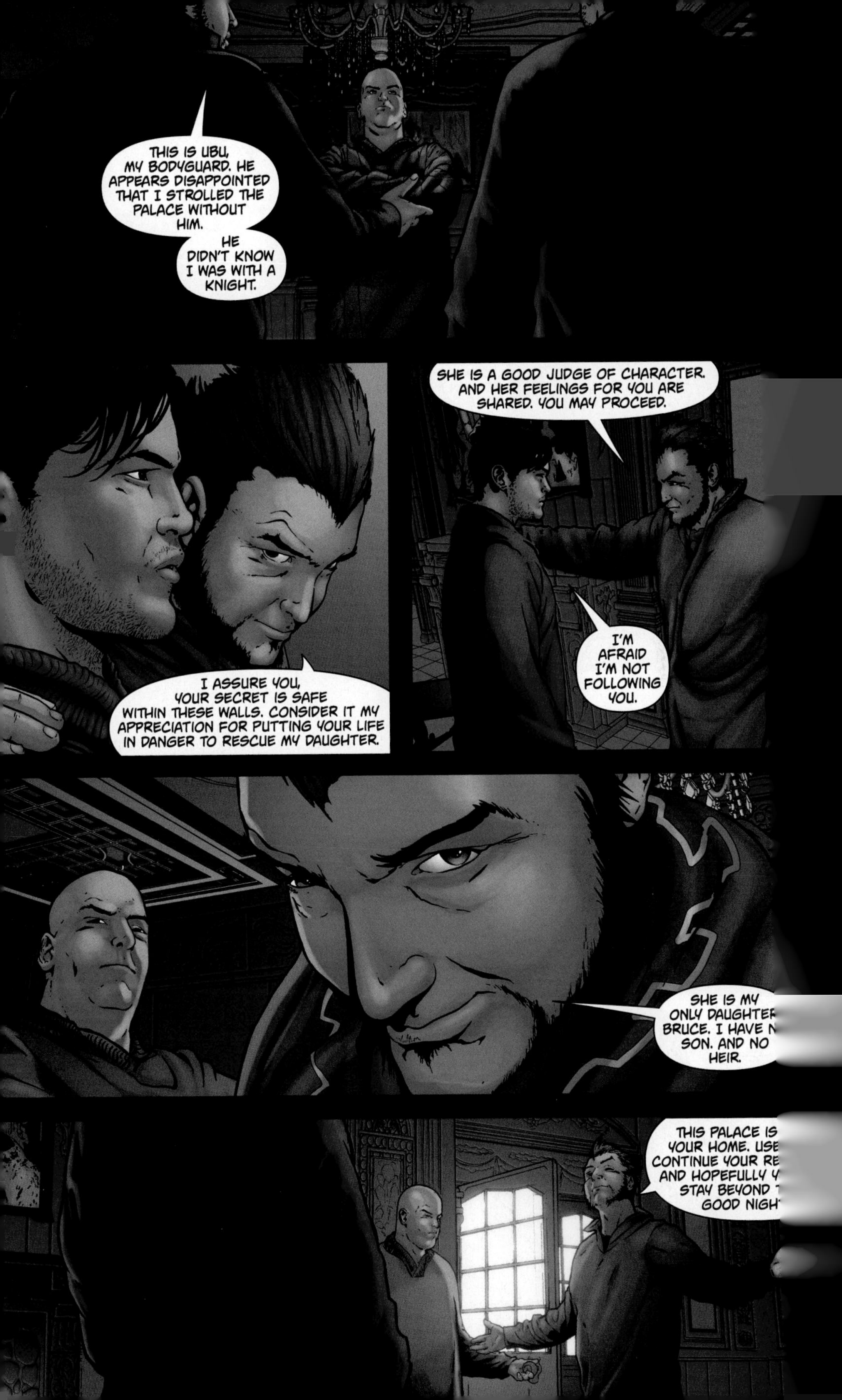
THIS IS UBU, MY BODYGUARD. HE APPEARS DISAPPOINTED THAT I STROLLED THE PALACE WITHOUT HIM.
HE DIDN'T KNOW I WAS WITH A KNIGHT.
I ASSURE YOU, YOUR SECRET IS SAFE WITHIN THESE WALLS. CONSIDER IT MY APPRECIATION FOR PUTTING YOUR LIFE IN DANGER TO RESCUE MY DAUGHTER.
SHE IS A GOOD JUDGE OF CHARACTER. AND HER FEELINGS FOR YOU ARE SHARED. YOU MAY PROCEED.
I'M AFRAID I'M NOT FOLLOWING YOU.
SHE IS MY ONLY DAUGHTER BRUCE. I HAVE N SON. AND NO HEIR.
THIS PALACE IS YOUR HOME. USE CONTINUE YOUR RE AND HOPEFULLY Y STAY BEYOND GOOD NIGH

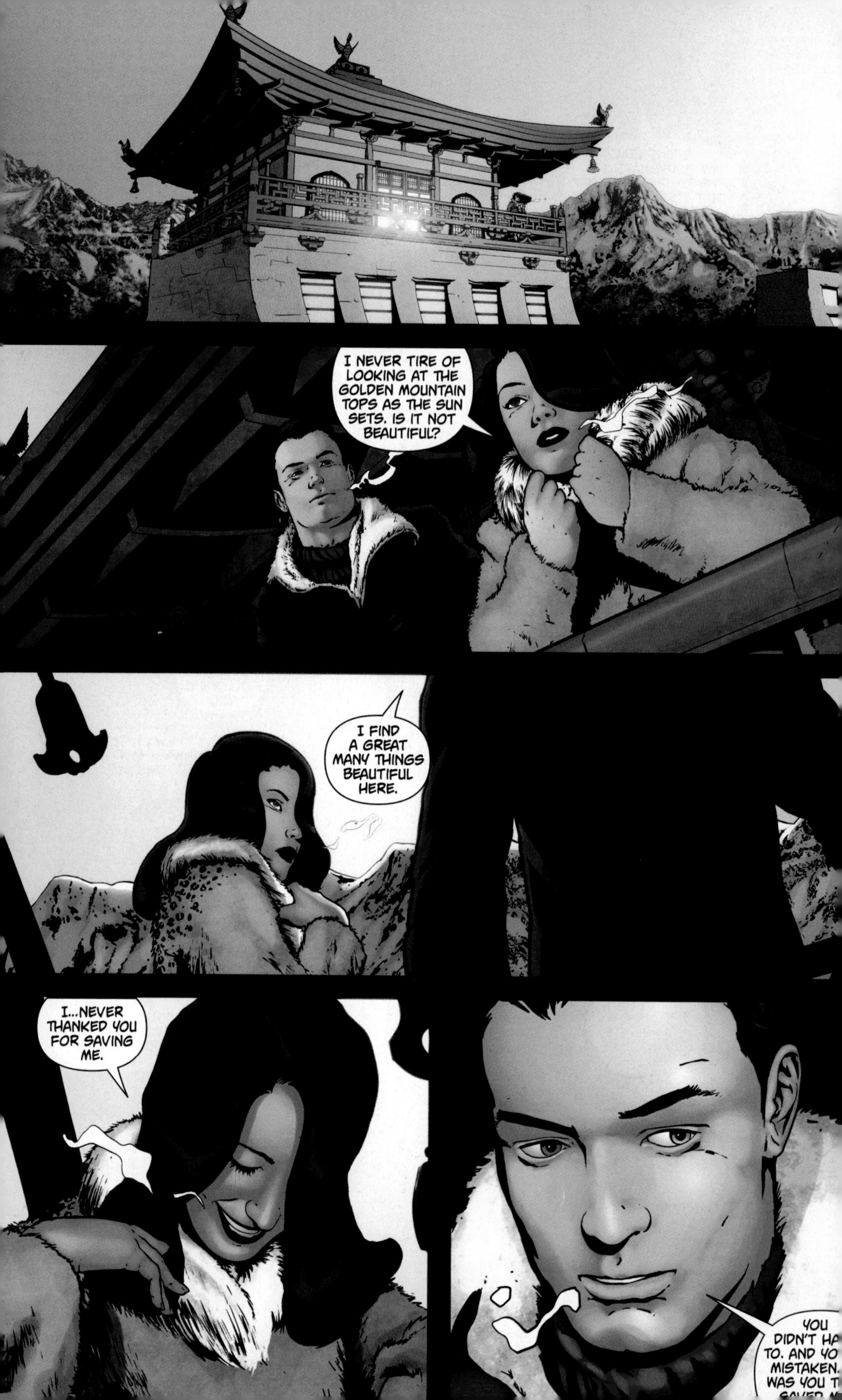
I NEVER TIRE OF LOOKING AT THE GOLDEN MOUNTAIN TOPS AS THE SUN SETS. IS IT NOT BEAUTIFUL?
I FIND A GREAT MANY THINGS BEAUTIFUL HERE.
I...NEVER THANKED YOU FOR SAVING ME.
YOU DIDN'T HA TO. AND YO MISTAKEN. WAS YOU T

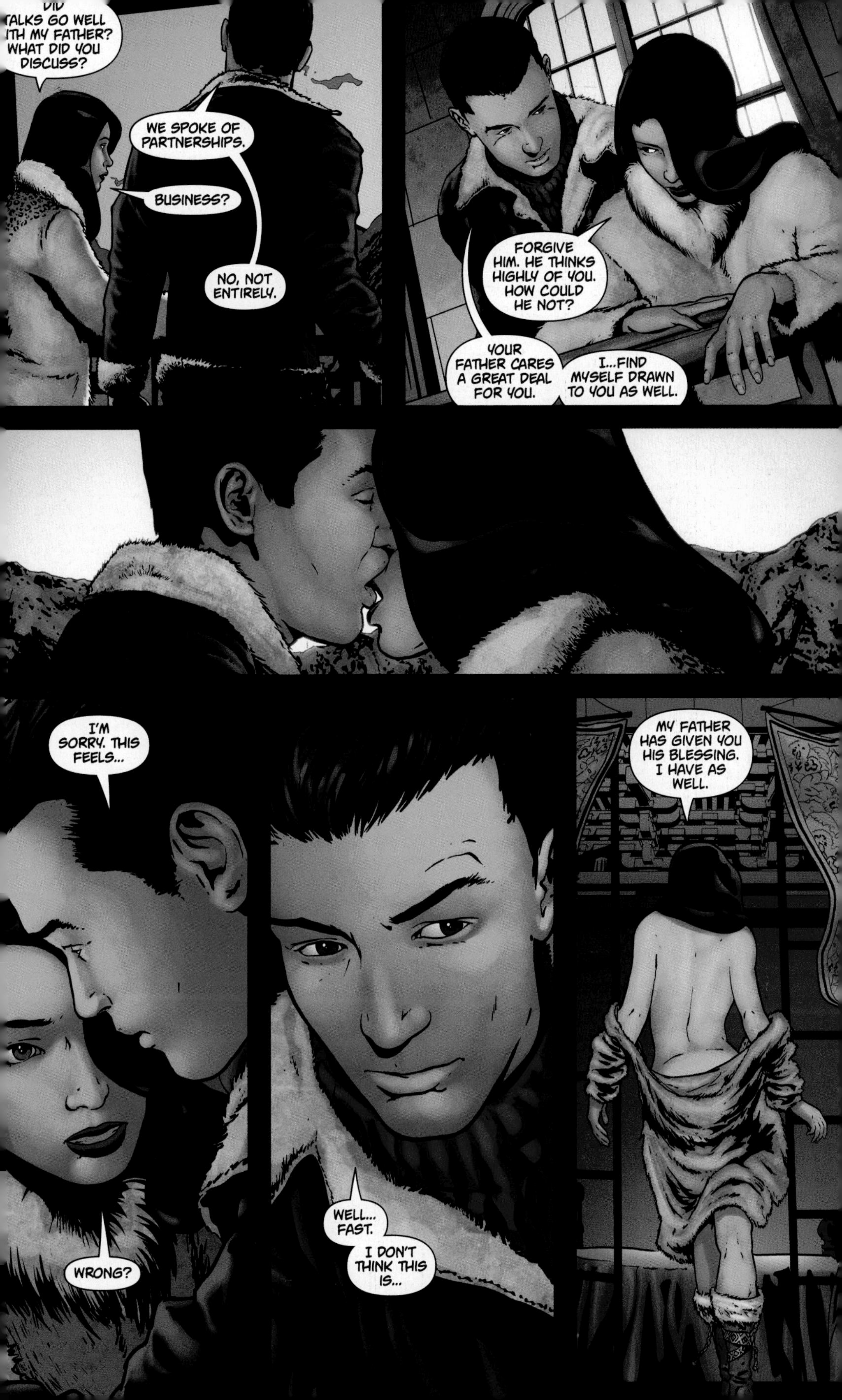
DID
TALKS GO WELL
ITH MY FATHER?
WHAT DID YOU
DISCUSS?
WE SPOKE OF
PARTNERSHIPS.
BUSINESS?
NO, NOT
ENTIRELY.
FORGIVE
HIM. HE THINKS
HIGHLY OF YOU.
HOW COULD
HE NOT?
YOUR
FATHER CARES
A GREAT DEAL
FOR YOU.
I...FIND
MYSELF DRAWN
TO YOU AS WELL.
I'M
SORRY. THIS
FEELS...
WRONG?
WELL...
FAST.
I DON'T
THINK THIS
IS...
MY FATHER
HAS GIVEN YOU
HIS BLESSING.
I HAVE AS
WELL.

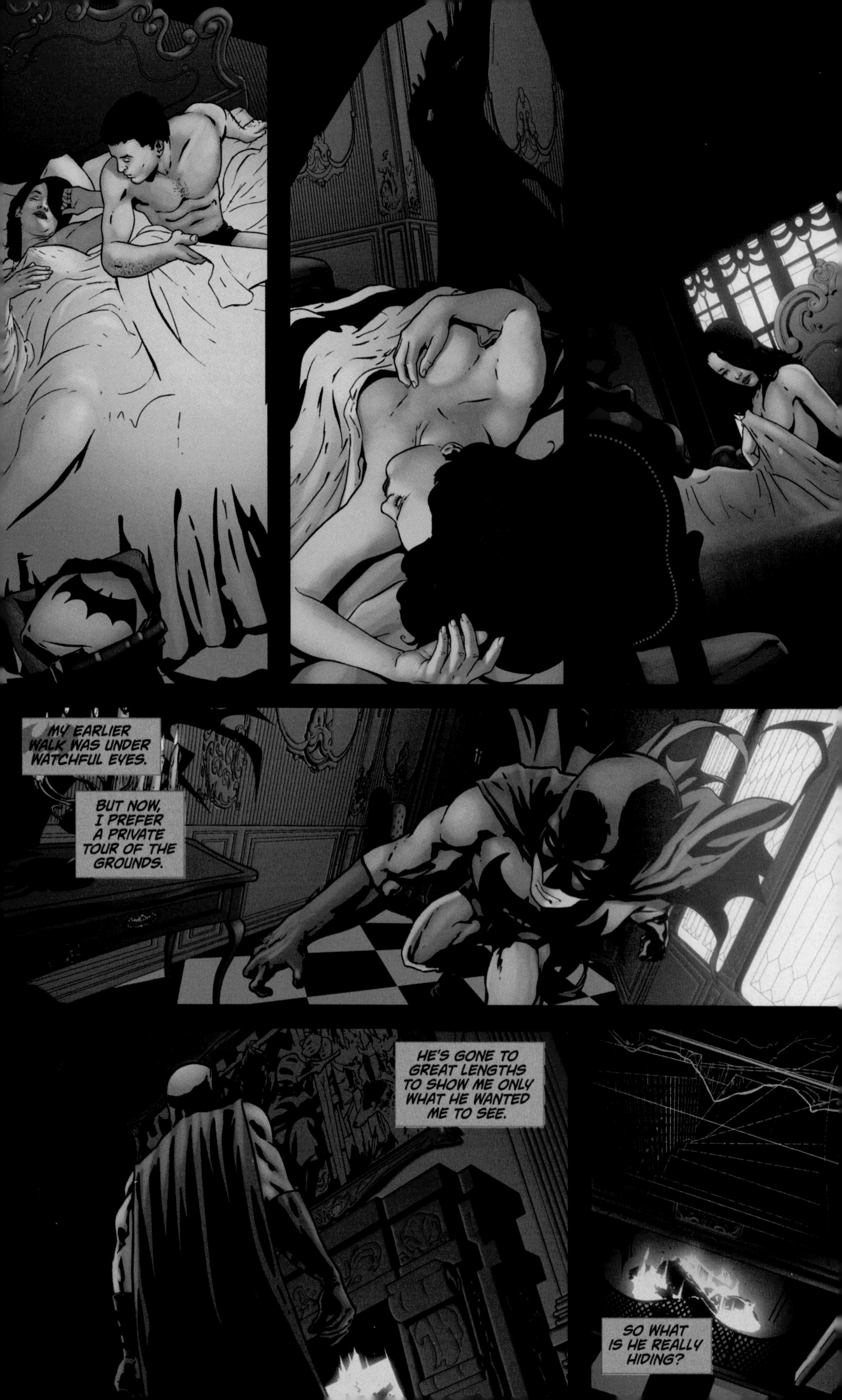

MY EARLIER WALK WAS UNDER WATCHFUL EYES.
BUT NOW, I PREFER A PRIVATE TOUR OF THE GROUNDS.
HE'S GONE TO GREAT LENGTHS TO SHOW ME ONLY WHAT HE WANTED ME TO SEE.
SO WHAT IS HE REALLY HIDING?

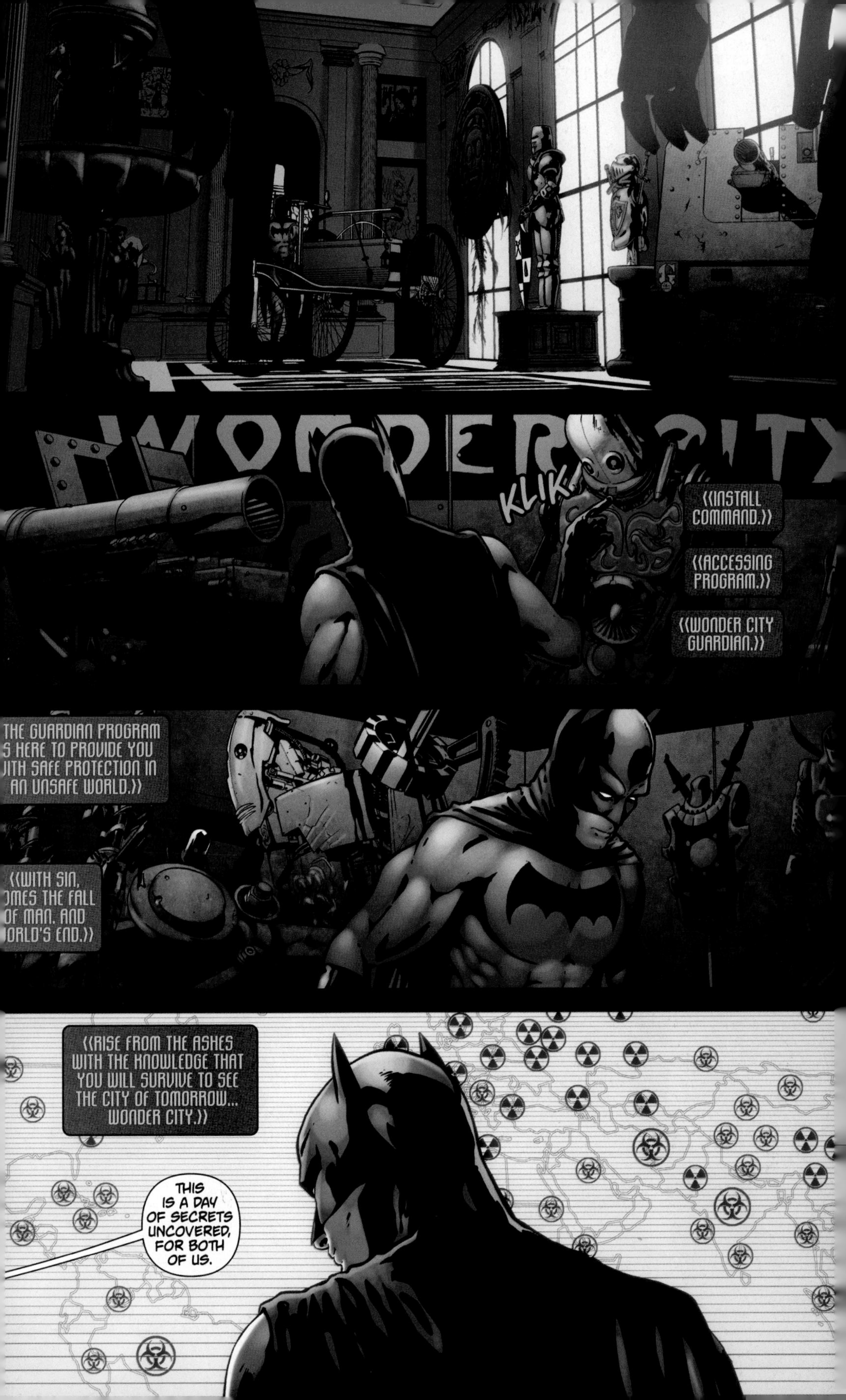
WONDER CITY
KLIK
((INSTALL COMMAND.))
((ACCESSING PROGRAM.))
((WONDER CITY GUARDIAN.))
THE GUARDIAN PROGRAM S HERE TO PROVIDE YOU ITH SAFE PROTECTION IN AN UNSAFE WORLD.))
((WITH SIN, OMES THE FALL OF MAN. AND ORLD'S END.))
((RISE FROM THE ASHES WITH THE KNOWLEDGE THAT YOU WILL SURVIVE TO SEE THE CITY OF TOMORROW... WONDER CITY.))
THIS IS A DAY OF SECRETS UNCOVERED, FOR BOTH OF US.

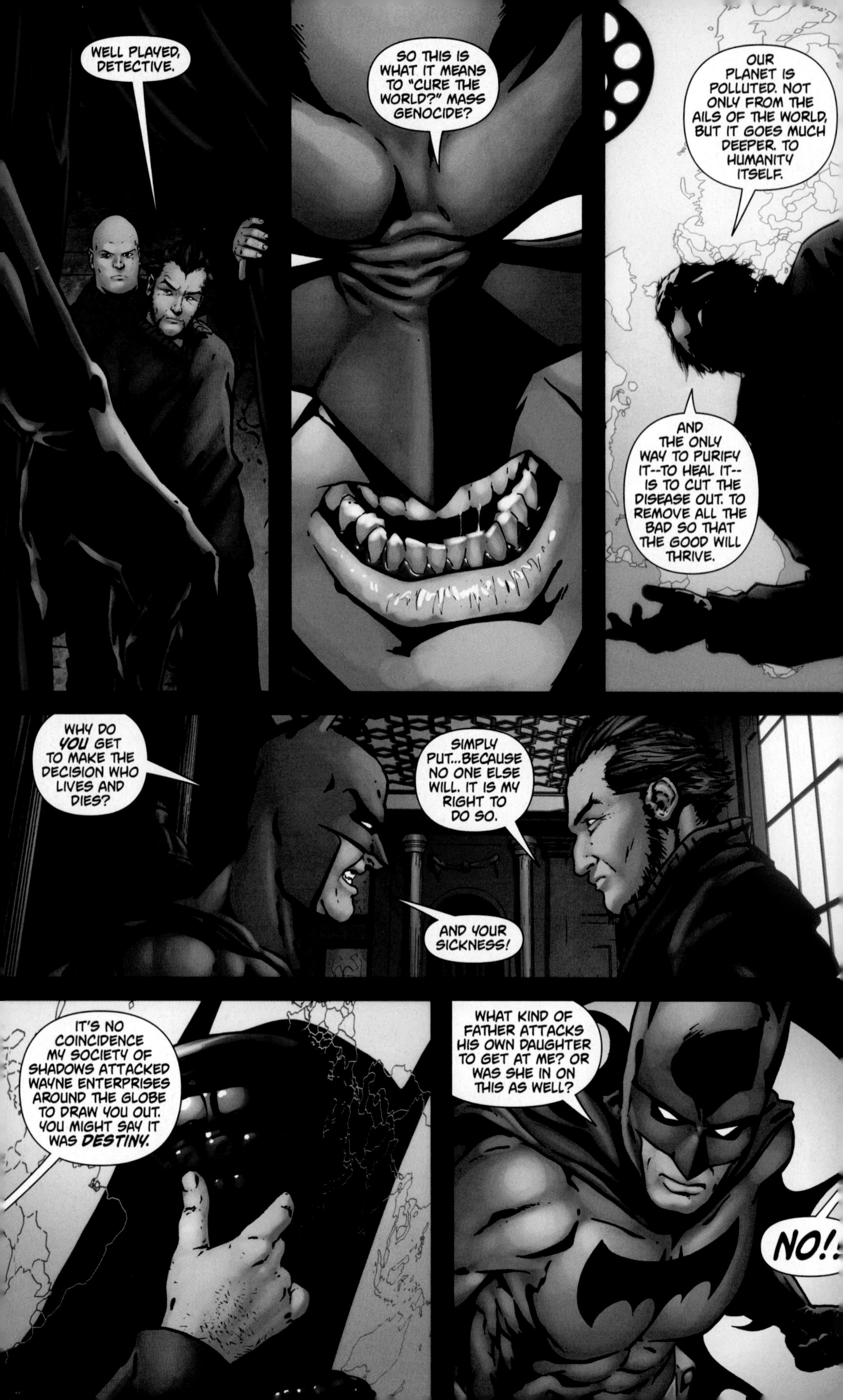
WELL PLAYED, DETECTIVE.
SO THIS IS WHAT IT MEANS TO "CURE THE WORLD?" MASS GENOCIDE?
OUR PLANET IS POLLUTED. NOT ONLY FROM THE AILS OF THE WORLD, BUT IT GOES MUCH DEEPER. TO HUMANITY ITSELF.
AND THE ONLY WAY TO PURIFY IT--TO HEAL IT--IS TO CUT THE DISEASE OUT. TO REMOVE ALL THE BAD SO THAT THE GOOD WILL THRIVE.
WHY DO *YOU* GET TO MAKE THE DECISION WHO LIVES AND DIES?
SIMPLY PUT...BECAUSE NO ONE ELSE WILL. IT IS MY RIGHT TO DO SO.
AND YOUR SICKNESS!
IT'S NO COINCIDENCE MY SOCIETY OF SHADOWS ATTACKED WAYNE ENTERPRISES AROUND THE GLOBE TO DRAW YOU OUT. YOU MIGHT SAY IT WAS *DESTINY.*
WHAT KIND OF FATHER ATTACKS HIS OWN DAUGHTER TO GET AT ME? OR WAS SHE IN ON THIS AS WELL?
NO!

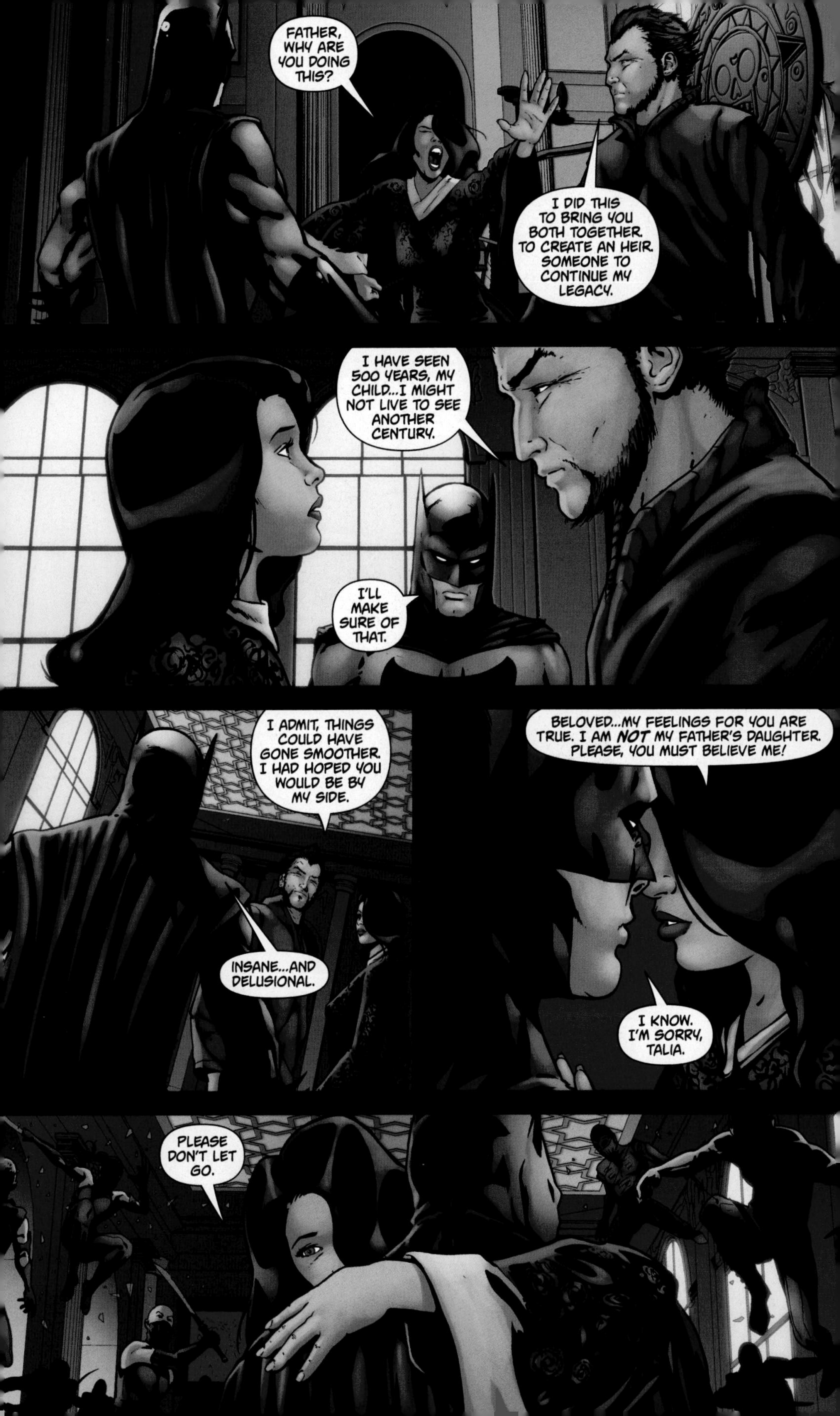
FATHER, WHY ARE YOU DOING THIS?
I DID THIS TO BRING YOU BOTH TOGETHER. TO CREATE AN HEIR. SOMEONE TO CONTINUE MY LEGACY.
I HAVE SEEN 500 YEARS, MY CHILD...I MIGHT NOT LIVE TO SEE ANOTHER CENTURY.
I'LL MAKE SURE OF THAT.
I ADMIT, THINGS COULD HAVE GONE SMOOTHER. I HAD HOPED YOU WOULD BE BY MY SIDE.
INSANE...AND DELUSIONAL.
BELOVED...MY FEELINGS FOR YOU ARE TRUE. I AM *NOT* MY FATHER'S DAUGHTER. PLEASE, YOU MUST BELIEVE ME!
I KNOW. I'M SORRY, TALIA.
PLEASE DON'T LET GO.

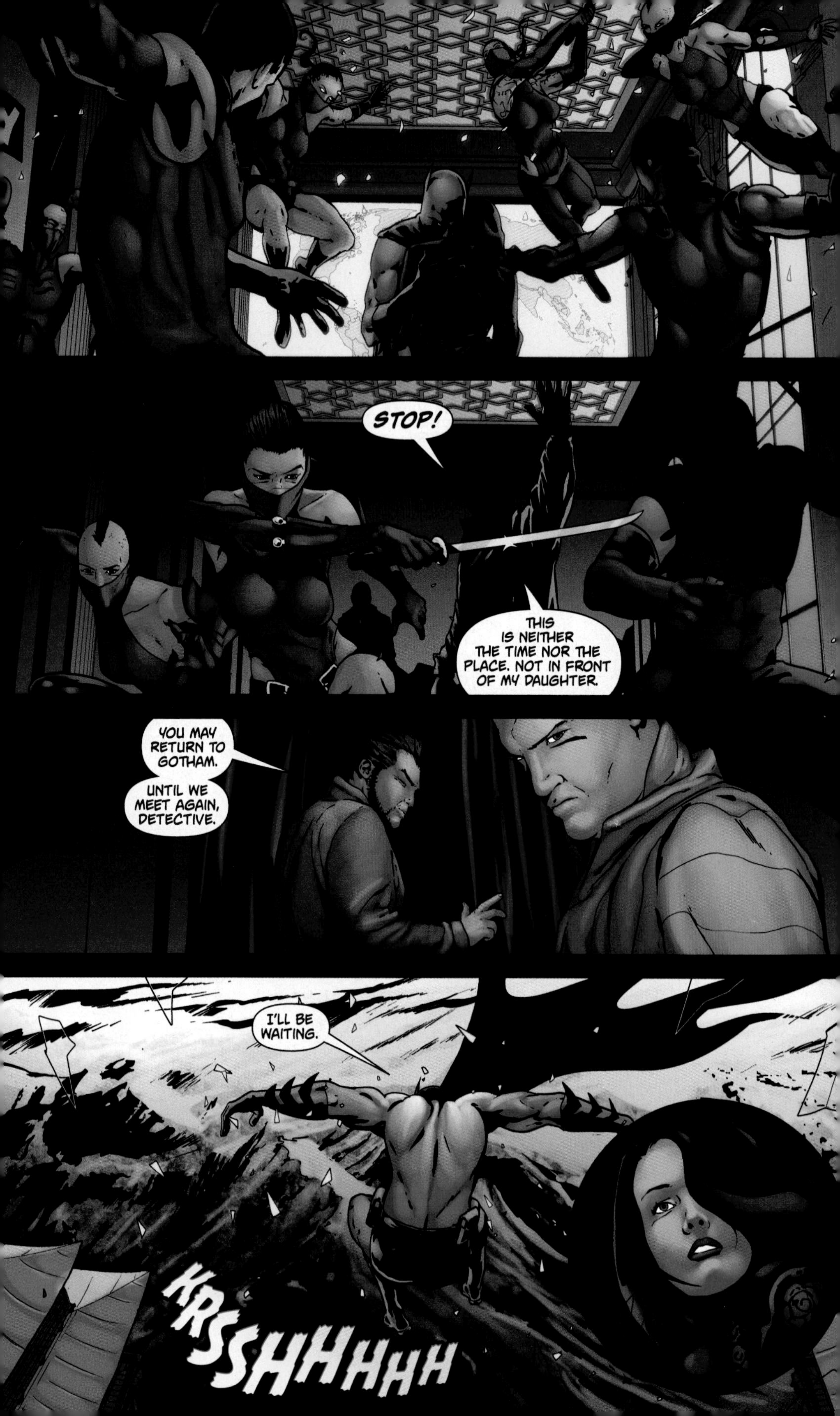
STOP!
THIS IS NEITHER THE TIME NOR THE PLACE. NOT IN FRONT OF MY DAUGHTER.
YOU MAY RETURN TO GOTHAM.
UNTIL WE MEET AGAIN, DETECTIVE.
I'LL BE WAITING.
KRSSHHHHHH

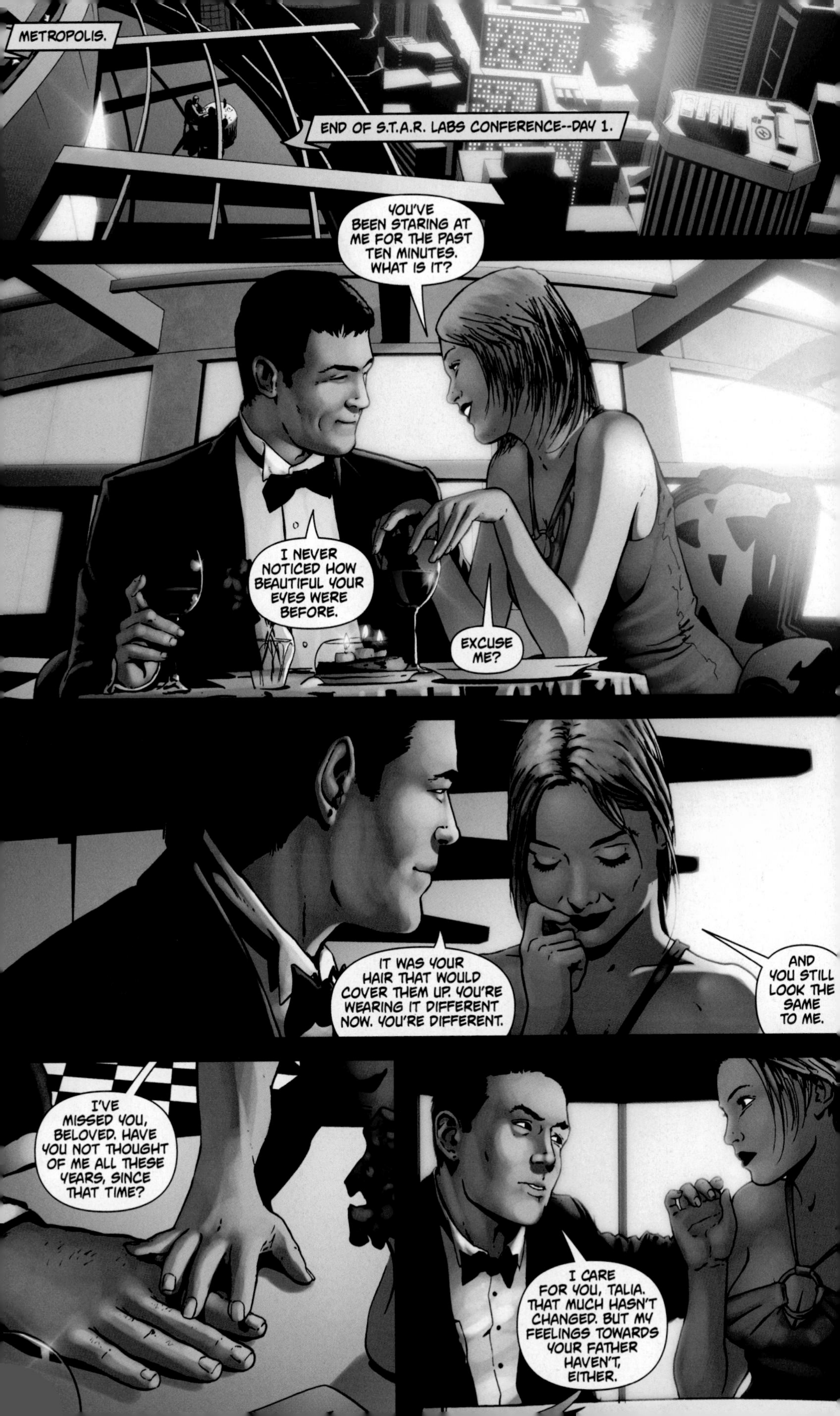
METROPOLIS.
END OF S.T.A.R. LABS CONFERENCE--DAY 1.
YOU'VE BEEN STARING AT ME FOR THE PAST TEN MINUTES. WHAT IS IT?
I NEVER NOTICED HOW BEAUTIFUL YOUR EYES WERE BEFORE.
EXCUSE ME?
IT WAS YOUR HAIR THAT WOULD COVER THEM UP. YOU'RE WEARING IT DIFFERENT NOW. YOU'RE DIFFERENT.
AND YOU STILL LOOK THE SAME TO ME.
I'VE MISSED YOU, BELOVED. HAVE YOU NOT THOUGHT OF ME ALL THESE YEARS, SINCE THAT TIME?
I CARE FOR YOU, TALIA. THAT MUCH HASN'T CHANGED. BUT MY FEELINGS TOWARDS YOUR FATHER HAVEN'T, EITHER.

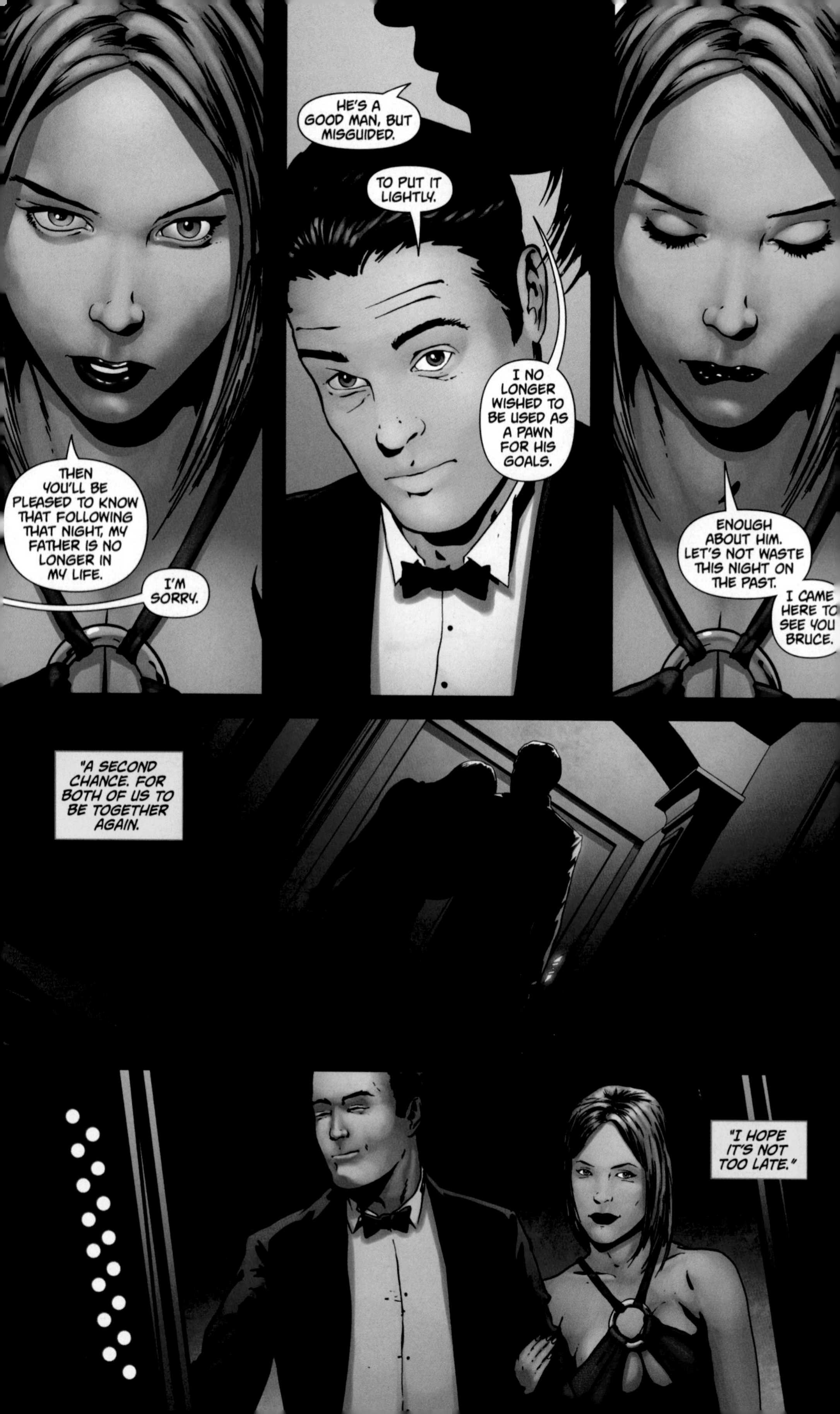
HE'S A GOOD MAN, BUT MISGUIDED.
TO PUT IT LIGHTLY.
I NO LONGER WISHED TO BE USED AS A PAWN FOR HIS GOALS.
THEN YOU'LL BE PLEASED TO KNOW THAT FOLLOWING THAT NIGHT, MY FATHER IS NO LONGER IN MY LIFE.
I'M SORRY.
ENOUGH ABOUT HIM. LET'S NOT WASTE THIS NIGHT ON THE PAST.
I CAME HERE TO SEE YOU BRUCE.
"A SECOND CHANCE. FOR BOTH OF US TO BE TOGETHER AGAIN.
"I HOPE IT'S NOT TOO LATE."

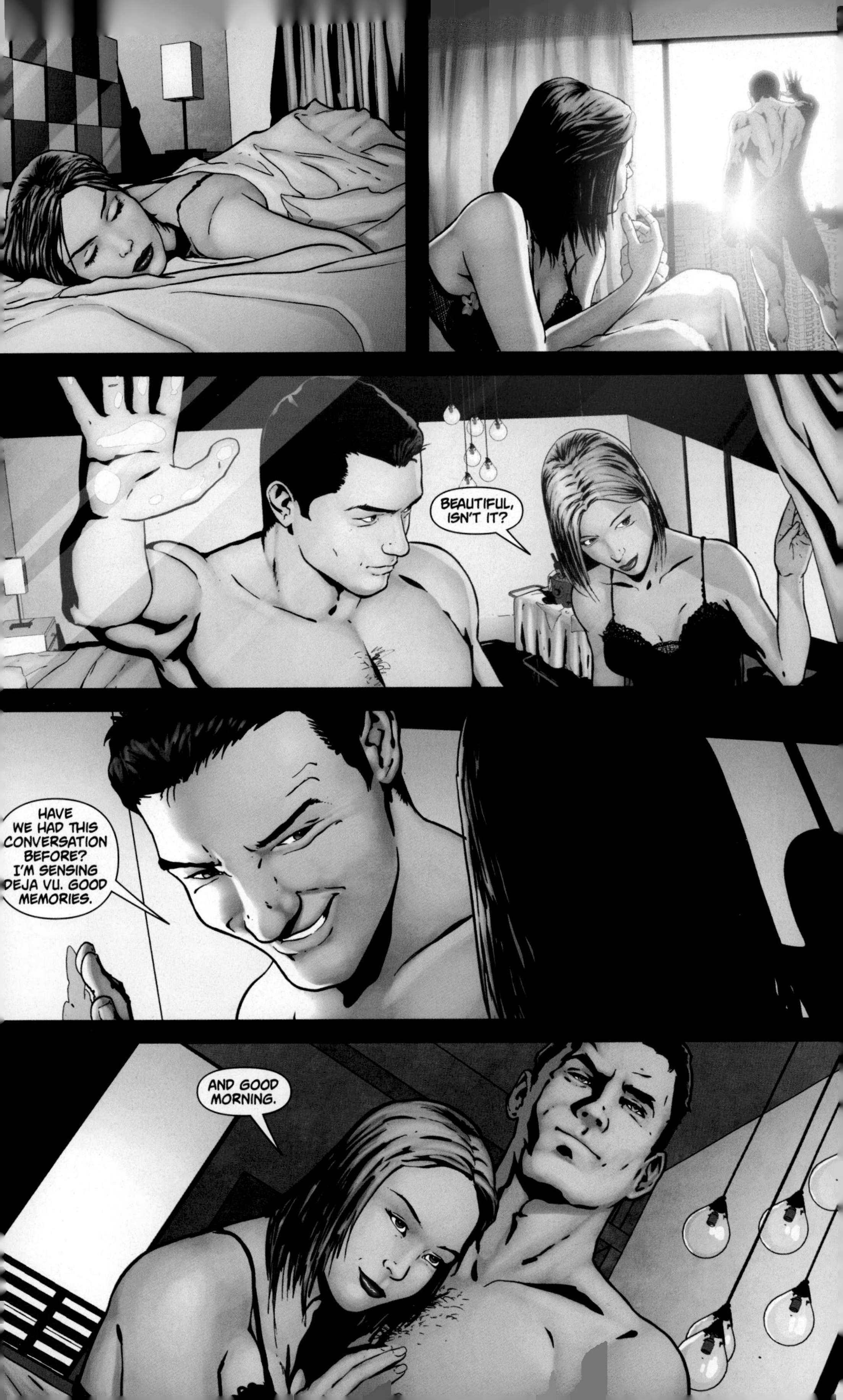
BEAUTIFUL, ISN'T IT?
HAVE WE HAD THIS CONVERSATION BEFORE? I'M SENSING DEJA VU. GOOD MEMORIES.
AND GOOD MORNING.

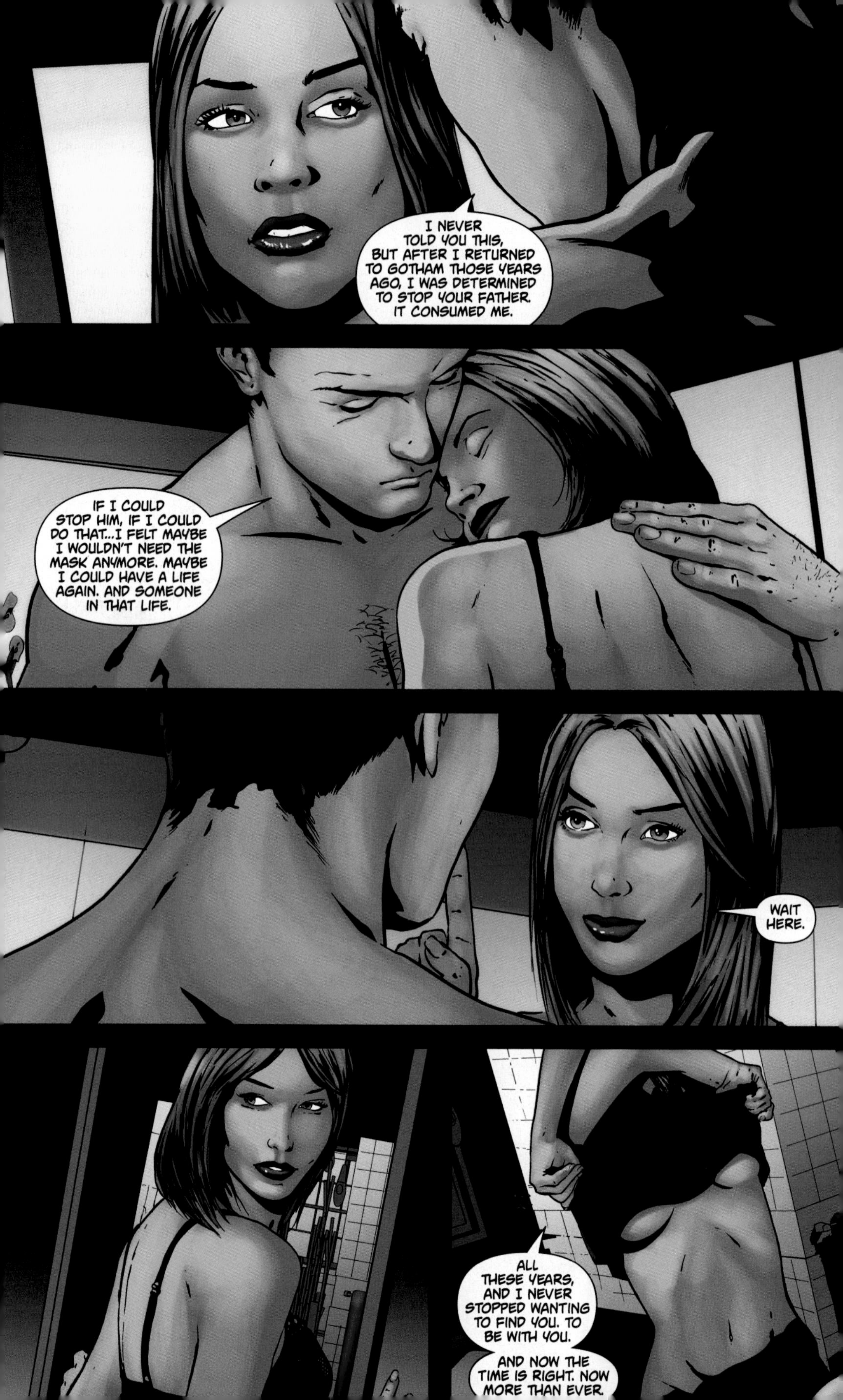
I NEVER TOLD YOU THIS, BUT AFTER I RETURNED TO GOTHAM THOSE YEARS AGO, I WAS DETERMINED TO STOP YOUR FATHER. IT CONSUMED ME.
IF I COULD STOP HIM, IF I COULD DO THAT...I FELT MAYBE I WOULDN'T NEED THE MASK ANYMORE. MAYBE I COULD HAVE A LIFE AGAIN. AND SOMEONE IN THAT LIFE.
WAIT HERE.
ALL THESE YEARS, AND I NEVER STOPPED WANTING TO FIND YOU. TO BE WITH YOU.
AND NOW THE TIME IS RIGHT. NOW MORE THAN EVER.

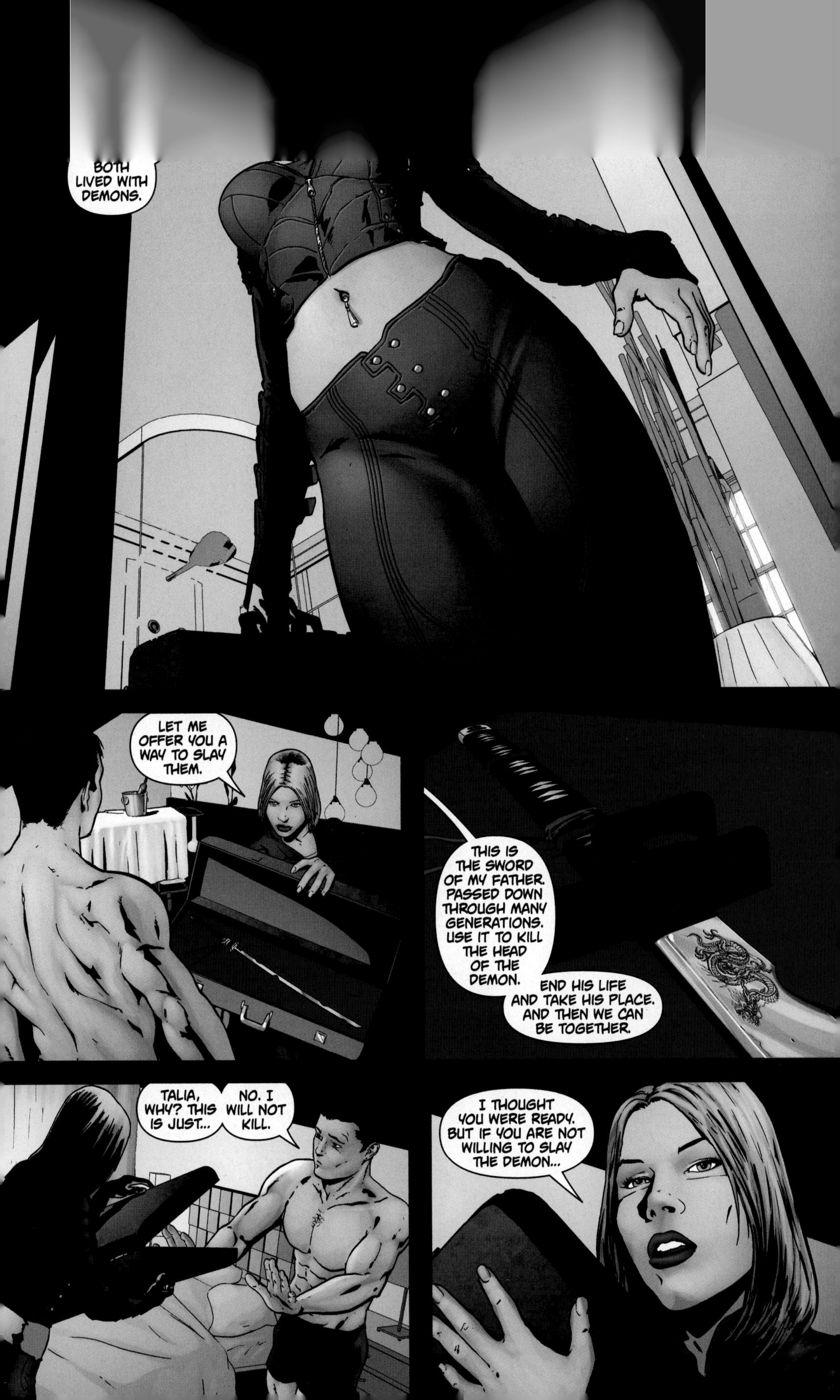

BOTH LIVED WITH DEMONS.
LET ME OFFER YOU A WAY TO SLAY THEM.
THIS IS THE SWORD OF MY FATHER. PASSED DOWN THROUGH MANY GENERATIONS. USE IT TO KILL THE HEAD OF THE DEMON.
END HIS LIFE AND TAKE HIS PLACE. AND THEN WE CAN BE TOGETHER.
TALIA, WHY? THIS IS JUST...
NO. I WILL NOT KILL.
I THOUGHT YOU WERE READY. BUT IF YOU ARE NOT WILLING TO SLAY THE DEMON...

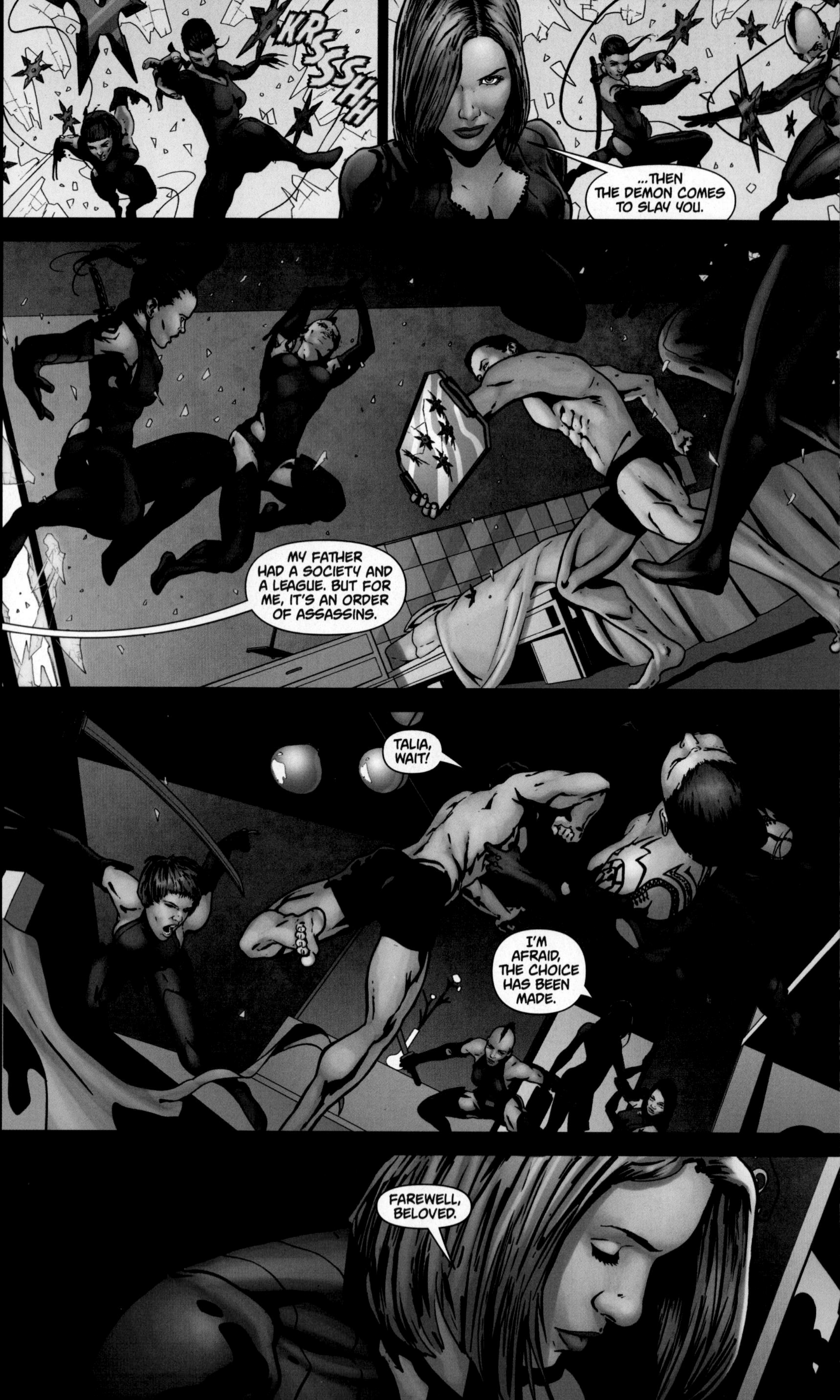
KRSSHH
...THEN THE DEMON COMES TO SLAY YOU.
MY FATHER HAD A SOCIETY AND A LEAGUE. BUT FOR ME, IT'S AN ORDER OF ASSASSINS.
TALIA, WAIT!
I'M AFRAID, THE CHOICE HAS BEEN MADE.
FAREWELL, BELOVED.

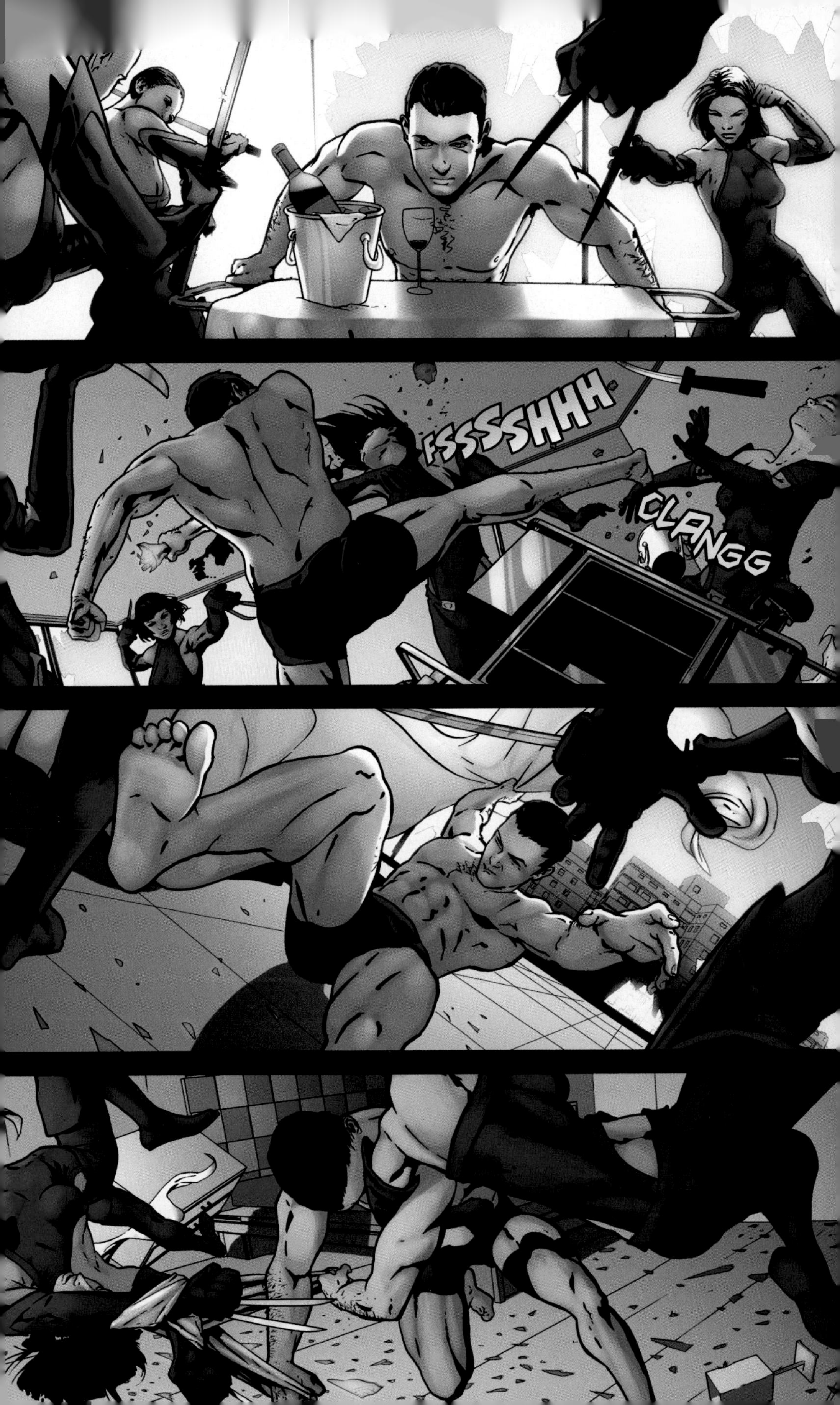
FSSSSHHH
CLANGG

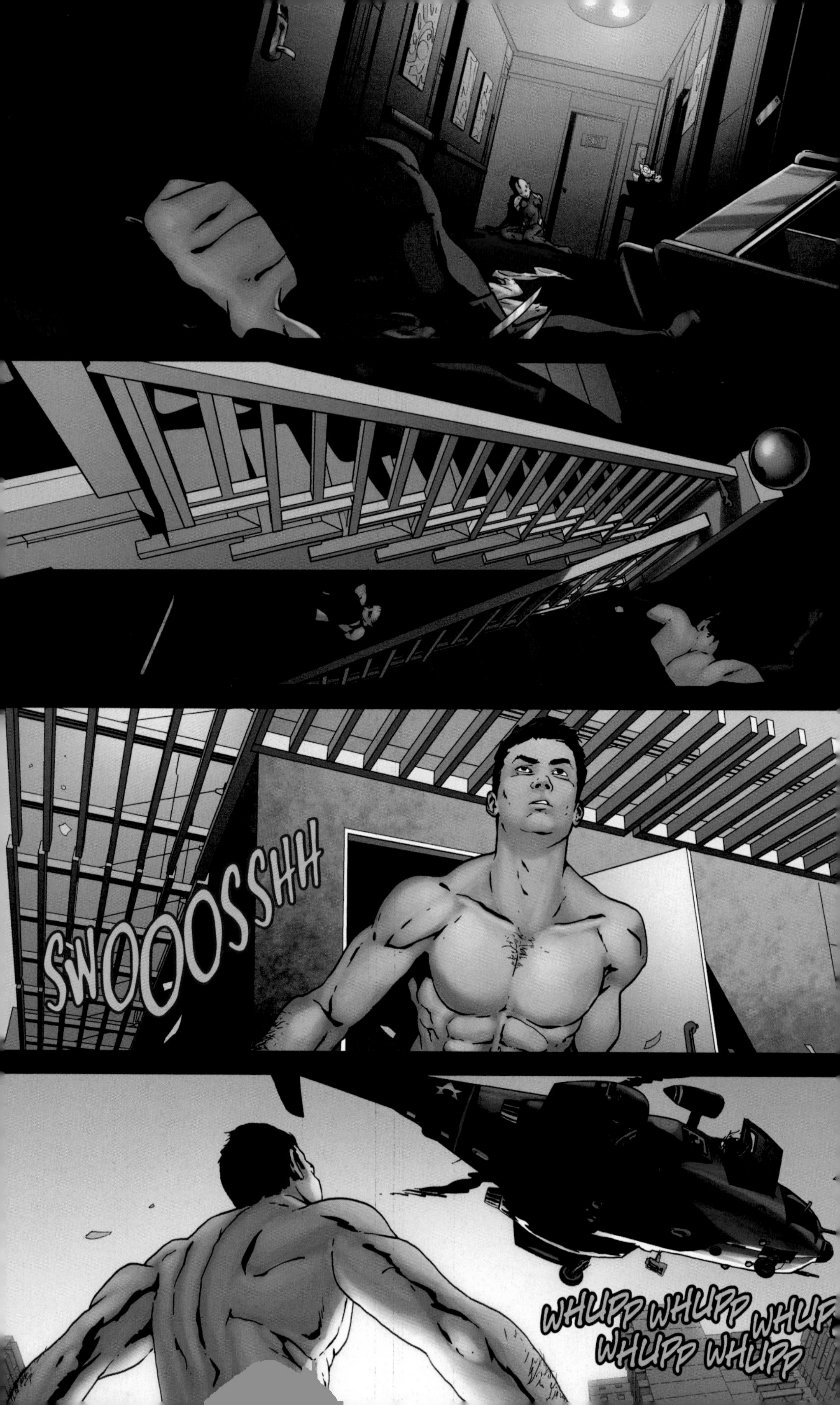
EXIT
SWOOOSSHH
WHUPP WHUPP WHUPP
WHUPP WHUPP

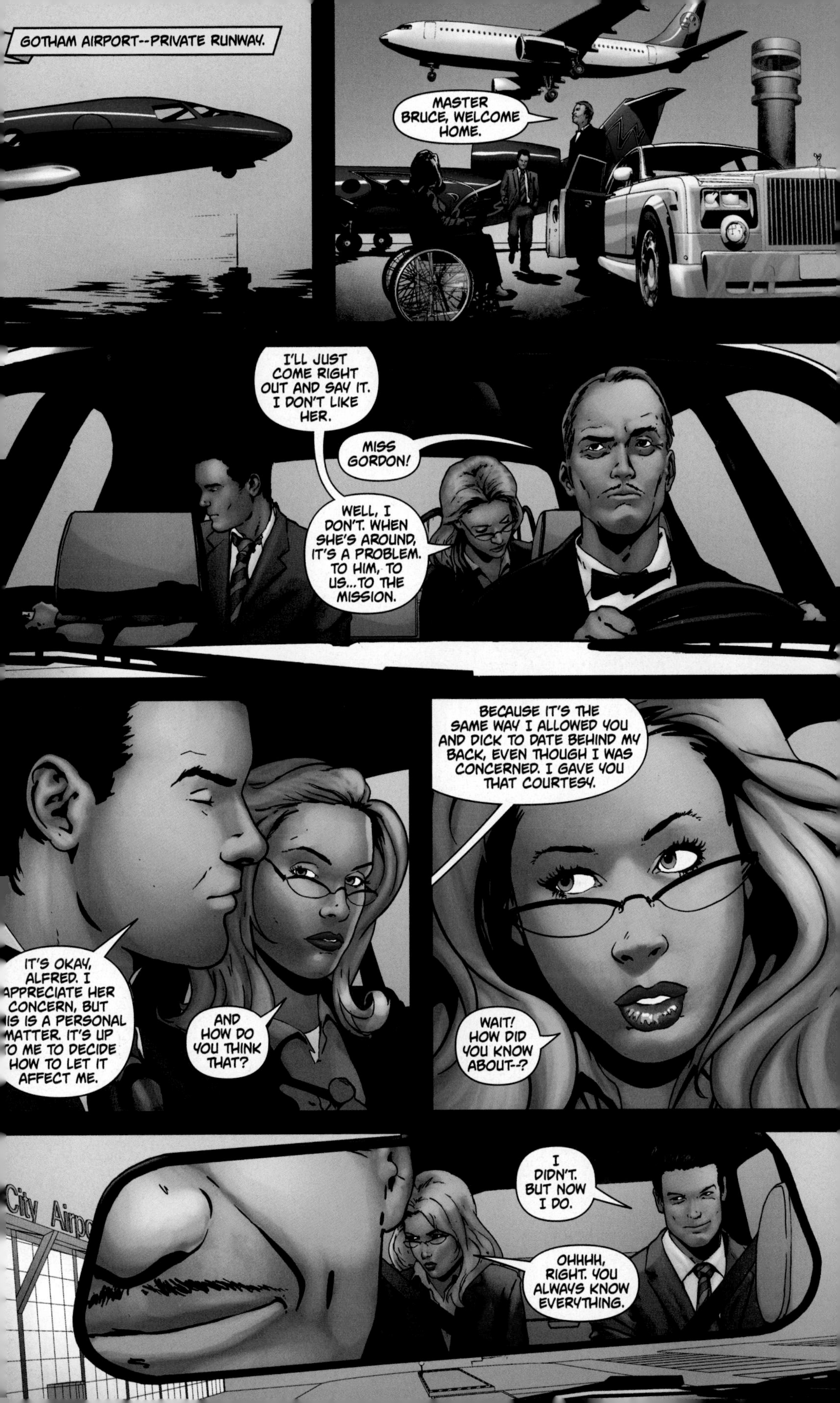
GOTHAM AIRPORT--PRIVATE RUNWAY.
MASTER BRUCE, WELCOME HOME.
I'LL JUST COME RIGHT OUT AND SAY IT. I DON'T LIKE HER.
MISS GORDON!
WELL, I DON'T. WHEN SHE'S AROUND, IT'S A PROBLEM. TO HIM, TO US...TO THE MISSION.
IT'S OKAY, ALFRED. I APPRECIATE HER CONCERN, BUT IS IS A PERSONAL MATTER. IT'S UP TO ME TO DECIDE HOW TO LET IT AFFECT ME.
AND HOW DO YOU THINK THAT?
BECAUSE IT'S THE SAME WAY I ALLOWED YOU AND DICK TO DATE BEHIND MY BACK, EVEN THOUGH I WAS CONCERNED. I GAVE YOU THAT COURTESY.
WAIT! HOW DID YOU KNOW ABOUT--?
City Airpo
I DIDN'T. BUT NOW I DO.
OHHHH, RIGHT. YOU ALWAYS KNOW EVERYTHING.

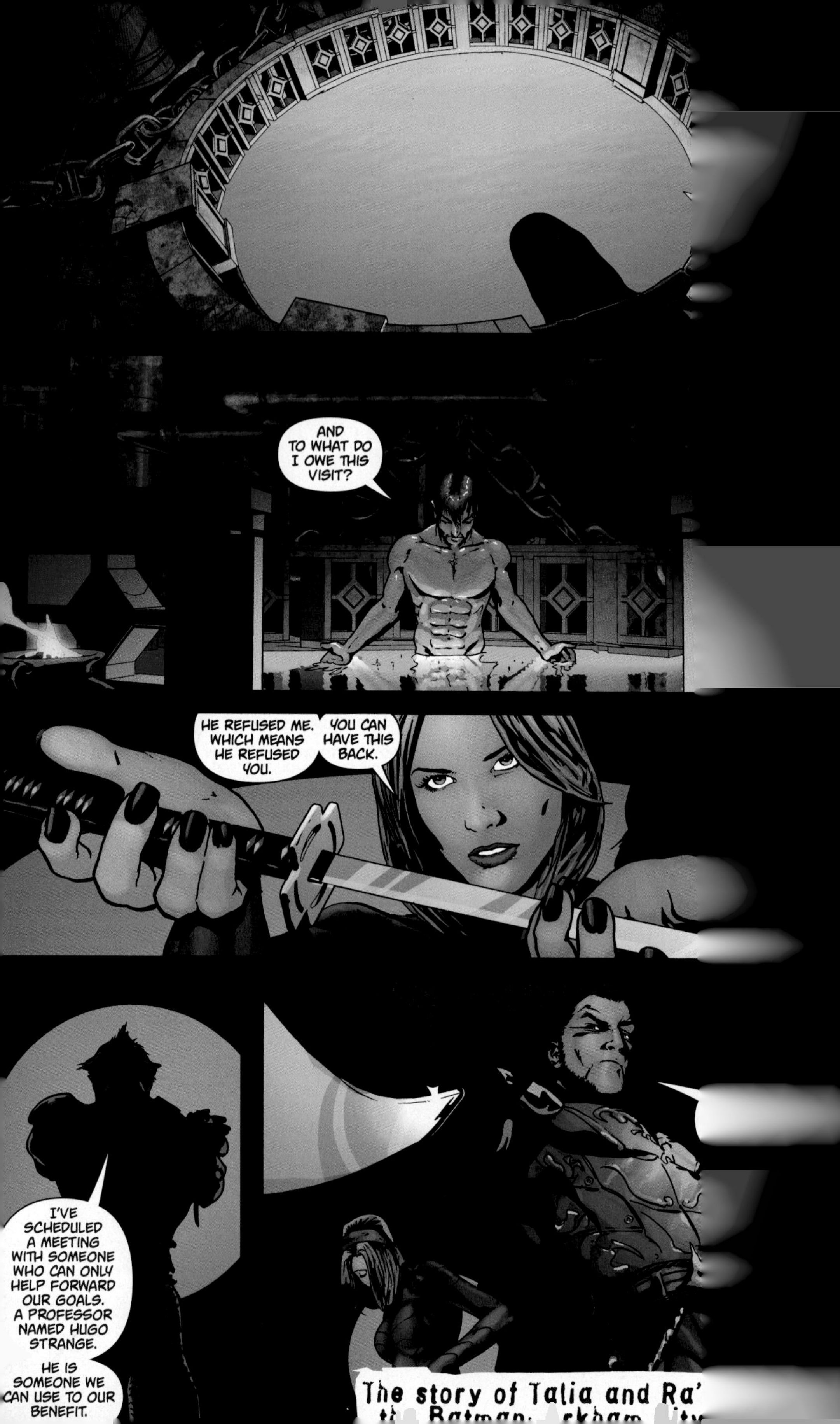
AND TO WHAT DO I OWE THIS VISIT?
HE REFUSED ME. WHICH MEANS HE REFUSED YOU.
YOU CAN HAVE THIS BACK.
I'VE SCHEDULED A MEETING WITH SOMEONE WHO CAN ONLY HELP FORWARD OUR GOALS. A PROFESSOR NAMED HUGO STRANGE.
HE IS SOMEONE WE CAN USE TO OUR BENEFIT.
The story of Talia and Ra'

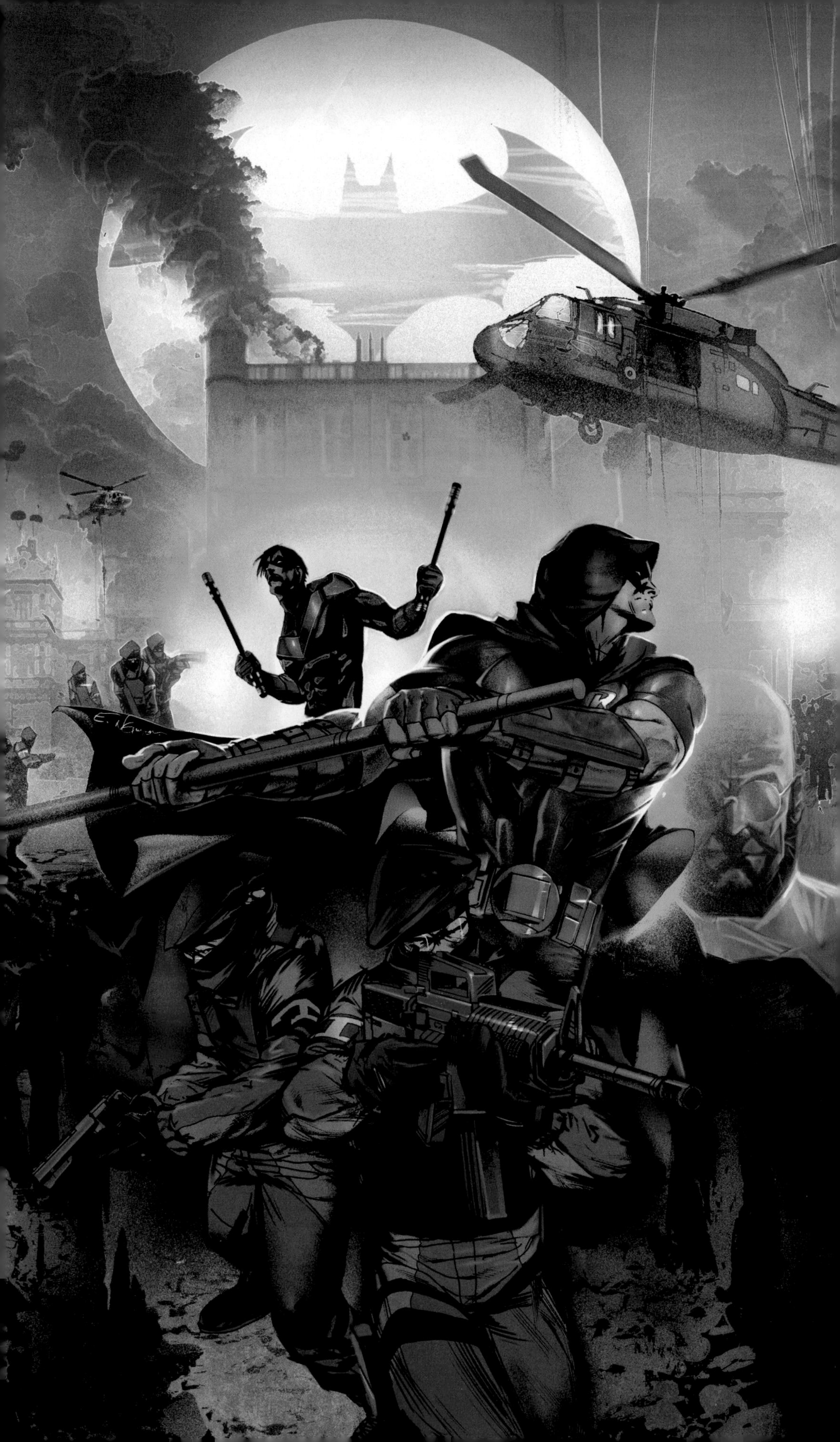

UNINVITED GUESTS

WRITTEN BY: **DEREK FRIDOLFS**

ART BY: **DAVIDE FABBRI**

COLORS BY: **ALEJANDRO SANCHEZ**

COVER ART BY: ERIC NGUYEN

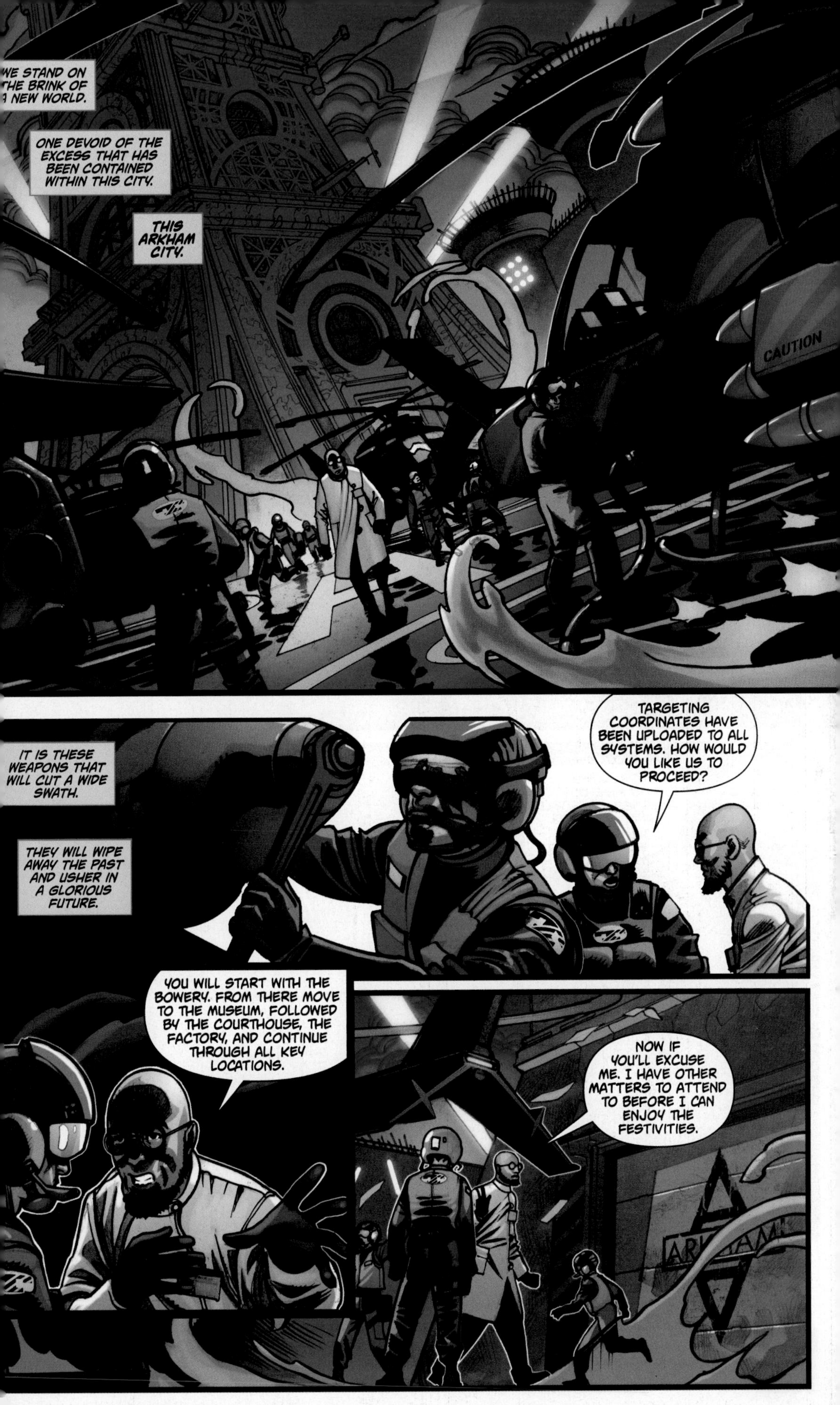
WE STAND ON THE BRINK OF A NEW WORLD.
ONE DEVOID OF THE EXCESS THAT HAS BEEN CONTAINED WITHIN THIS CITY.
THIS ARKHAM CITY.
CAUTION
IT IS THESE WEAPONS THAT WILL CUT A WIDE SWATH.
THEY WILL WIPE AWAY THE PAST AND USHER IN A GLORIOUS FUTURE.
TARGETING COORDINATES HAVE BEEN UPLOADED TO ALL SYSTEMS. HOW WOULD YOU LIKE US TO PROCEED?
YOU WILL START WITH THE BOWERY. FROM THERE MOVE TO THE MUSEUM, FOLLOWED BY THE COURTHOUSE, THE FACTORY, AND CONTINUE THROUGH ALL KEY LOCATIONS.
NOW IF YOU'LL EXCUSE ME. I HAVE OTHER MATTERS TO ATTEND TO BEFORE I CAN ENJOY THE FESTIVITIES.

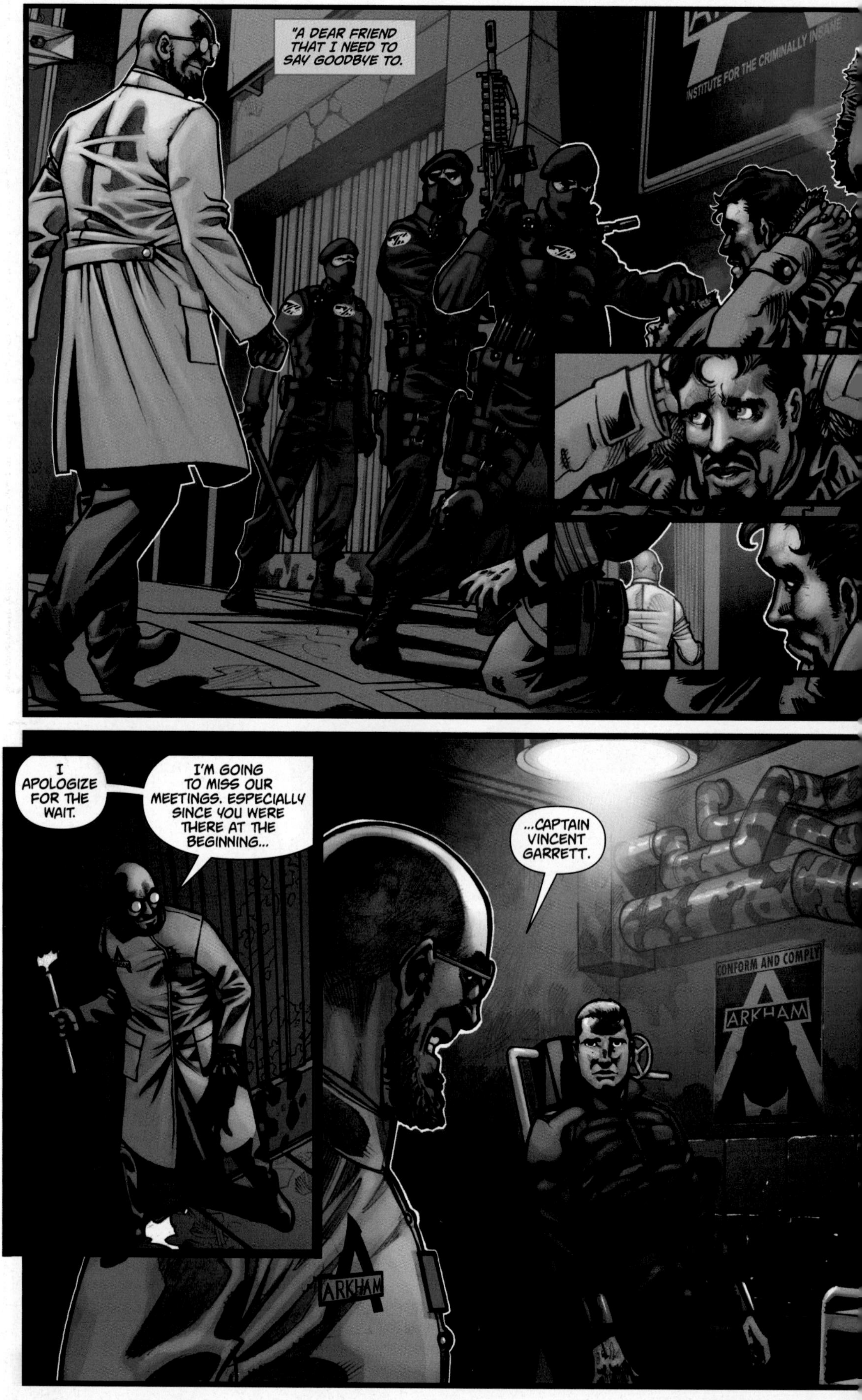
"A DEAR FRIEND THAT I NEED TO SAY GOODBYE TO.
INSTITUTE FOR THE CRIMINALLY INSANE
I APOLOGIZE FOR THE WAIT.
I'M GOING TO MISS OUR MEETINGS. ESPECIALLY SINCE YOU WERE THERE AT THE BEGINNING...
...CAPTAIN VINCENT GARRETT.
CONFORM AND COMPLY
ARKHAM
ARKHAM

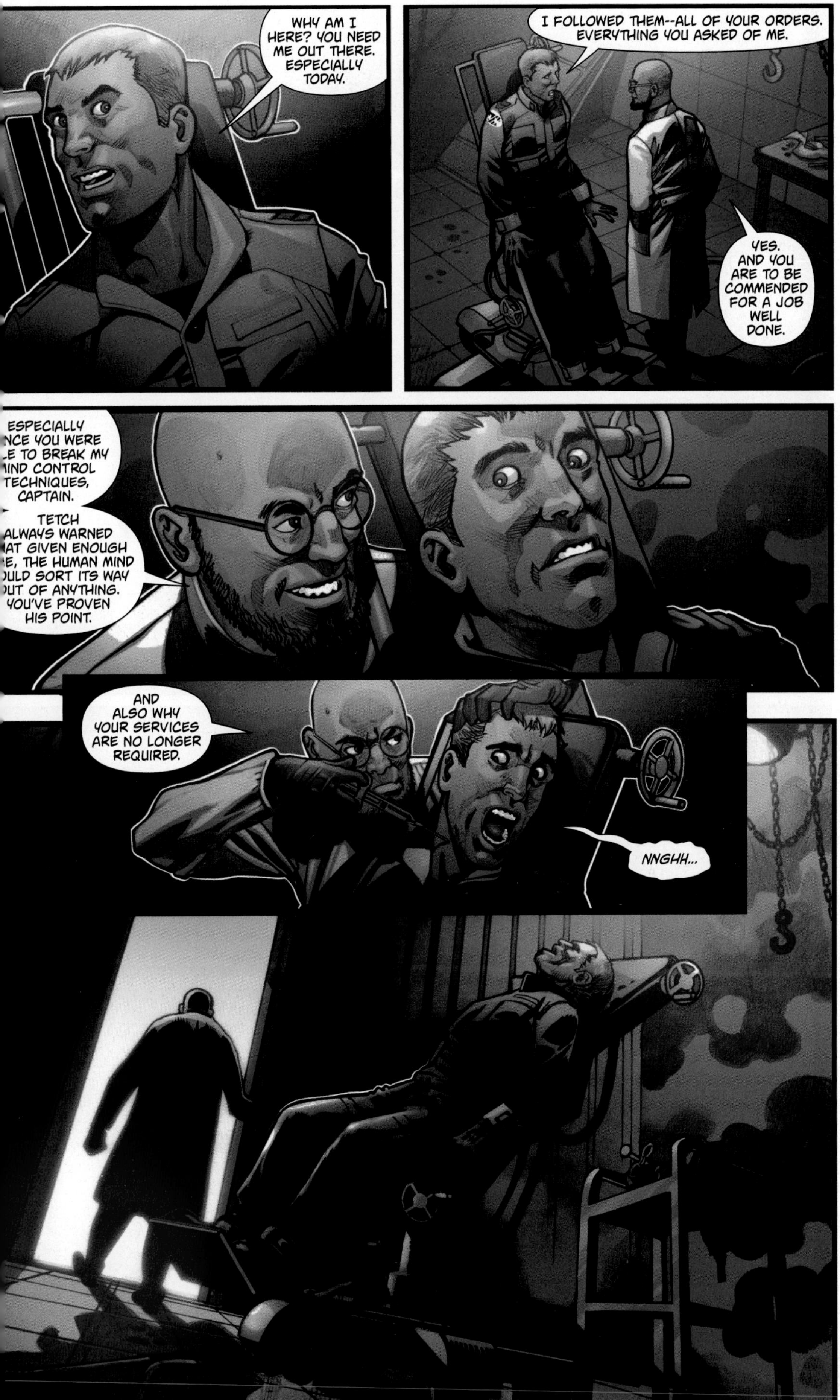
WHY AM I HERE? YOU NEED ME OUT THERE. ESPECIALLY TODAY.
I FOLLOWED THEM--ALL OF YOUR ORDERS. EVERYTHING YOU ASKED OF ME.
YES. AND YOU ARE TO BE COMMENDED FOR A JOB WELL DONE.
ESPECIALLY NCE YOU WERE LE TO BREAK MY IIND CONTROL TECHNIQUES, CAPTAIN.
TETCH ALWAYS WARNED IAT GIVEN ENOUGH E, THE HUMAN MIND OULD SORT ITS WAY UT OF ANYTHING. YOU'VE PROVEN HIS POINT.
AND ALSO WHY YOUR SERVICES ARE NO LONGER REQUIRED.
NNGHH...

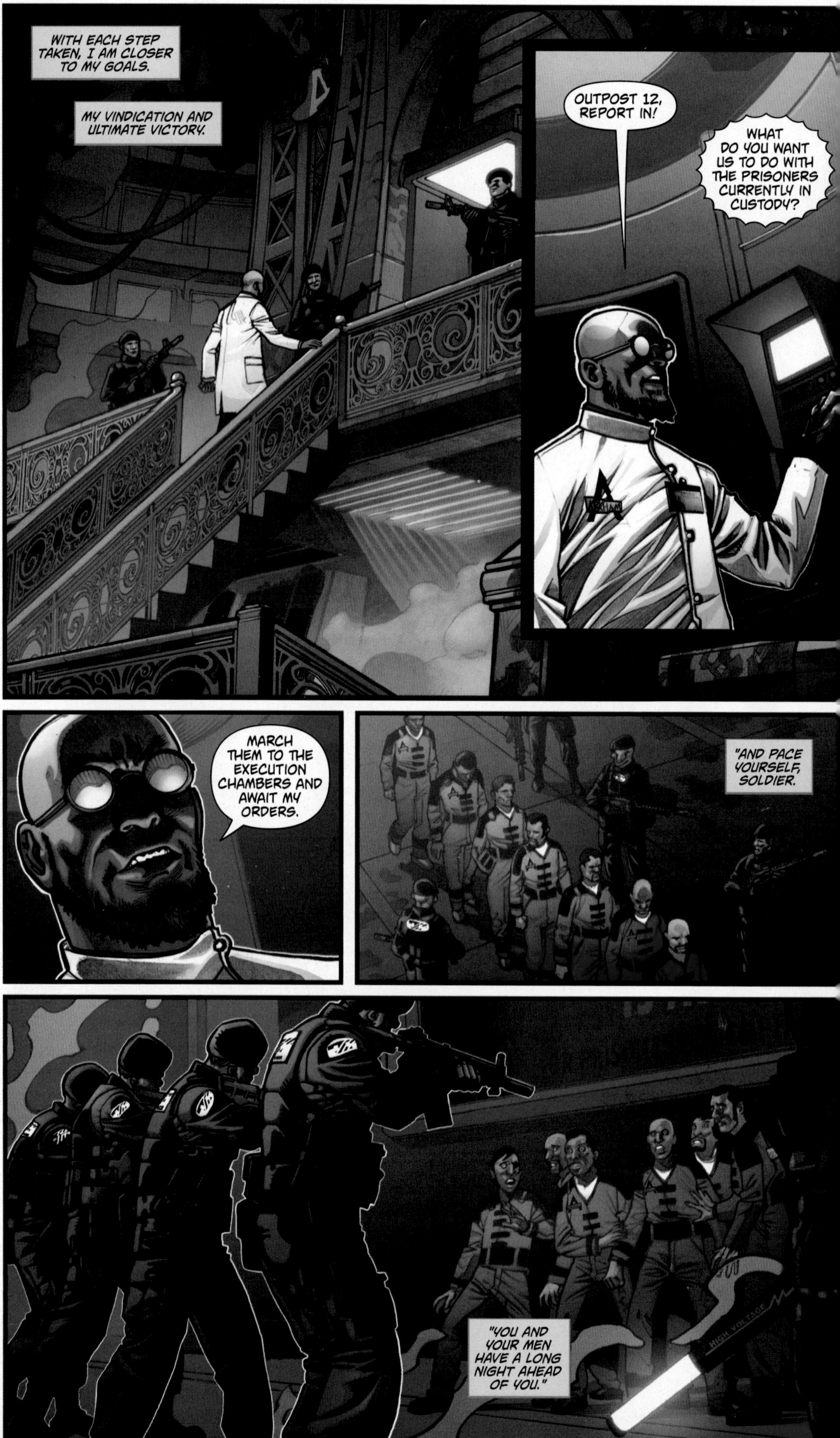
WITH EACH STEP TAKEN, I AM CLOSER TO MY GOALS.
MY VINDICATION AND ULTIMATE VICTORY.
OUTPOST 12, REPORT IN!
WHAT DO YOU WANT US TO DO WITH THE PRISONERS CURRENTLY IN CUSTODY?
MARCH THEM TO THE EXECUTION CHAMBERS AND AWAIT MY ORDERS.
"AND PACE YOURSELF, SOLDIER.
"YOU AND YOUR MEN HAVE A LONG NIGHT AHEAD OF YOU."
HIGH VOLTAGE

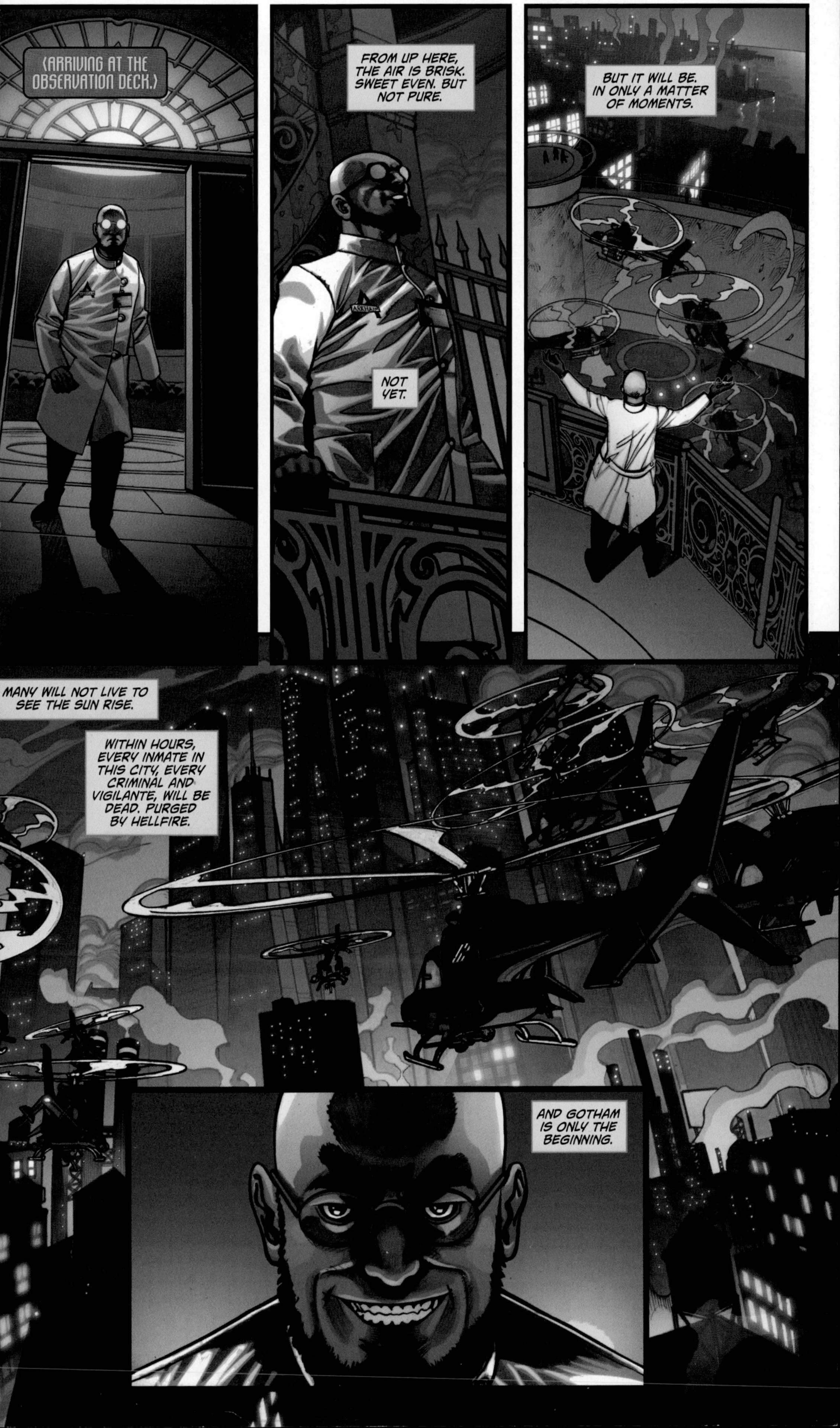
(ARRIVING AT THE OBSERVATION DECK.)
FROM UP HERE, THE AIR IS BRISK. SWEET EVEN. BUT NOT PURE.
NOT YET.
BUT IT WILL BE. IN ONLY A MATTER OF MOMENTS.
MANY WILL NOT LIVE TO SEE THE SUN RISE.
WITHIN HOURS, EVERY INMATE IN THIS CITY, EVERY CRIMINAL AND VIGILANTE, WILL BE DEAD. PURGED BY HELLFIRE.
AND GOTHAM IS ONLY THE BEGINNING.

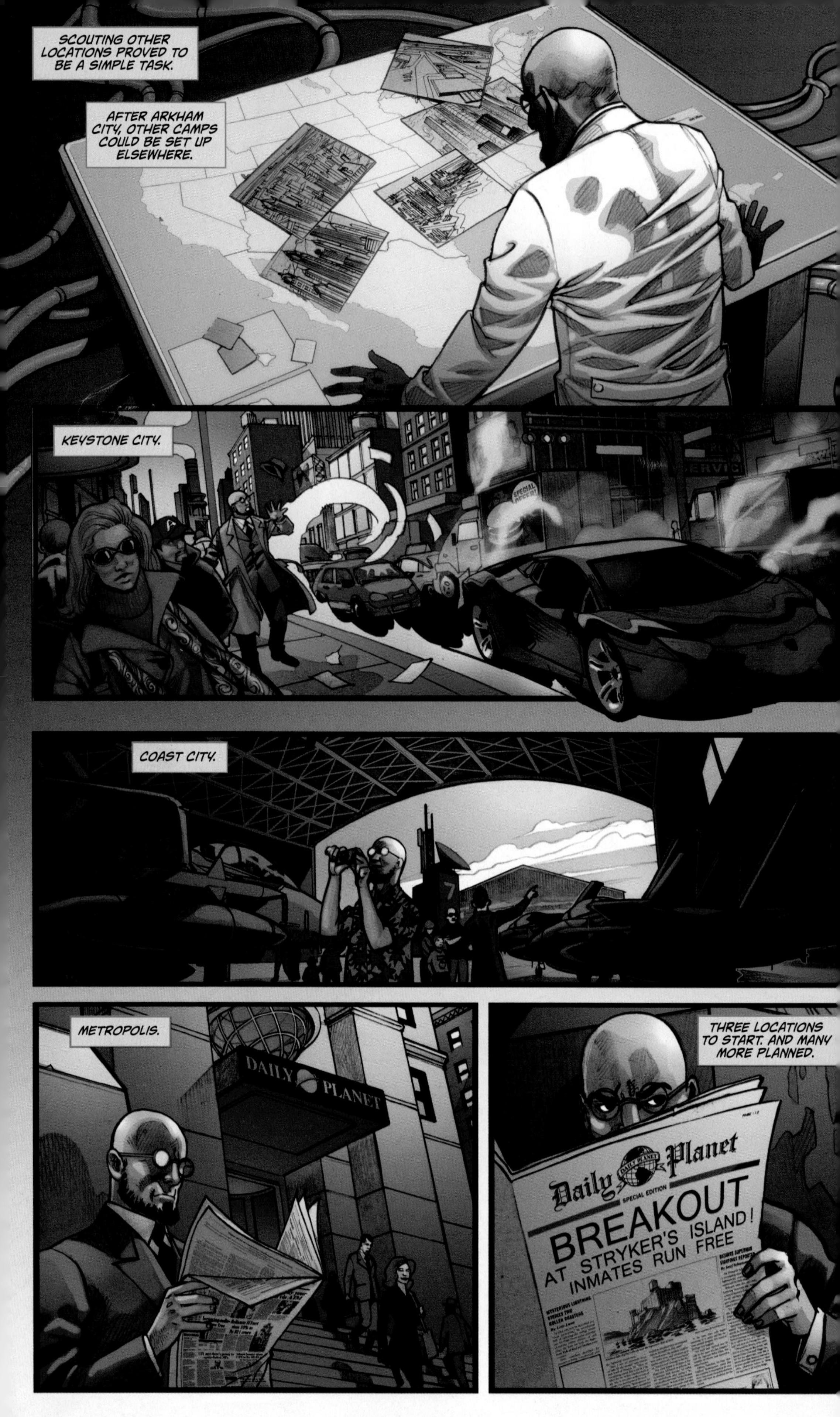
SCOUTING OTHER LOCATIONS PROVED TO BE A SIMPLE TASK.
AFTER ARKHAM CITY, OTHER CAMPS COULD BE SET UP ELSEWHERE.
KEYSTONE CITY.
SPECIAL OFFER!
COAST CITY.
METROPOLIS.
DAILY PLANET
THREE LOCATIONS TO START. AND MANY MORE PLANNED.
Daily Planet
SPECIAL EDITION
BREAKOUT AT STRYKER'S ISLAND! INMATES RUN FREE

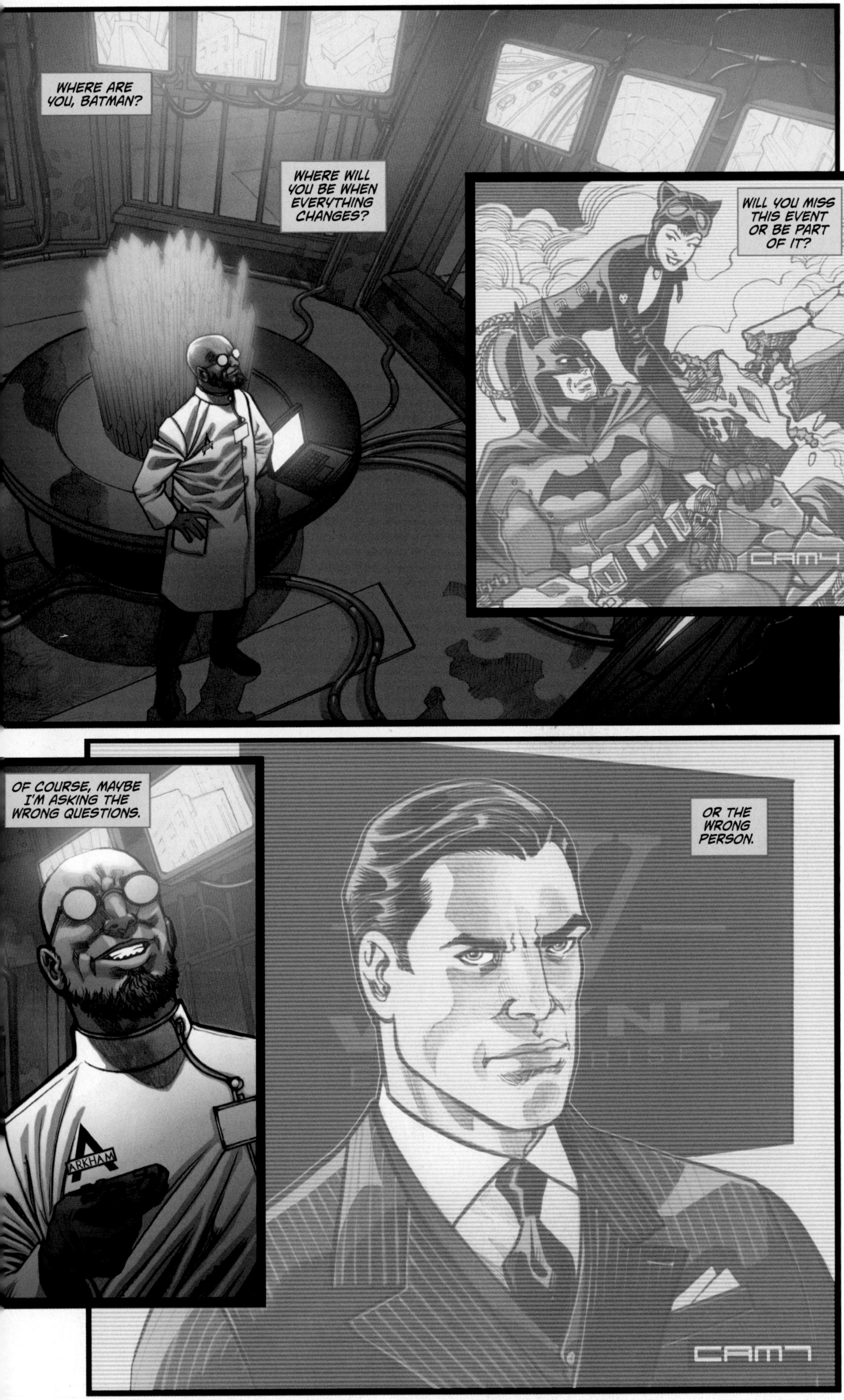
WHERE ARE YOU, BATMAN?
WHERE WILL YOU BE WHEN EVERYTHING CHANGES?
WILL YOU MISS THIS EVENT OR BE PART OF IT?
CAM4
OF COURSE, MAYBE I'M ASKING THE WRONG QUESTIONS.
ARKHAM
OR THE WRONG PERSON.
CAM7

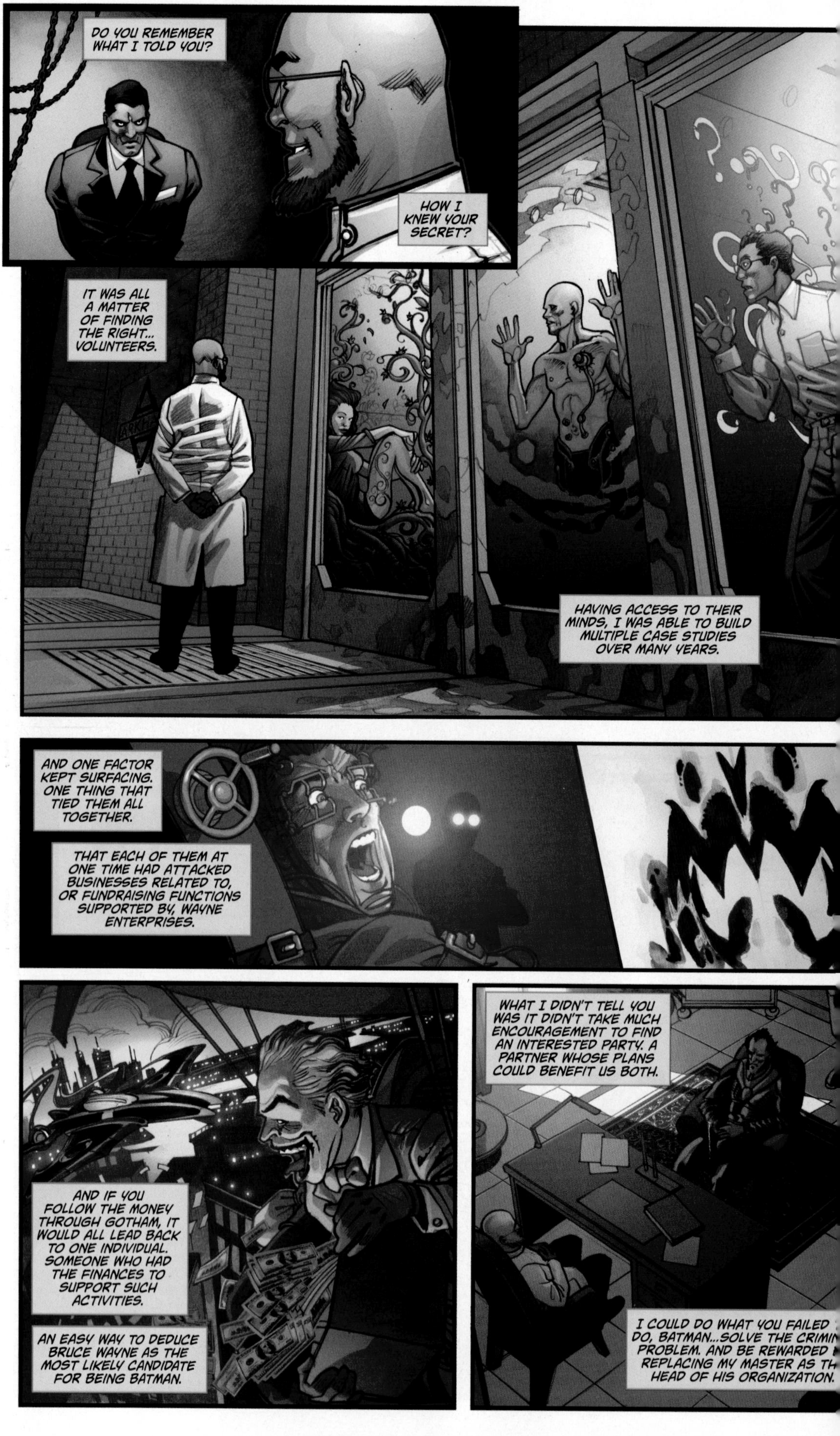
DO YOU REMEMBER WHAT I TOLD YOU?
HOW I KNEW YOUR SECRET?
IT WAS ALL A MATTER OF FINDING THE RIGHT... VOLUNTEERS.
HAVING ACCESS TO THEIR MINDS, I WAS ABLE TO BUILD MULTIPLE CASE STUDIES OVER MANY YEARS.
AND ONE FACTOR KEPT SURFACING. ONE THING THAT TIED THEM ALL TOGETHER.
THAT EACH OF THEM AT ONE TIME HAD ATTACKED BUSINESSES RELATED TO, OR FUNDRAISING FUNCTIONS SUPPORTED BY, WAYNE ENTERPRISES.
AND IF YOU FOLLOW THE MONEY THROUGH GOTHAM, IT WOULD ALL LEAD BACK TO ONE INDIVIDUAL. SOMEONE WHO HAD THE FINANCES TO SUPPORT SUCH ACTIVITIES.
AN EASY WAY TO DEDUCE BRUCE WAYNE AS THE MOST LIKELY CANDIDATE FOR BEING BATMAN.
WHAT I DIDN'T TELL YOU WAS IT DIDN'T TAKE MUCH ENCOURAGEMENT TO FIND AN INTERESTED PARTY. A PARTNER WHOSE PLANS COULD BENEFIT US BOTH.
I COULD DO WHAT YOU FAILED DO, BATMAN...SOLVE THE CRIMI PROBLEM. AND BE REWARDED REPLACING MY MASTER AS TH HEAD OF HIS ORGANIZATION.

HE WOULD FUND THE OPERATION AS A SILENT PARTNER, PROVIDING THE MONEY TO GET SHARP ELECTED FOR MAYOR.

HE WOULD PROVIDE THE MEANS TO ARM MY SOLDIERS WITH THE BEST FIREARMS.

M'136-AT4
ANTI AIRCRAFT MISSILE LAUNCHER

HE WOULD EVEN PROVIDE GROUND SUPPORT. EYES AND EARS TO GAIN ACCESS INSIDE LESS DESIRABLE LOCATIONS WITHIN ARKHAM CITY.

THE REST WOULD BE LEFT UP TO ME.

AND NOW COMPLETES THE CIRCLE. I'VE ATTACKED YOUR PRIVATE LIFE, ONCE I DISCOVERED YOUR SECRET IDENTITY. YOUR PUBLIC LIFE, WHEN I CAPTURED YOU AT THE PRESS CONFERENCE.

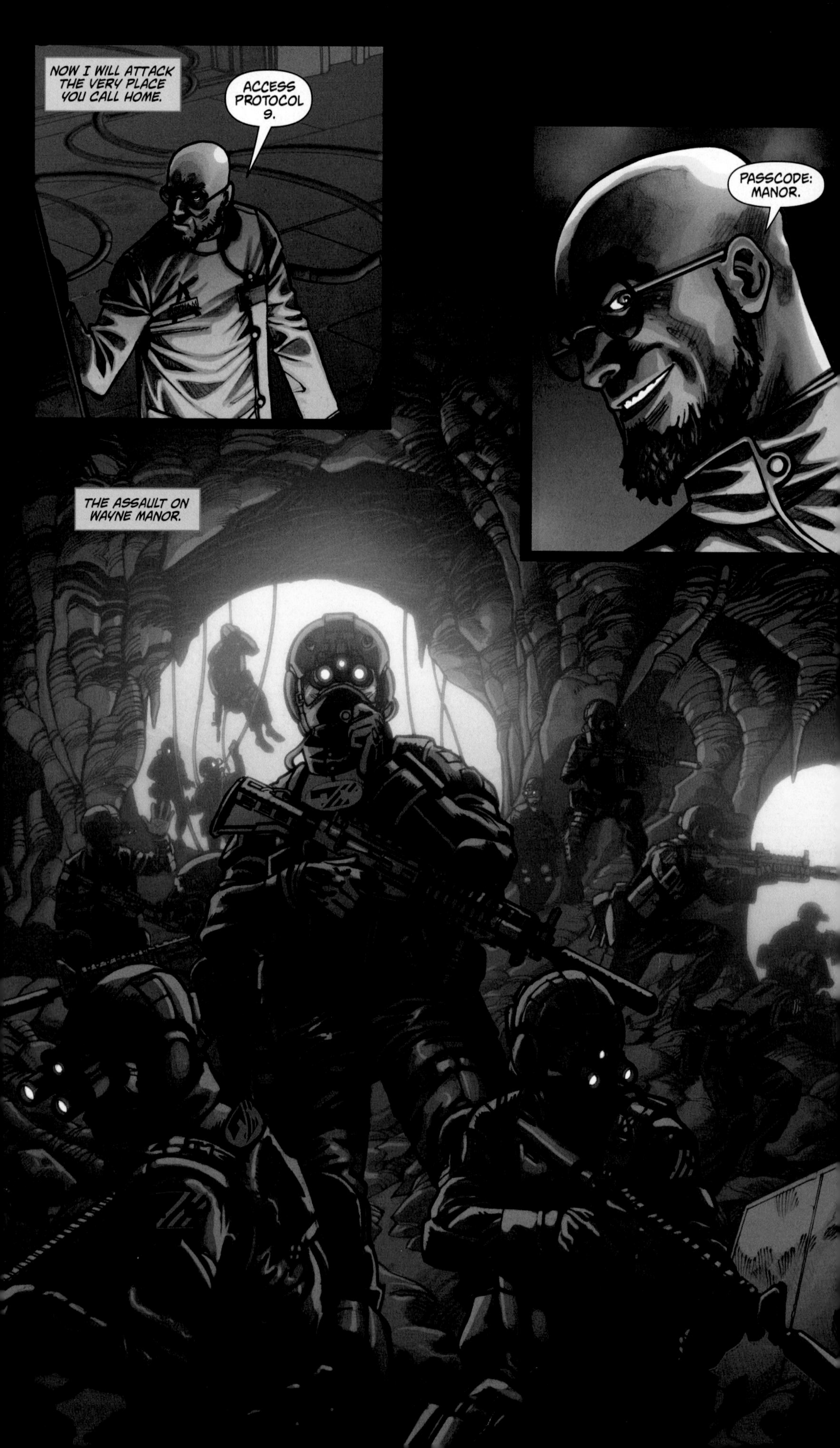
NOW I WILL ATTACK THE VERY PLACE YOU CALL HOME.
ACCESS PROTOCOL 9.
PASSCODE: MANOR.
THE ASSAULT ON WAYNE MANOR.

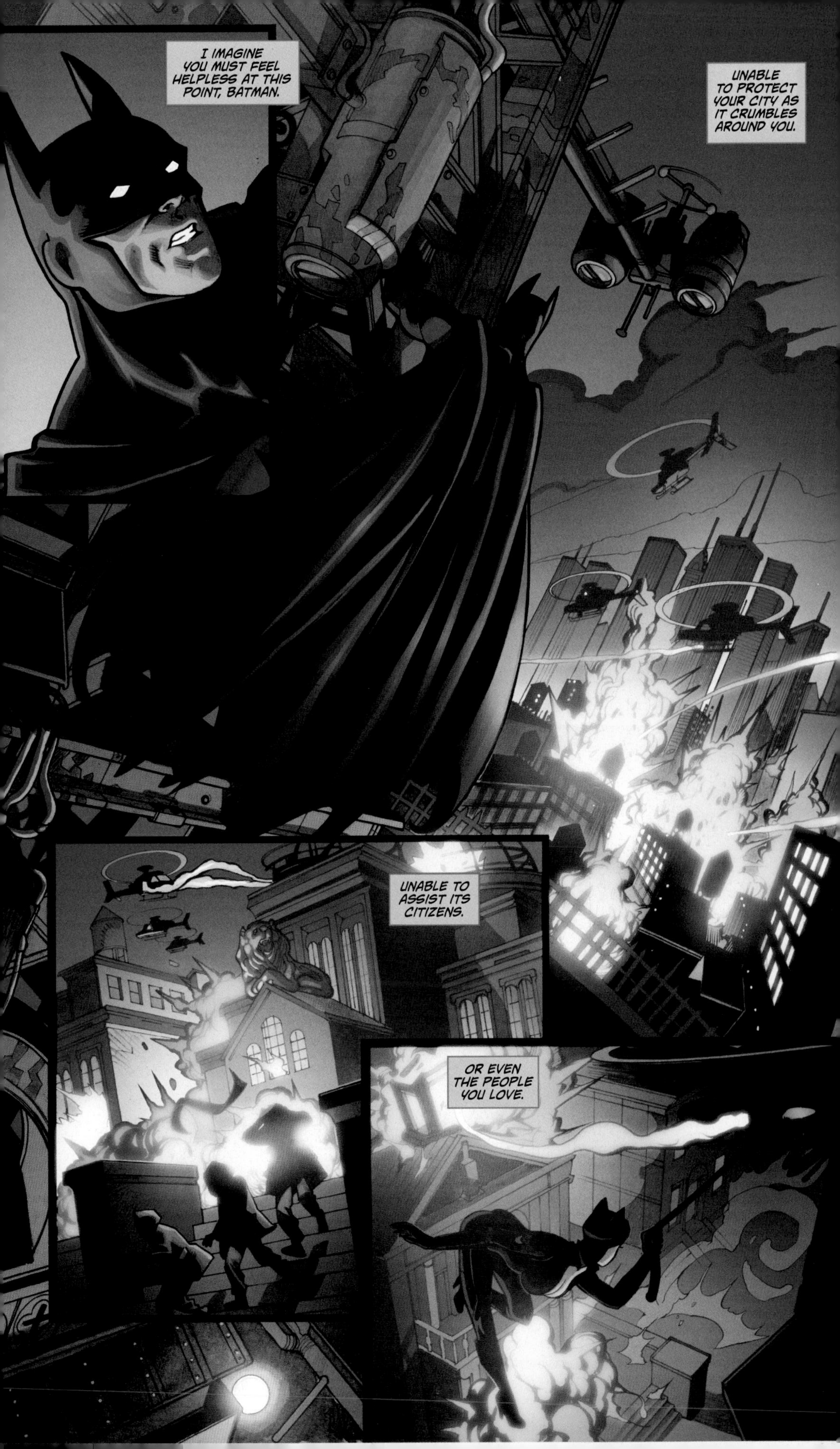
I IMAGINE YOU MUST FEEL HELPLESS AT THIS POINT, BATMAN.
UNABLE TO PROTECT YOUR CITY AS IT CRUMBLES AROUND YOU.
UNABLE TO ASSIST ITS CITIZENS.
OR EVEN THE PEOPLE YOU LOVE.

I ALSO KNOW THERE ARE STILL SECRETS YET TO BE UNCOVERED.

LAYERS YET TO BE PEELED BACK.

YOU CONCEAL YOUR IDENTITY IN PUBLIC.

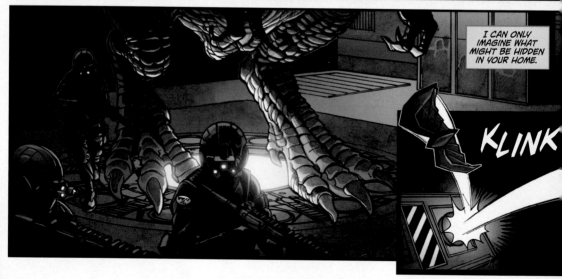

I CAN ONLY IMAGINE WHAT MIGHT BE HIDDEN IN YOUR HOME.

KLINK

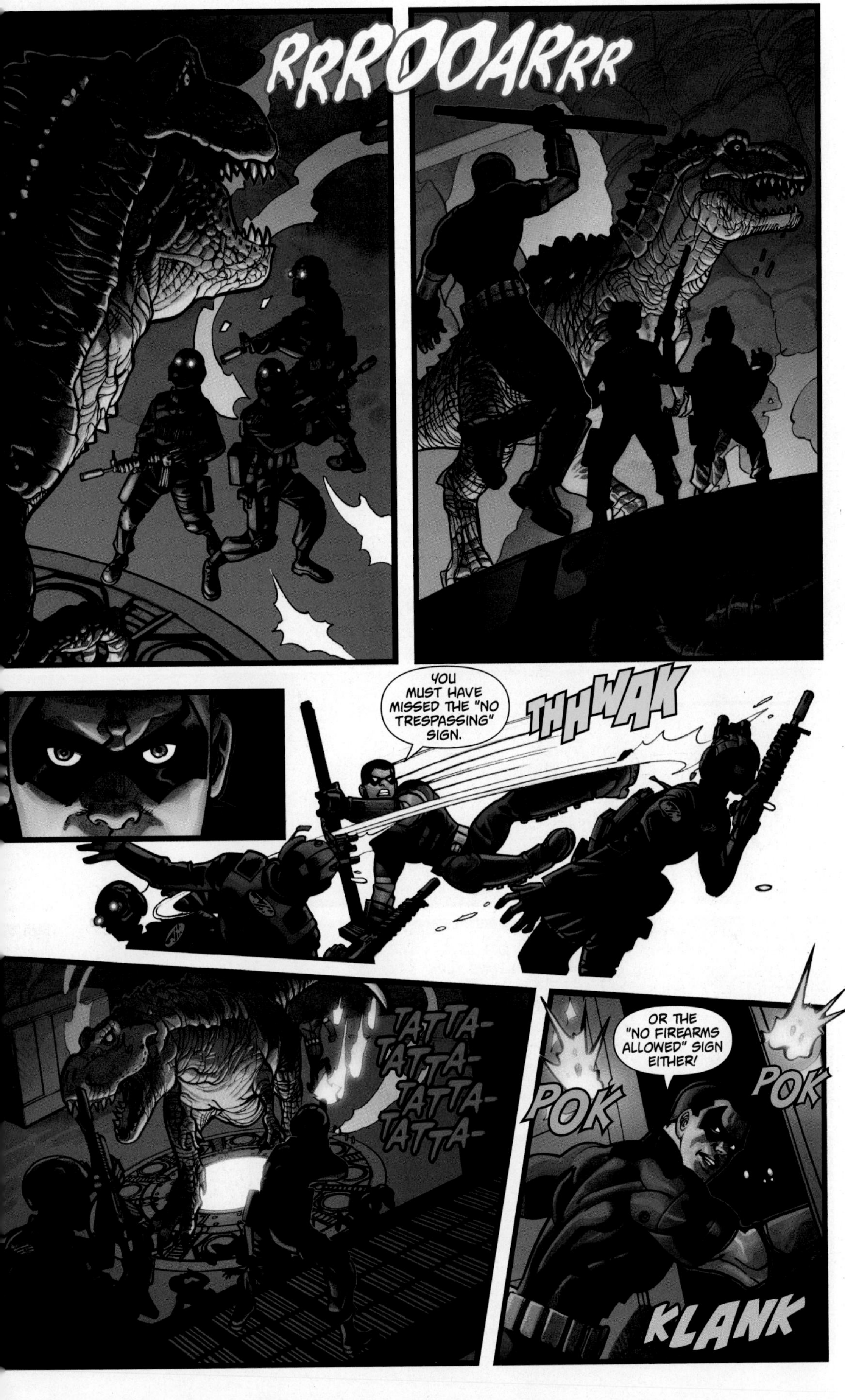
RRROOARRR
YOU MUST HAVE MISSED THE "NO TRESPASSING" SIGN.
THHWAK
TATTA-TATTA-TATTA-TATTA-
OR THE "NO FIREARMS ALLOWED" SIGN EITHER!
POK
POK
KLANK

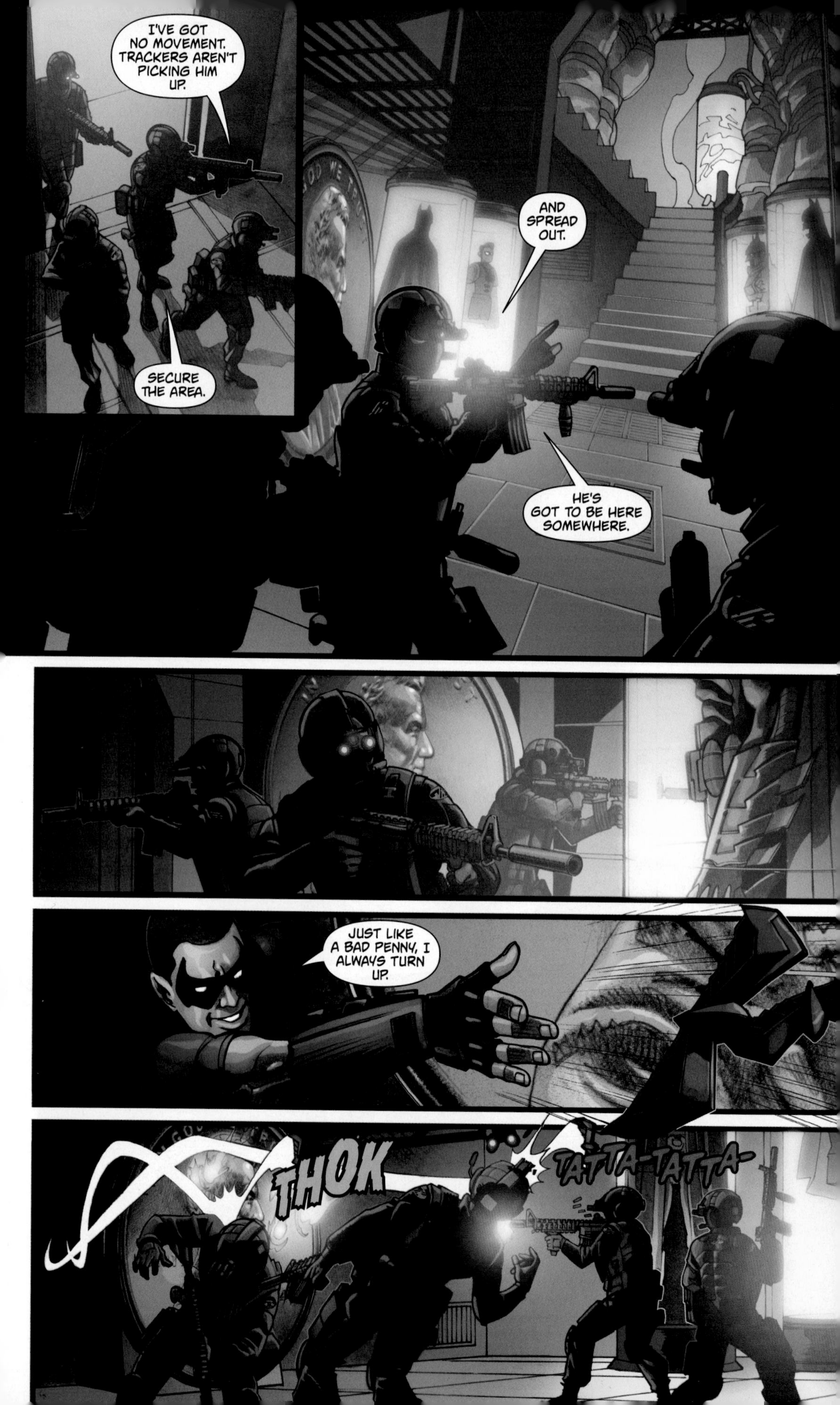
I'VE GOT NO MOVEMENT. TRACKERS AREN'T PICKING HIM UP.
SECURE THE AREA.
AND SPREAD OUT.
HE'S GOT TO BE HERE SOMEWHERE.
JUST LIKE A BAD PENNY, I ALWAYS TURN UP.
THOK
TATTA-TATTA-

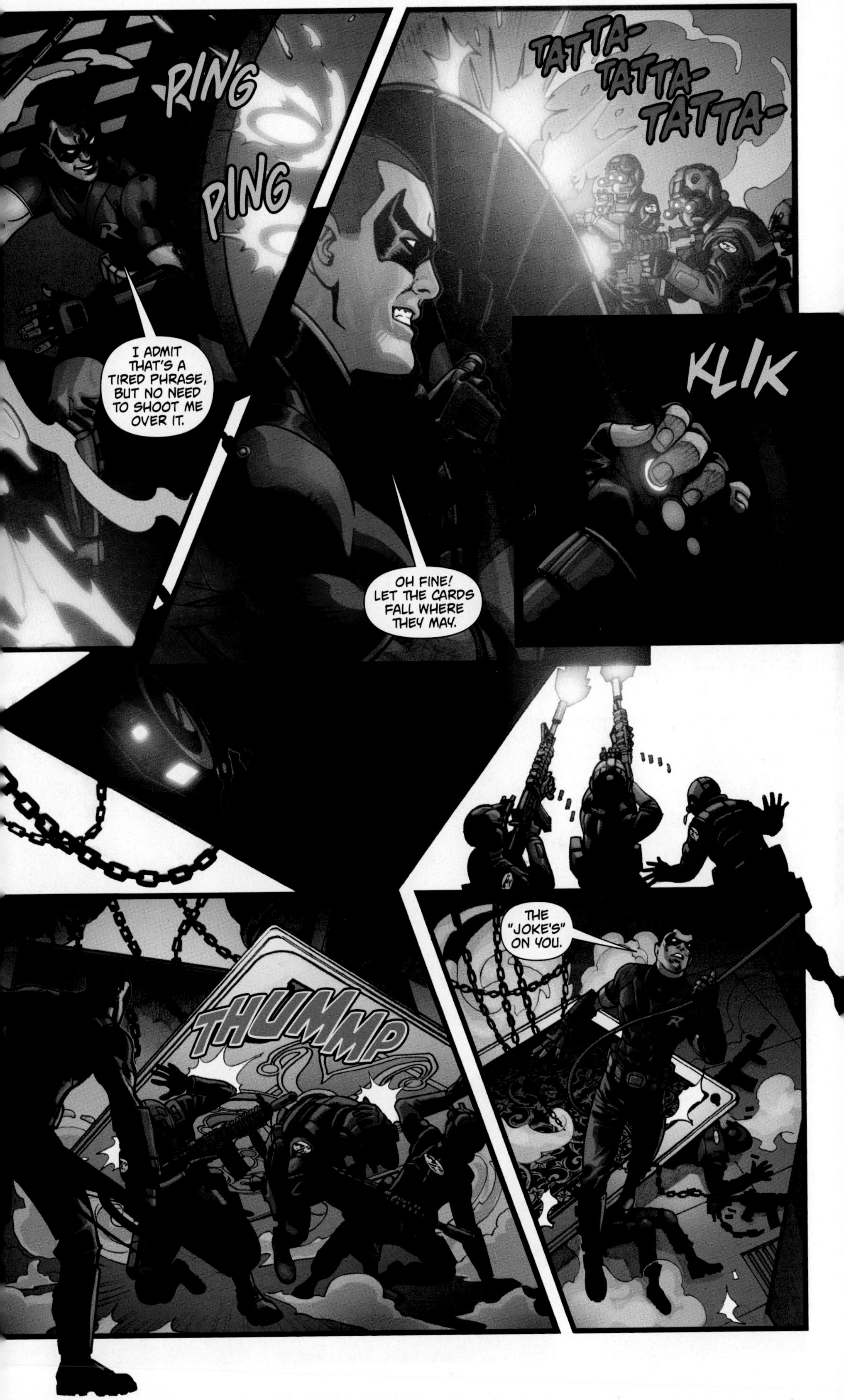
PING
PING
I ADMIT THAT'S A TIRED PHRASE, BUT NO NEED TO SHOOT ME OVER IT.
TATTA-TATTA-TATTA-
OH FINE! LET THE CARDS FALL WHERE THEY MAY.
KLIK
THUMMP
THE "JOKE'S" ON YOU.

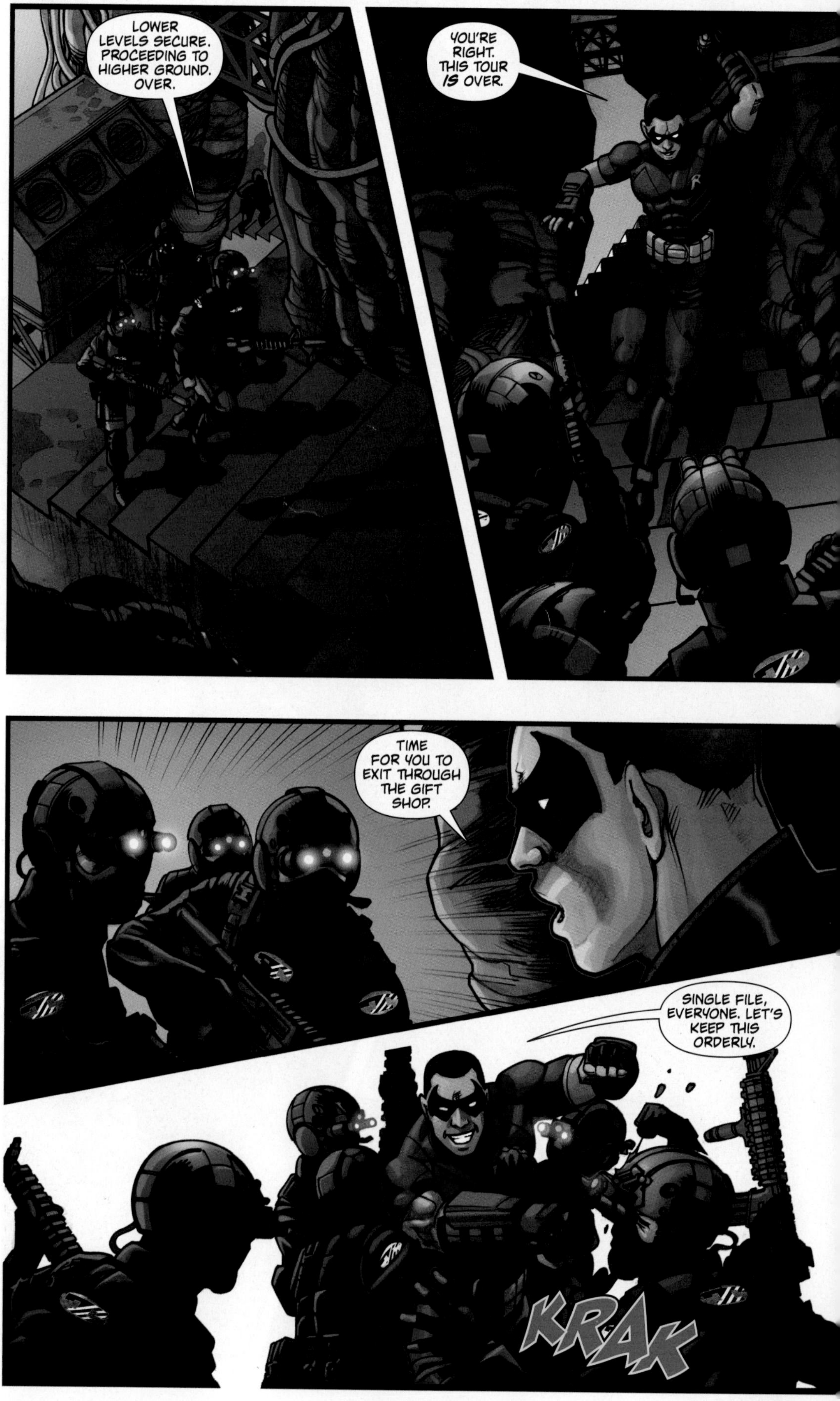
LOWER LEVELS SECURE. PROCEEDING TO HIGHER GROUND. OVER.
YOU'RE RIGHT. THIS TOUR *IS* OVER.
TIME FOR YOU TO EXIT THROUGH THE GIFT SHOP.
SINGLE FILE, EVERYONE. LET'S KEEP THIS ORDERLY.
KRAK

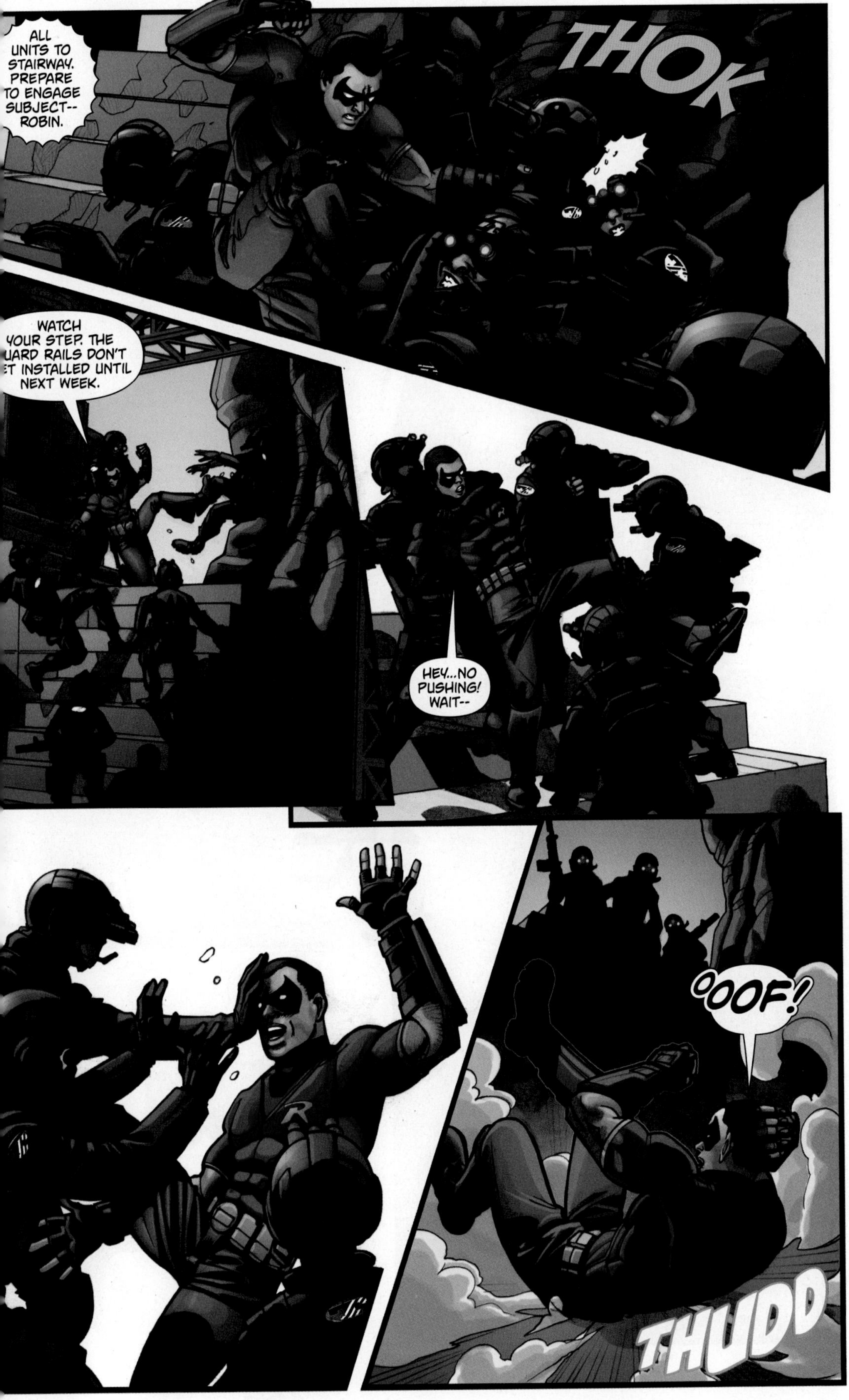
ALL UNITS TO STAIRWAY. PREPARE TO ENGAGE SUBJECT-- ROBIN.
THOK
WATCH YOUR STEP. THE UARD RAILS DON'T ET INSTALLED UNTIL NEXT WEEK.
HEY...NO PUSHING! WAIT--
OOOF!
THUDD

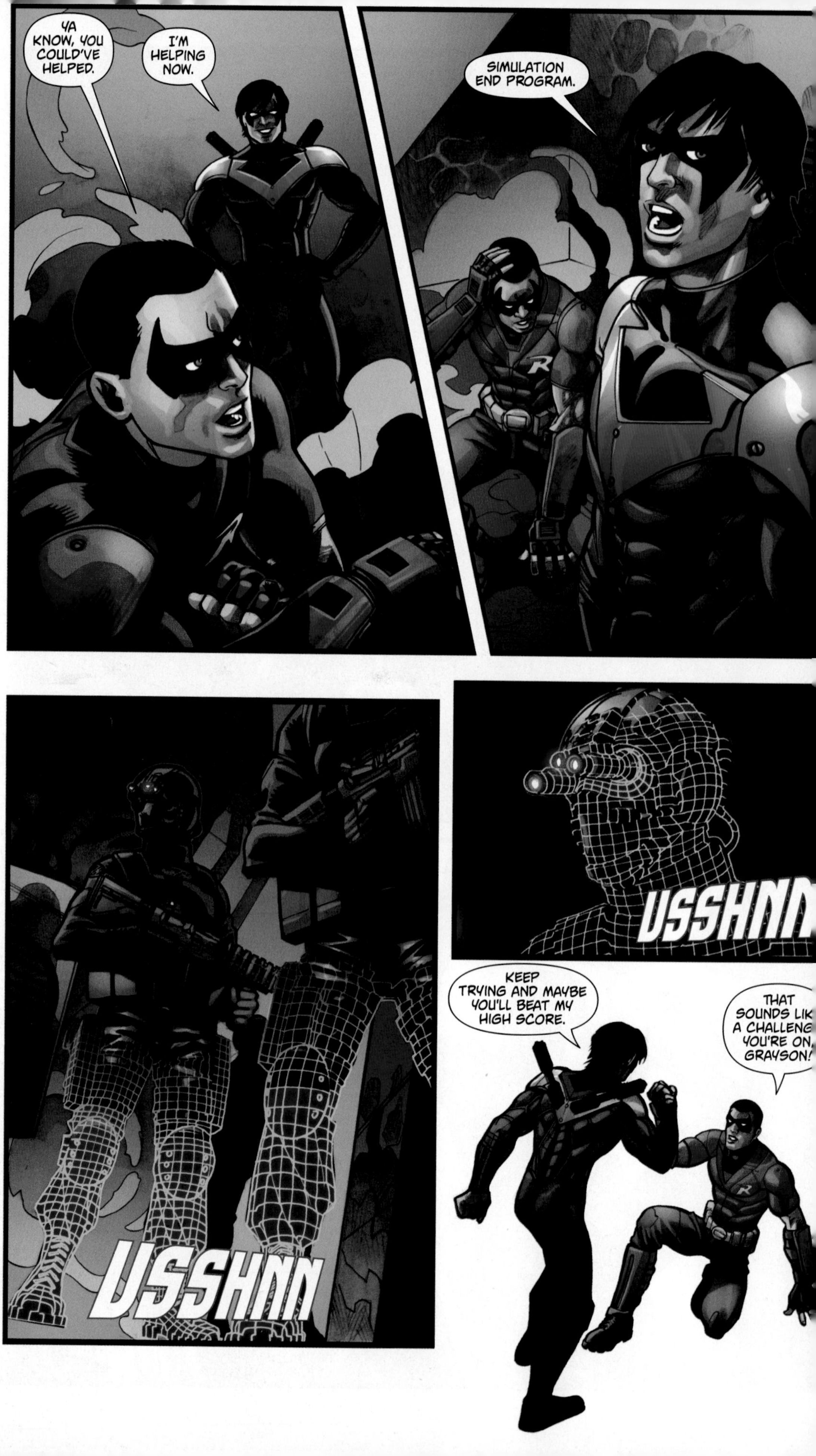
YA KNOW, YOU COULD'VE HELPED.
I'M HELPING NOW.
SIMULATION END PROGRAM.
USSHNN
USSHNN
KEEP TRYING AND MAYBE YOU'LL BEAT MY HIGH SCORE.
THAT SOUNDS LIK A CHALLENG YOU'RE ON, GRAYSON!

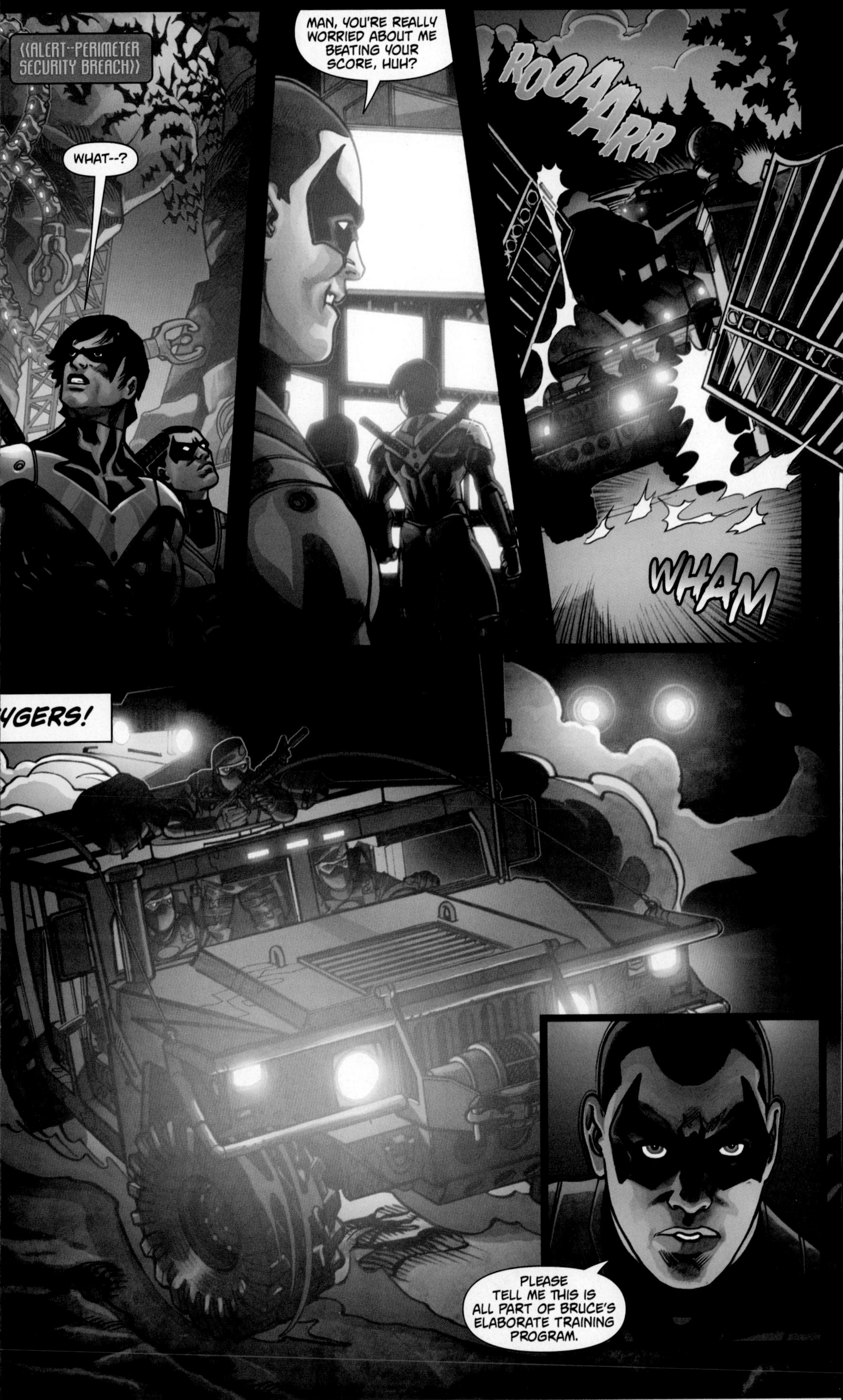
((ALERT--PERIMETER SECURITY BREACH))
WHAT--?
MAN, YOU'RE REALLY WORRIED ABOUT ME BEATING YOUR SCORE, HUH?
ROOAARR
WHAM
YGERS!
PLEASE TELL ME THIS IS ALL PART OF BRUCE'S ELABORATE TRAINING PROGRAM.

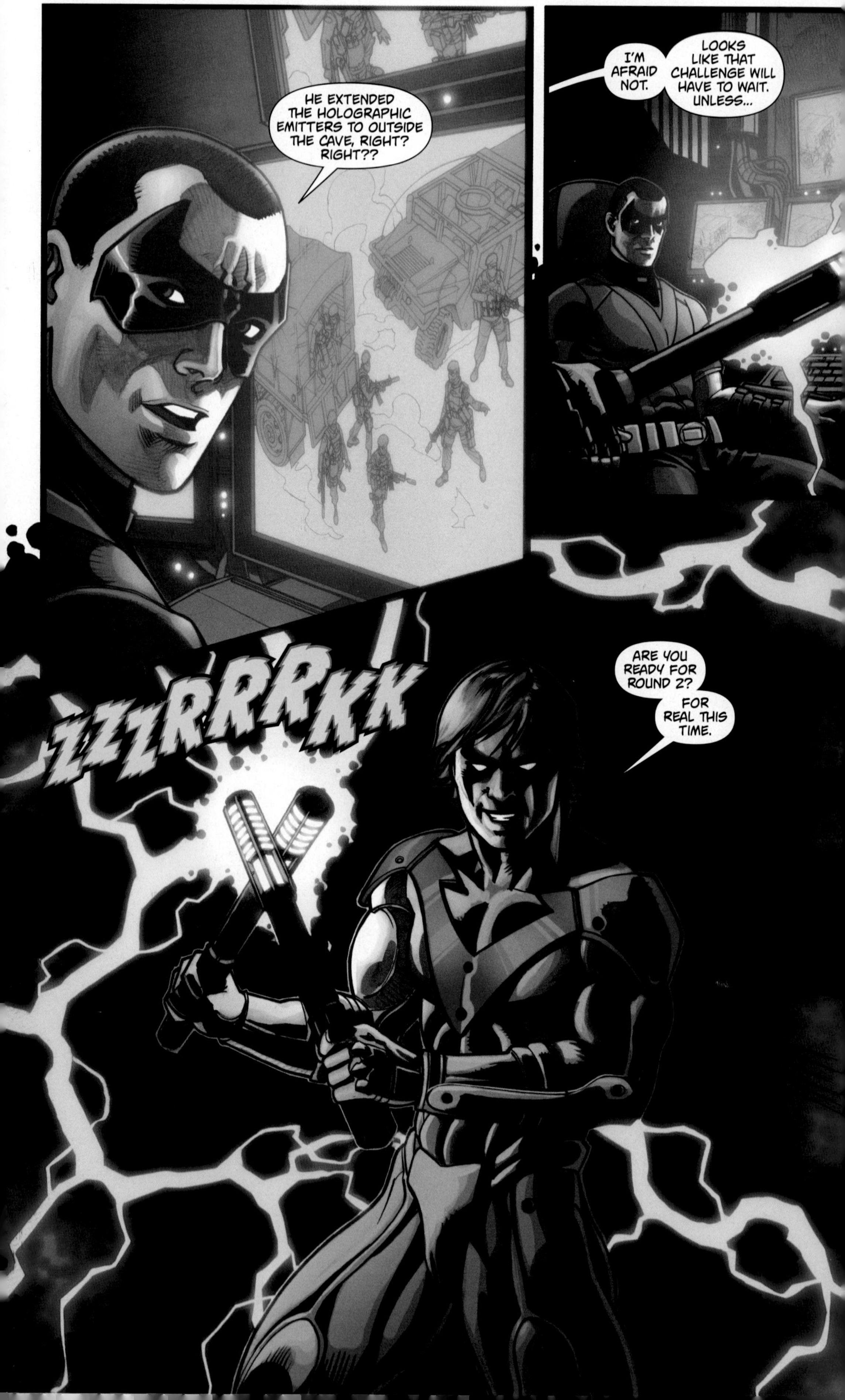
HE EXTENDED THE HOLOGRAPHIC EMITTERS TO OUTSIDE THE CAVE, RIGHT? RIGHT??
I'M AFRAID NOT.
LOOKS LIKE THAT CHALLENGE WILL HAVE TO WAIT. UNLESS...
ZZZRRRRKK
ARE YOU READY FOR ROUND 2?
FOR REAL THIS TIME.

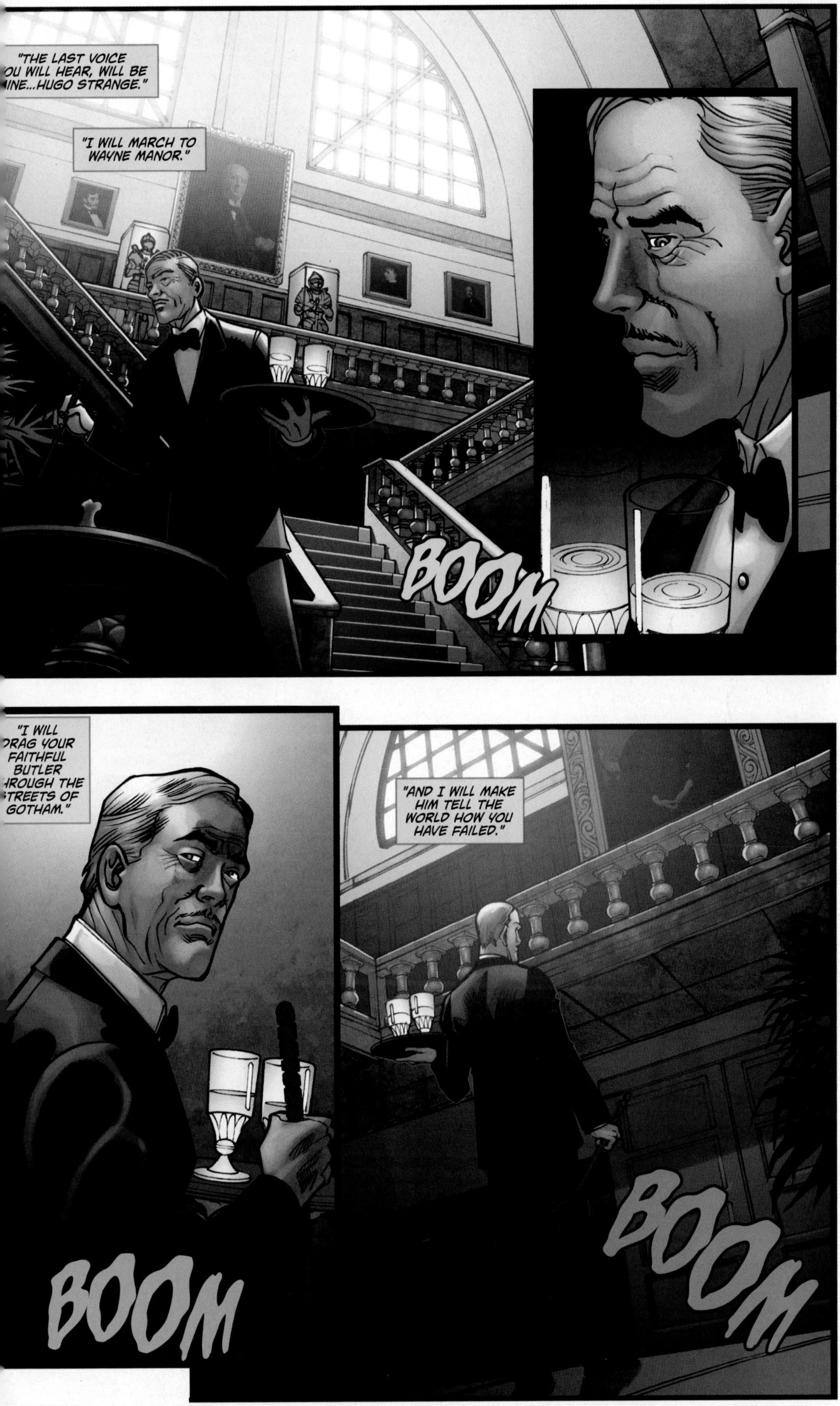
"THE LAST VOICE
OU WILL HEAR, WILL BE
INE...HUGO STRANGE."
"I WILL MARCH TO
WAYNE MANOR."
BOOM
"I WILL
RAG YOUR
FAITHFUL
BUTLER
HROUGH THE
TREETS OF
GOTHAM."
BOOM
"AND I WILL MAKE
HIM TELL THE
WORLD HOW YOU
HAVE FAILED."
BOOM

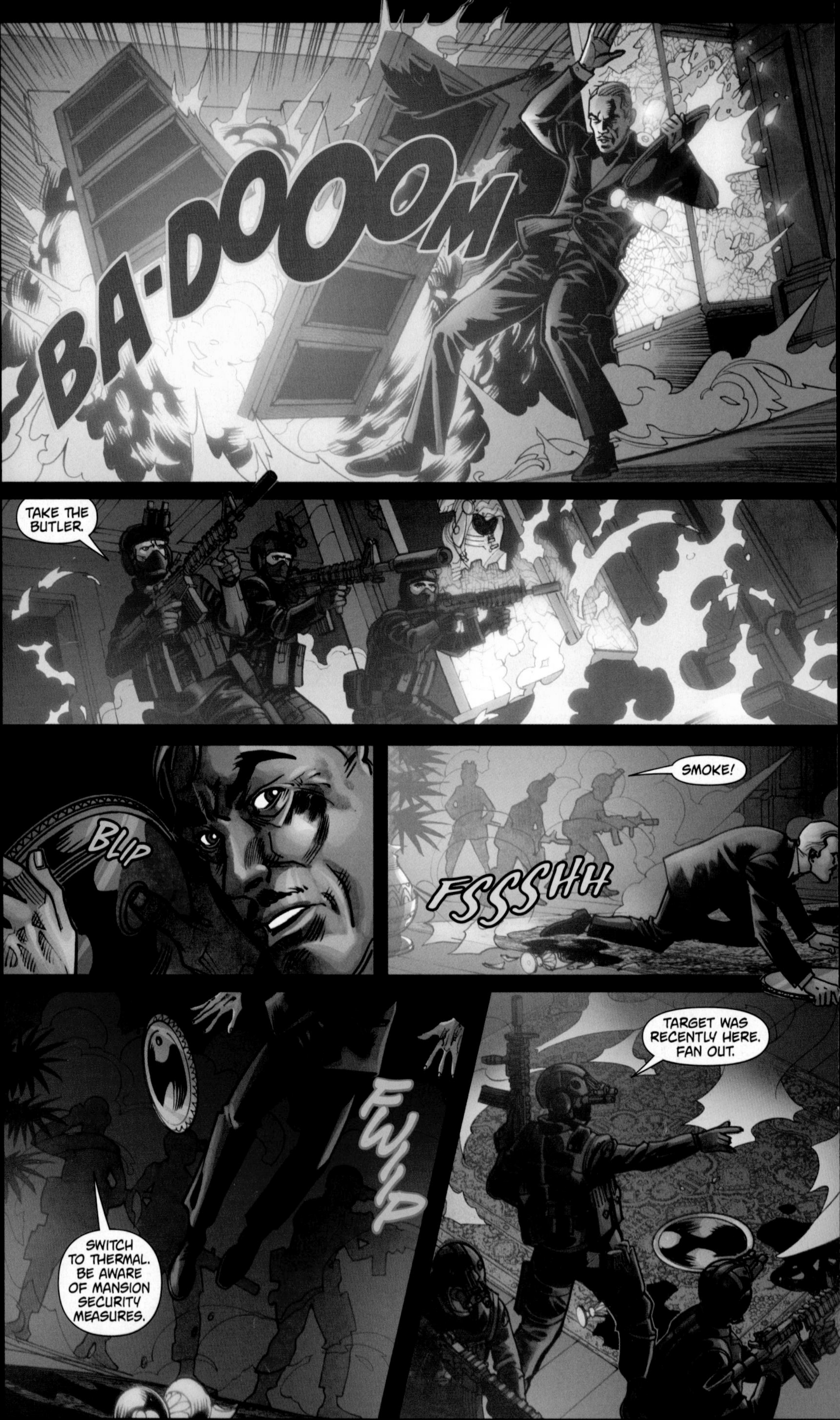
BA-DOOOM
TAKE THE BUTLER.
BLIP
SMOKE!
FSSSHH
SWITCH TO THERMAL. BE AWARE OF MANSION SECURITY MEASURES.
FWIP
TARGET WAS RECENTLY HERE. FAN OUT.

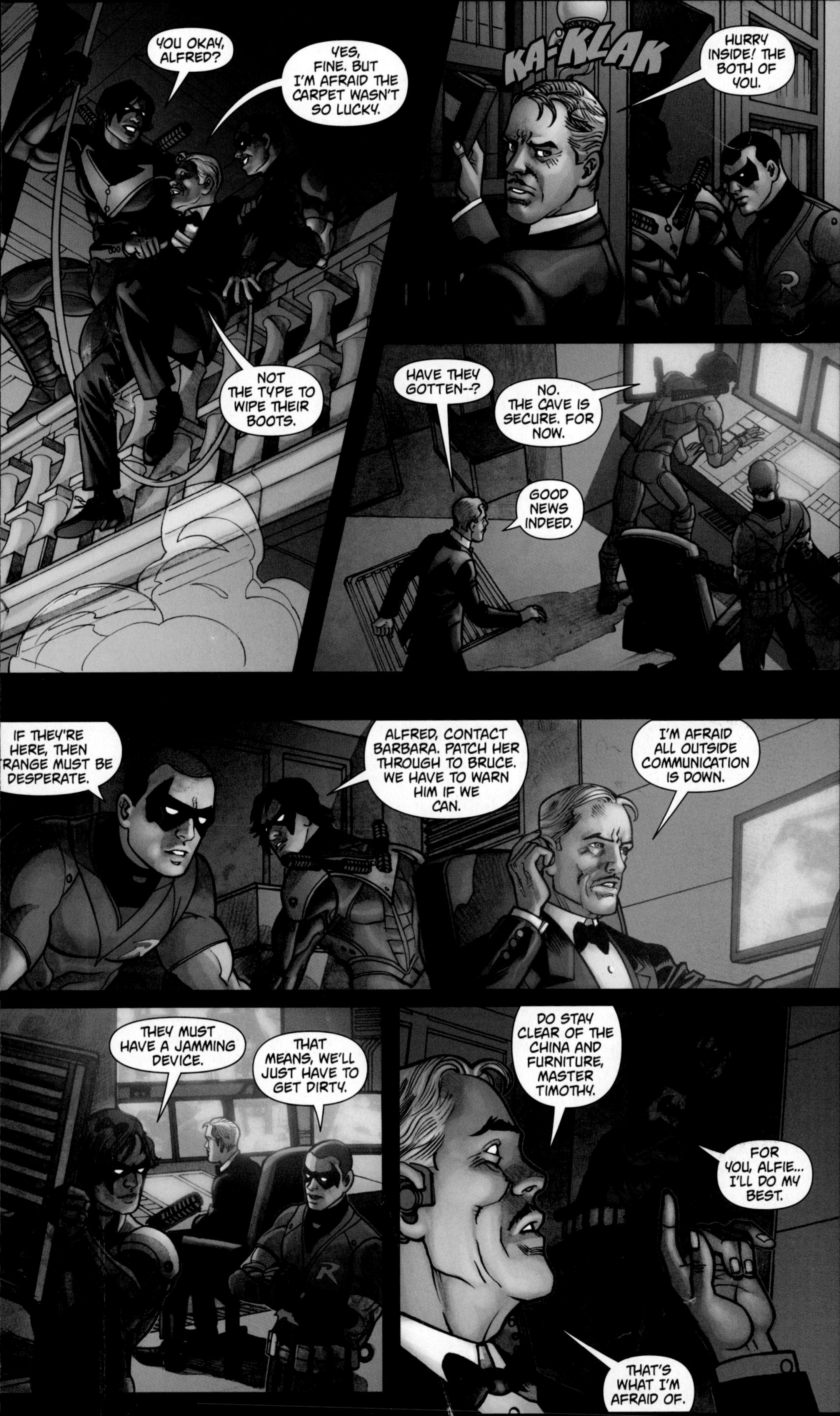
YOU OKAY, ALFRED?
YES, FINE. BUT I'M AFRAID THE CARPET WASN'T SO LUCKY.
NOT THE TYPE TO WIPE THEIR BOOTS.
KA-KLAK
HURRY INSIDE! THE BOTH OF YOU.
HAVE THEY GOTTEN--?
NO. THE CAVE IS SECURE. FOR NOW.
GOOD NEWS INDEED.
IF THEY'RE HERE, THEN RANGE MUST BE DESPERATE.
ALFRED, CONTACT BARBARA. PATCH HER THROUGH TO BRUCE. WE HAVE TO WARN HIM IF WE CAN.
I'M AFRAID ALL OUTSIDE COMMUNICATION IS DOWN.
THEY MUST HAVE A JAMMING DEVICE.
THAT MEANS, WE'LL JUST HAVE TO GET DIRTY.
DO STAY CLEAR OF THE CHINA AND FURNITURE, MASTER TIMOTHY.
FOR YOU, ALFIE... I'LL DO MY BEST.
THAT'S WHAT I'M AFRAID OF.

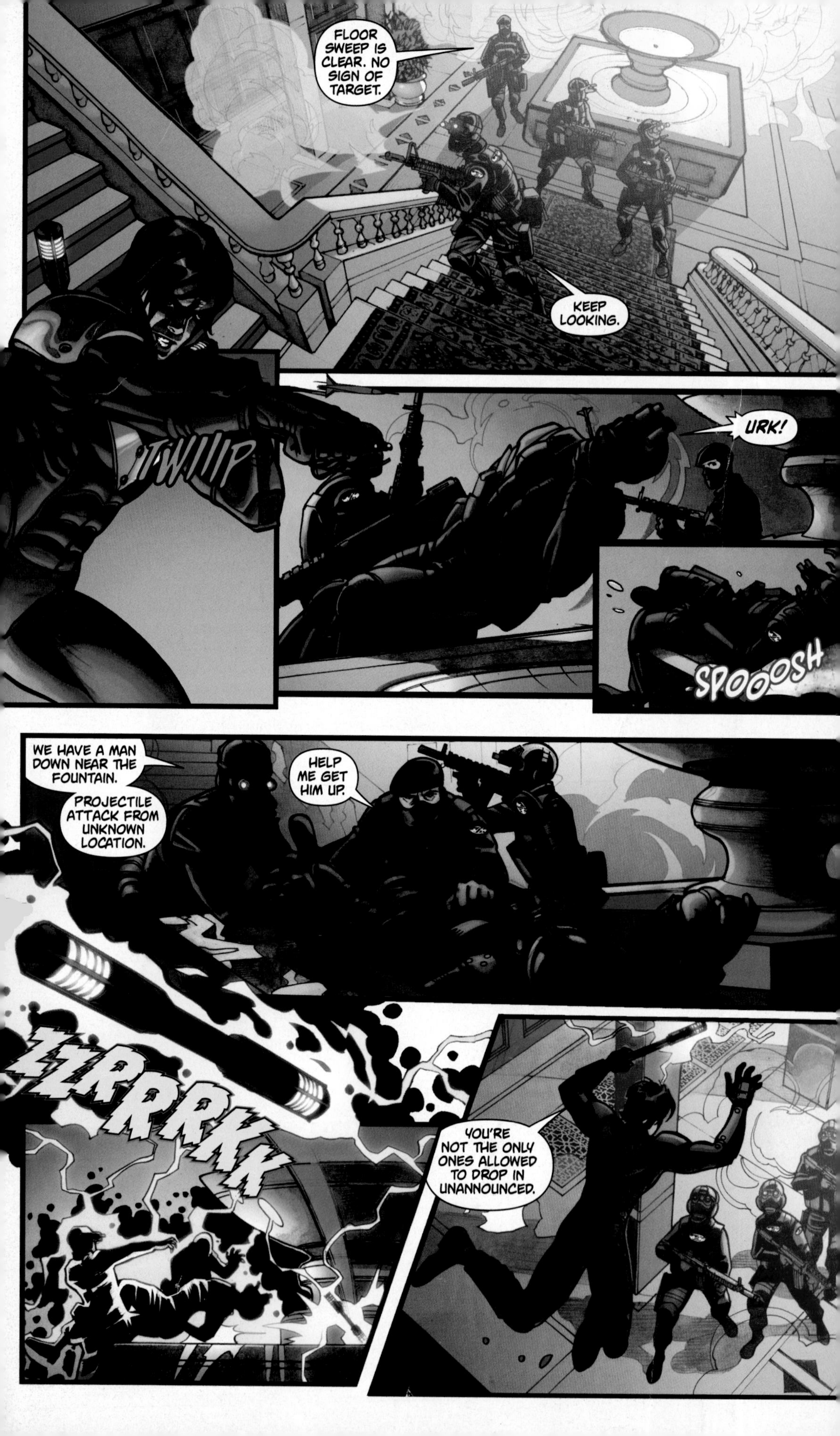
FLOOR SWEEP IS CLEAR. NO SIGN OF TARGET.
KEEP LOOKING.
TWIIIP
URK!
SPOOOSH
WE HAVE A MAN DOWN NEAR THE FOUNTAIN.
PROJECTILE ATTACK FROM UNKNOWN LOCATION.
HELP ME GET HIM UP.
ZZRRRKK
YOU'RE NOT THE ONLY ONES ALLOWED TO DROP IN UNANNOUNCED.

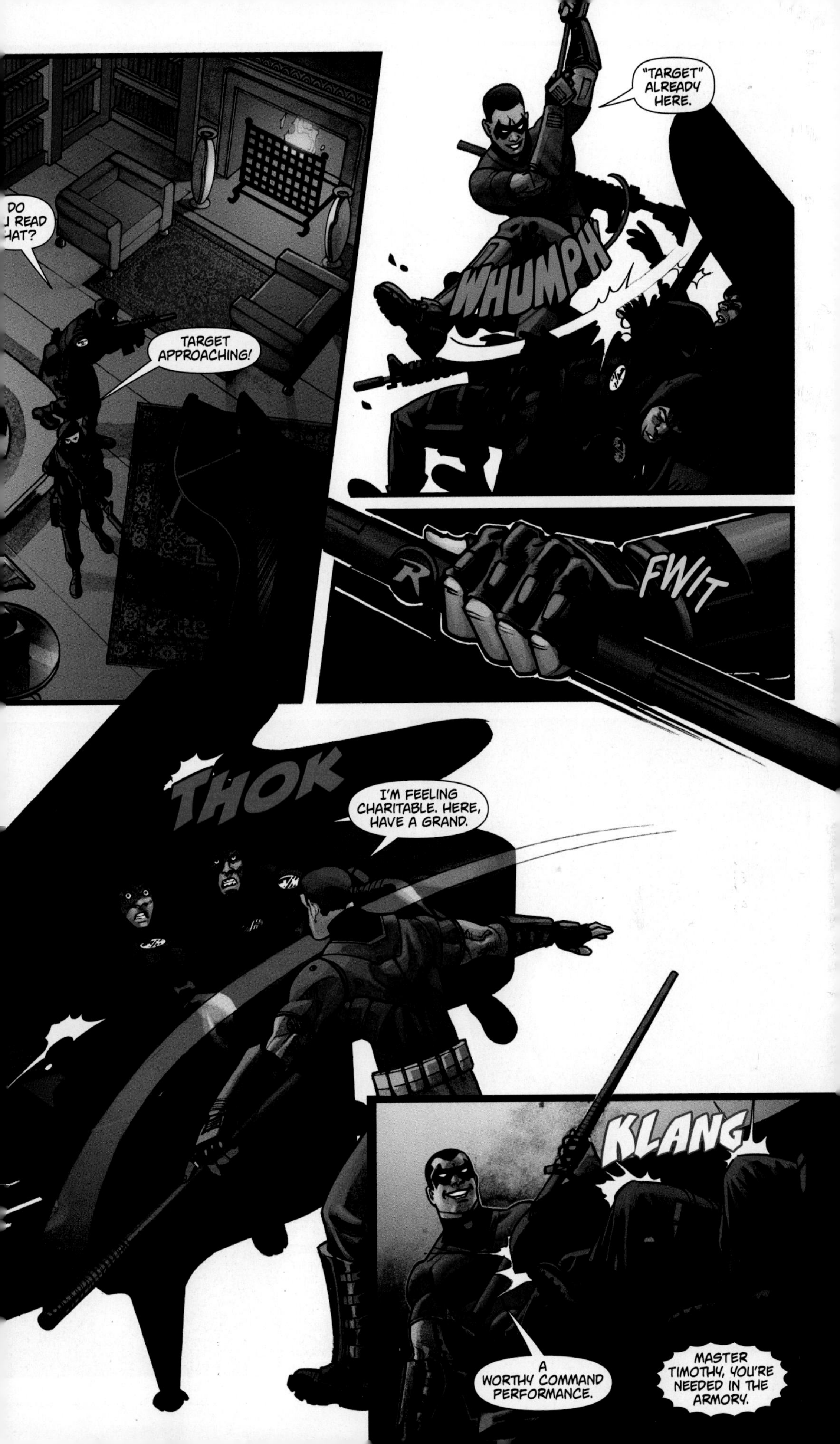

DO
U READ
HAT?
TARGET
APPROACHING!
"TARGET"
ALREADY
HERE.
WHUMPH
FWIT
THOK
I'M FEELING
CHARITABLE. HERE,
HAVE A GRAND.
KLANG
A
WORTHY COMMAND
PERFORMANCE.
MASTER
TIMOTHY, YOU'RE
NEEDED IN THE
ARMORY.

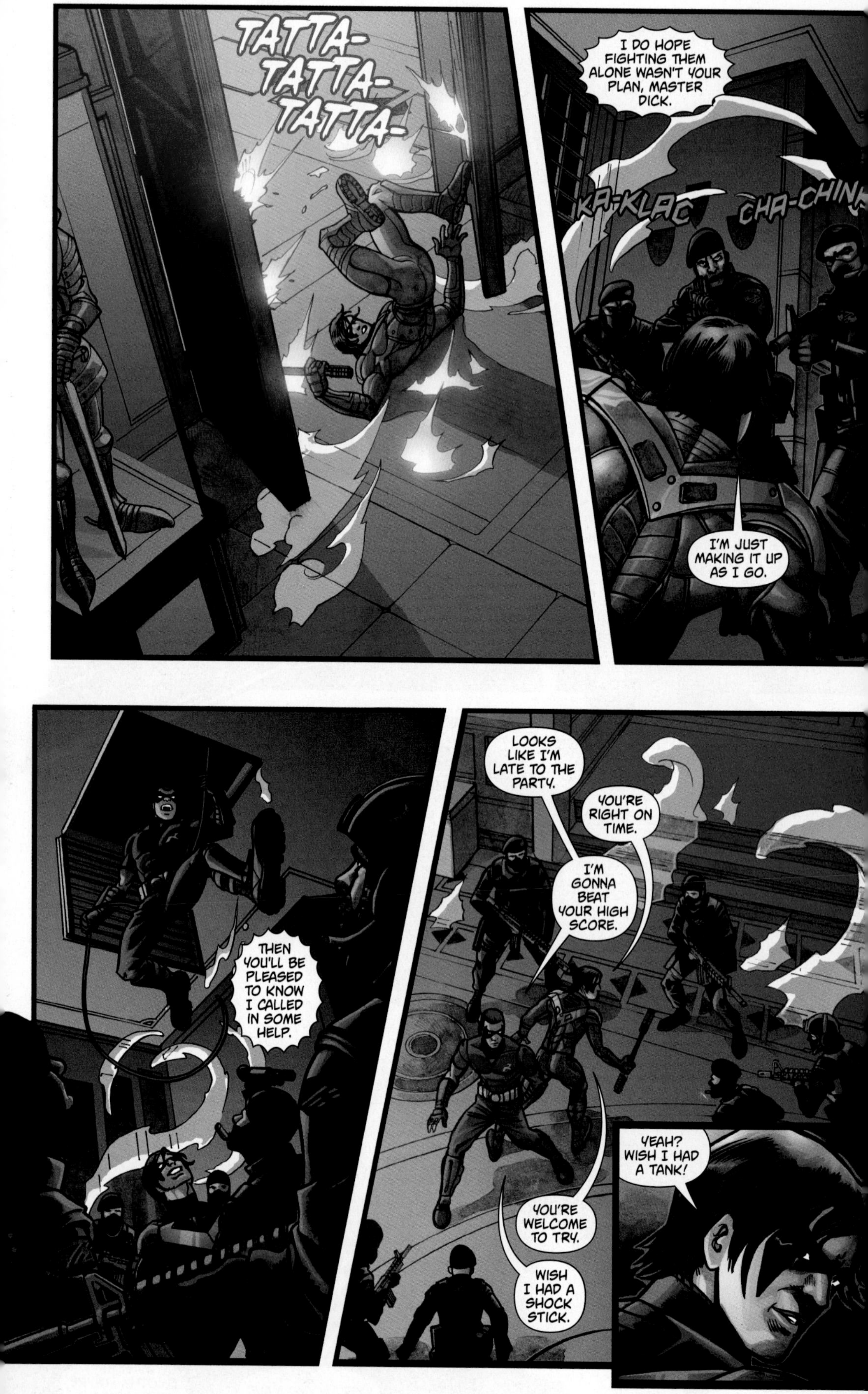
TATTA-TATTA-TATTA-
I DO HOPE FIGHTING THEM ALONE WASN'T YOUR PLAN, MASTER DICK.
KA-KLAC
CHA-CHINK
I'M JUST MAKING IT UP AS I GO.
THEN YOU'LL BE PLEASED TO KNOW I CALLED IN SOME HELP.
LOOKS LIKE I'M LATE TO THE PARTY.
YOU'RE RIGHT ON TIME.
I'M GONNA BEAT YOUR HIGH SCORE.
YOU'RE WELCOME TO TRY.
WISH I HAD A SHOCK STICK.
YEAH? WISH I HAD A TANK!

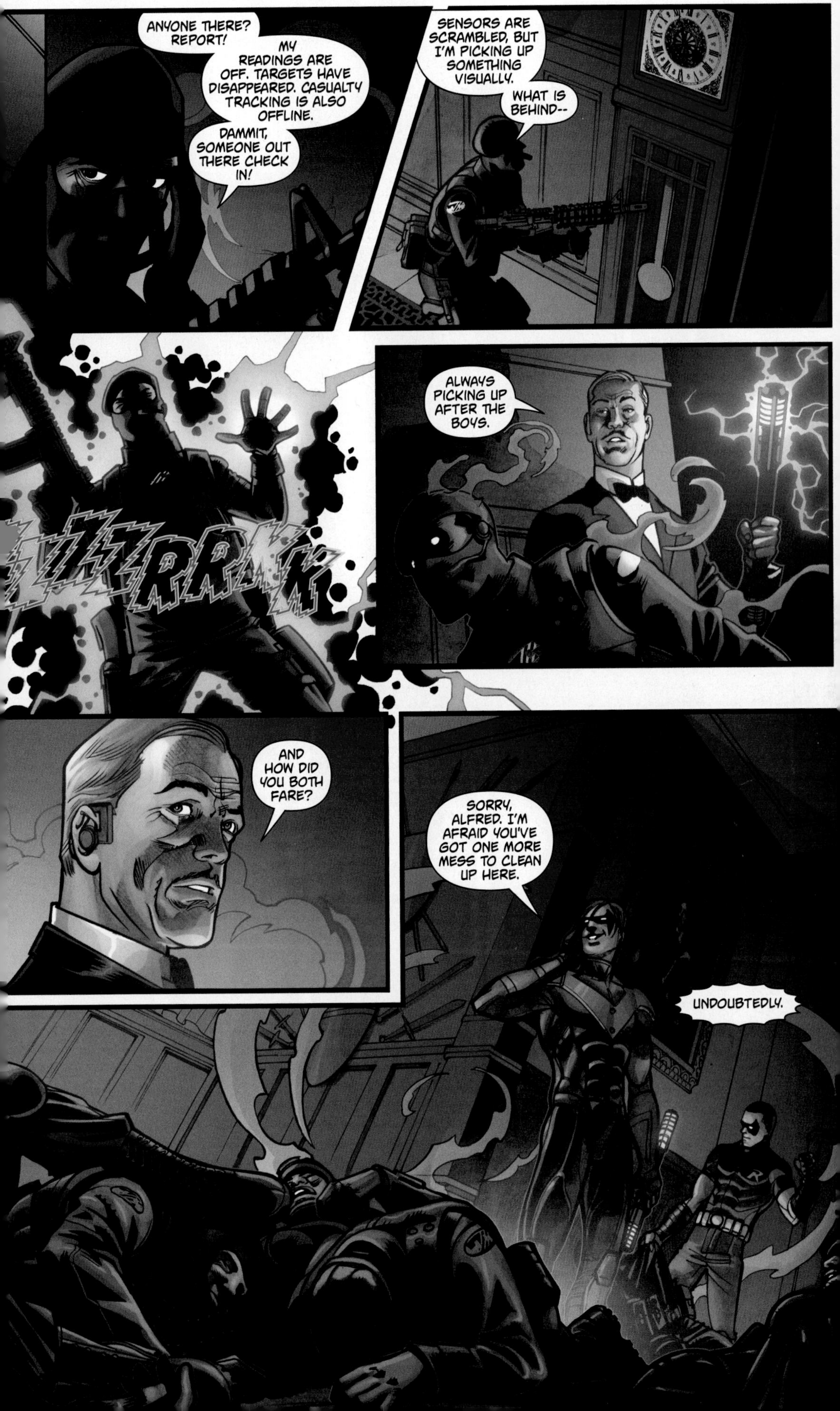
ANYONE THERE? REPORT!
MY READINGS ARE OFF. TARGETS HAVE DISAPPEARED. CASUALTY TRACKING IS ALSO OFFLINE.
DAMMIT, SOMEONE OUT THERE CHECK IN!
SENSORS ARE SCRAMBLED, BUT I'M PICKING UP SOMETHING VISUALLY.
WHAT IS BEHIND--
ZZZRRKK
ALWAYS PICKING UP AFTER THE BOYS.
AND HOW DID YOU BOTH FARE?
SORRY, ALFRED. I'M AFRAID YOU'VE GOT ONE MORE MESS TO CLEAN UP HERE.
UNDOUBTEDLY.

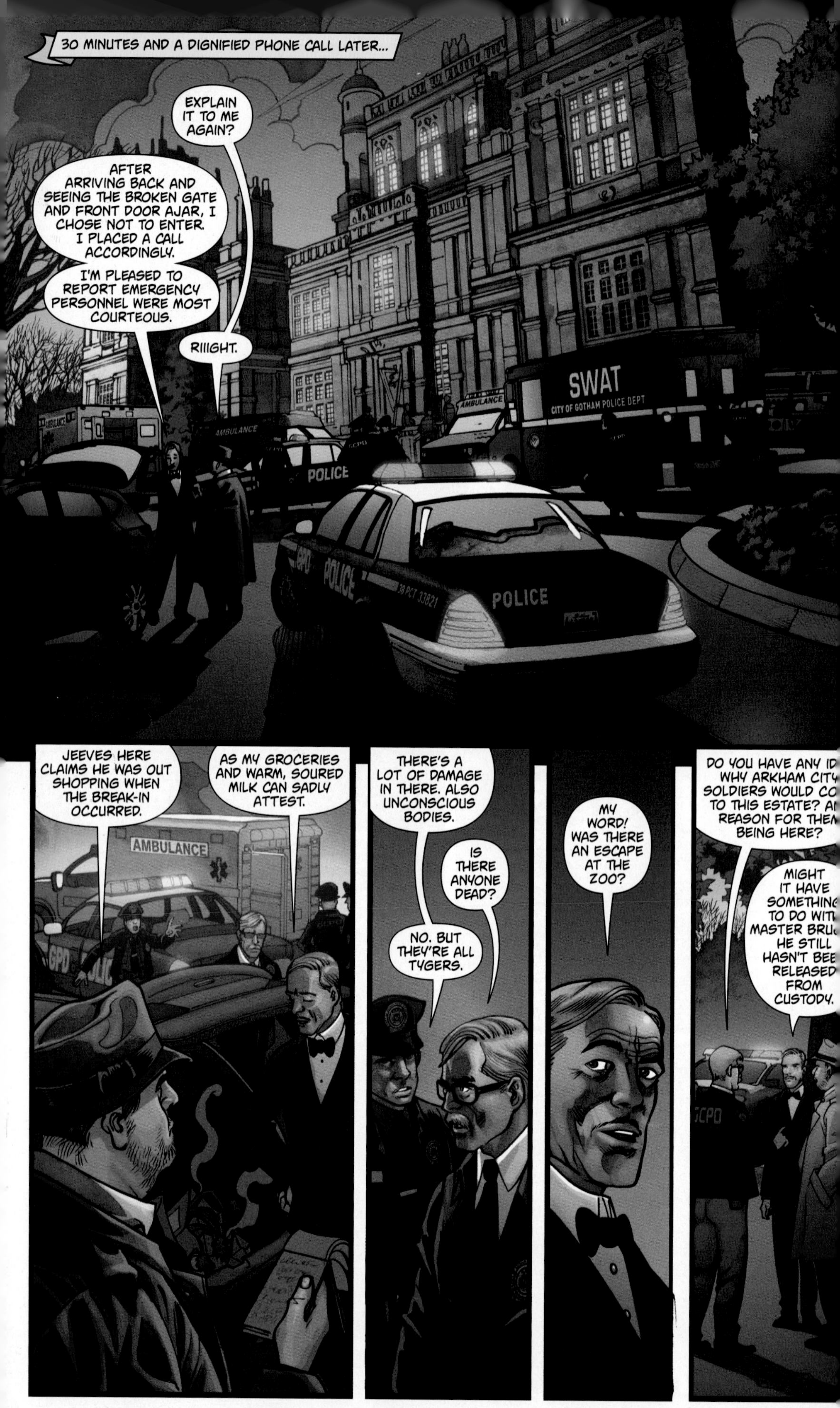

30 MINUTES AND A DIGNIFIED PHONE CALL LATER...
EXPLAIN IT TO ME AGAIN?
AFTER ARRIVING BACK AND SEEING THE BROKEN GATE AND FRONT DOOR AJAR, I CHOSE NOT TO ENTER. I PLACED A CALL ACCORDINGLY.
I'M PLEASED TO REPORT EMERGENCY PERSONNEL WERE MOST COURTEOUS.
RIIIGHT.
SWAT
CITY OF GOTHAM POLICE DEPT
AMBULANCE
POLICE
JEEVES HERE CLAIMS HE WAS OUT SHOPPING WHEN THE BREAK-IN OCCURRED.
AS MY GROCERIES AND WARM, SOURED MILK CAN SADLY ATTEST.
AMBULANCE
THERE'S A LOT OF DAMAGE IN THERE. ALSO UNCONSCIOUS BODIES.
IS THERE ANYONE DEAD?
NO. BUT THEY'RE ALL TYGERS.
MY WORD! WAS THERE AN ESCAPE AT THE ZOO?
DO YOU HAVE ANY ID WHY ARKHAM CITY SOLDIERS WOULD CO TO THIS ESTATE? AN REASON FOR THEM BEING HERE?
MIGHT IT HAVE SOMETHIN TO DO WIT MASTER BRU HE STILL HASN'T BEE RELEASED FROM CUSTODY.

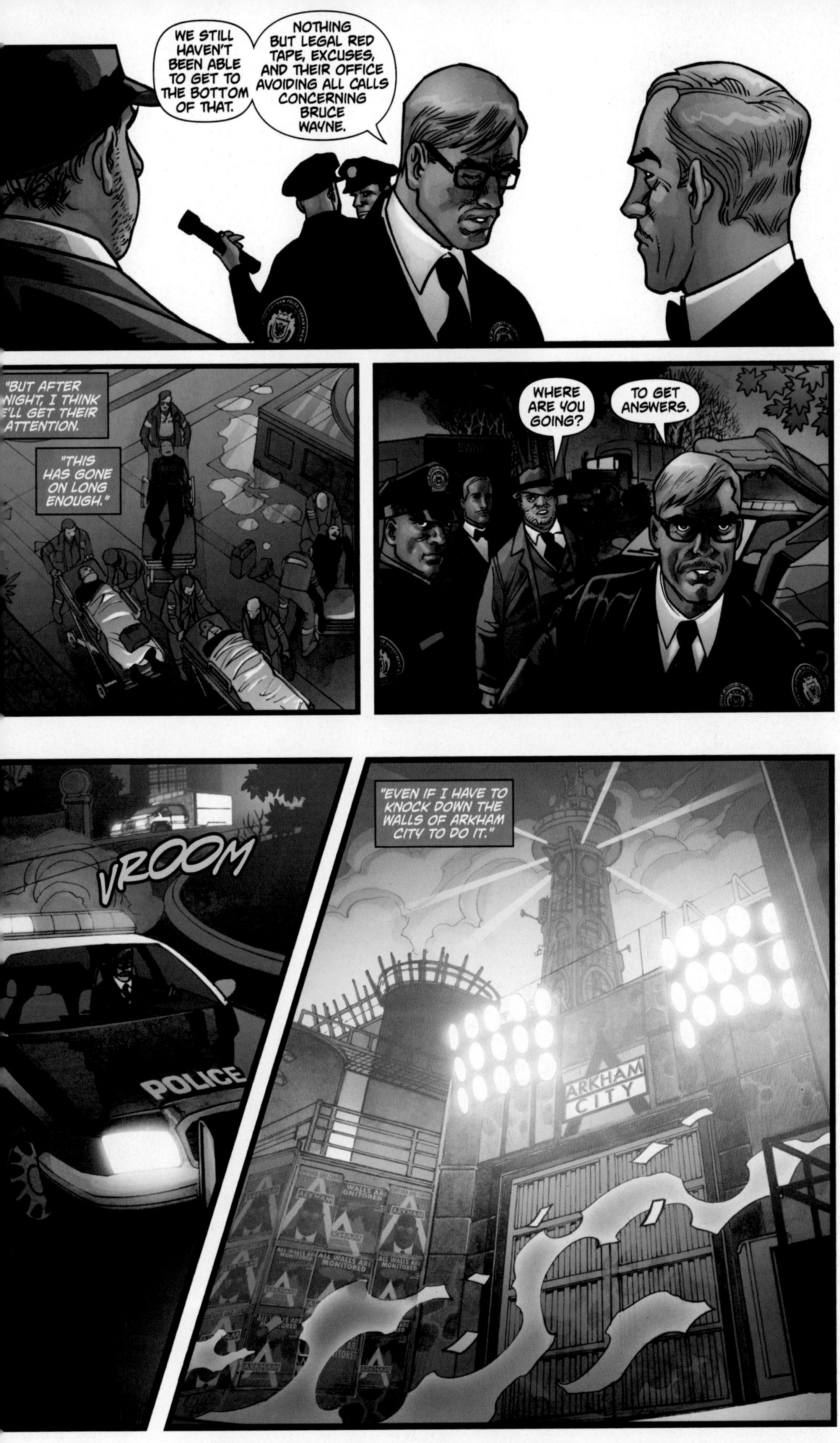
WE STILL HAVEN'T BEEN ABLE TO GET TO THE BOTTOM OF THAT.
NOTHING BUT LEGAL RED TAPE, EXCUSES, AND THEIR OFFICE AVOIDING ALL CALLS CONCERNING BRUCE WAYNE.
"BUT AFTER NIGHT, I THINK 'LL GET THEIR ATTENTION.
"THIS HAS GONE ON LONG ENOUGH."
WHERE ARE YOU GOING?
TO GET ANSWERS.
VROOM
POLICE
"EVEN IF I HAVE TO KNOCK DOWN THE WALLS OF ARKHAM CITY TO DO IT."
ARKHAM CITY
ALL WALLS ARE MONITORED

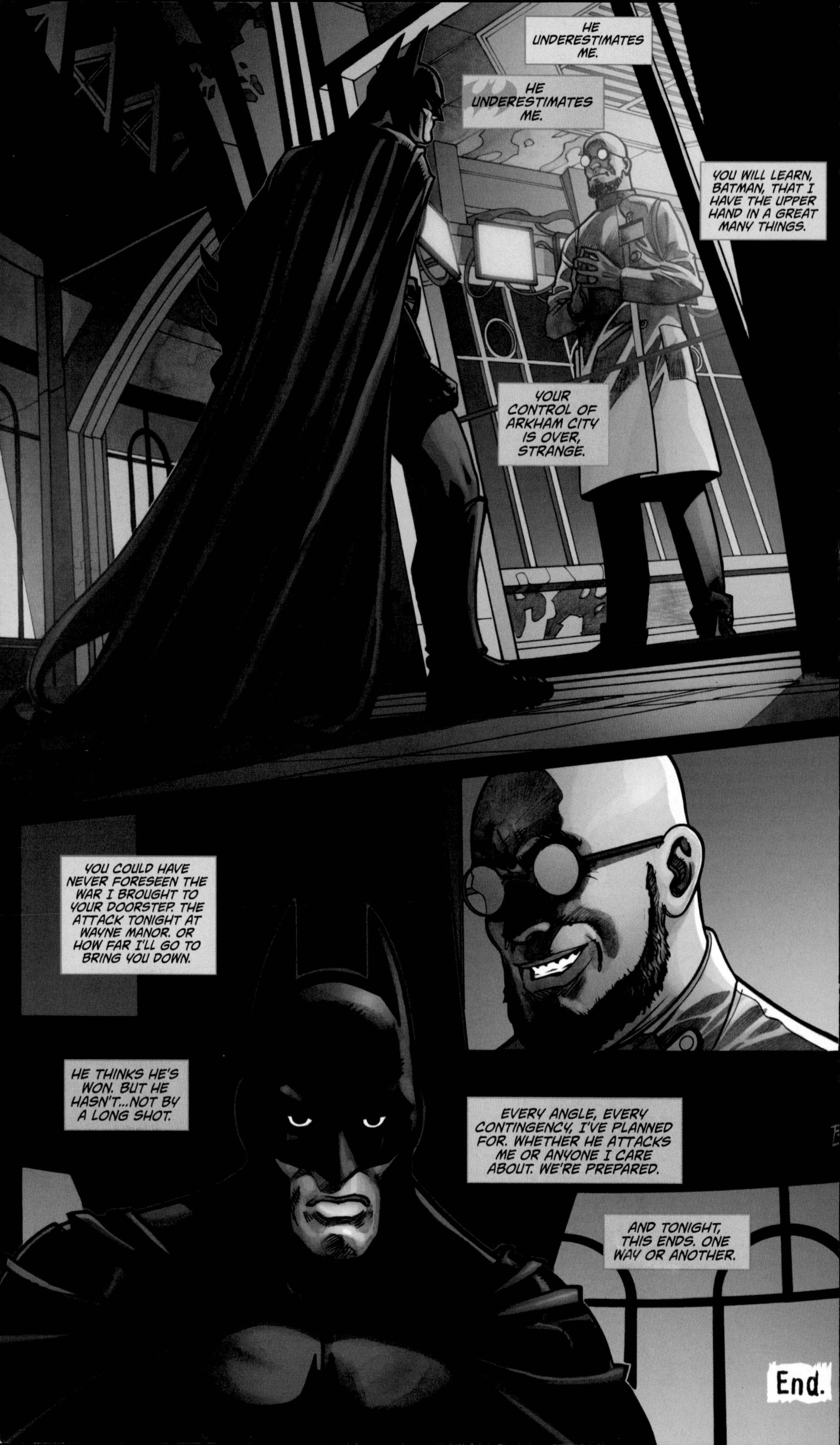

HE UNDERESTIMATES ME.
HE UNDERESTIMATES ME.
YOU WILL LEARN, BATMAN, THAT I HAVE THE UPPER HAND IN A GREAT MANY THINGS.
YOUR CONTROL OF ARKHAM CITY IS OVER, STRANGE.
YOU COULD HAVE NEVER FORESEEN THE WAR I BROUGHT TO YOUR DOORSTEP. THE ATTACK TONIGHT AT WAYNE MANOR. OR HOW FAR I'LL GO TO BRING YOU DOWN.
HE THINKS HE'S WON. BUT HE HASN'T...NOT BY A LONG SHOT.
EVERY ANGLE, EVERY CONTINGENCY, I'VE PLANNED FOR. WHETHER HE ATTACKS ME OR ANYONE I CARE ABOUT. WE'RE PREPARED.
AND TONIGHT, THIS ENDS. ONE WAY OR ANOTHER.
End.

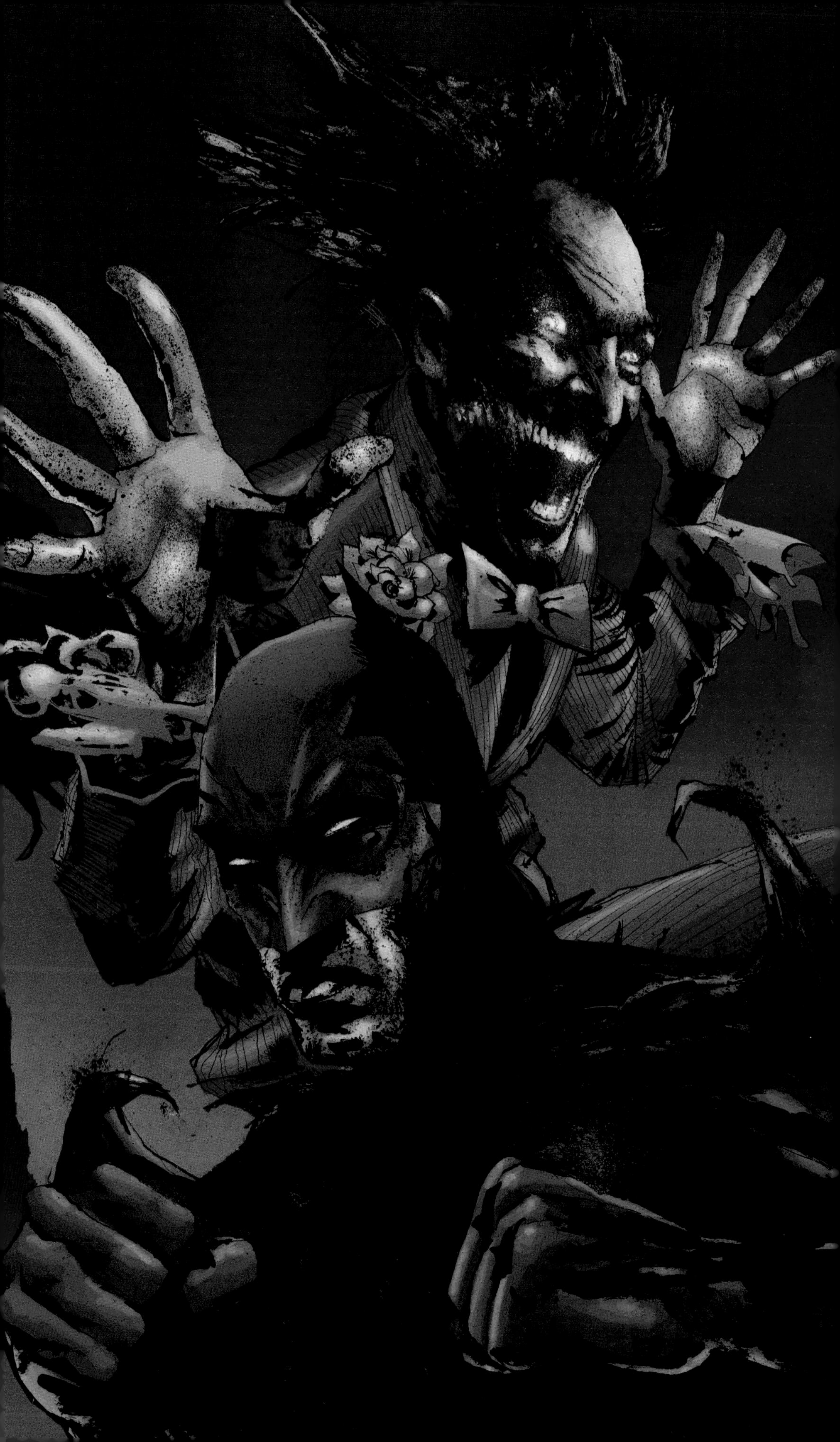

END GAME

WRITER: DEREK FRIDOLFS
ARTIST: JASON SHAWN ALEXANDER
COLORIST: LEE LOUGHRIDGE
LETTERER: TRAVIS LANHAM
COVER ART BY: JASON SHAWN ALEXANDER
COVER COLORS BY: LEE LOUGHRIDGE
VARIANT COVER PENCILS BY: PAT GLEASON
VARIANT COVER INKS BY: DEREK FRIDOLFS
VARIANT COVER COLORS BY: GABE ELTAEB

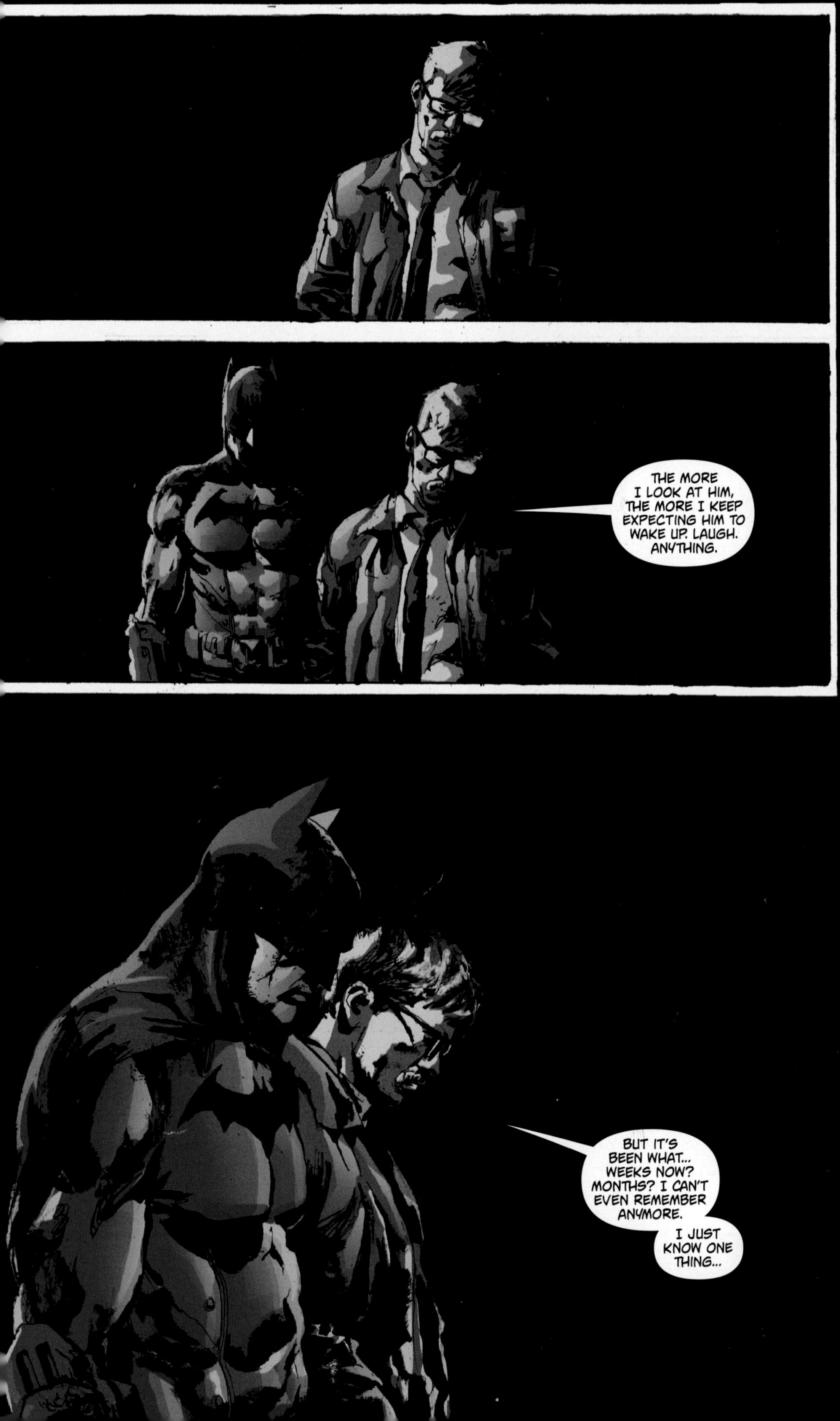
THE MORE I LOOK AT HIM, THE MORE I KEEP EXPECTING HIM TO WAKE UP. LAUGH. ANYTHING.
BUT IT'S BEEN WHAT... WEEKS NOW? MONTHS? I CAN'T EVEN REMEMBER ANYMORE.
I JUST KNOW ONE THING...

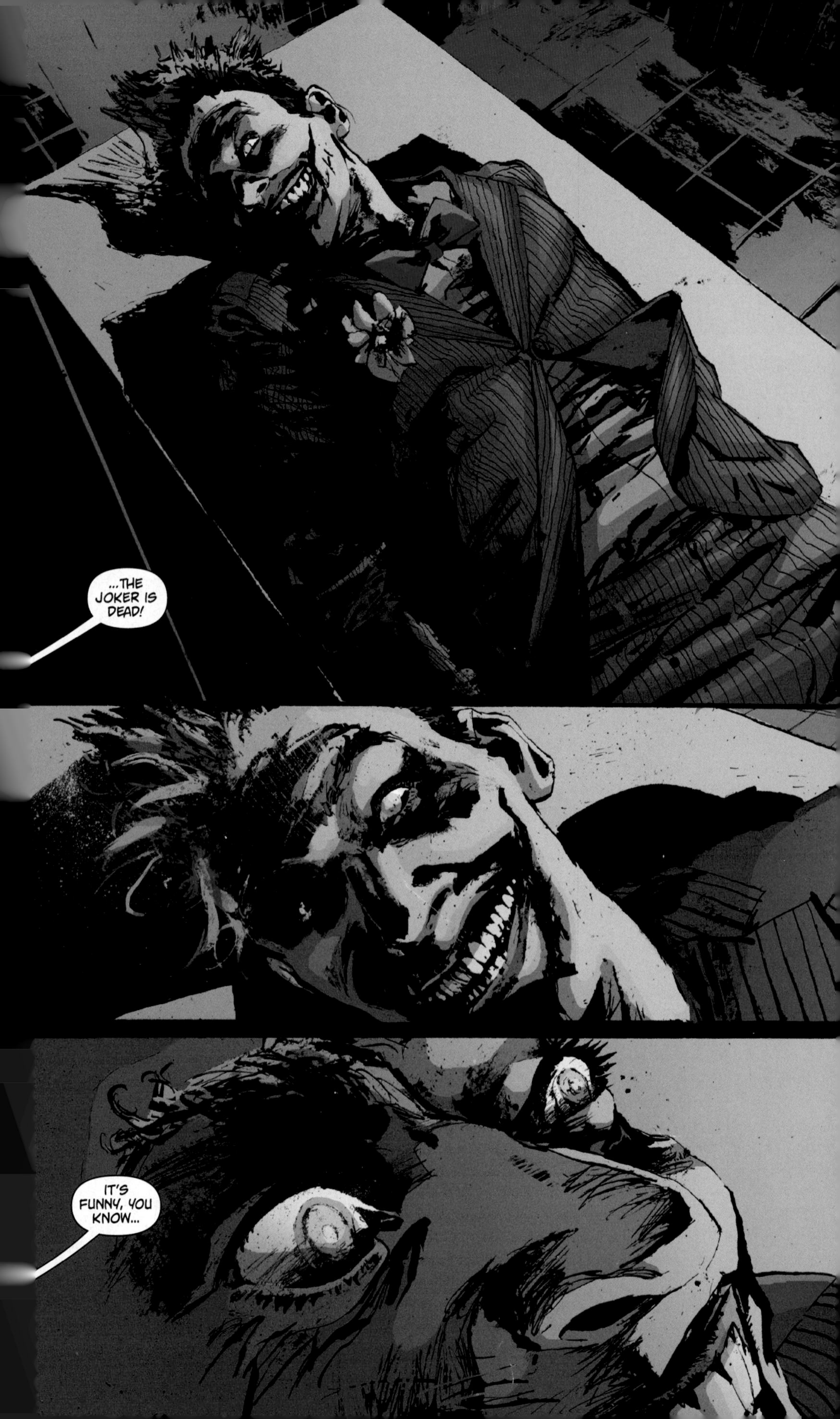
...THE JOKER IS DEAD!
IT'S FUNNY, YOU KNOW...

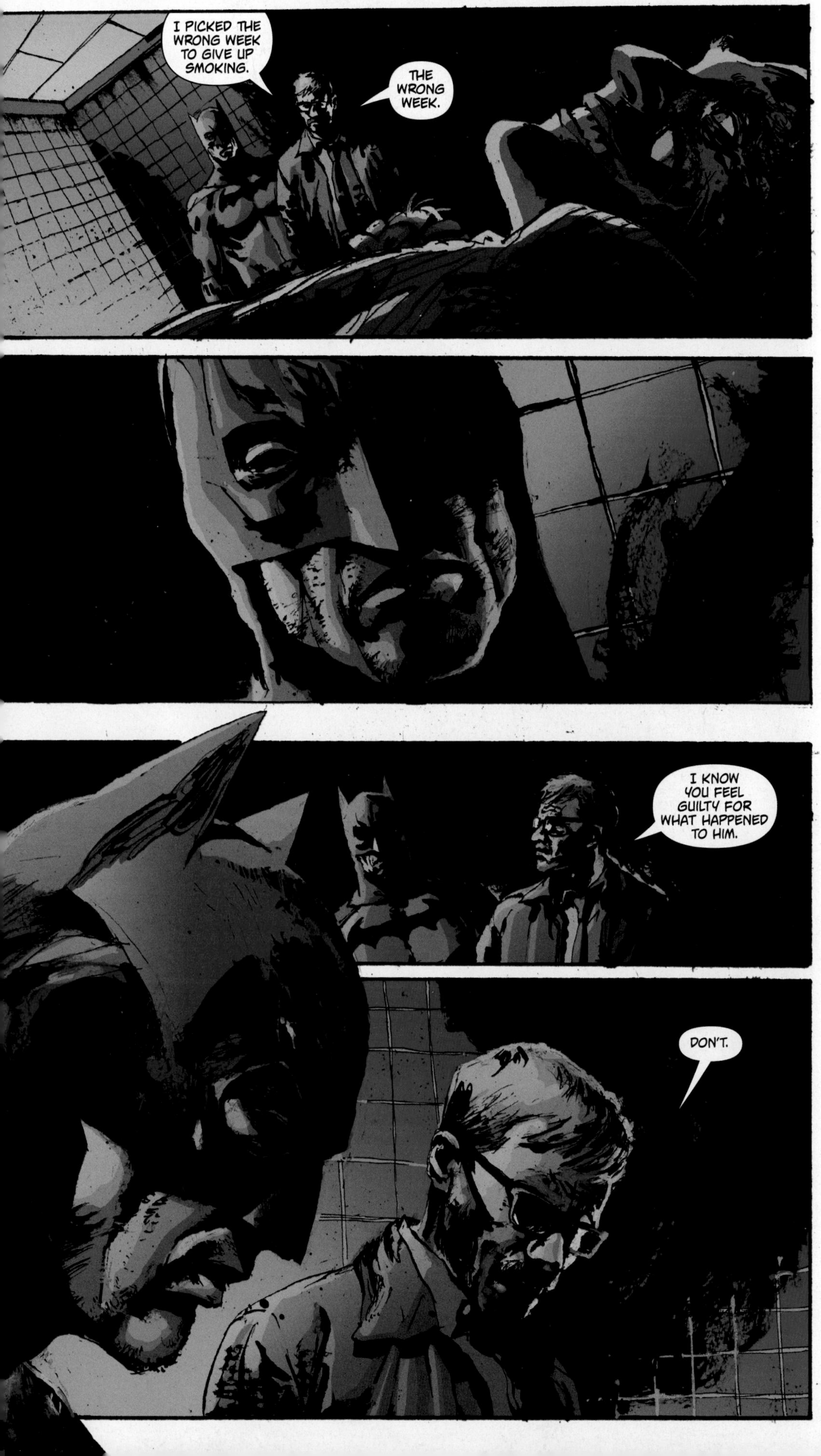
I PICKED THE WRONG WEEK TO GIVE UP SMOKING.
THE WRONG WEEK.
I KNOW YOU FEEL GUILTY FOR WHAT HAPPENED TO HIM.
DON'T.

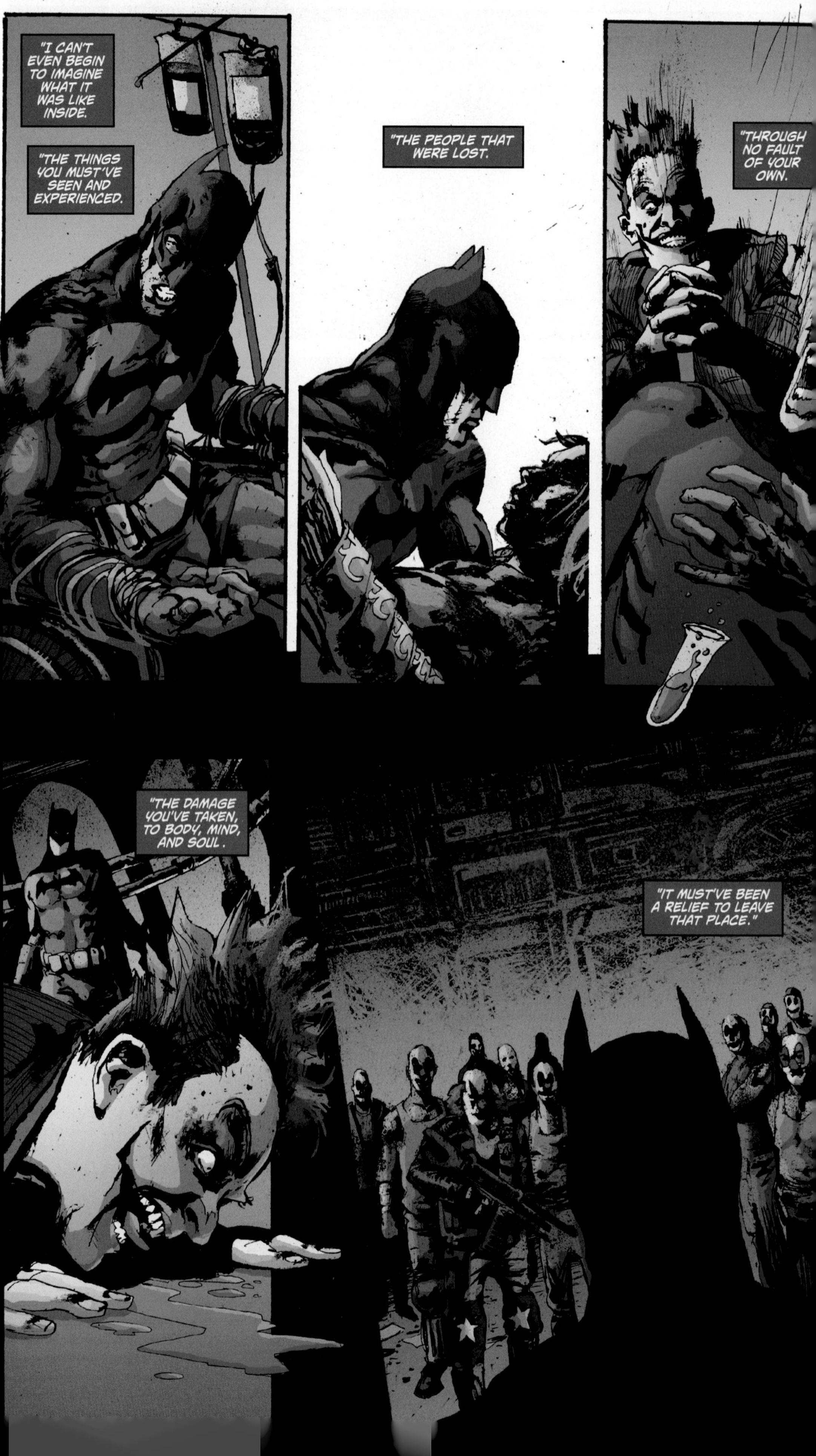
"I CAN'T EVEN BEGIN TO IMAGINE WHAT IT WAS LIKE INSIDE.
"THE THINGS YOU MUST'VE SEEN AND EXPERIENCED.
"THE PEOPLE THAT WERE LOST.
"THROUGH NO FAULT OF YOUR OWN.
"THE DAMAGE YOU'VE TAKEN, TO BODY, MIND, AND SOUL.
"IT MUST'VE BEEN A RELIEF TO LEAVE THAT PLACE."

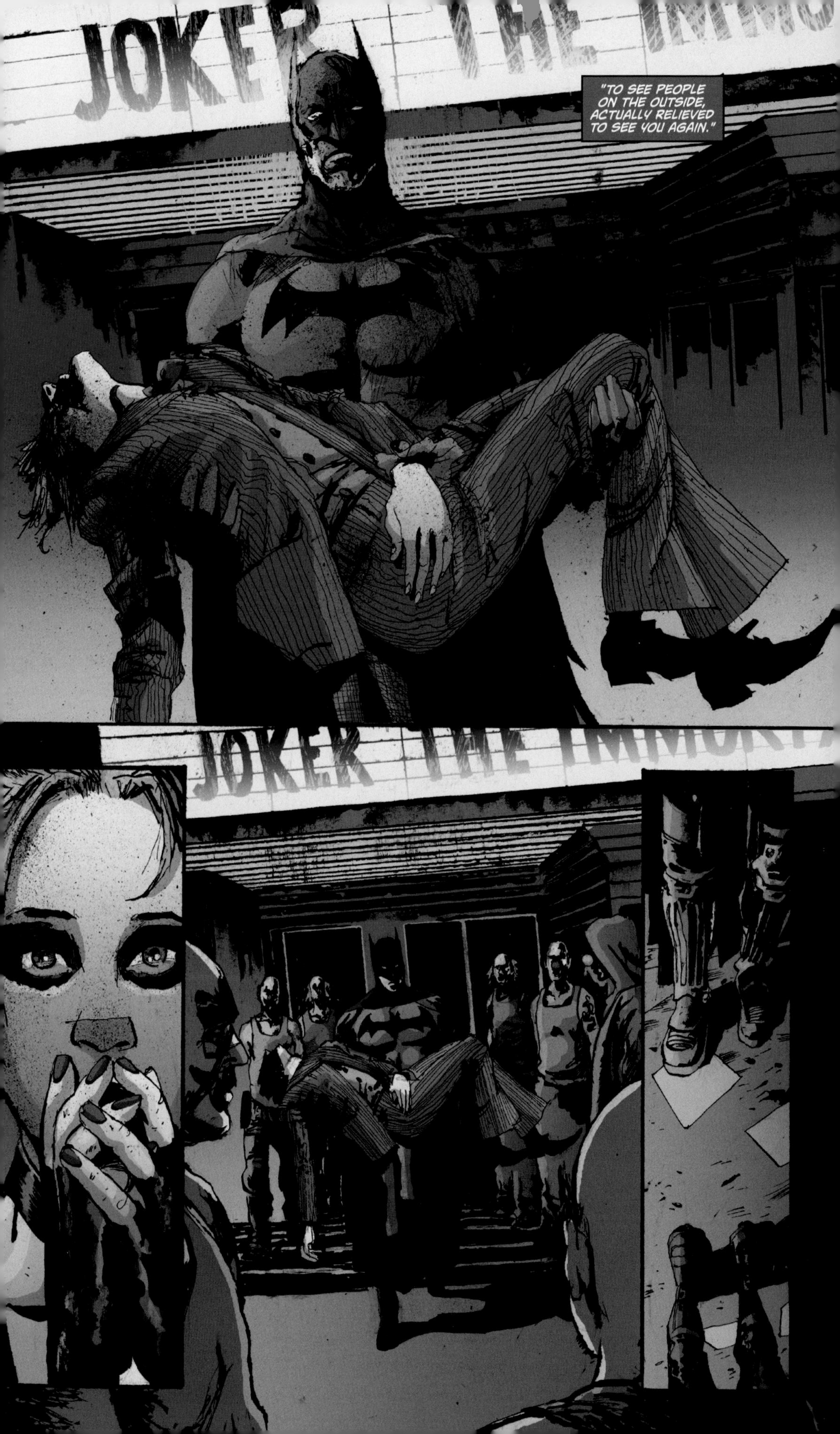
JOKER
"TO SEE PEOPLE ON THE OUTSIDE, ACTUALLY RELIEVED TO SEE YOU AGAIN."

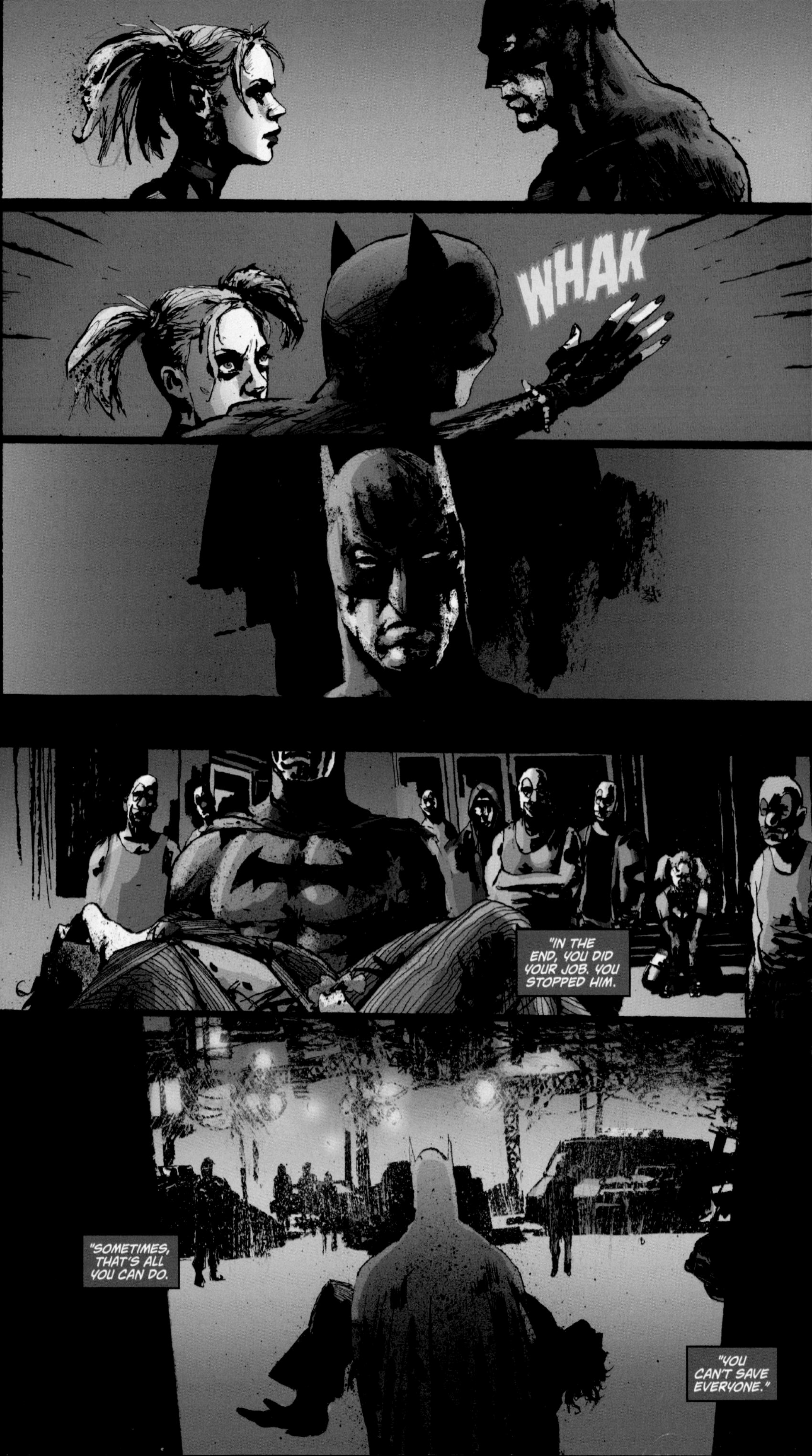
WHAK
"IN THE END, YOU DID YOUR JOB. YOU STOPPED HIM.
"SOMETIMES, THAT'S ALL YOU CAN DO.
"YOU CAN'T SAVE EVERYONE."

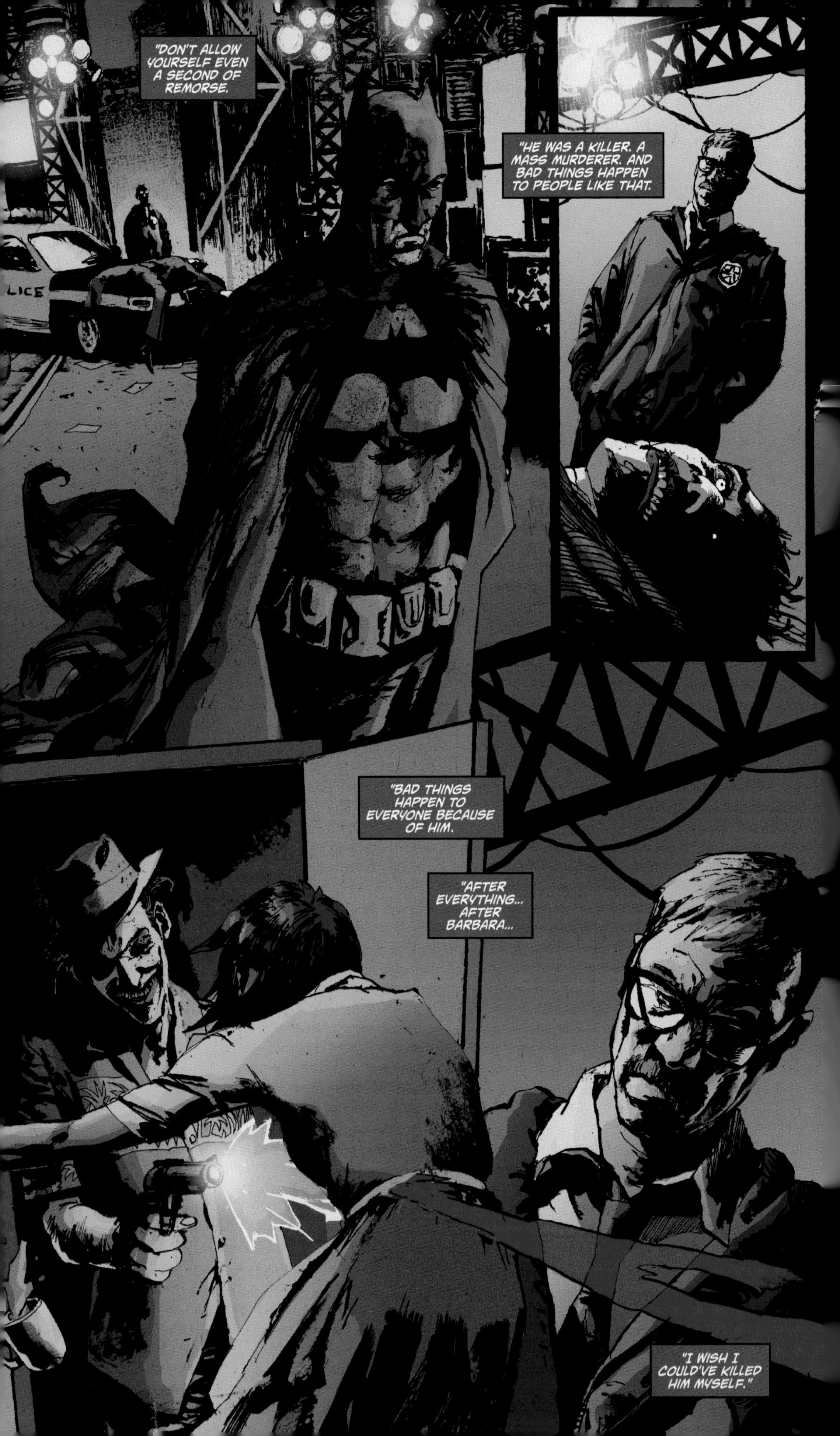
"DON'T ALLOW YOURSELF EVEN A SECOND OF REMORSE.
LICE
"HE WAS A KILLER. A MASS MURDERER. AND BAD THINGS HAPPEN TO PEOPLE LIKE THAT.
"BAD THINGS HAPPEN TO EVERYONE BECAUSE OF HIM.
"AFTER EVERYTHING... AFTER BARBARA...
"I WISH I COULD'VE KILLED HIM MYSELF."

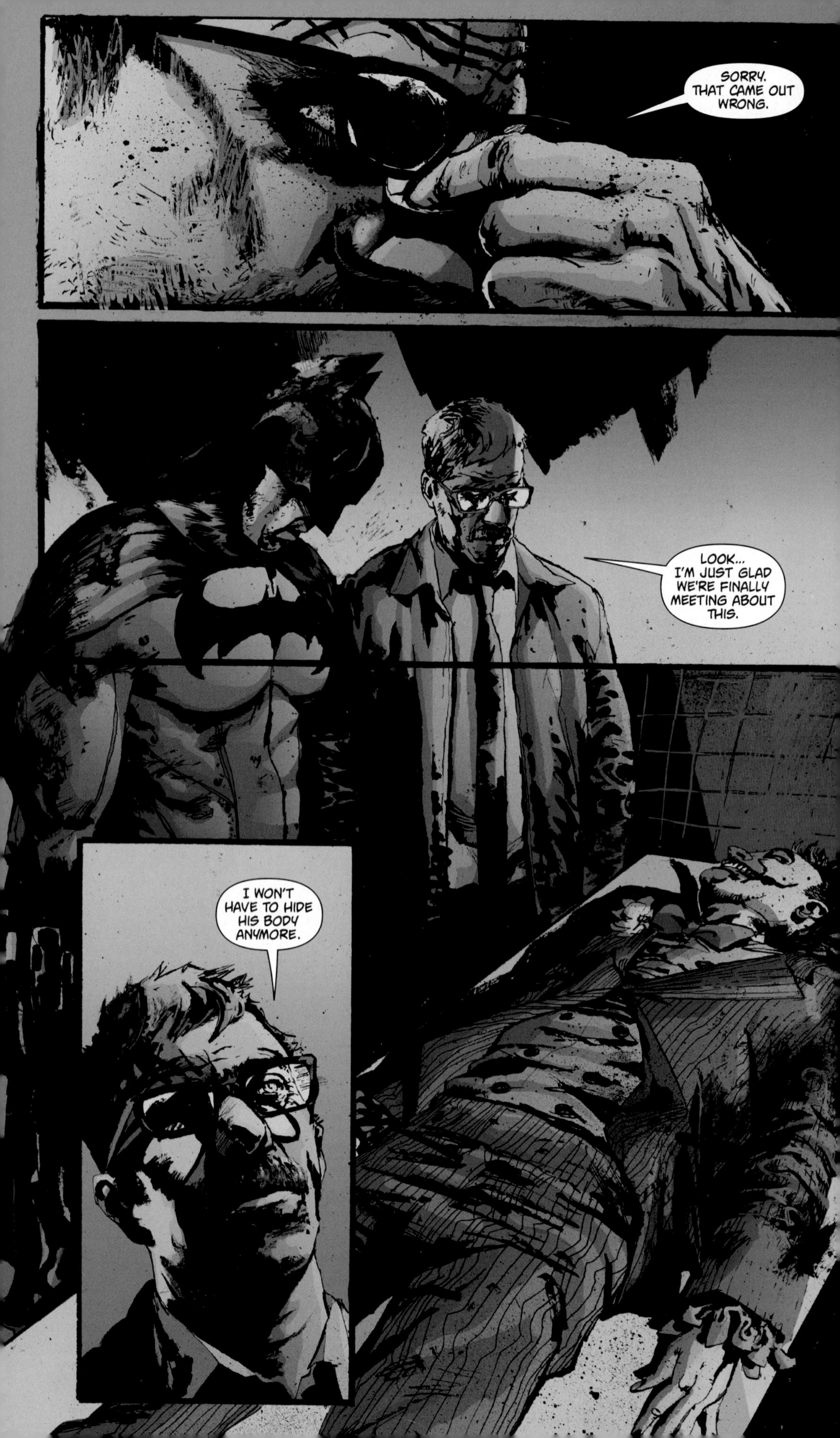
SORRY. THAT CAME OUT WRONG.
LOOK... I'M JUST GLAD WE'RE FINALLY MEETING ABOUT THIS.
I WON'T HAVE TO HIDE HIS BODY ANYMORE.

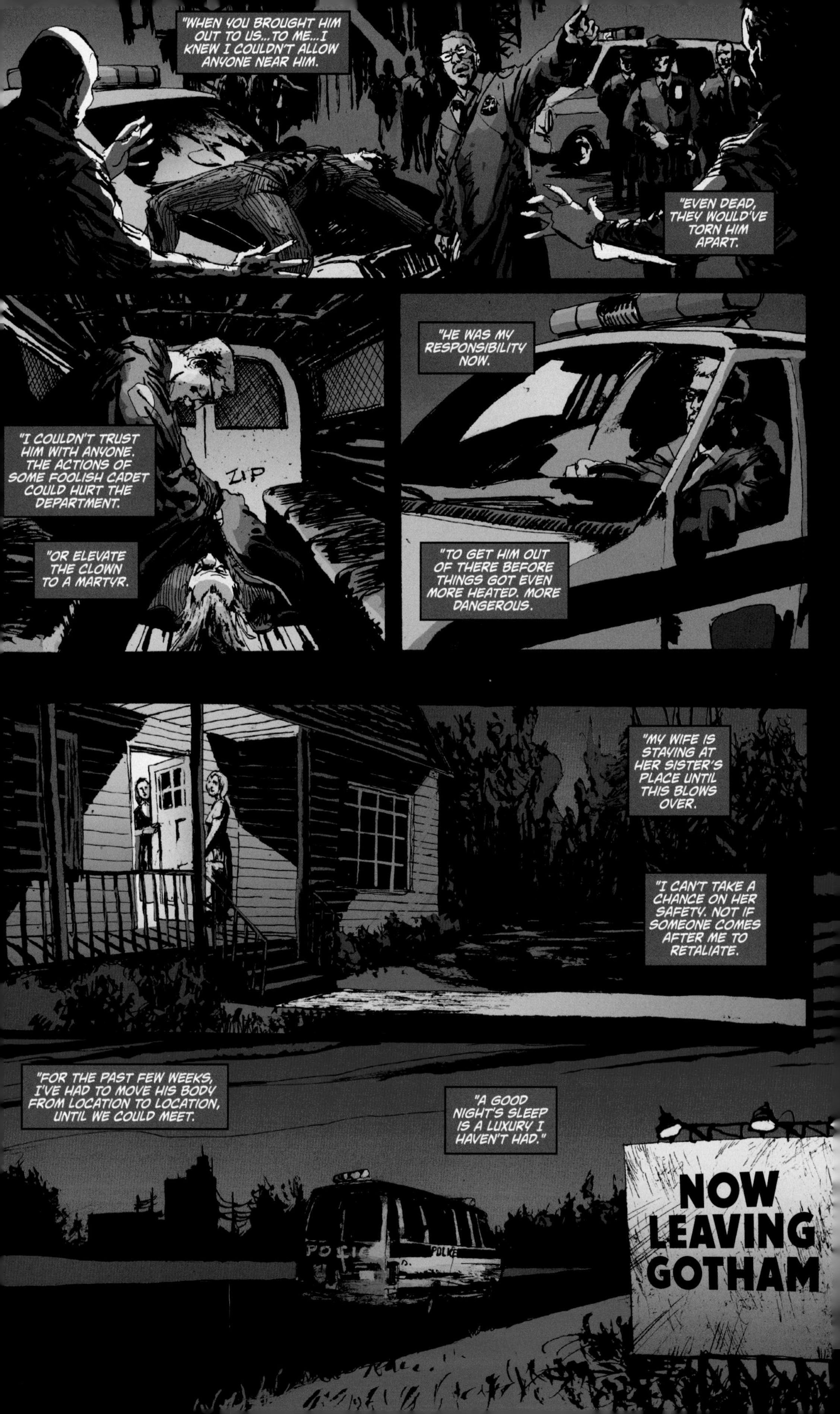
"WHEN YOU BROUGHT HIM OUT TO US...TO ME...I KNEW I COULDN'T ALLOW ANYONE NEAR HIM.
"EVEN DEAD, THEY WOULD'VE TORN HIM APART.
"I COULDN'T TRUST HIM WITH ANYONE. THE ACTIONS OF SOME FOOLISH CADET COULD HURT THE DEPARTMENT.
"OR ELEVATE THE CLOWN TO A MARTYR.
ZIP
"HE WAS MY RESPONSIBILITY NOW.
"TO GET HIM OUT OF THERE BEFORE THINGS GOT EVEN MORE HEATED. MORE DANGEROUS.
"MY WIFE IS STAYING AT HER SISTER'S PLACE UNTIL THIS BLOWS OVER.
"I CAN'T TAKE A CHANCE ON HER SAFETY. NOT IF SOMEONE COMES AFTER ME TO RETALIATE.
"FOR THE PAST FEW WEEKS, I'VE HAD TO MOVE HIS BODY FROM LOCATION TO LOCATION, UNTIL WE COULD MEET.
"A GOOD NIGHT'S SLEEP IS A LUXURY I HAVEN'T HAD."
NOW LEAVING GOTHAM

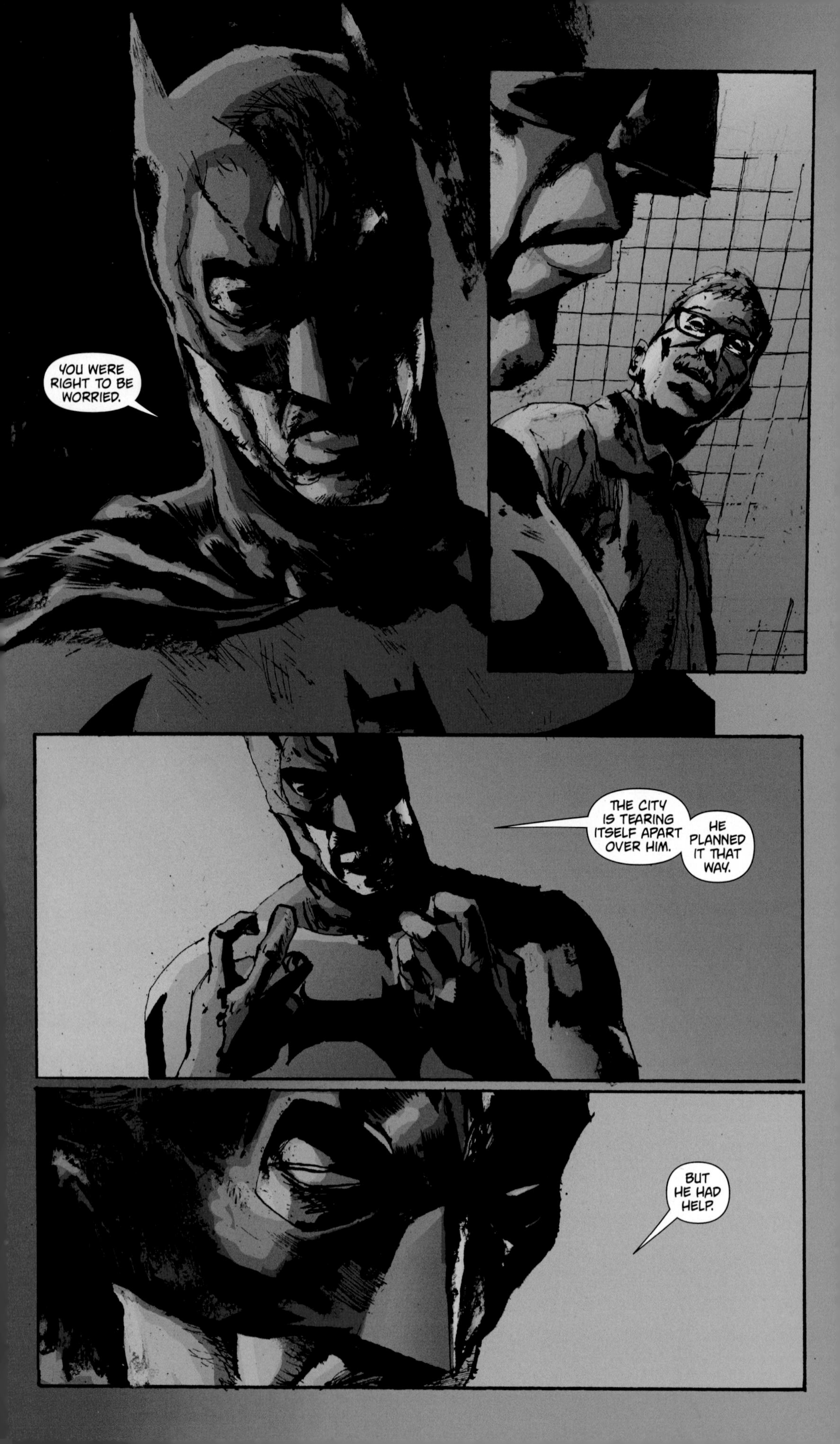
YOU WERE RIGHT TO BE WORRIED.
THE CITY IS TEARING ITSELF APART OVER HIM.
HE PLANNED IT THAT WAY.
BUT HE HAD HELP.

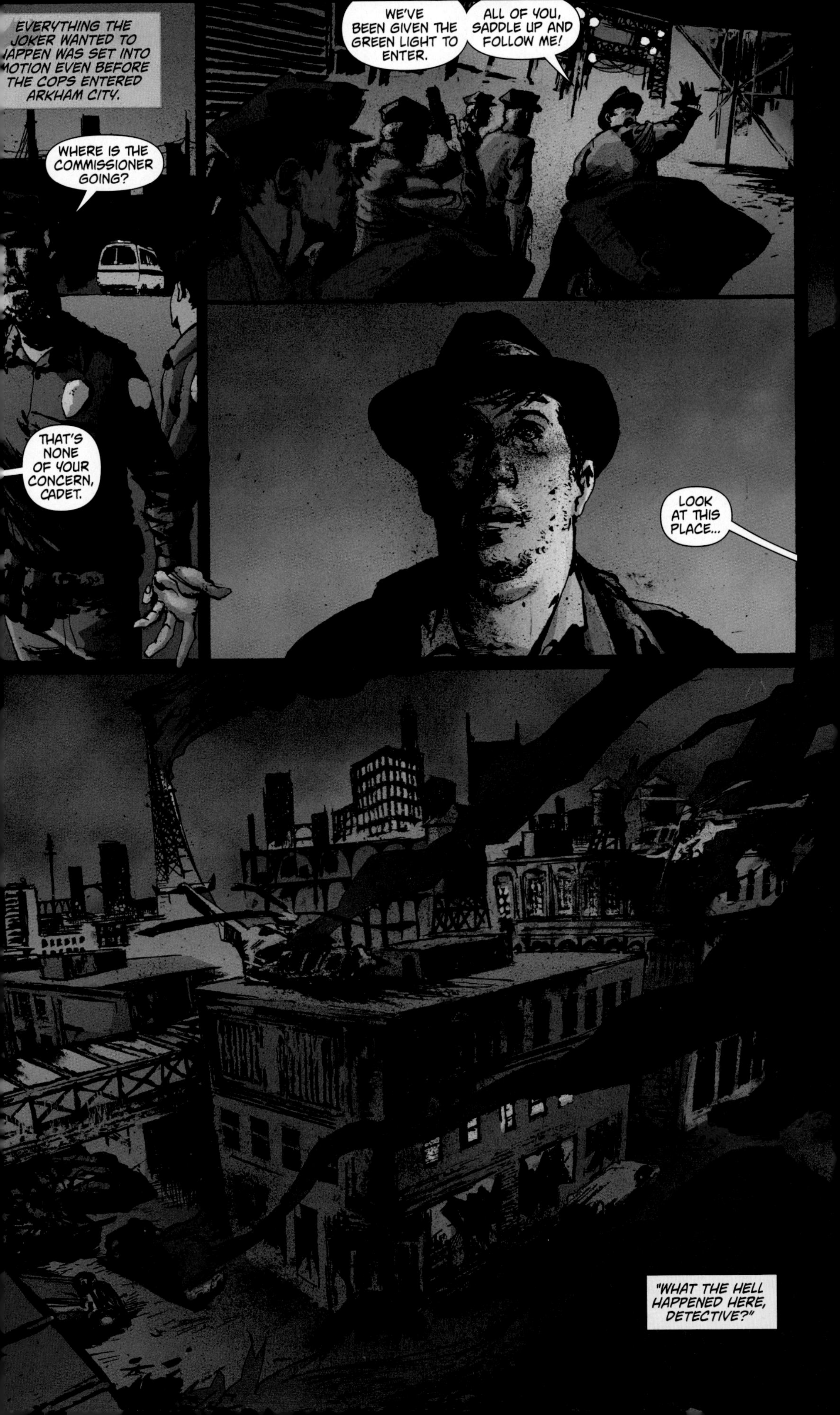

EVERYTHING THE JOKER WANTED TO HAPPEN WAS SET INTO MOTION EVEN BEFORE THE COPS ENTERED ARKHAM CITY.
WE'VE BEEN GIVEN THE GREEN LIGHT TO ENTER.
ALL OF YOU, SADDLE UP AND FOLLOW ME!
WHERE IS THE COMMISSIONER GOING?
THAT'S NONE OF YOUR CONCERN, CADET.
LOOK AT THIS PLACE...
"WHAT THE HELL HAPPENED HERE, DETECTIVE?"

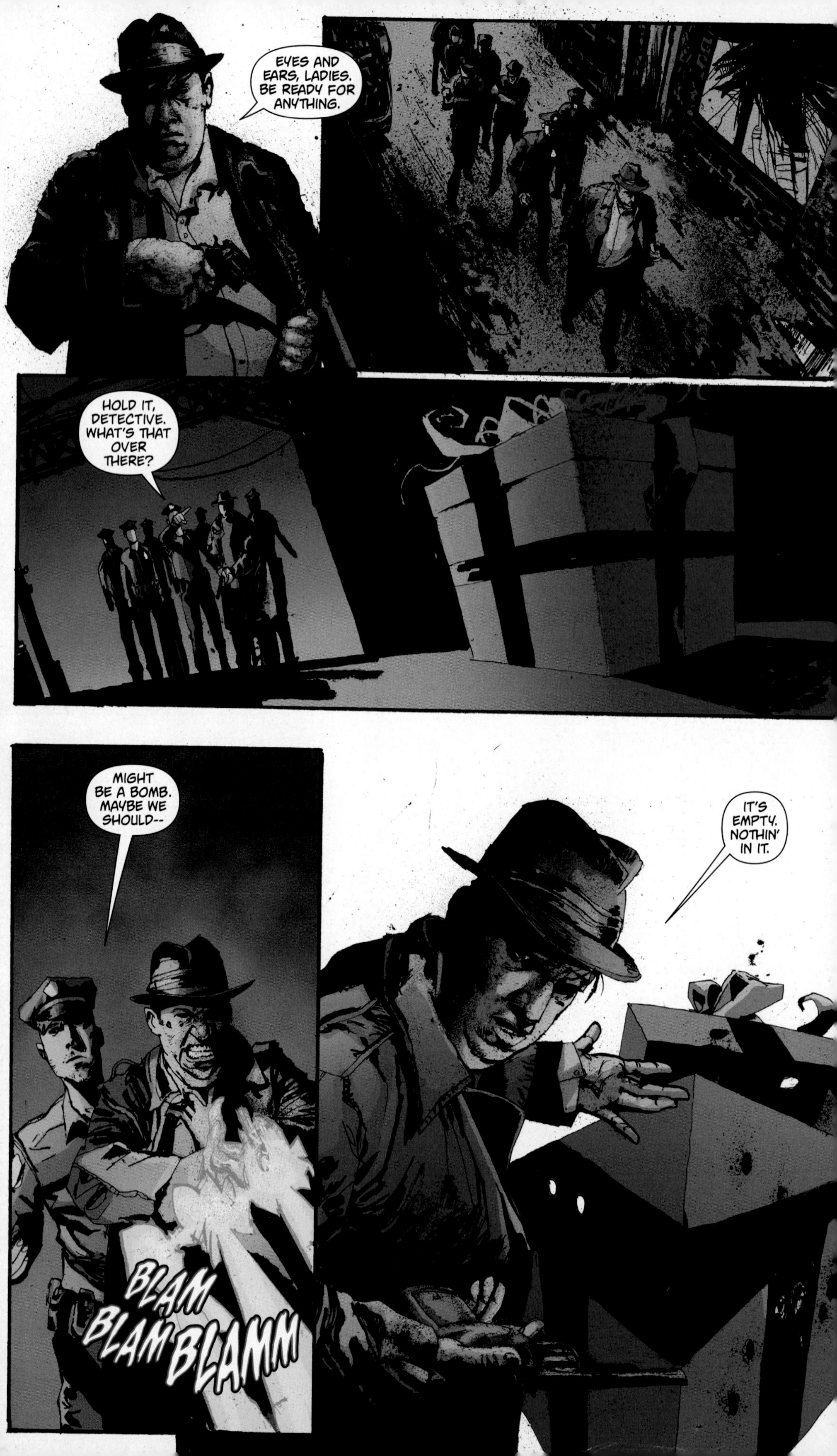
EYES AND EARS, LADIES. BE READY FOR ANYTHING.
HOLD IT, DETECTIVE. WHAT'S THAT OVER THERE?
MIGHT BE A BOMB. MAYBE WE SHOULD--
IT'S EMPTY. NOTHIN' IN IT.
BLAM BLAM BLAMM

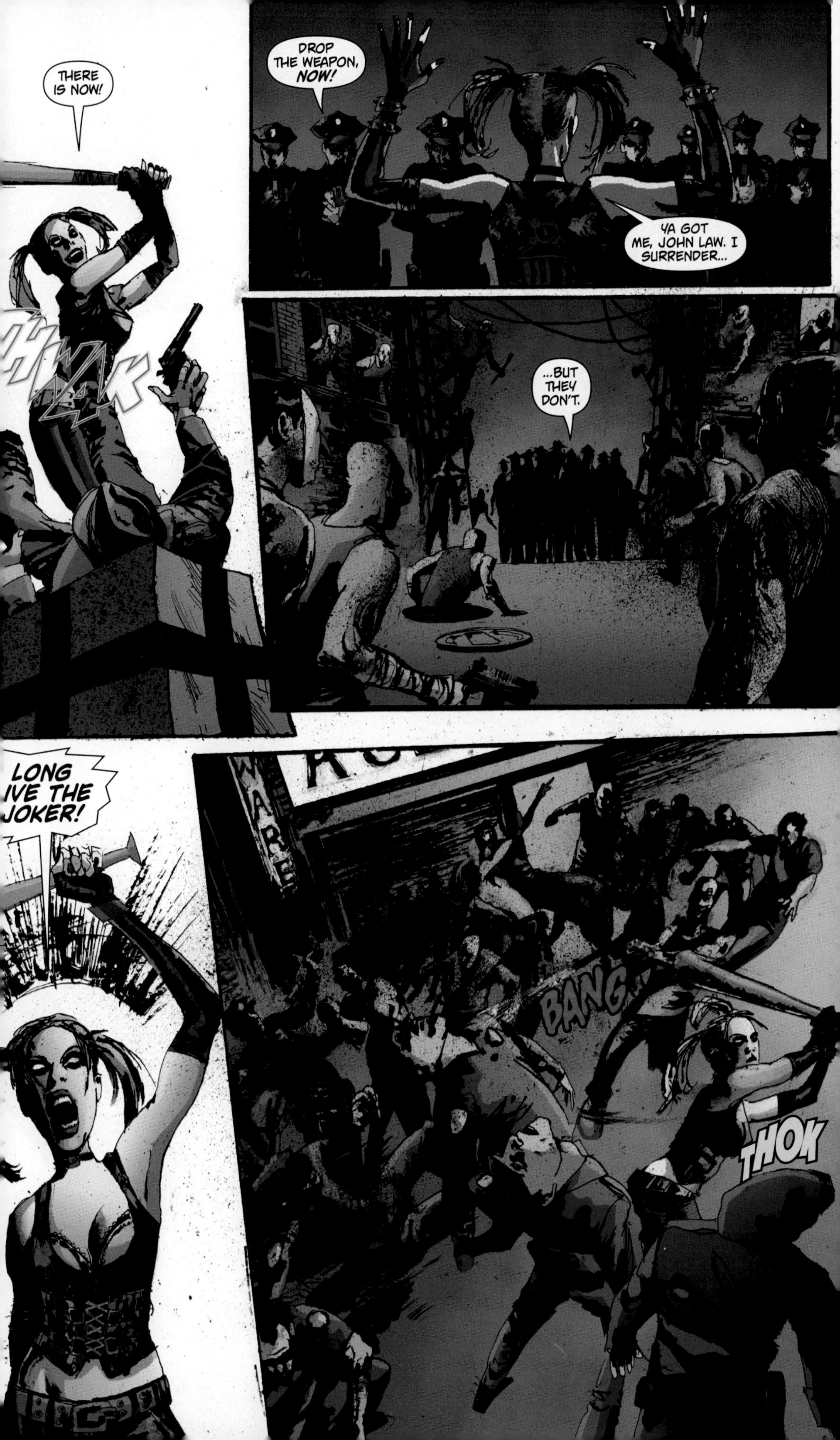
DROP THE WEAPON, NOW!
THERE IS NOW!
THWAK
YA GOT ME, JOHN LAW. I SURRENDER...
...BUT THEY DON'T.
LONG LIVE THE JOKER!
BANG
THOK

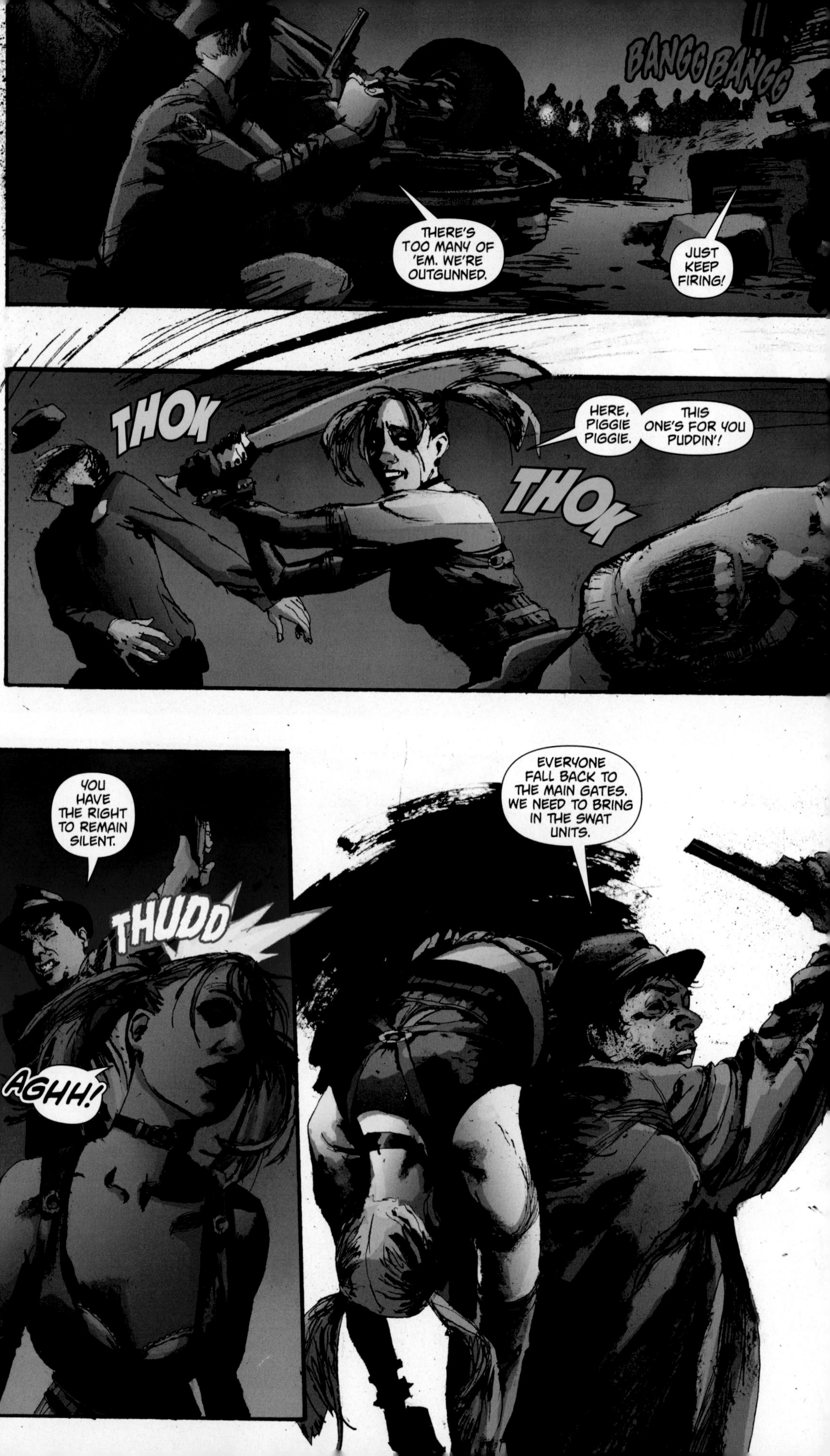
BANGG BANGG
THERE'S TOO MANY OF 'EM. WE'RE OUTGUNNED.
JUST KEEP FIRING!
THOK
HERE, PIGGIE PIGGIE.
THIS ONE'S FOR YOU PUDDIN'!
THOK
YOU HAVE THE RIGHT TO REMAIN SILENT.
THUDD
AGHH!
EVERYONE FALL BACK TO THE MAIN GATES. WE NEED TO BRING IN THE SWAT UNITS.

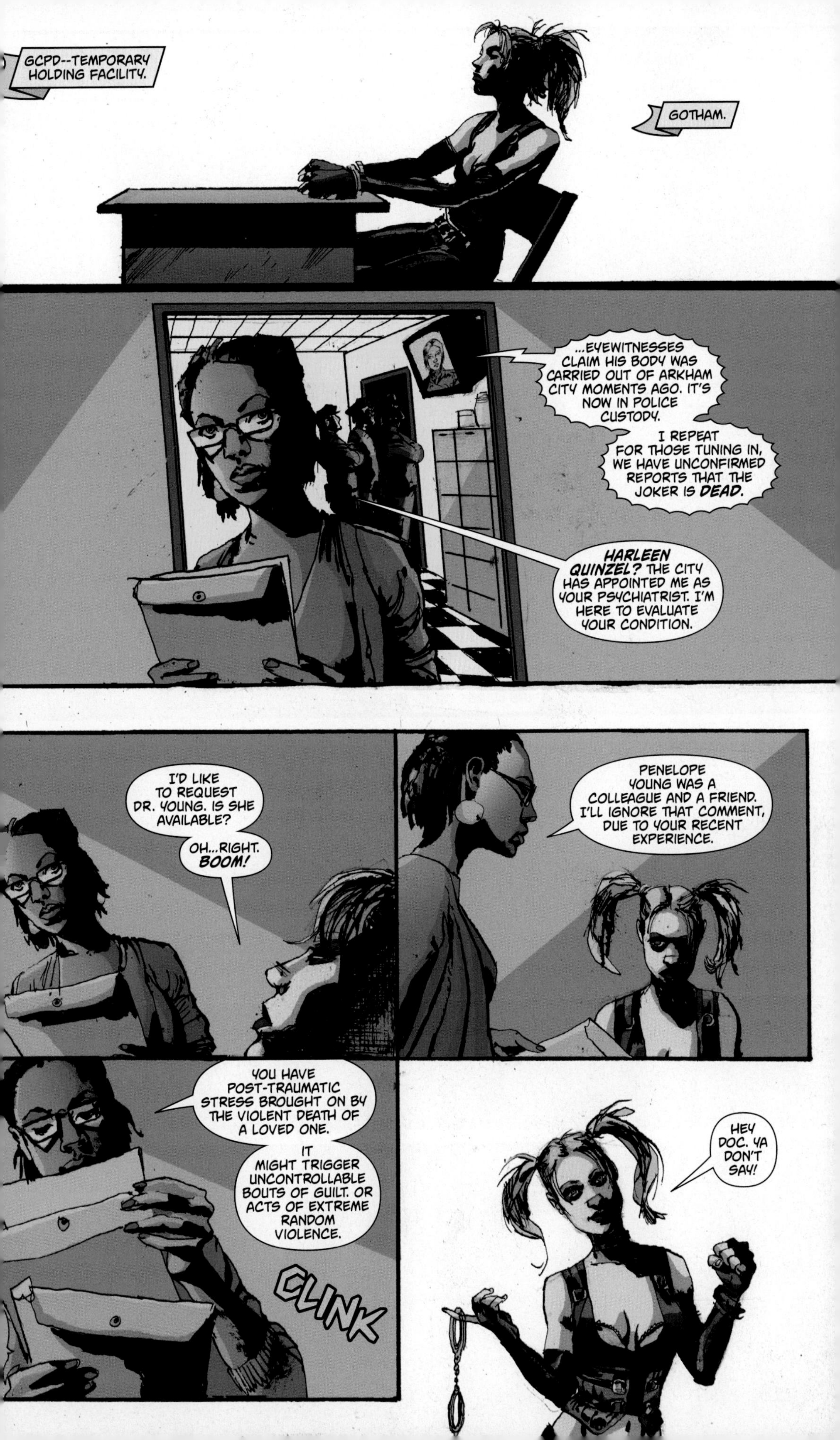
GCPD--TEMPORARY HOLDING FACILITY.
GOTHAM.
...EYEWITNESSES CLAIM HIS BODY WAS CARRIED OUT OF ARKHAM CITY MOMENTS AGO. IT'S NOW IN POLICE CUSTODY.
I REPEAT FOR THOSE TUNING IN, WE HAVE UNCONFIRMED REPORTS THAT THE JOKER IS DEAD.
HARLEEN QUINZEL? THE CITY HAS APPOINTED ME AS YOUR PSYCHIATRIST. I'M HERE TO EVALUATE YOUR CONDITION.
I'D LIKE TO REQUEST DR. YOUNG. IS SHE AVAILABLE?
OH...RIGHT. BOOM!
PENELOPE YOUNG WAS A COLLEAGUE AND A FRIEND. I'LL IGNORE THAT COMMENT, DUE TO YOUR RECENT EXPERIENCE.
YOU HAVE POST-TRAUMATIC STRESS BROUGHT ON BY THE VIOLENT DEATH OF A LOVED ONE.
IT MIGHT TRIGGER UNCONTROLLABLE BOUTS OF GUILT. OR ACTS OF EXTREME RANDOM VIOLENCE.
CLINK
HEY DOC. YA DON'T SAY!

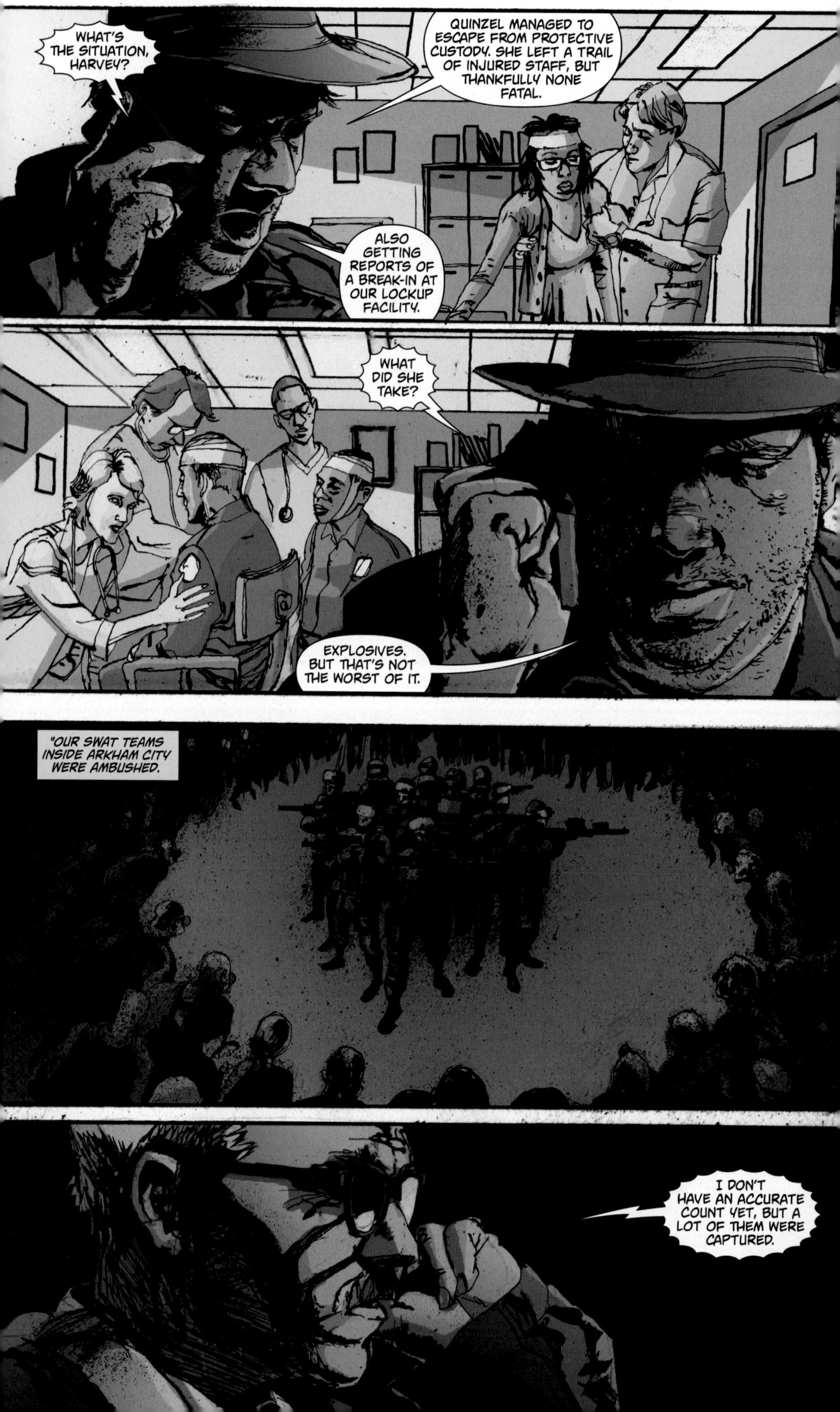
WHAT'S THE SITUATION, HARVEY?
QUINZEL MANAGED TO ESCAPE FROM PROTECTIVE CUSTODY. SHE LEFT A TRAIL OF INJURED STAFF, BUT THANKFULLY NONE FATAL.
ALSO GETTING REPORTS OF A BREAK-IN AT OUR LOCKUP FACILITY.
WHAT DID SHE TAKE?
EXPLOSIVES. BUT THAT'S NOT THE WORST OF IT.
"OUR SWAT TEAMS INSIDE ARKHAM CITY WERE AMBUSHED.
I DON'T HAVE AN ACCURATE COUNT YET, BUT A LOT OF THEM WERE CAPTURED.

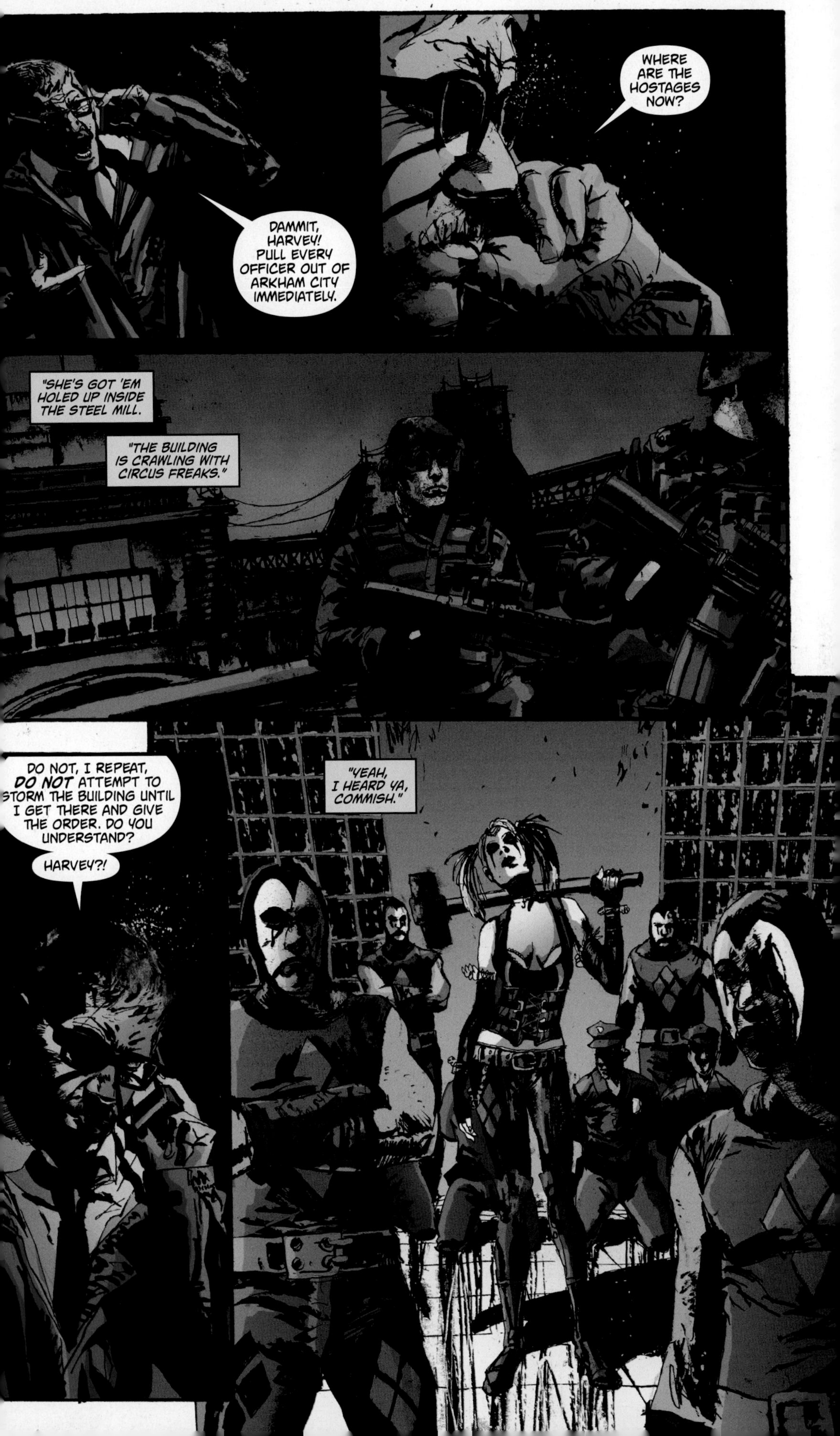
WHERE ARE THE HOSTAGES NOW?
DAMMIT, HARVEY! PULL EVERY OFFICER OUT OF ARKHAM CITY IMMEDIATELY.
"SHE'S GOT 'EM HOLED UP INSIDE THE STEEL MILL.
"THE BUILDING IS CRAWLING WITH CIRCUS FREAKS."
DO NOT, I REPEAT, DO NOT ATTEMPT TO STORM THE BUILDING UNTIL I GET THERE AND GIVE THE ORDER. DO YOU UNDERSTAND?
HARVEY?!
"YEAH, I HEARD YA, COMMISH."

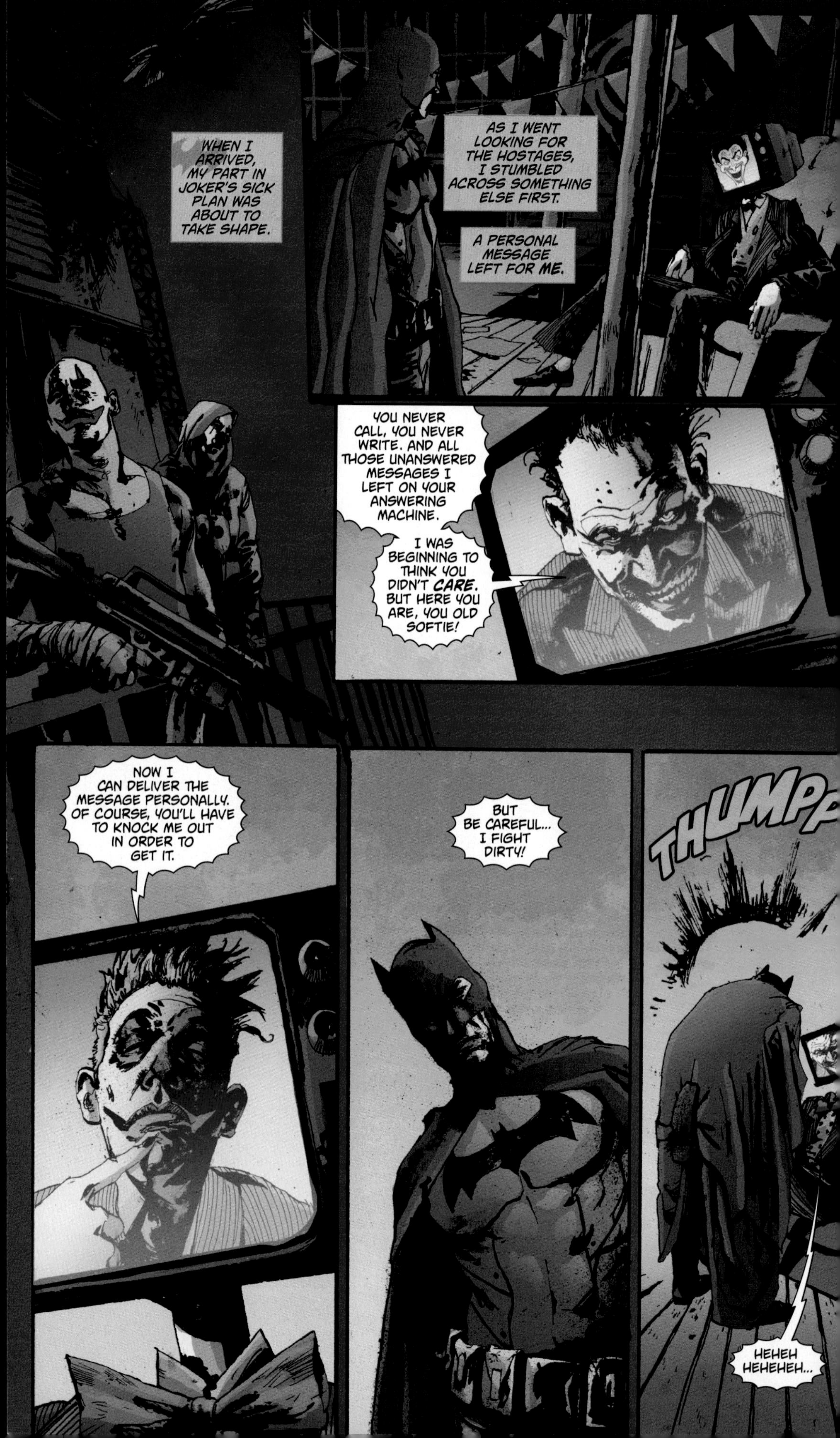
WHEN I ARRIVED, MY PART IN JOKER'S SICK PLAN WAS ABOUT TO TAKE SHAPE.
AS I WENT LOOKING FOR THE HOSTAGES, I STUMBLED ACROSS SOMETHING ELSE FIRST.
A PERSONAL MESSAGE LEFT FOR ME.
YOU NEVER CALL, YOU NEVER WRITE. AND ALL THOSE UNANSWERED MESSAGES I LEFT ON YOUR ANSWERING MACHINE.
I WAS BEGINNING TO THINK YOU DIDN'T CARE. BUT HERE YOU ARE, YOU OLD SOFTIE!
NOW I CAN DELIVER THE MESSAGE PERSONALLY. OF COURSE, YOU'LL HAVE TO KNOCK ME OUT IN ORDER TO GET IT.
BUT BE CAREFUL... I FIGHT DIRTY!
THUMP
HEHEH HEHEHEH...

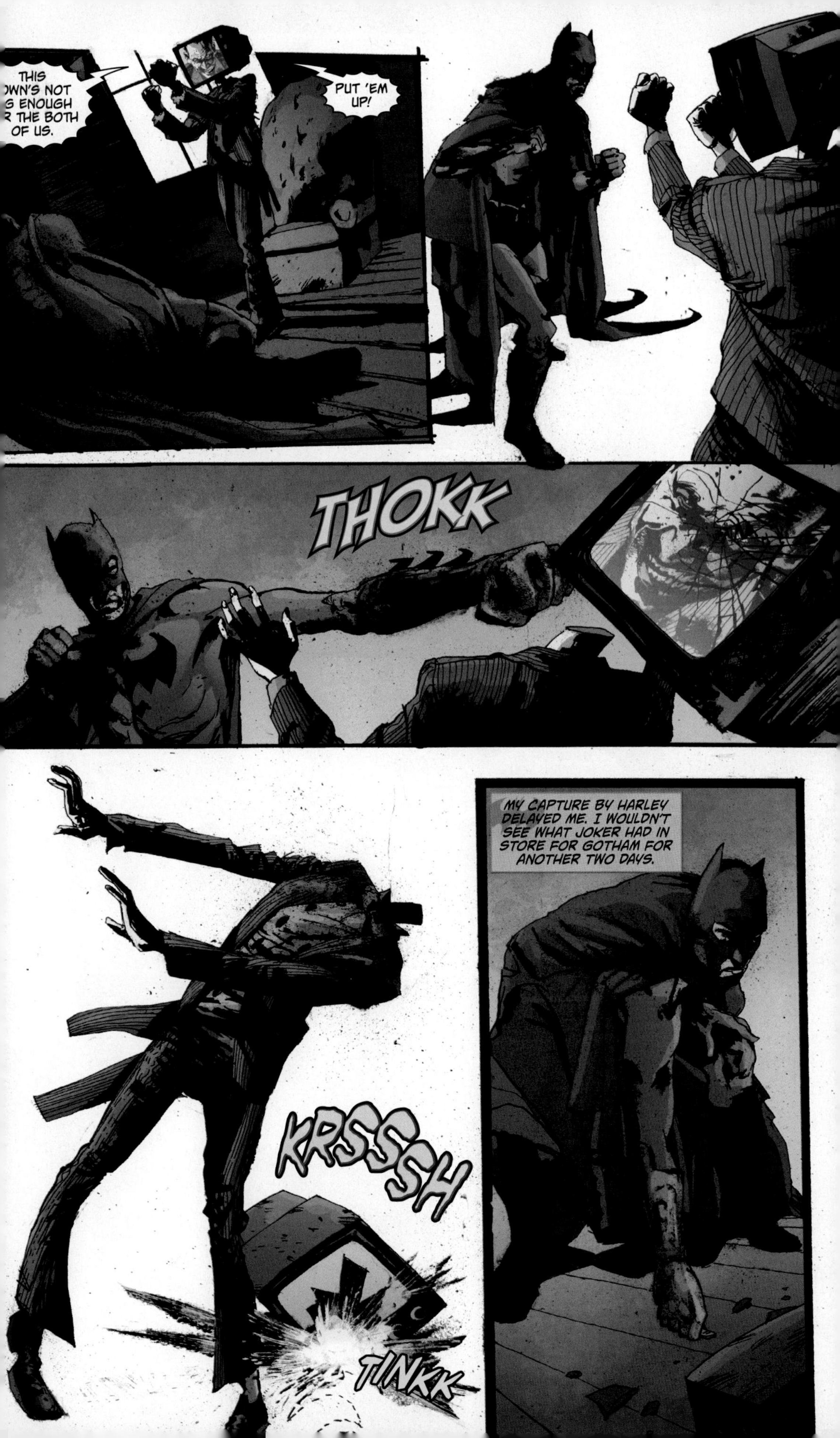
THIS
OWN'S NOT
G ENOUGH
R THE BOTH
OF US.
PUT 'EM UP!
THOKK
KRSSSH
TINKK
MY CAPTURE BY HARLEY DELAYED ME. I WOULDN'T SEE WHAT JOKER HAD IN STORE FOR GOTHAM FOR ANOTHER TWO DAYS.

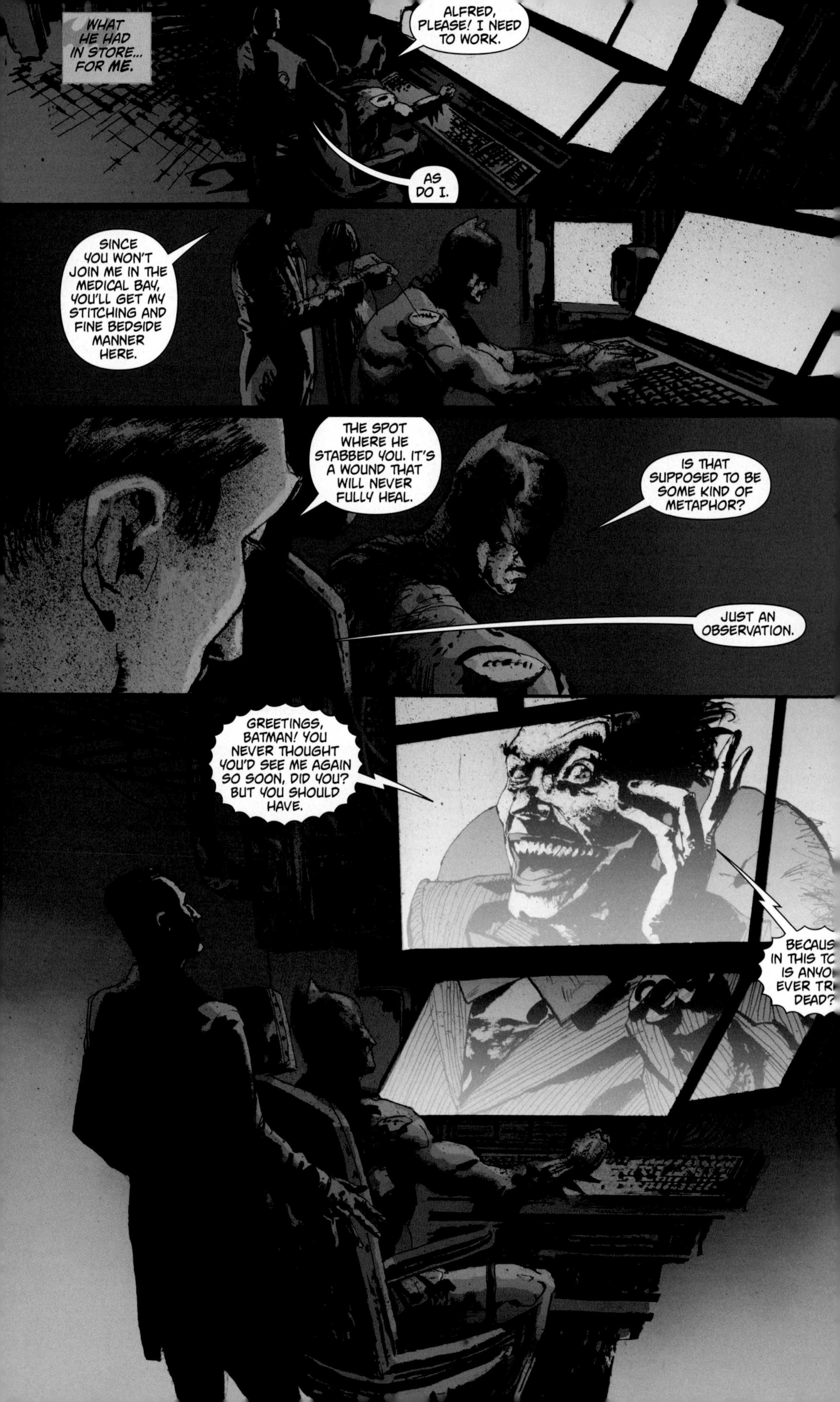
WHAT HE HAD IN STORE... FOR ME.
ALFRED, PLEASE! I NEED TO WORK.
AS DO I.
SINCE YOU WON'T JOIN ME IN THE MEDICAL BAY, YOU'LL GET MY STITCHING AND FINE BEDSIDE MANNER HERE.
THE SPOT WHERE HE STABBED YOU. IT'S A WOUND THAT WILL NEVER FULLY HEAL.
IS THAT SUPPOSED TO BE SOME KIND OF METAPHOR?
JUST AN OBSERVATION.
GREETINGS, BATMAN! YOU NEVER THOUGHT YOU'D SEE ME AGAIN SO SOON, DID YOU? BUT YOU SHOULD HAVE.

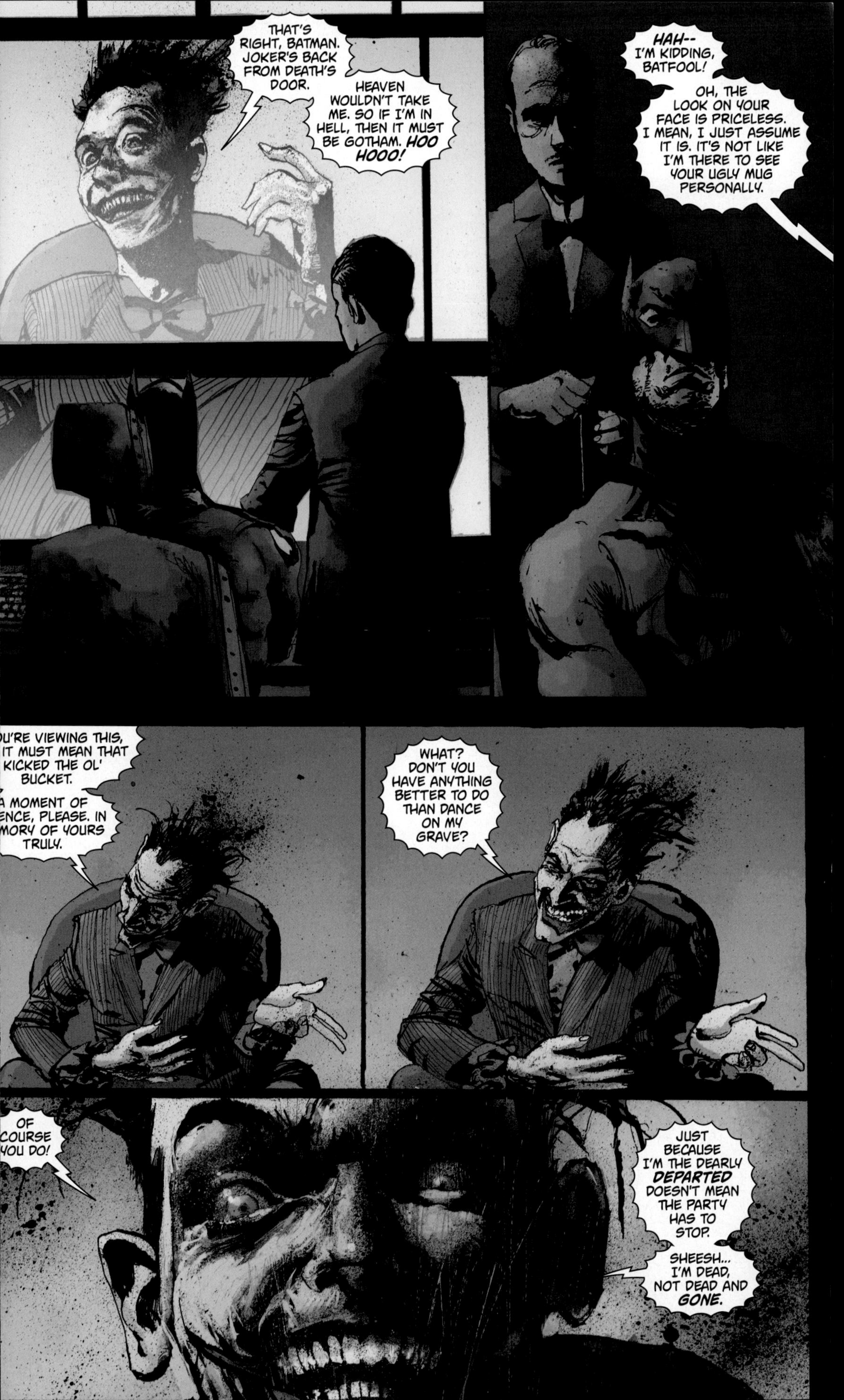
THAT'S RIGHT, BATMAN. JOKER'S BACK FROM DEATH'S DOOR.
HEAVEN WOULDN'T TAKE ME. SO IF I'M IN HELL, THEN IT MUST BE GOTHAM. **HOO HOOO!**
HAH-- I'M KIDDING, BATFOOL!
OH, THE LOOK ON YOUR FACE IS PRICELESS. I MEAN, I JUST ASSUME IT IS. IT'S NOT LIKE I'M THERE TO SEE YOUR UGLY MUG PERSONALLY.
OU'RE VIEWING THIS, IT MUST MEAN THAT KICKED THE OL' BUCKET.
A MOMENT OF ENCE, PLEASE. IN MORY OF YOURS TRULY.
WHAT? DON'T YOU HAVE ANYTHING BETTER TO DO THAN DANCE ON MY GRAVE?
OF COURSE YOU DO!
JUST BECAUSE I'M THE DEARLY **DEPARTED** DOESN'T MEAN THE PARTY HAS TO STOP.
SHEESH... I'M DEAD, NOT DEAD AND **GONE.**

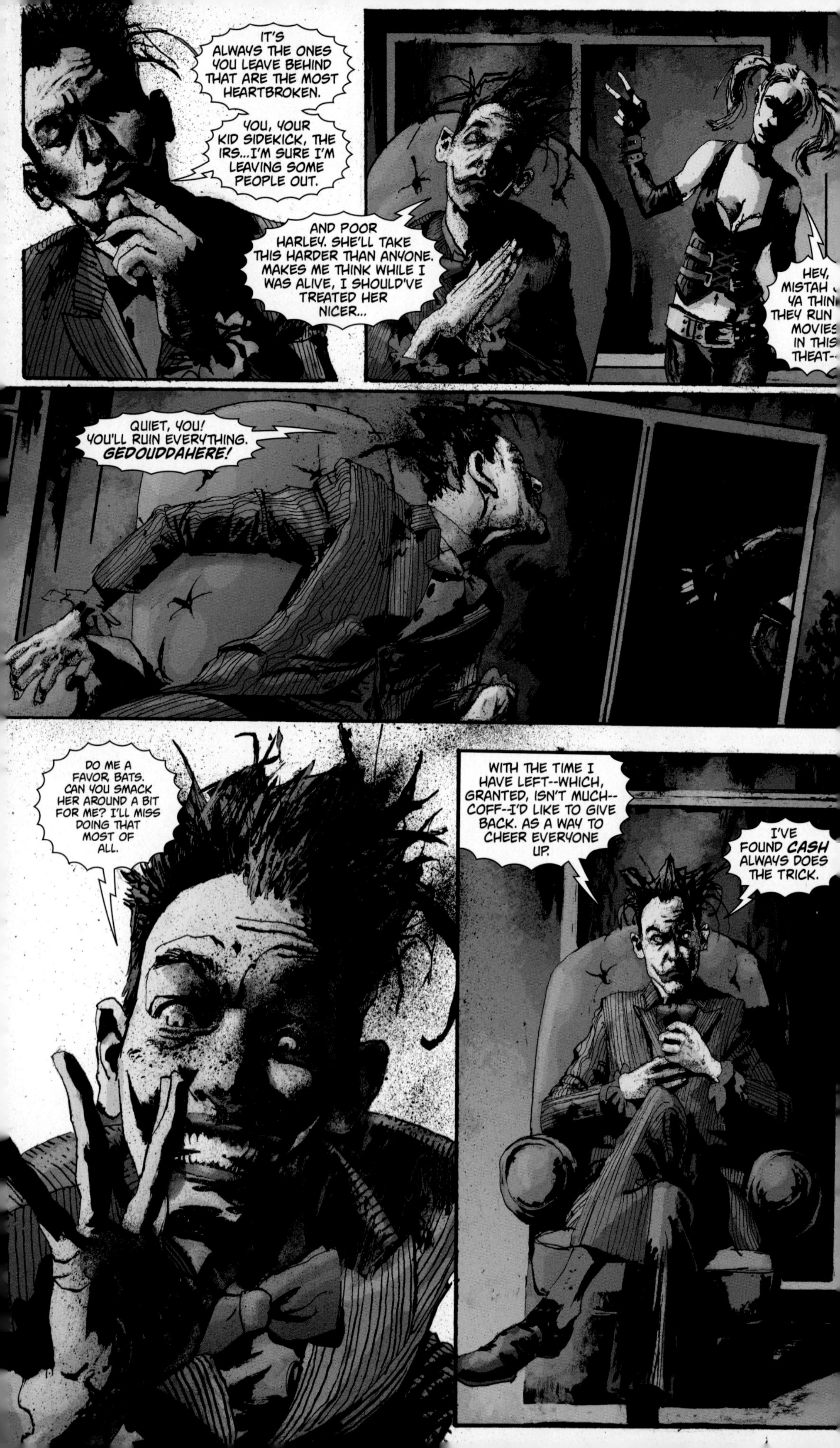
IT'S ALWAYS THE ONES YOU LEAVE BEHIND THAT ARE THE MOST HEARTBROKEN.
YOU, YOUR KID SIDEKICK, THE IRS...I'M SURE I'M LEAVING SOME PEOPLE OUT.
AND POOR HARLEY. SHE'LL TAKE THIS HARDER THAN ANYONE. MAKES ME THINK WHILE I WAS ALIVE, I SHOULD'VE TREATED HER NICER...
HEY, MISTAH J, YA THINK THEY RUN MOVIES IN THIS THEAT--
QUIET, YOU! YOU'LL RUIN EVERYTHING. GEDOUDDAHERE!
DO ME A FAVOR, BATS. CAN YOU SMACK HER AROUND A BIT FOR ME? I'LL MISS DOING THAT MOST OF ALL.
WITH THE TIME I HAVE LEFT--WHICH, GRANTED, ISN'T MUCH--COFF--I'D LIKE TO GIVE BACK. AS A WAY TO CHEER EVERYONE UP.
I'VE FOUND CASH ALWAYS DOES THE TRICK.

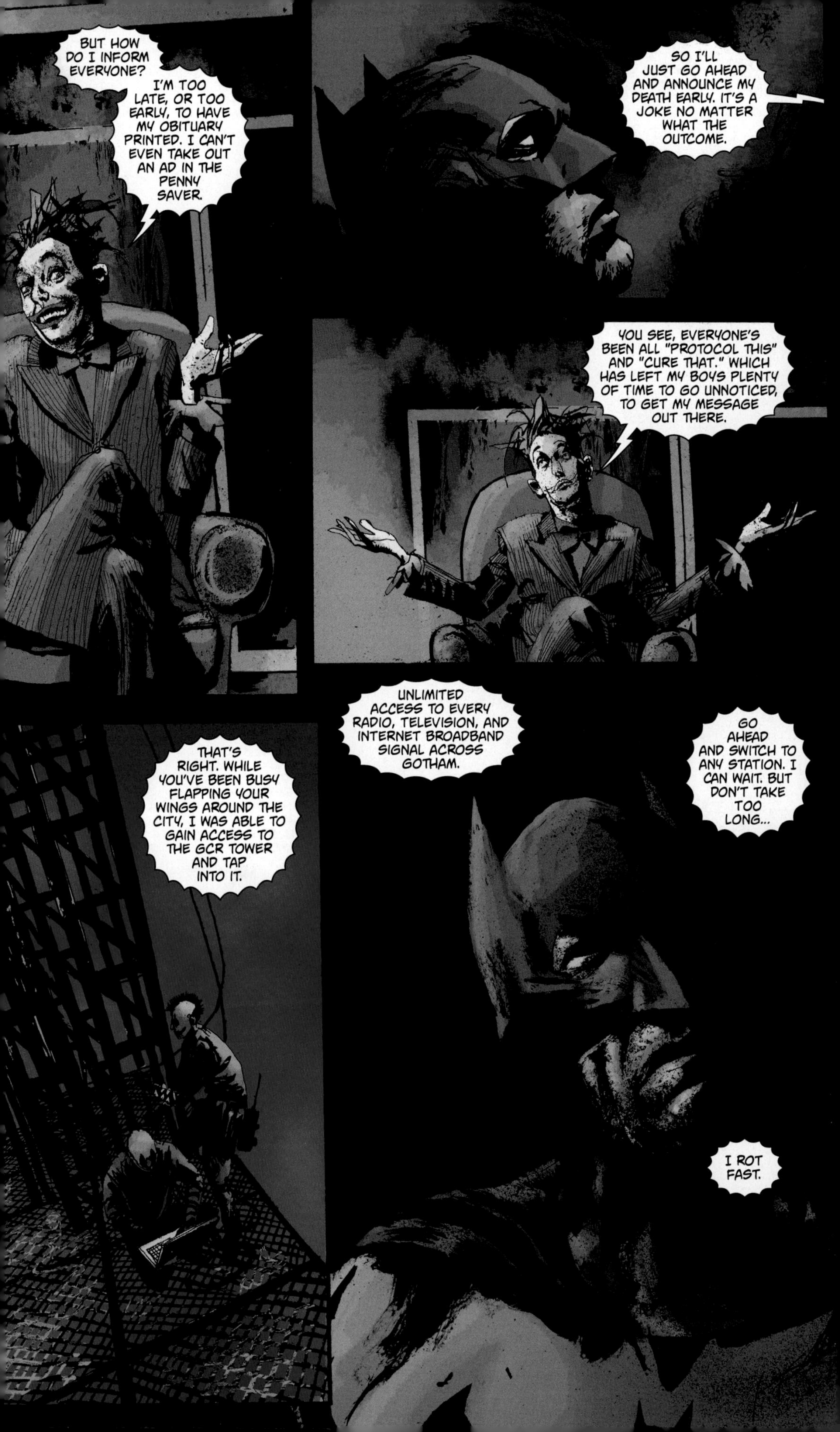
BUT HOW DO I INFORM EVERYONE?
I'M TOO LATE, OR TOO EARLY, TO HAVE MY OBITUARY PRINTED. I CAN'T EVEN TAKE OUT AN AD IN THE PENNY SAVER.
SO I'LL JUST GO AHEAD AND ANNOUNCE MY DEATH EARLY. IT'S A JOKE NO MATTER WHAT THE OUTCOME.
YOU SEE, EVERYONE'S BEEN ALL "PROTOCOL THIS" AND "CURE THAT." WHICH HAS LEFT MY BOYS PLENTY OF TIME TO GO UNNOTICED, TO GET MY MESSAGE OUT THERE.
THAT'S RIGHT. WHILE YOU'VE BEEN BUSY FLAPPING YOUR WINGS AROUND THE CITY, I WAS ABLE TO GAIN ACCESS TO THE GCR TOWER AND TAP INTO IT.
UNLIMITED ACCESS TO EVERY RADIO, TELEVISION, AND INTERNET BROADBAND SIGNAL ACROSS GOTHAM.
GO AHEAD AND SWITCH TO ANY STATION. I CAN WAIT. BUT DON'T TAKE TOO LONG...
I ROT FAST.

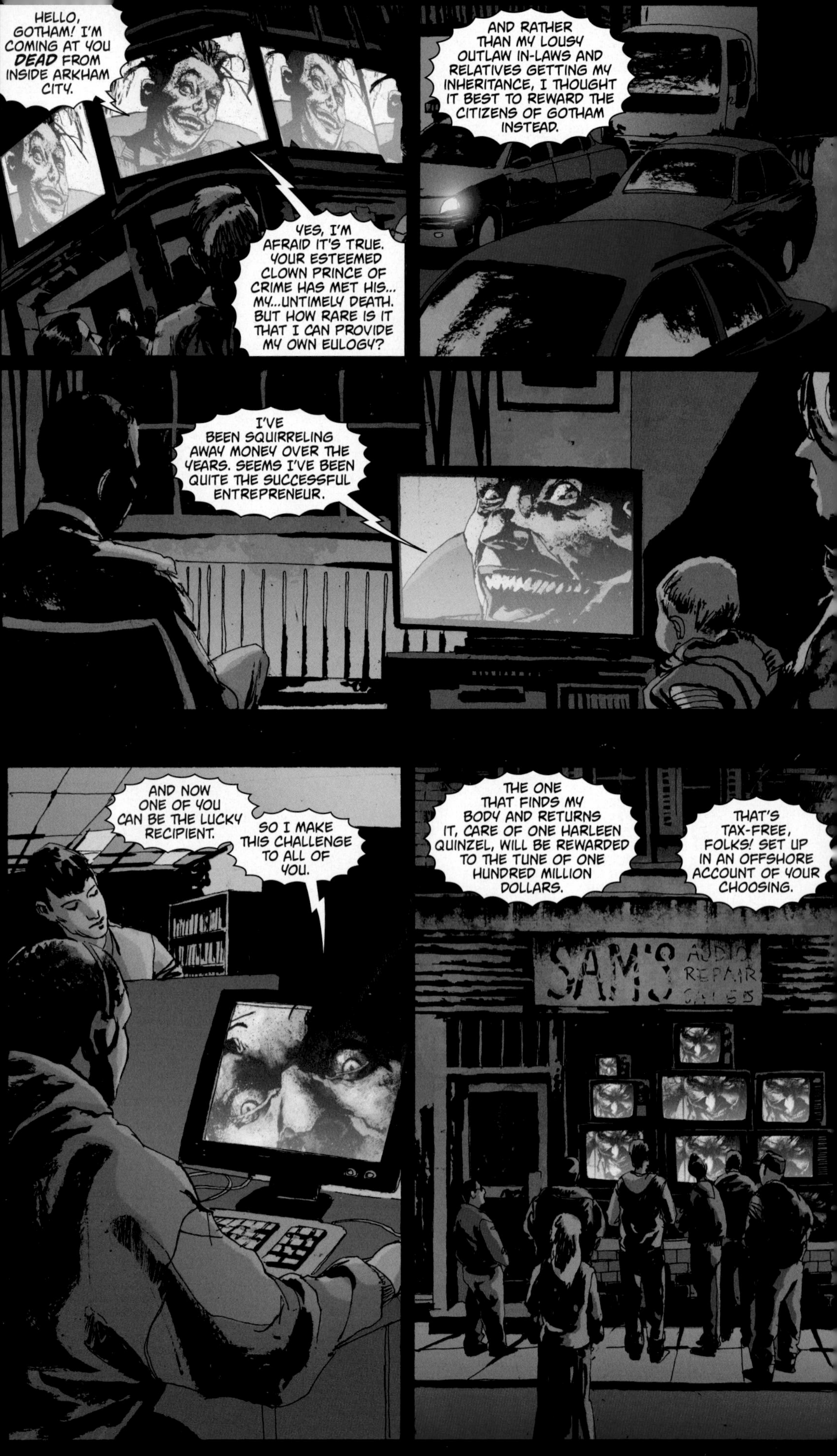
HELLO, GOTHAM! I'M COMING AT YOU **DEAD** FROM INSIDE ARKHAM CITY.
YES, I'M AFRAID IT'S TRUE. YOUR ESTEEMED CLOWN PRINCE OF CRIME HAS MET HIS... MY...UNTIMELY DEATH. BUT HOW RARE IS IT THAT I CAN PROVIDE MY OWN EULOGY?
AND RATHER THAN MY LOUSY OUTLAW IN-LAWS AND RELATIVES GETTING MY INHERITANCE, I THOUGHT IT BEST TO REWARD THE CITIZENS OF GOTHAM INSTEAD.
I'VE BEEN SQUIRRELING AWAY MONEY OVER THE YEARS. SEEMS I'VE BEEN QUITE THE SUCCESSFUL ENTREPRENEUR.
AND NOW ONE OF YOU CAN BE THE LUCKY RECIPIENT.
SO I MAKE THIS CHALLENGE TO ALL OF YOU.
THE ONE THAT FINDS MY BODY AND RETURNS IT, CARE OF ONE HARLEEN QUINZEL, WILL BE REWARDED TO THE TUNE OF ONE HUNDRED MILLION DOLLARS.
THAT'S TAX-FREE, FOLKS! SET UP IN AN OFFSHORE ACCOUNT OF YOUR CHOOSING.
SAM'S

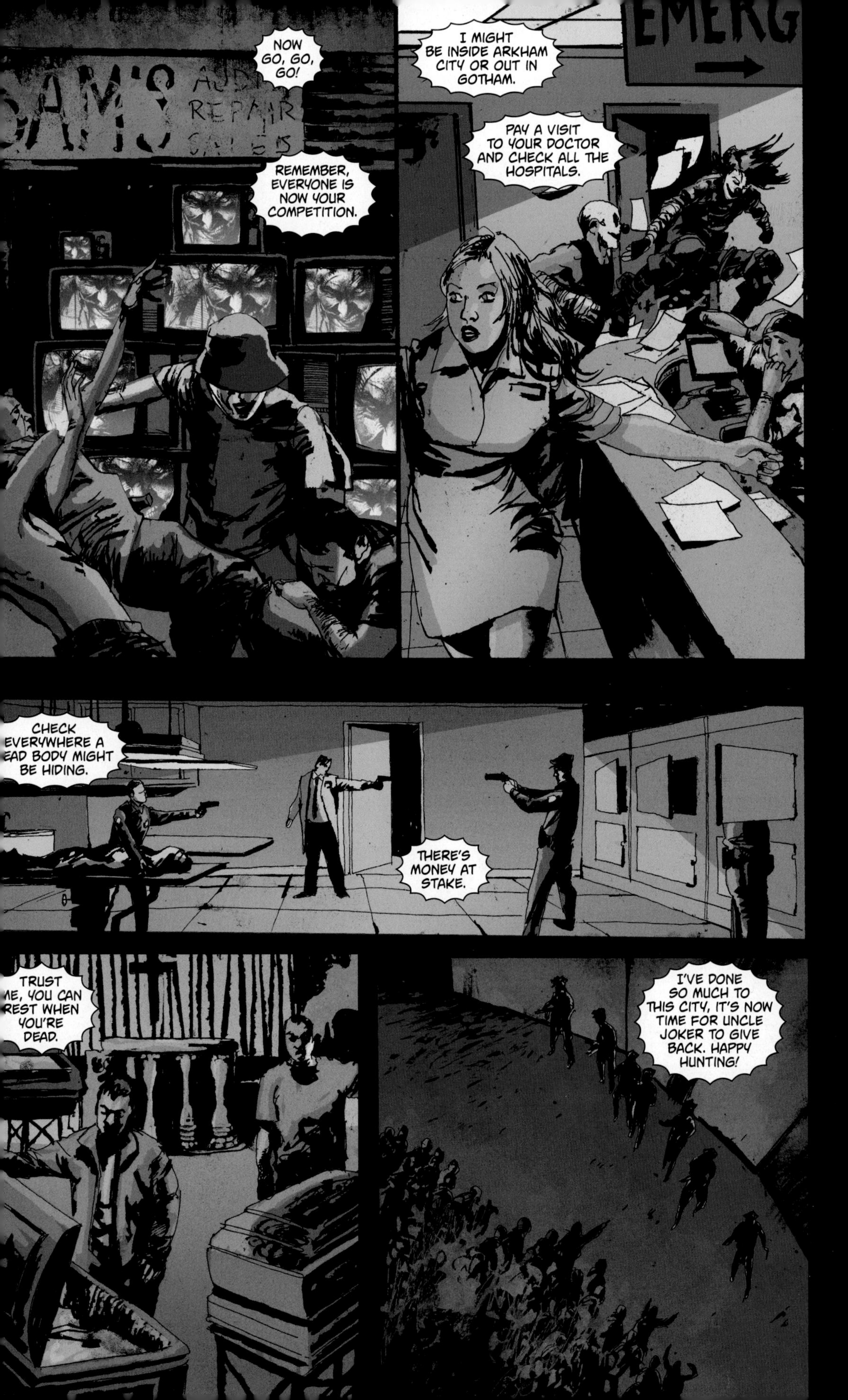

NOW GO, GO, GO!
REMEMBER, EVERYONE IS NOW YOUR COMPETITION.
EMERG
I MIGHT BE INSIDE ARKHAM CITY OR OUT IN GOTHAM.
PAY A VISIT TO YOUR DOCTOR AND CHECK ALL THE HOSPITALS.
CHECK EVERYWHERE A EAD BODY MIGHT BE HIDING.
THERE'S MONEY AT STAKE.
TRUST ME, YOU CAN REST WHEN YOU'RE DEAD.
I'VE DONE SO MUCH TO THIS CITY, IT'S NOW TIME FOR UNCLE JOKER TO GIVE BACK. HAPPY HUNTING!

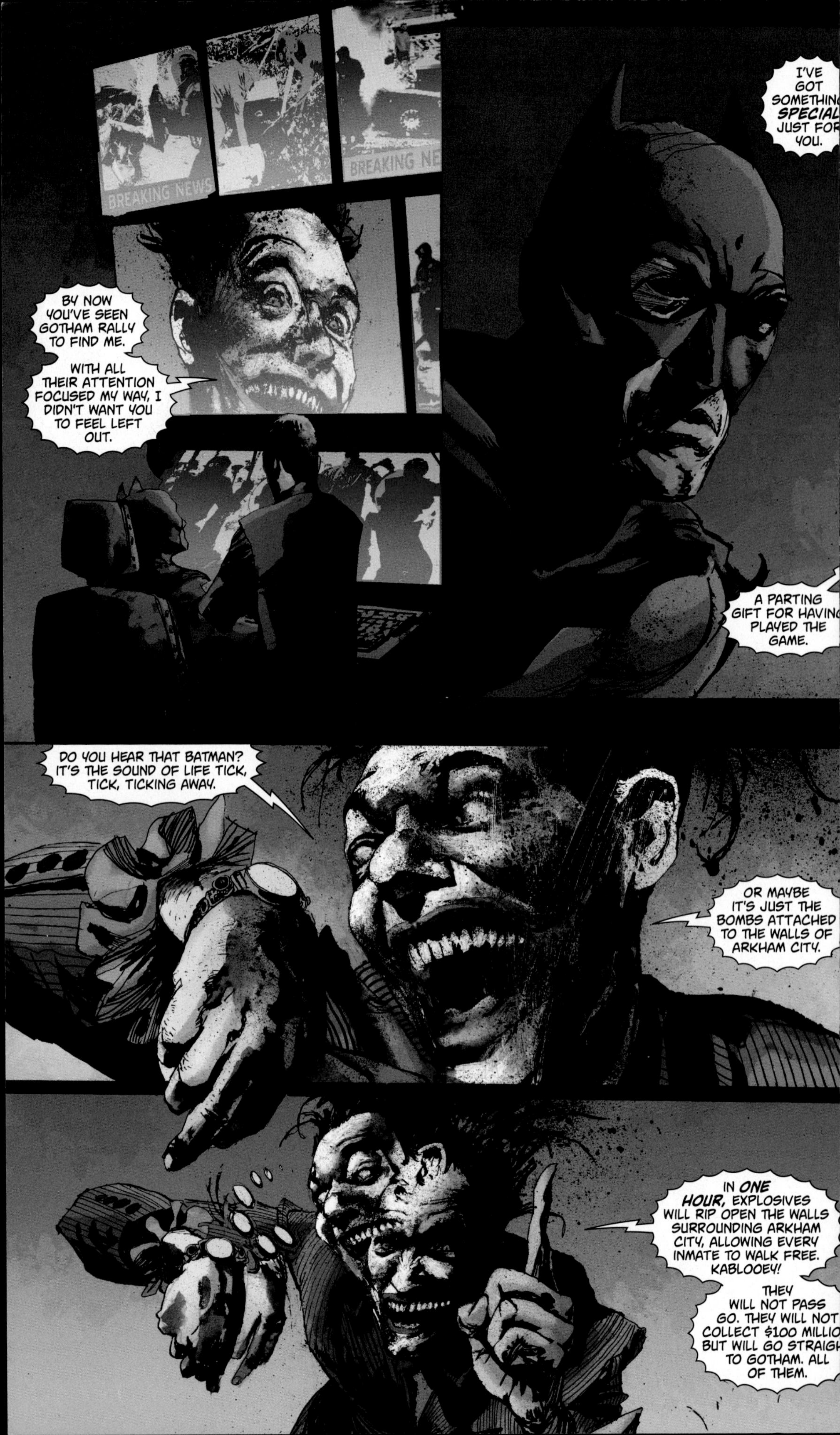
BREAKING NEWS
BREAKING NE
I'VE GOT SOMETHING SPECIAL JUST FOR YOU.
BY NOW YOU'VE SEEN GOTHAM RALLY TO FIND ME.
WITH ALL THEIR ATTENTION FOCUSED MY WAY, I DIDN'T WANT YOU TO FEEL LEFT OUT.
A PARTING GIFT FOR HAVING PLAYED THE GAME.
DO YOU HEAR THAT BATMAN? IT'S THE SOUND OF LIFE TICK, TICK, TICKING AWAY.
OR MAYBE IT'S JUST THE BOMBS ATTACHED TO THE WALLS OF ARKHAM CITY.
IN ONE HOUR, EXPLOSIVES WILL RIP OPEN THE WALLS SURROUNDING ARKHAM CITY, ALLOWING EVERY INMATE TO WALK FREE. KABLOOEY!
THEY WILL NOT PASS GO. THEY WILL NOT COLLECT $100 MILLION BUT WILL GO STRAIGHT TO GOTHAM. ALL OF THEM.

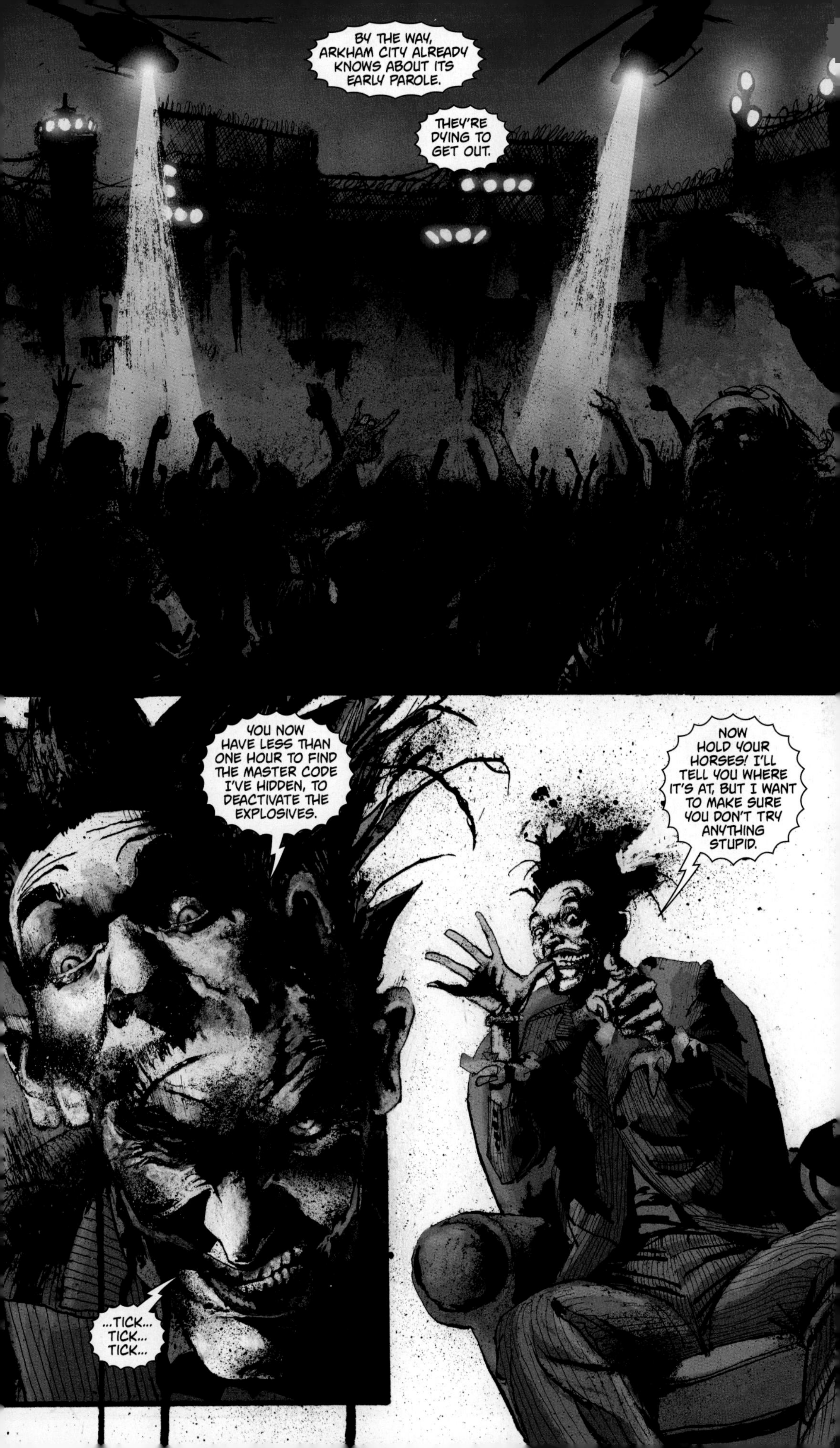
BY THE WAY, ARKHAM CITY ALREADY KNOWS ABOUT ITS EARLY PAROLE.
THEY'RE DYING TO GET OUT.
YOU NOW HAVE LESS THAN ONE HOUR TO FIND THE MASTER CODE I'VE HIDDEN, TO DEACTIVATE THE EXPLOSIVES.
...TICK... TICK... TICK...
NOW HOLD YOUR HORSES! I'LL TELL YOU WHERE IT'S AT, BUT I WANT TO MAKE SURE YOU DON'T TRY ANYTHING STUPID.

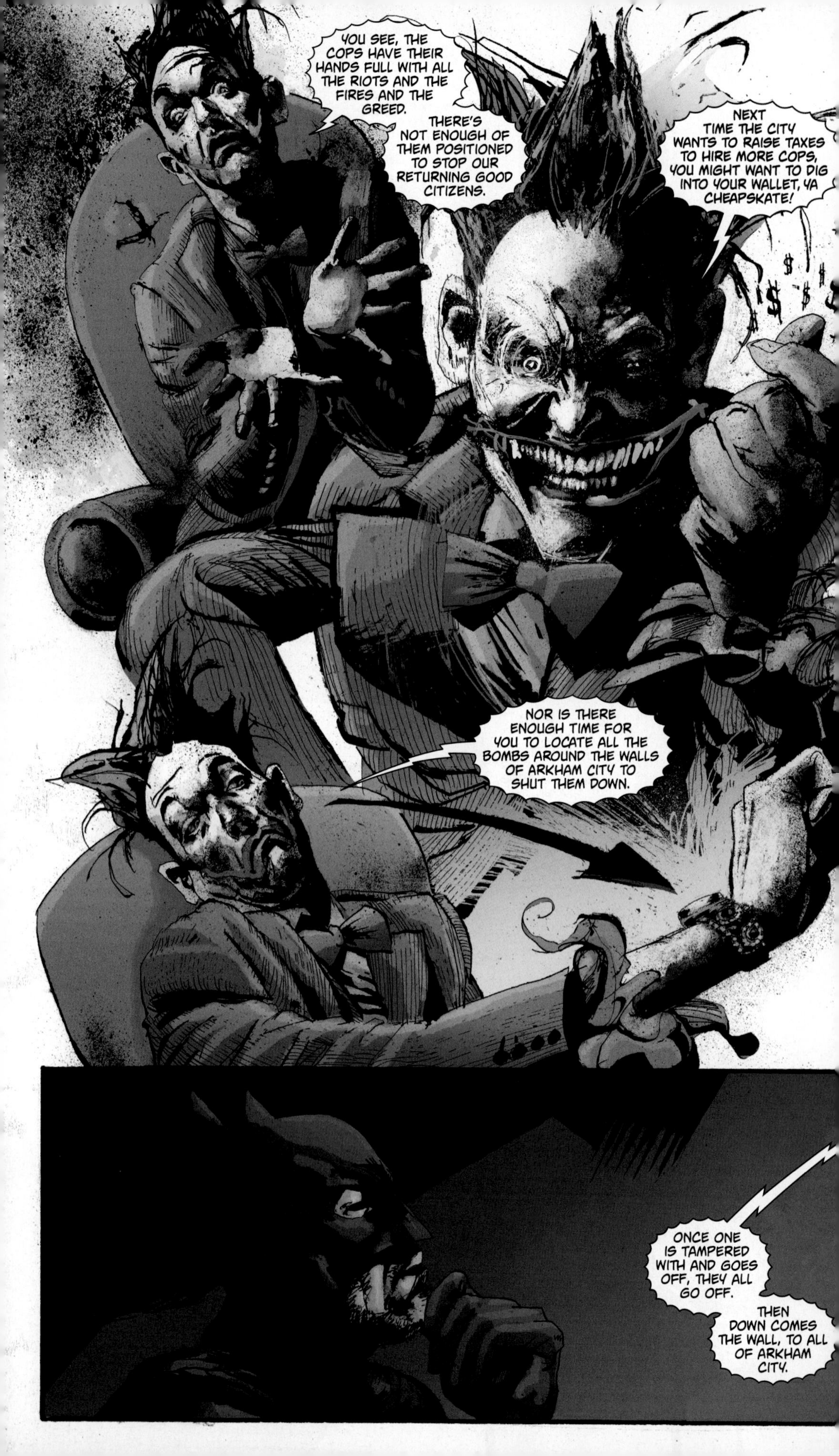
YOU SEE, THE COPS HAVE THEIR HANDS FULL WITH ALL THE RIOTS AND THE FIRES AND THE GREED.
THERE'S NOT ENOUGH OF THEM POSITIONED TO STOP OUR RETURNING GOOD CITIZENS.
NEXT TIME THE CITY WANTS TO RAISE TAXES TO HIRE MORE COPS, YOU MIGHT WANT TO DIG INTO YOUR WALLET, YA CHEAPSKATE!
NOR IS THERE ENOUGH TIME FOR YOU TO LOCATE ALL THE BOMBS AROUND THE WALLS OF ARKHAM CITY TO SHUT THEM DOWN.
ONCE ONE IS TAMPERED WITH AND GOES OFF, THEY ALL GO OFF.
THEN DOWN COMES THE WALL, TO ALL OF ARKHAM CITY.

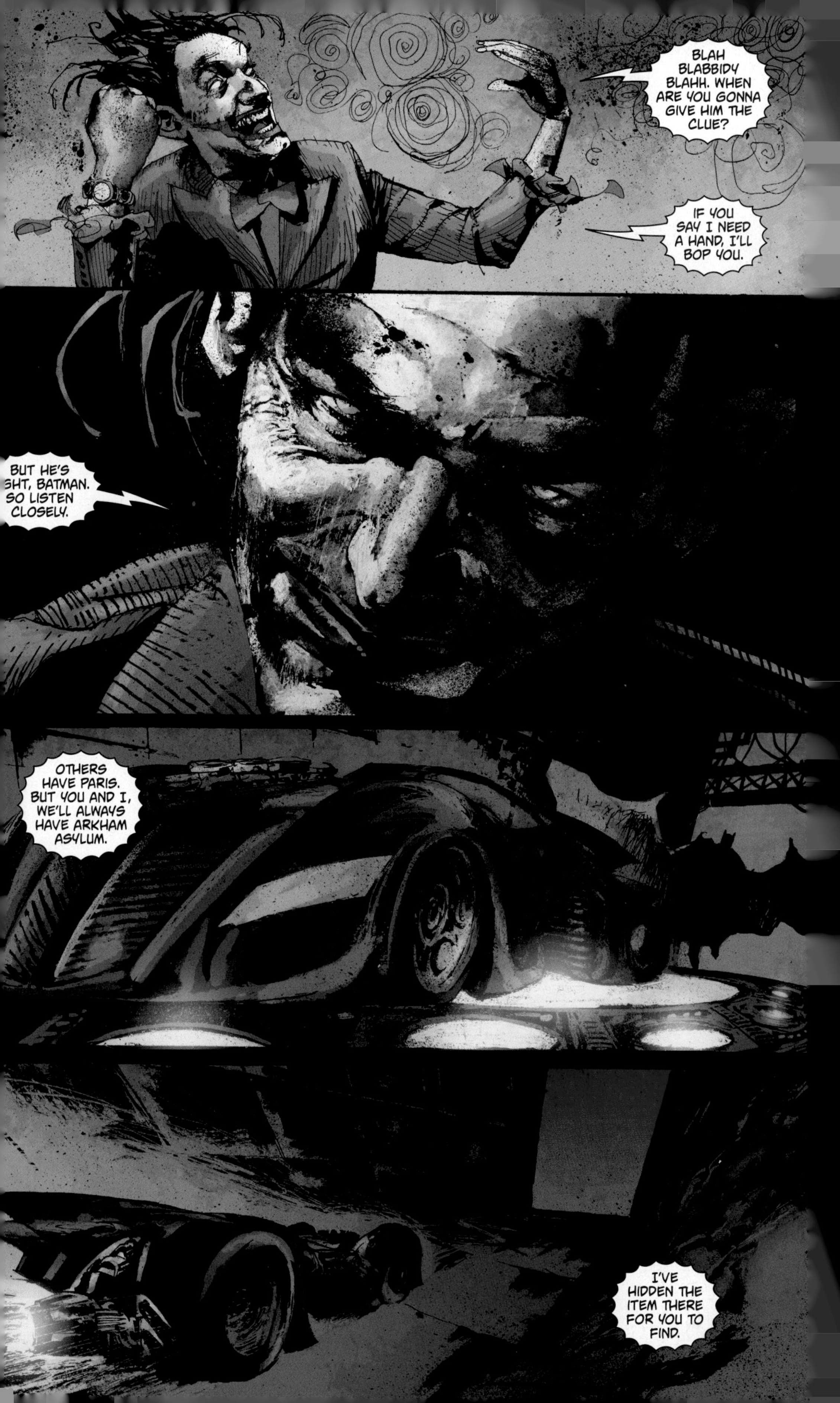
BLAH BLABBIDY BLAHH. WHEN ARE YOU GONNA GIVE HIM THE CLUE?
IF YOU SAY I NEED A HAND, I'LL BOP YOU.
BUT HE'S GHT, BATMAN. SO LISTEN CLOSELY.
OTHERS HAVE PARIS. BUT YOU AND I, WE'LL ALWAYS HAVE ARKHAM ASYLUM.
I'VE HIDDEN THE ITEM THERE FOR YOU TO FIND.

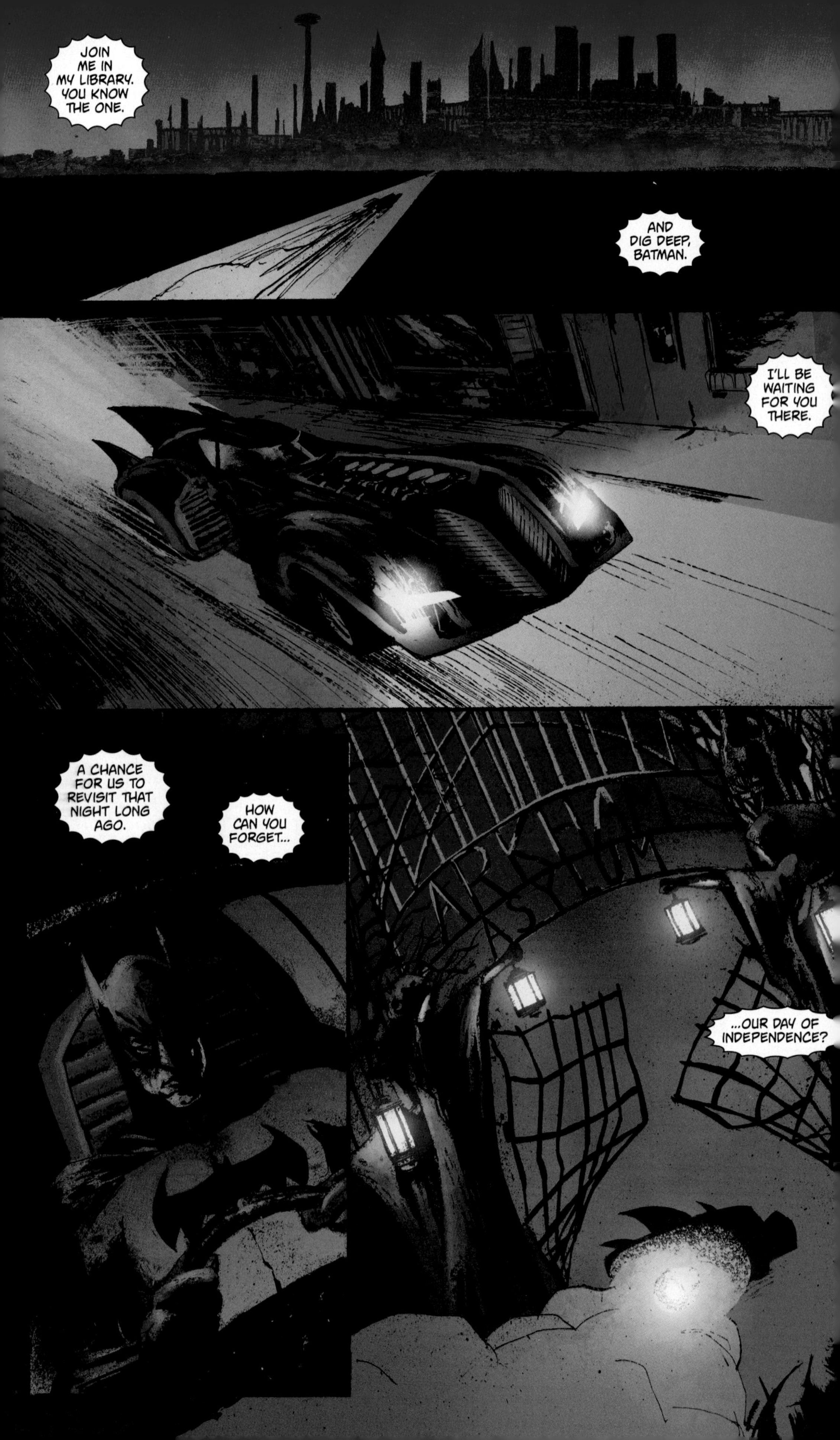
JOIN ME IN MY LIBRARY. YOU KNOW THE ONE.
AND DIG DEEP, BATMAN.
I'LL BE WAITING FOR YOU THERE.
A CHANCE FOR US TO REVISIT THAT NIGHT LONG AGO.
HOW CAN YOU FORGET...
...OUR DAY OF INDEPENDENCE?

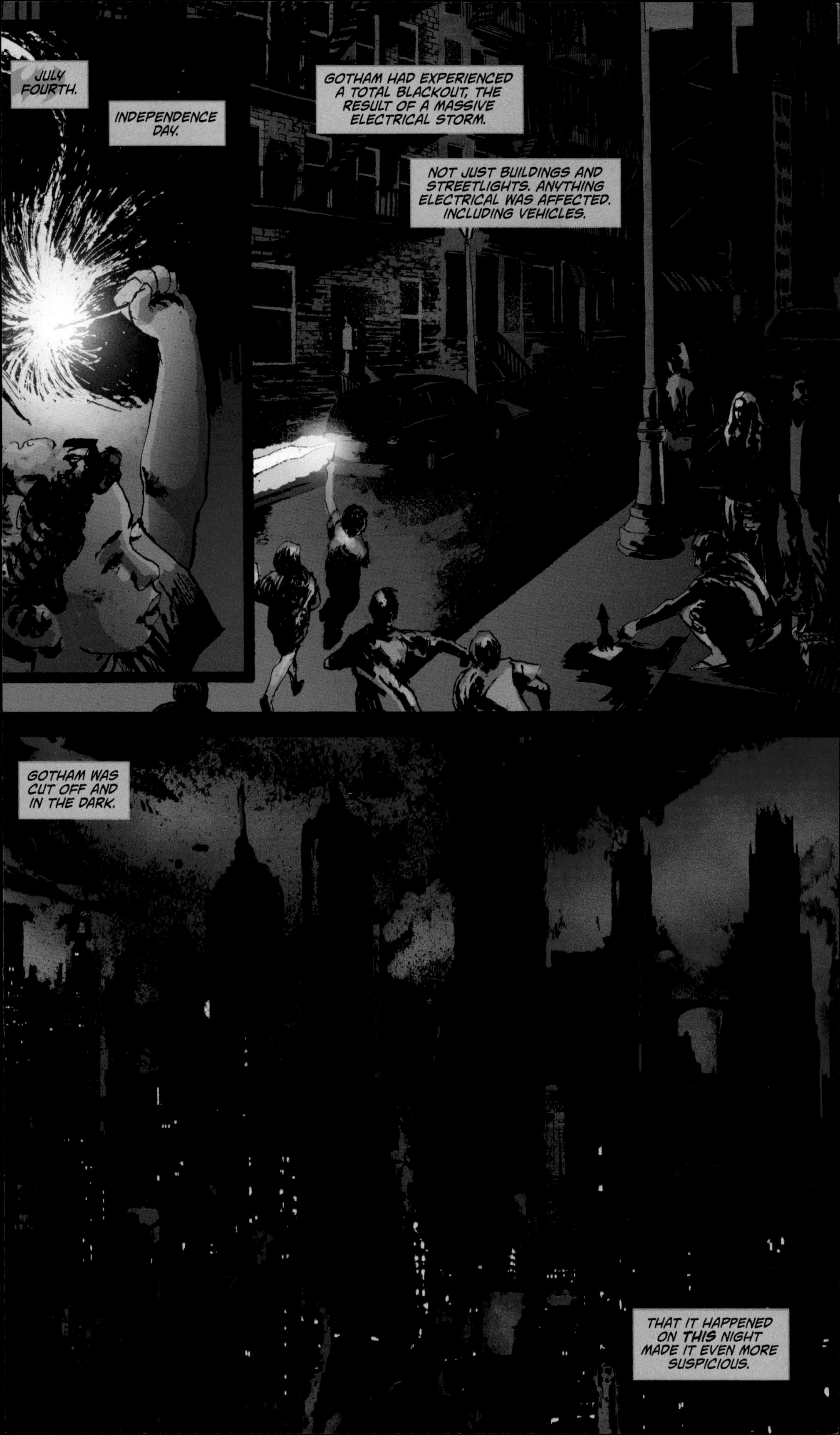
JULY FOURTH.
INDEPENDENCE DAY.
GOTHAM HAD EXPERIENCED A TOTAL BLACKOUT, THE RESULT OF A MASSIVE ELECTRICAL STORM.
NOT JUST BUILDINGS AND STREETLIGHTS. ANYTHING ELECTRICAL WAS AFFECTED. INCLUDING VEHICLES.
GOTHAM WAS CUT OFF AND IN THE DARK.
THAT IT HAPPENED ON **THIS** NIGHT MADE IT EVEN MORE SUSPICIOUS.

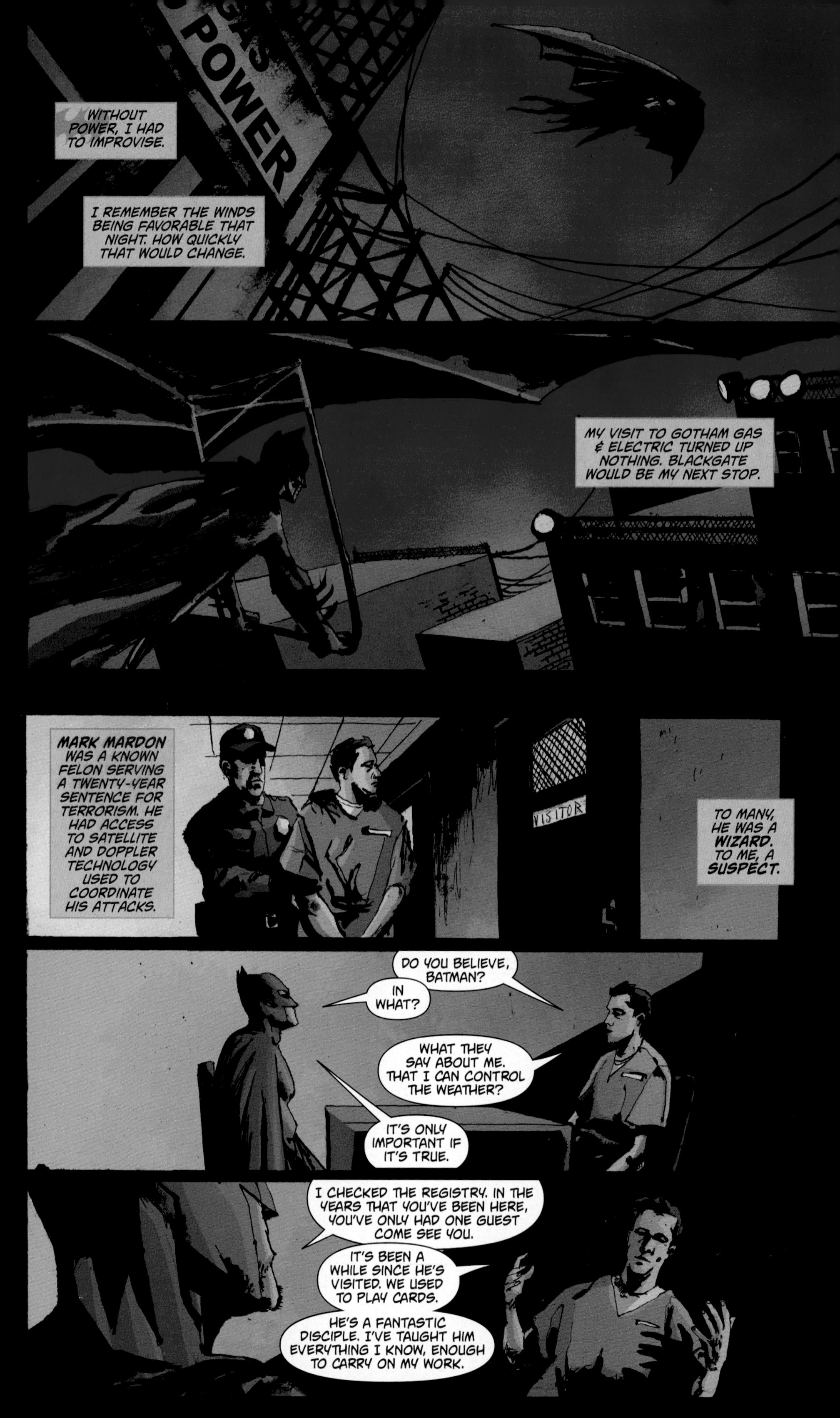
GAS
POWER
WITHOUT POWER, I HAD TO IMPROVISE.
I REMEMBER THE WINDS BEING FAVORABLE THAT NIGHT. HOW QUICKLY THAT WOULD CHANGE.
MY VISIT TO GOTHAM GAS & ELECTRIC TURNED UP NOTHING. BLACKGATE WOULD BE MY NEXT STOP.
MARK MARDON WAS A KNOWN FELON SERVING A TWENTY-YEAR SENTENCE FOR TERRORISM. HE HAD ACCESS TO SATELLITE AND DOPPLER TECHNOLOGY USED TO COORDINATE HIS ATTACKS.
VISITOR
TO MANY, HE WAS A WIZARD. TO ME, A SUSPECT.
DO YOU BELIEVE, BATMAN?
IN WHAT?
WHAT THEY SAY ABOUT ME. THAT I CAN CONTROL THE WEATHER?
IT'S ONLY IMPORTANT IF IT'S TRUE.
I CHECKED THE REGISTRY. IN THE YEARS THAT YOU'VE BEEN HERE, YOU'VE ONLY HAD ONE GUEST COME SEE YOU.
IT'S BEEN A WHILE SINCE HE'S VISITED. WE USED TO PLAY CARDS.
HE'S A FANTASTIC DISCIPLE. I'VE TAUGHT HIM EVERYTHING I KNOW, ENOUGH TO CARRY ON MY WORK.

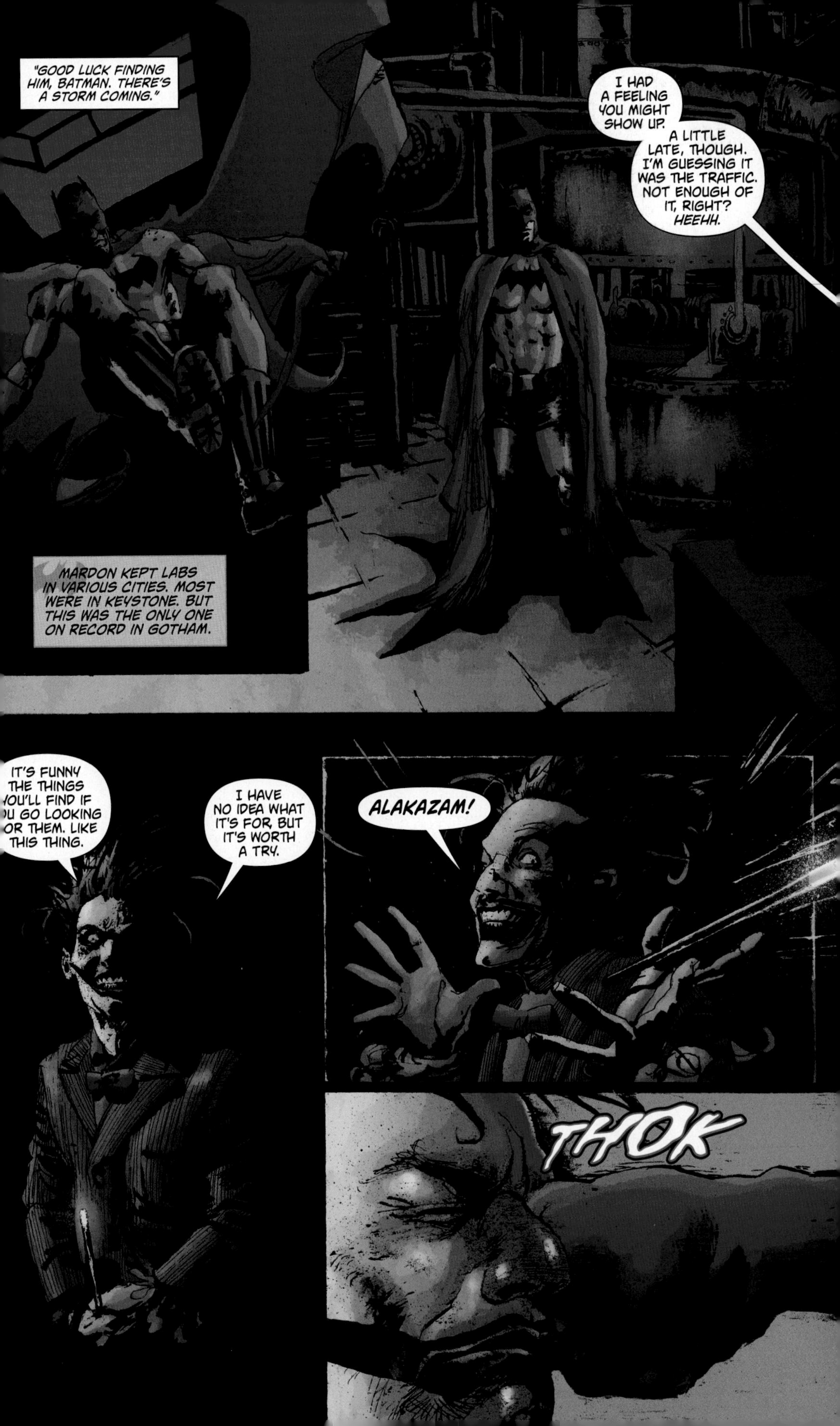
"GOOD LUCK FINDING HIM, BATMAN. THERE'S A STORM COMING."
I HAD A FEELING YOU MIGHT SHOW UP.
A LITTLE LATE, THOUGH. I'M GUESSING IT WAS THE TRAFFIC. NOT ENOUGH OF IT, RIGHT? HEEHH.
MARDON KEPT LABS IN VARIOUS CITIES. MOST WERE IN KEYSTONE. BUT THIS WAS THE ONLY ONE ON RECORD IN GOTHAM.
IT'S FUNNY THE THINGS YOU'LL FIND IF YOU GO LOOKING FOR THEM. LIKE THIS THING.
I HAVE NO IDEA WHAT IT'S FOR, BUT IT'S WORTH A TRY.
ALAKAZAM!
THOK

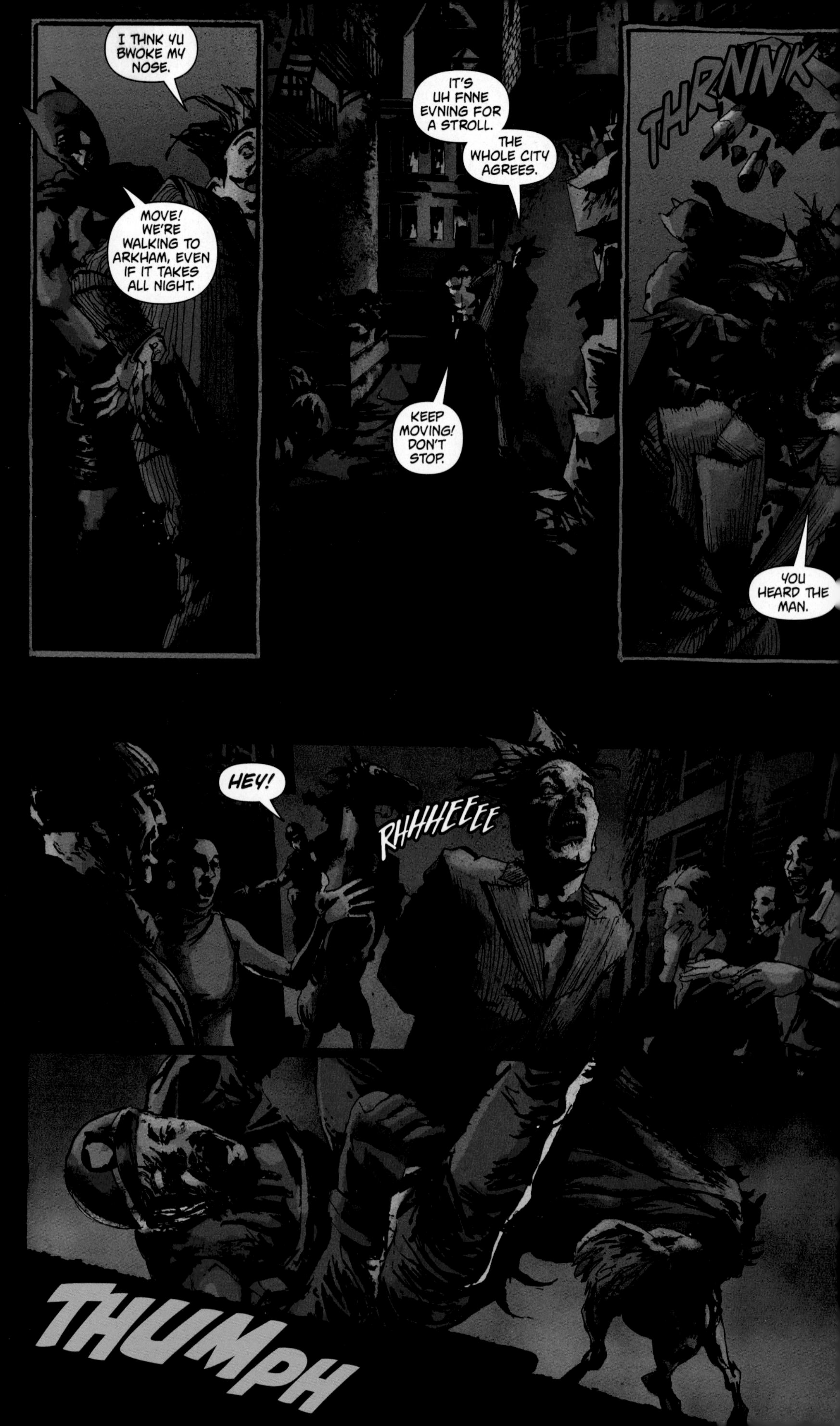
I THNK YU BWOKE MY NOSE.
MOVE! WE'RE WALKING TO ARKHAM, EVEN IF IT TAKES ALL NIGHT.
IT'S UH FNNE EVNING FOR A STROLL.
THE WHOLE CITY AGREES.
KEEP MOVING! DON'T STOP.
THRNNK
YOU HEARD THE MAN.
HEY!
RHHHEEEE
THUMPH

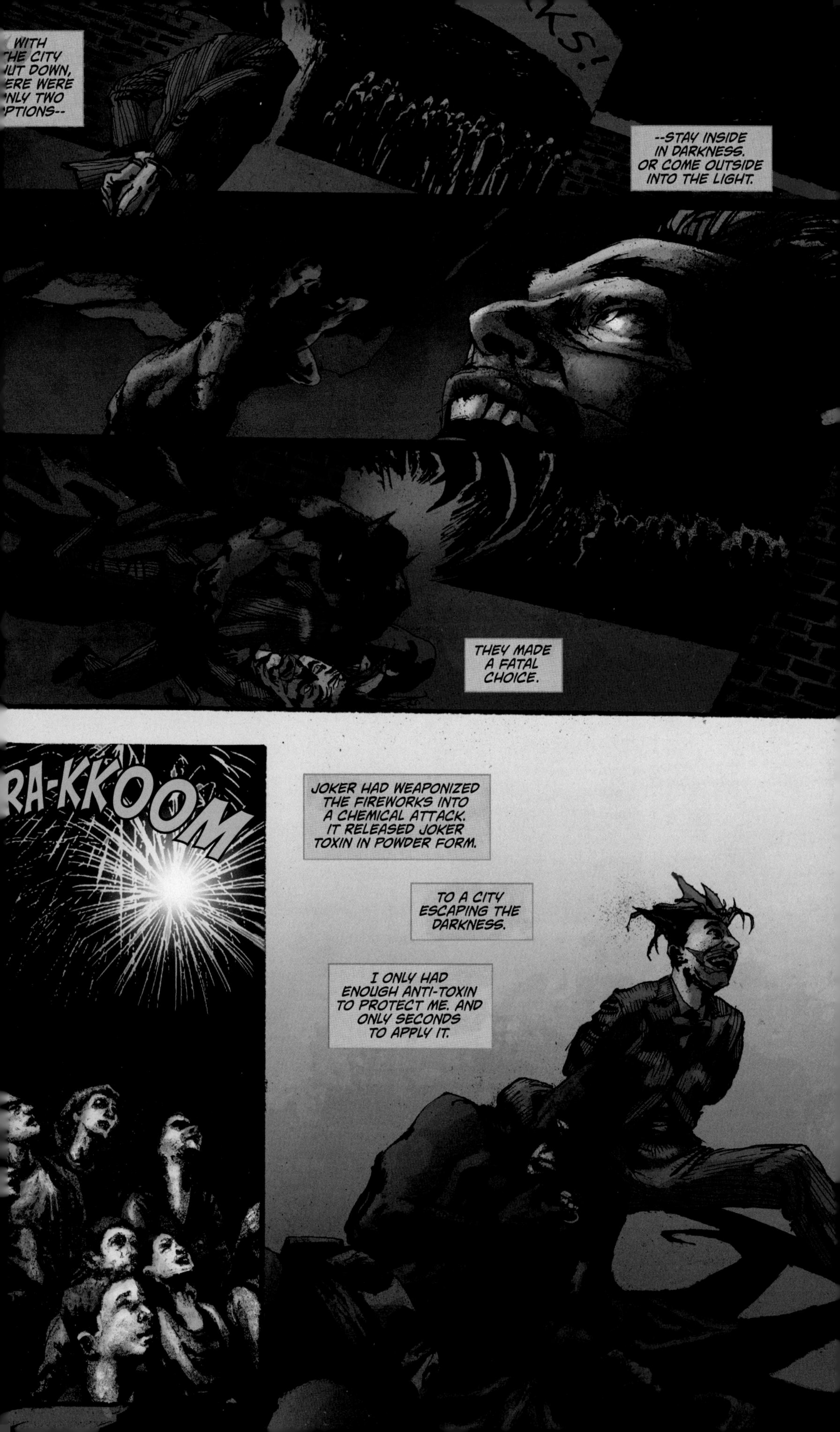

WITH
HE CITY
UT DOWN,
ERE WERE
NLY TWO
PTIONS--
--STAY INSIDE IN DARKNESS. OR COME OUTSIDE INTO THE LIGHT.
THEY MADE A FATAL CHOICE.
RA-KKOOM
JOKER HAD WEAPONIZED THE FIREWORKS INTO A CHEMICAL ATTACK. IT RELEASED JOKER TOXIN IN POWDER FORM.
TO A CITY ESCAPING THE DARKNESS.
I ONLY HAD ENOUGH ANTI-TOXIN TO PROTECT ME. AND ONLY SECONDS TO APPLY IT.

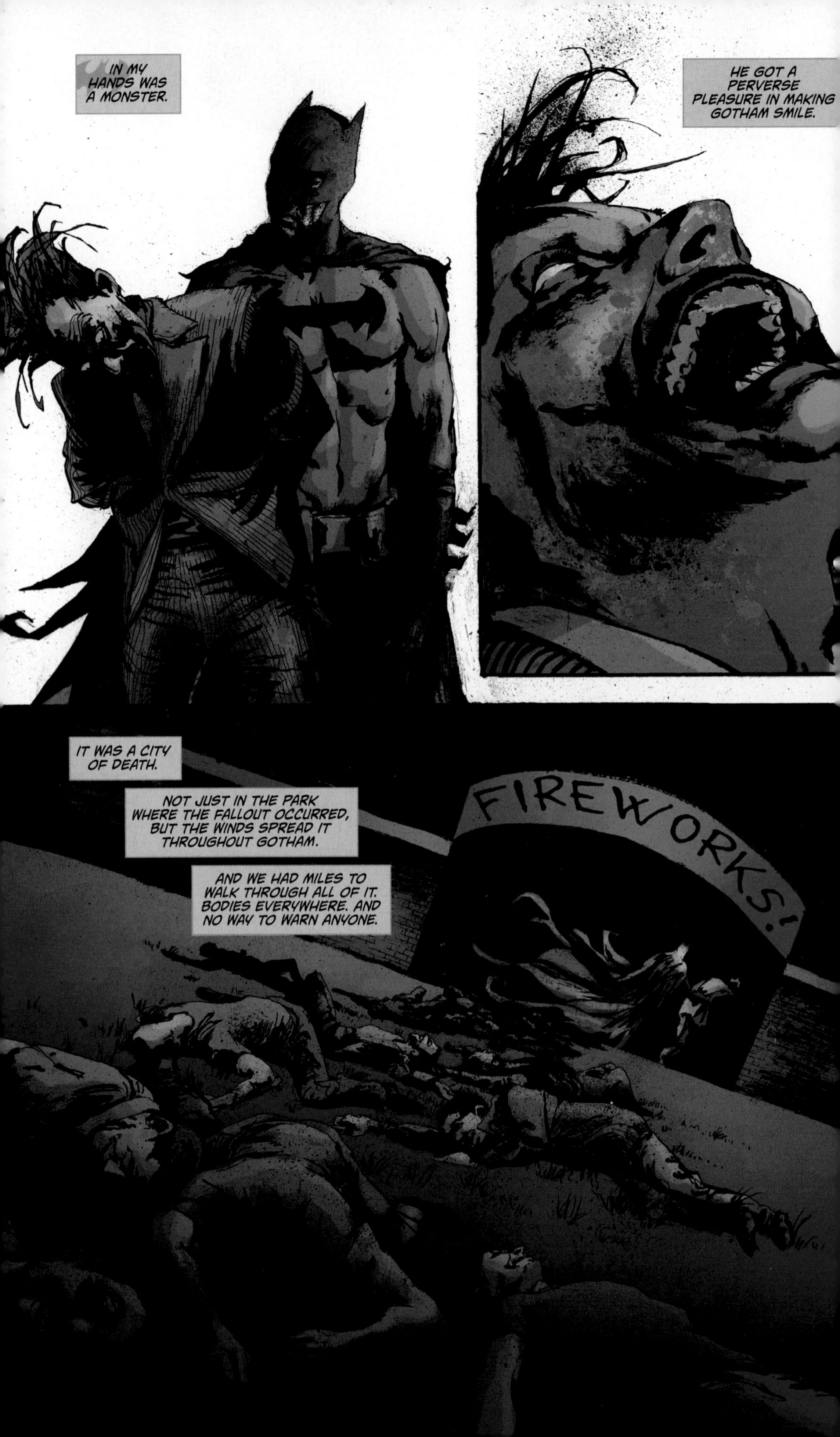
IN MY HANDS WAS A MONSTER.
HE GOT A PERVERSE PLEASURE IN MAKING GOTHAM SMILE.
IT WAS A CITY OF DEATH.
NOT JUST IN THE PARK WHERE THE FALLOUT OCCURRED, BUT THE WINDS SPREAD IT THROUGHOUT GOTHAM.
AND WE HAD MILES TO WALK THROUGH ALL OF IT. BODIES EVERYWHERE. AND NO WAY TO WARN ANYONE.
FIREWORKS!

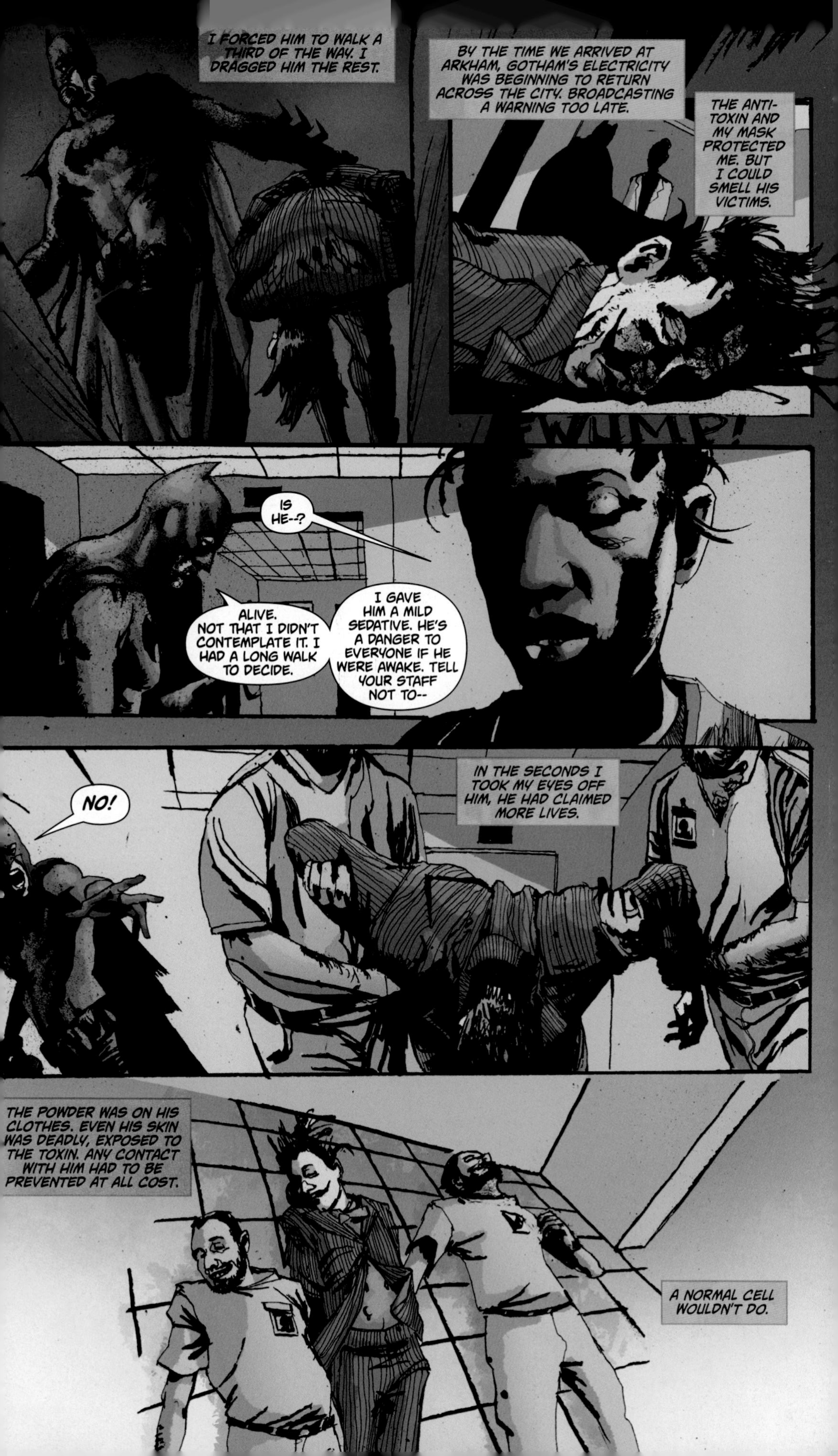
I FORCED HIM TO WALK A THIRD OF THE WAY. I DRAGGED HIM THE REST.
BY THE TIME WE ARRIVED AT ARKHAM, GOTHAM'S ELECTRICITY WAS BEGINNING TO RETURN ACROSS THE CITY. BROADCASTING A WARNING TOO LATE.
THE ANTI-TOXIN AND MY MASK PROTECTED ME. BUT I COULD SMELL HIS VICTIMS.
FWUMP!
IS HE--?
ALIVE. NOT THAT I DIDN'T CONTEMPLATE IT. I HAD A LONG WALK TO DECIDE.
I GAVE HIM A MILD SEDATIVE. HE'S A DANGER TO EVERYONE IF HE WERE AWAKE. TELL YOUR STAFF NOT TO--
NO!
IN THE SECONDS I TOOK MY EYES OFF HIM, HE HAD CLAIMED MORE LIVES.
THE POWDER WAS ON HIS CLOTHES. EVEN HIS SKIN WAS DEADLY, EXPOSED TO THE TOXIN. ANY CONTACT WITH HIM HAD TO BE PREVENTED AT ALL COST.
A NORMAL CELL WOULDN'T DO.

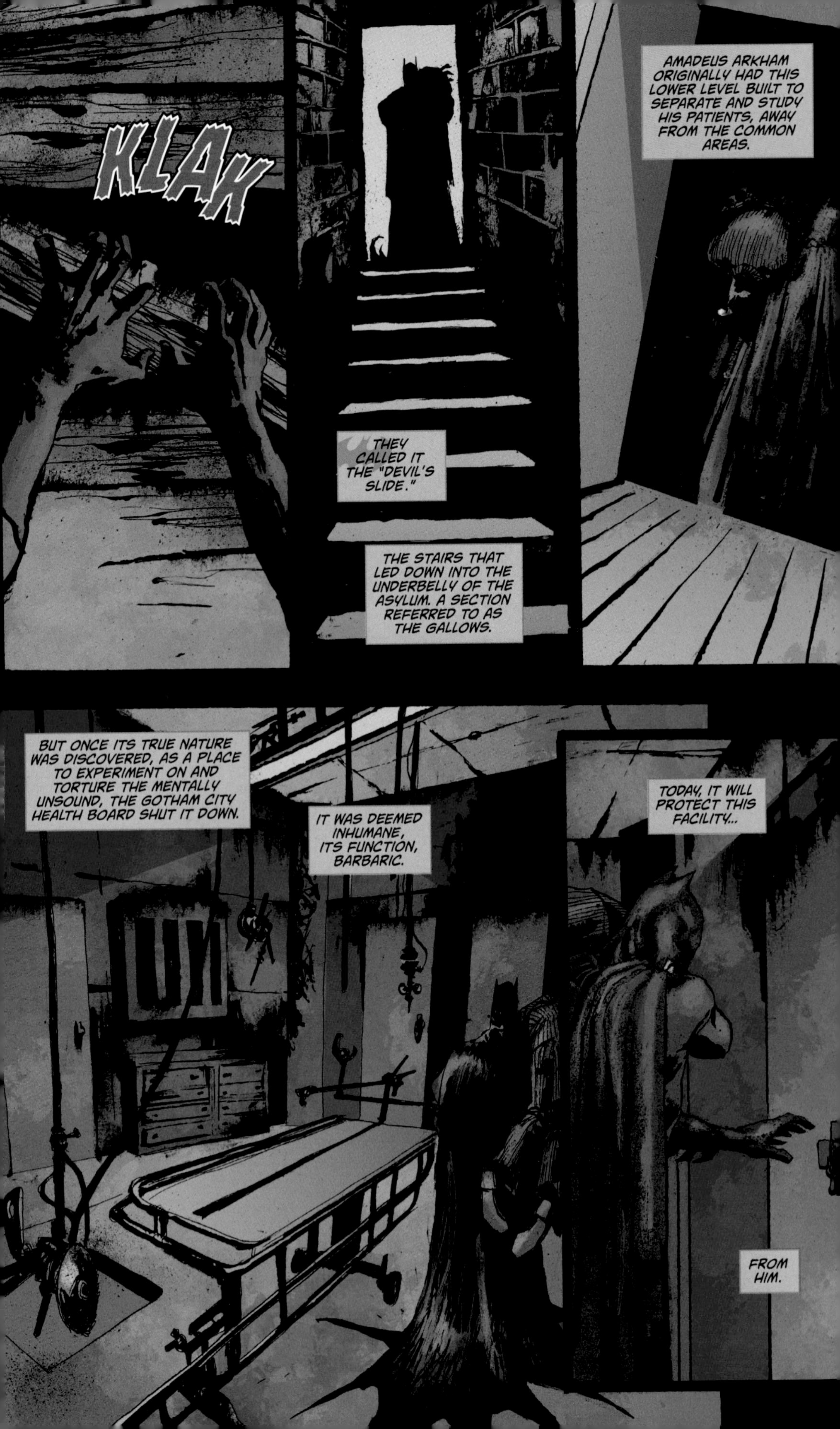
KLAK
THEY CALLED IT THE "DEVIL'S SLIDE."
THE STAIRS THAT LED DOWN INTO THE UNDERBELLY OF THE ASYLUM. A SECTION REFERRED TO AS THE GALLOWS.
AMADEUS ARKHAM ORIGINALLY HAD THIS LOWER LEVEL BUILT TO SEPARATE AND STUDY HIS PATIENTS, AWAY FROM THE COMMON AREAS.
BUT ONCE ITS TRUE NATURE WAS DISCOVERED, AS A PLACE TO EXPERIMENT ON AND TORTURE THE MENTALLY UNSOUND, THE GOTHAM CITY HEALTH BOARD SHUT IT DOWN.
IT WAS DEEMED INHUMANE, ITS FUNCTION, BARBARIC.
TODAY, IT WILL PROTECT THIS FACILITY...
FROM HIM.

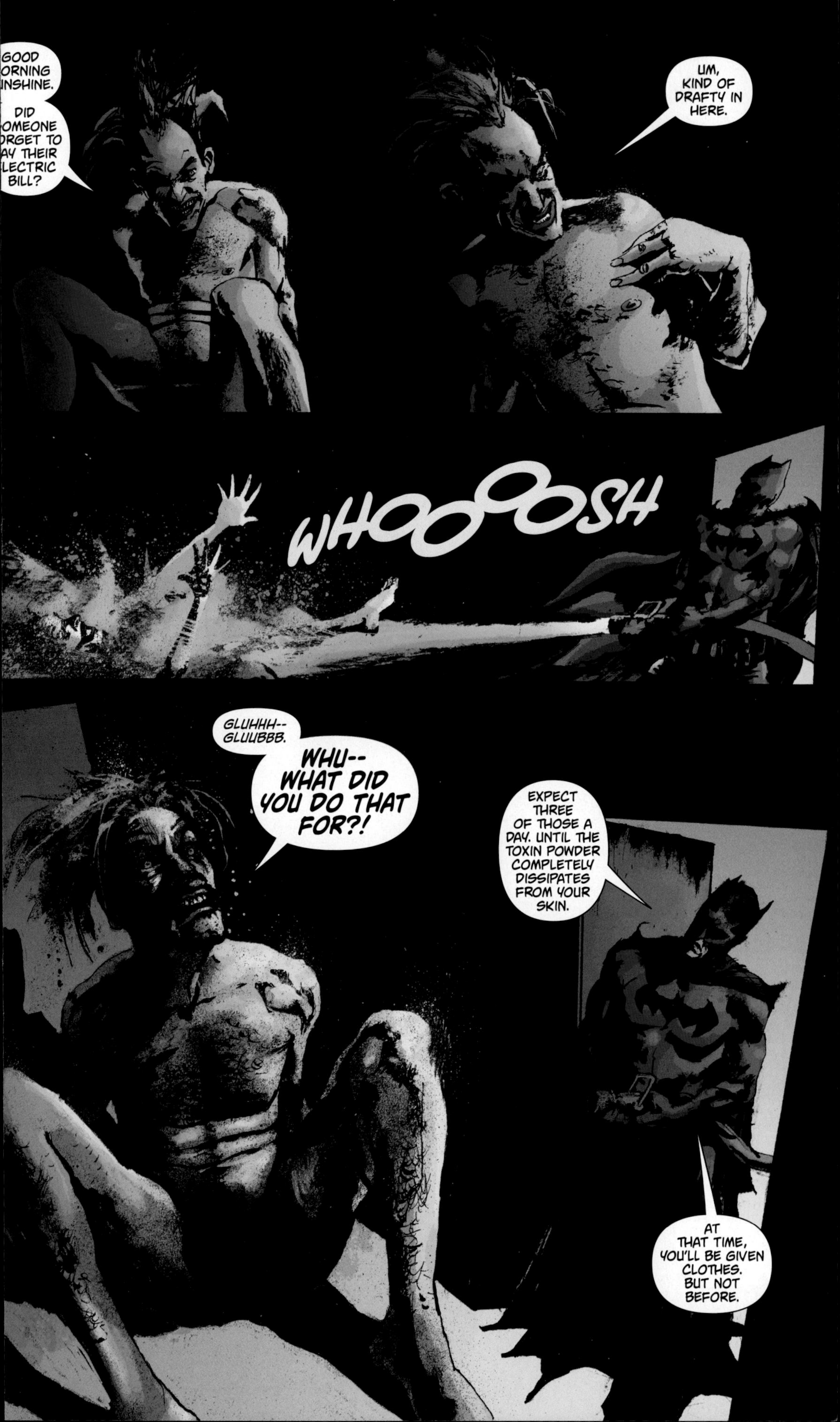
GOOD ORNING INSHINE.
DID OMEONE ORGET TO AY THEIR LECTRIC BILL?
UM, KIND OF DRAFTY IN HERE.
WHOOOOSH
GLUHHH-- GLUUBBB.
WHU-- WHAT DID YOU DO THAT FOR?!
EXPECT THREE OF THOSE A DAY. UNTIL THE TOXIN POWDER COMPLETELY DISSIPATES FROM YOUR SKIN.
AT THAT TIME, YOU'LL BE GIVEN CLOTHES. BUT NOT BEFORE.

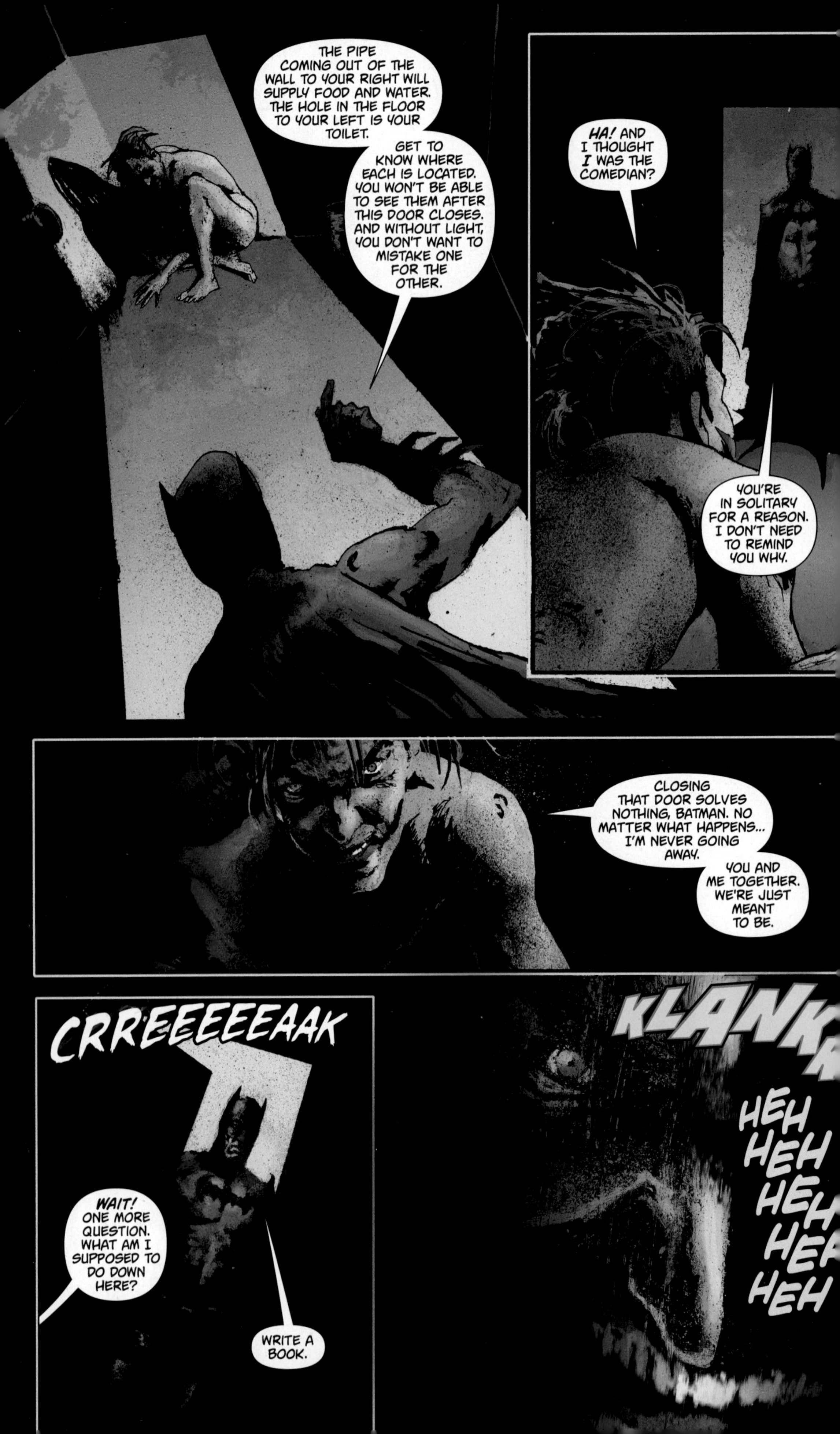

THE PIPE COMING OUT OF THE WALL TO YOUR RIGHT WILL SUPPLY FOOD AND WATER. THE HOLE IN THE FLOOR TO YOUR LEFT IS YOUR TOILET.
GET TO KNOW WHERE EACH IS LOCATED. YOU WON'T BE ABLE TO SEE THEM AFTER THIS DOOR CLOSES. AND WITHOUT LIGHT, YOU DON'T WANT TO MISTAKE ONE FOR THE OTHER.
HA! AND I THOUGHT I WAS THE COMEDIAN?
YOU'RE IN SOLITARY FOR A REASON. I DON'T NEED TO REMIND YOU WHY.
CLOSING THAT DOOR SOLVES NOTHING, BATMAN. NO MATTER WHAT HAPPENS... I'M NEVER GOING AWAY.
YOU AND ME TOGETHER. WE'RE JUST MEANT TO BE.
CRREEEEEEAAK
WAIT! ONE MORE QUESTION. WHAT AM I SUPPOSED TO DO DOWN HERE?
WRITE A BOOK.
HEH
HEH
HEH
HEH

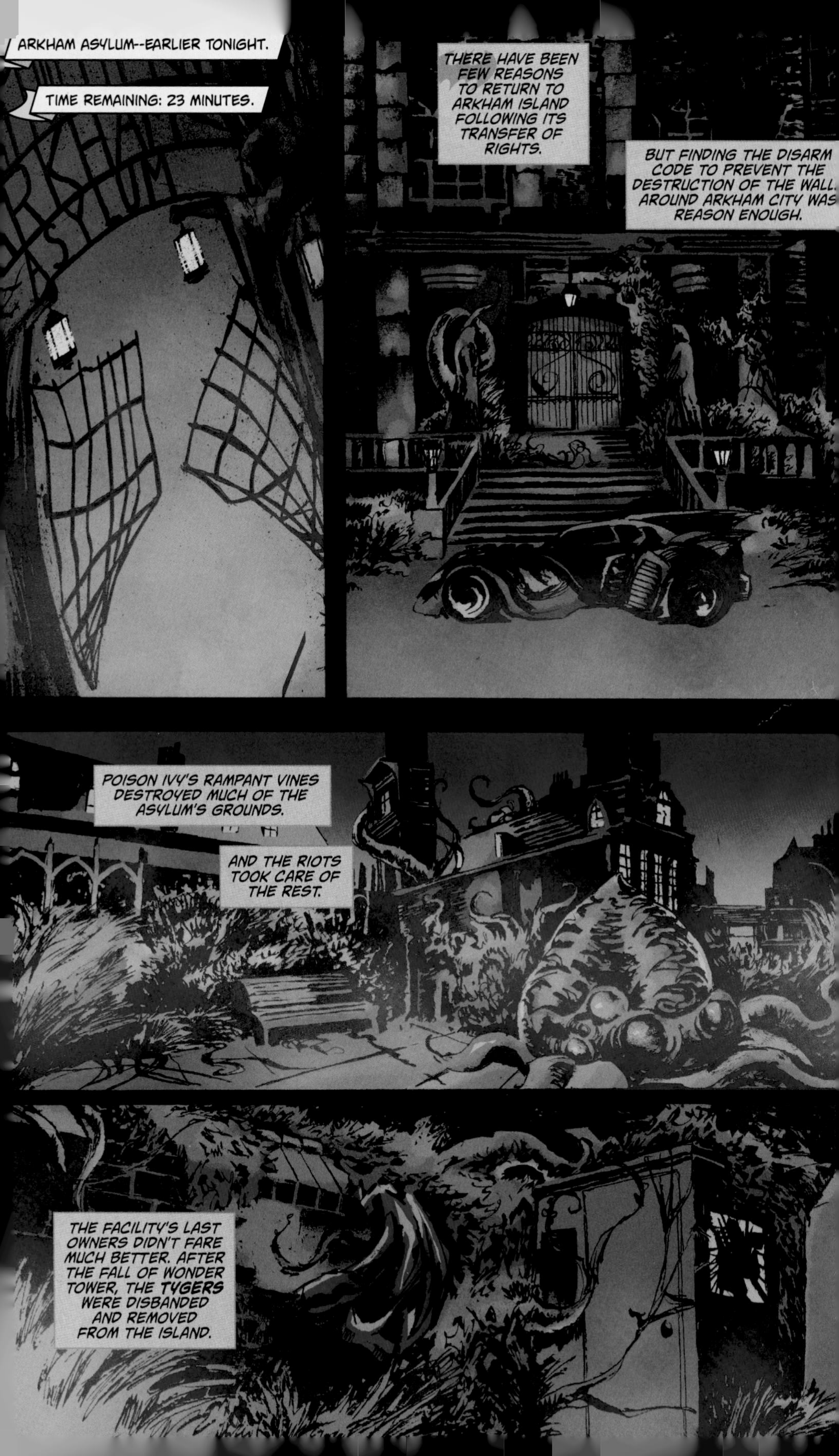
ARKHAM ASYLUM--EARLIER TONIGHT.
TIME REMAINING: 23 MINUTES.
ARKHAM ASYLUM
THERE HAVE BEEN FEW REASONS TO RETURN TO ARKHAM ISLAND FOLLOWING ITS TRANSFER OF RIGHTS.
BUT FINDING THE DISARM CODE TO PREVENT THE DESTRUCTION OF THE WALL AROUND ARKHAM CITY WAS REASON ENOUGH.
POISON IVY'S RAMPANT VINES DESTROYED MUCH OF THE ASYLUM'S GROUNDS.
AND THE RIOTS TOOK CARE OF THE REST.
THE FACILITY'S LAST OWNERS DIDN'T FARE MUCH BETTER. AFTER THE FALL OF WONDER TOWER, THE **TYGERS** WERE DISBANDED AND REMOVED FROM THE ISLAND.

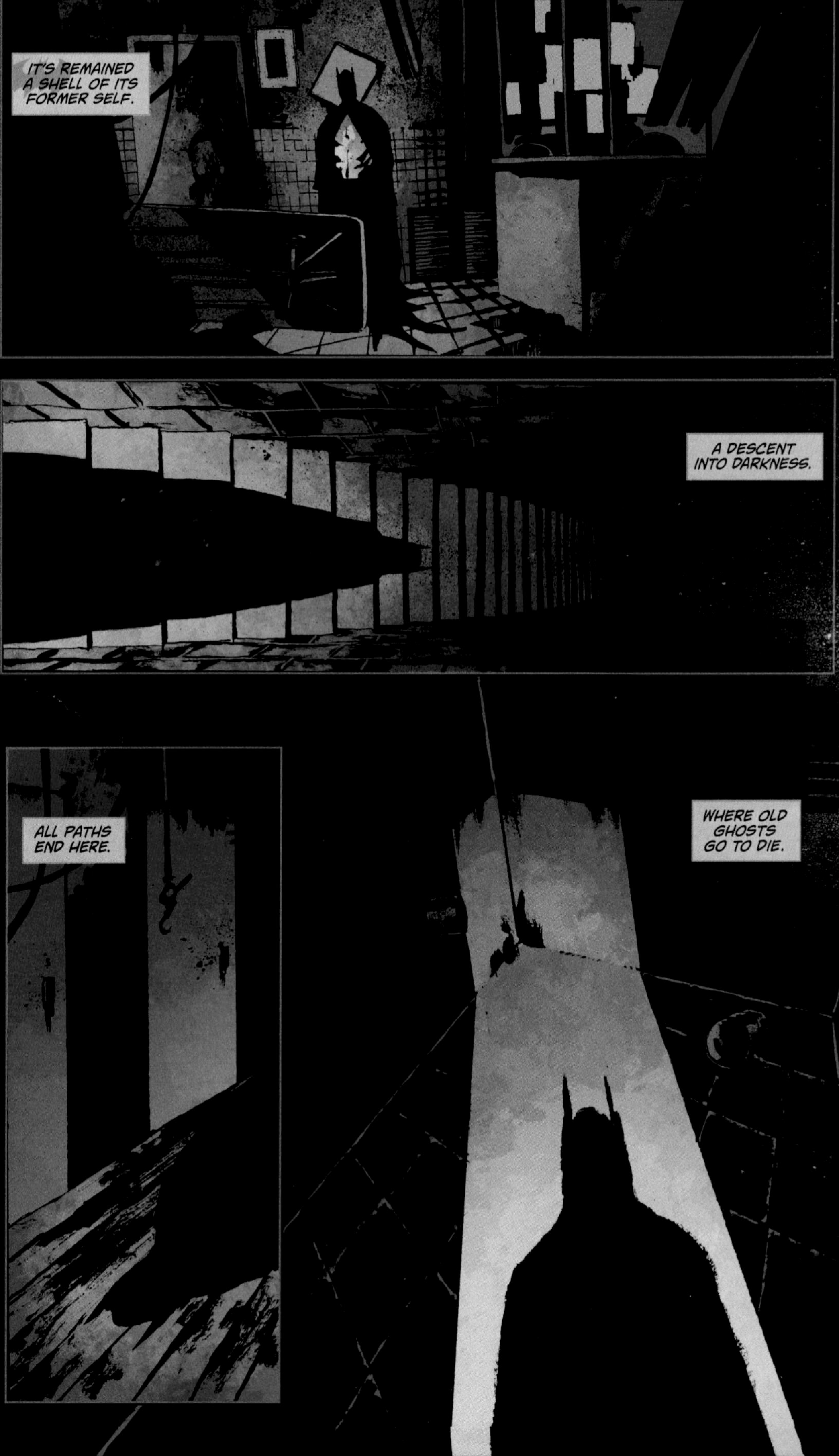
IT'S REMAINED A SHELL OF ITS FORMER SELF.
A DESCENT INTO DARKNESS.
ALL PATHS END HERE.
WHERE OLD GHOSTS GO TO DIE.

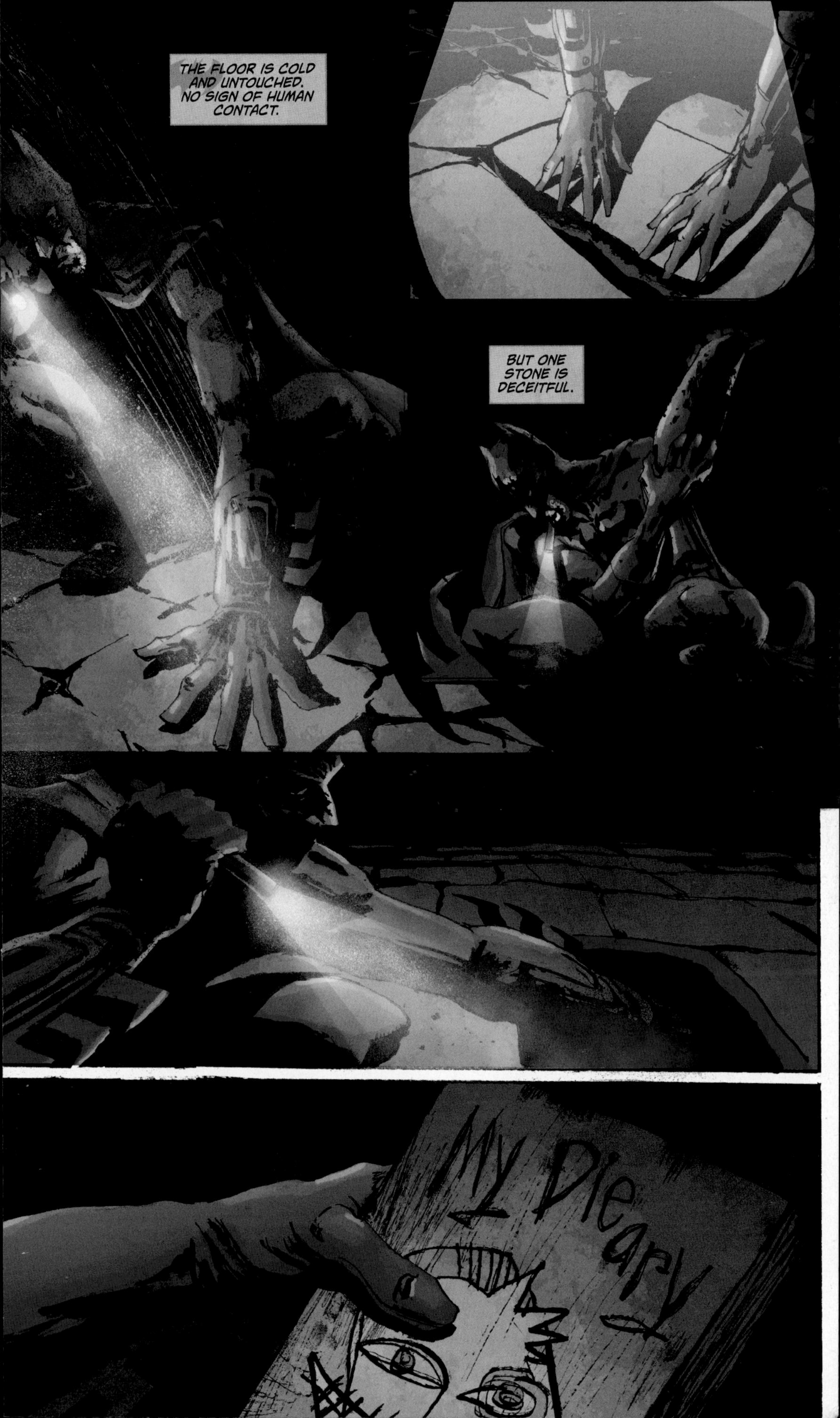
THE FLOOR IS COLD AND UNTOUCHED. NO SIGN OF HUMAN CONTACT.
BUT ONE STONE IS DECEITFUL.
My Dieary

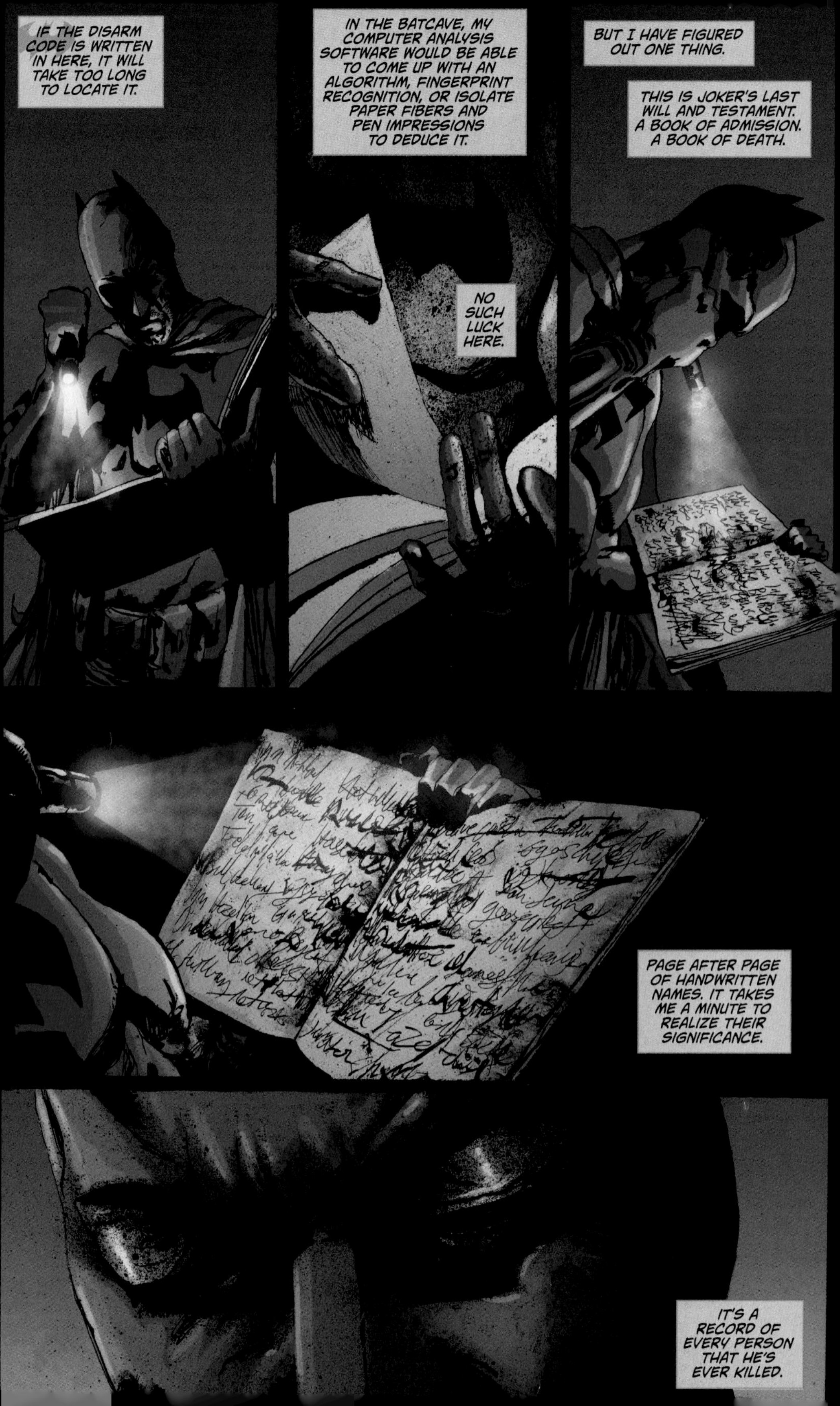
IF THE DISARM CODE IS WRITTEN IN HERE, IT WILL TAKE TOO LONG TO LOCATE IT.
IN THE BATCAVE, MY COMPUTER ANALYSIS SOFTWARE WOULD BE ABLE TO COME UP WITH AN ALGORITHM, FINGERPRINT RECOGNITION, OR ISOLATE PAPER FIBERS AND PEN IMPRESSIONS TO DEDUCE IT.
NO SUCH LUCK HERE.
BUT I HAVE FIGURED OUT ONE THING.
THIS IS JOKER'S LAST WILL AND TESTAMENT. A BOOK OF ADMISSION. A BOOK OF DEATH.
PAGE AFTER PAGE OF HANDWRITTEN NAMES. IT TAKES ME A MINUTE TO REALIZE THEIR SIGNIFICANCE.
IT'S A RECORD OF EVERY PERSON THAT HE'S EVER KILLED.

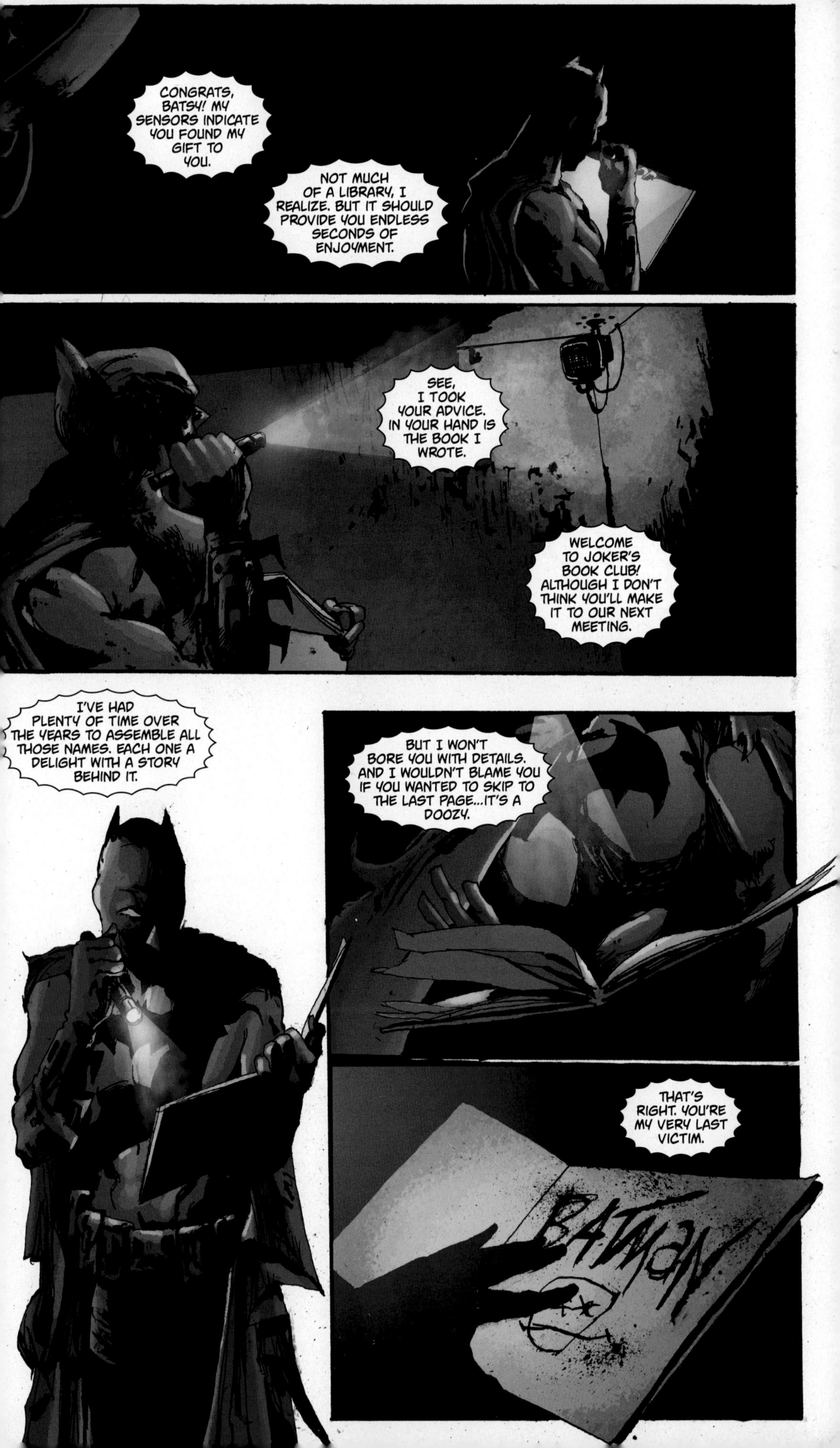
CONGRATS, BATSY! MY SENSORS INDICATE YOU FOUND MY GIFT TO YOU.
NOT MUCH OF A LIBRARY, I REALIZE. BUT IT SHOULD PROVIDE YOU ENDLESS SECONDS OF ENJOYMENT.
SEE, I TOOK YOUR ADVICE. IN YOUR HAND IS THE BOOK I WROTE.
WELCOME TO JOKER'S BOOK CLUB! ALTHOUGH I DON'T THINK YOU'LL MAKE IT TO OUR NEXT MEETING.
I'VE HAD PLENTY OF TIME OVER THE YEARS TO ASSEMBLE ALL THOSE NAMES. EACH ONE A DELIGHT WITH A STORY BEHIND IT.
BUT I WON'T BORE YOU WITH DETAILS. AND I WOULDN'T BLAME YOU IF YOU WANTED TO SKIP TO THE LAST PAGE...IT'S A DOOZY.
THAT'S RIGHT. YOU'RE MY VERY LAST VICTIM.
BATMAN

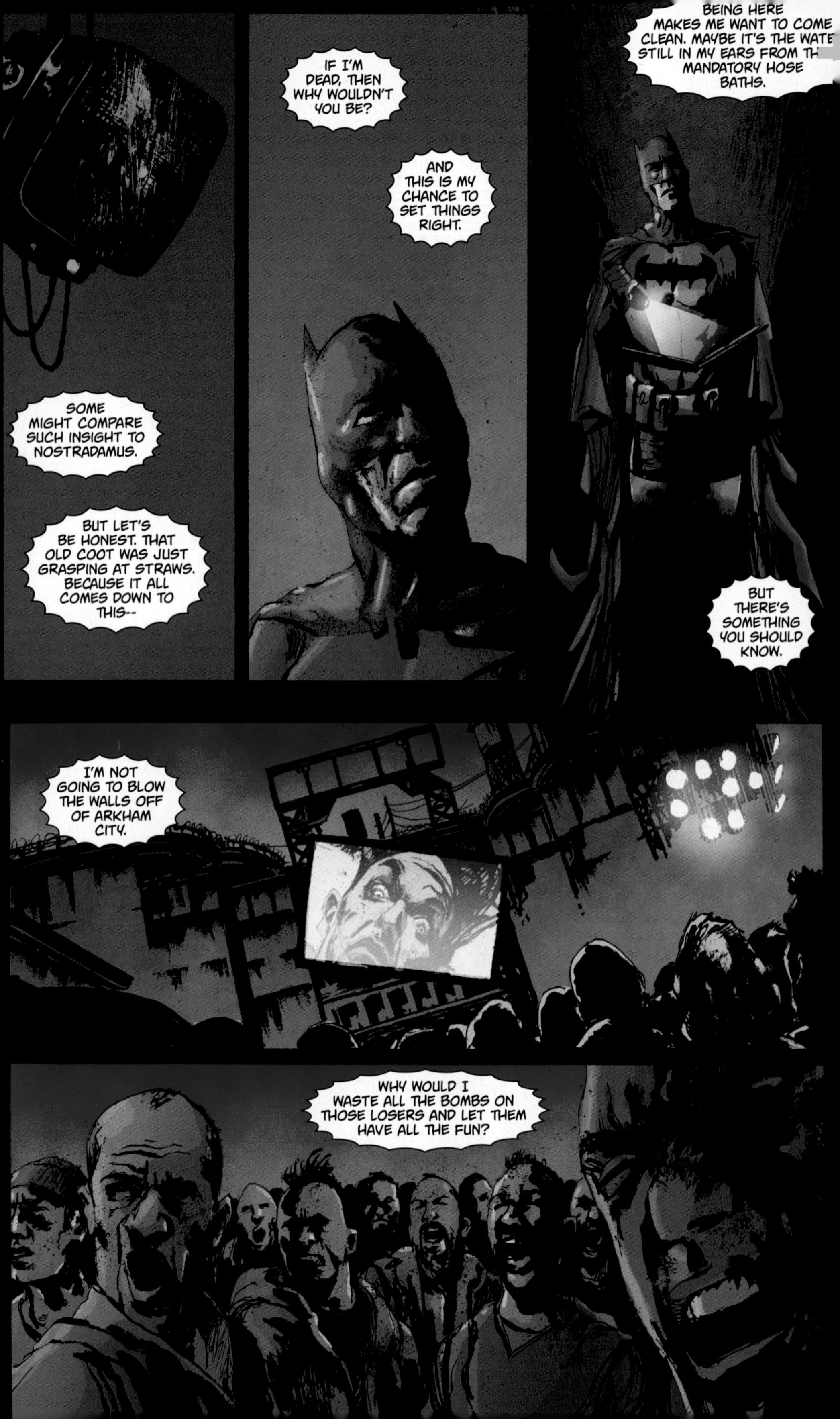
SOME MIGHT COMPARE SUCH INSIGHT TO NOSTRADAMUS.
BUT LET'S BE HONEST. THAT OLD COOT WAS JUST GRASPING AT STRAWS. BECAUSE IT ALL COMES DOWN TO THIS--
IF I'M DEAD, THEN WHY WOULDN'T YOU BE?
AND THIS IS MY CHANCE TO SET THINGS RIGHT.
BEING HERE MAKES ME WANT TO COME CLEAN. MAYBE IT'S THE WATE STILL IN MY EARS FROM TH MANDATORY HOSE BATHS.
BUT THERE'S SOMETHING YOU SHOULD KNOW.
I'M NOT GOING TO BLOW THE WALLS OFF OF ARKHAM CITY.
WHY WOULD I WASTE ALL THE BOMBS ON THOSE LOSERS AND LET THEM HAVE ALL THE FUN?

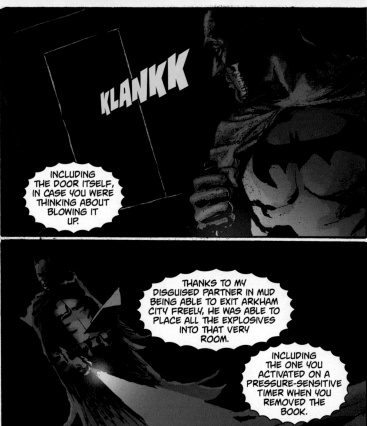

NOT WHEN I CAN CONCENTRATE ALL THE BOMBS RIGHT IN THIS VERY ROOM.

KLANKK

INCLUDING THE DOOR ITSELF, IN CASE YOU WERE THINKING ABOUT BLOWING IT UP.

THANKS TO MY DISGUISED PARTNER IN MUD BEING ABLE TO EXIT ARKHAM CITY FREELY, HE WAS ABLE TO PLACE ALL THE EXPLOSIVES INTO THAT VERY ROOM.

INCLUDING THE ONE YOU ACTIVATED ON A PRESSURE-SENSITIVE TIMER WHEN YOU REMOVED THE BOOK.

GET TO KNOW WHERE EACH IS LOCATED. YOU WON'T BE ABLE TO SEE THEM AFTER THIS DOOR CLOSES. AND WITHOUT LIGHT, YOU DON'T WANT TO MISTAKE ONE FOR THE OTHER.

SOUND FAMILIAR? THEY'RE WORDS TO DIE BY.

YOUR TIME IS UP. I'M AFRAID THERE ARE NO CHEAT CODES AND NO EXTRA LIFE.

IT'S GAME OVER.

SEE YOU IN HELL, BATSY! HEHEHEHEH--

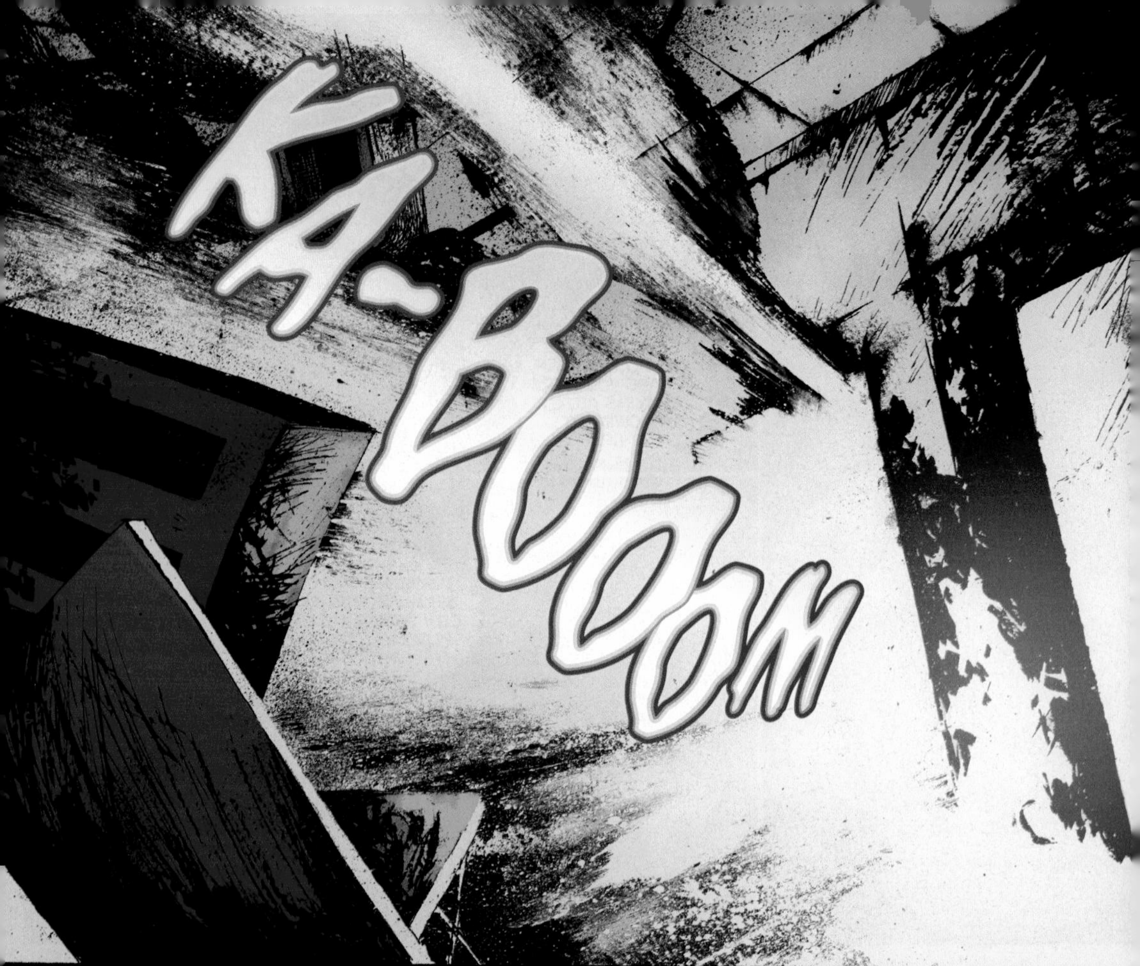
KA-BOOOOM
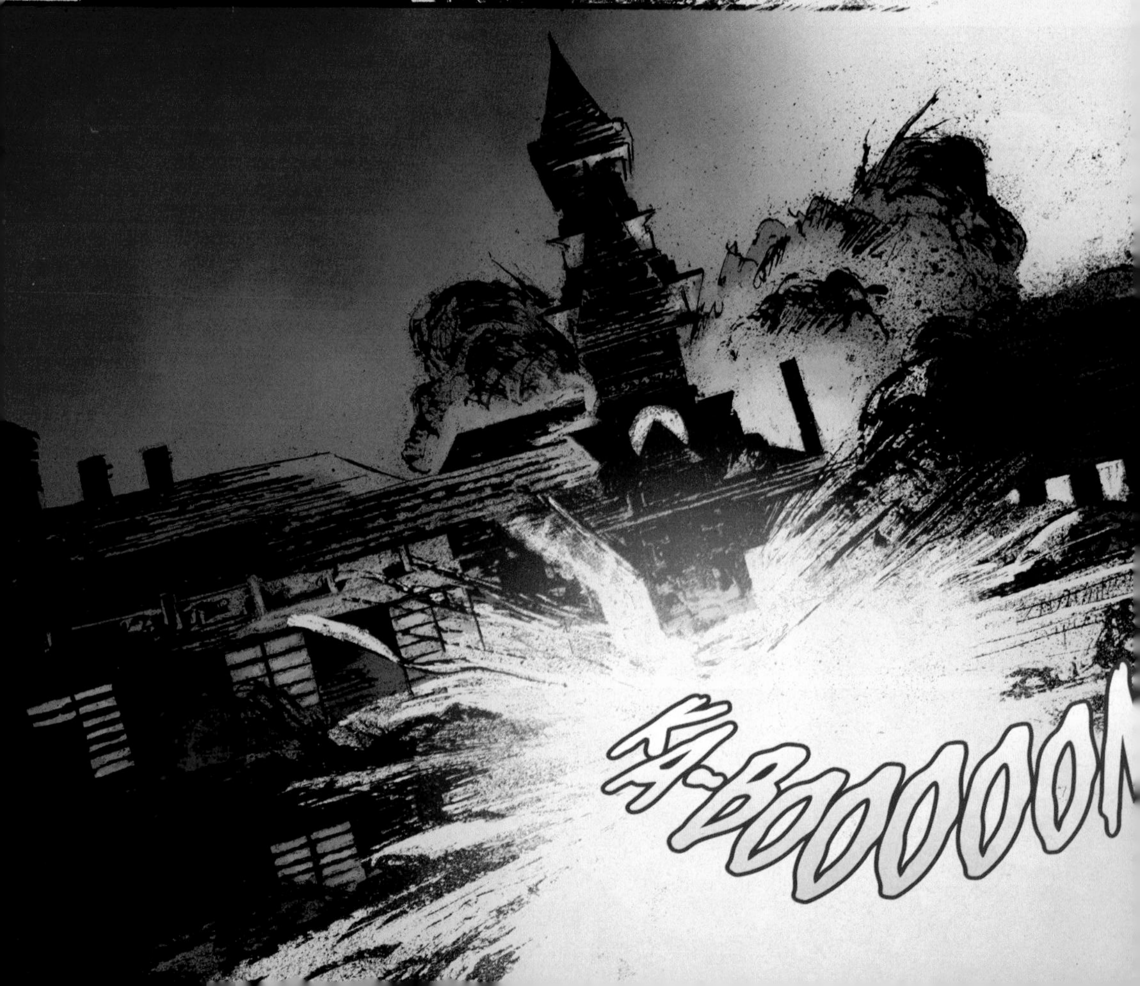
KA-BOOOOOOM

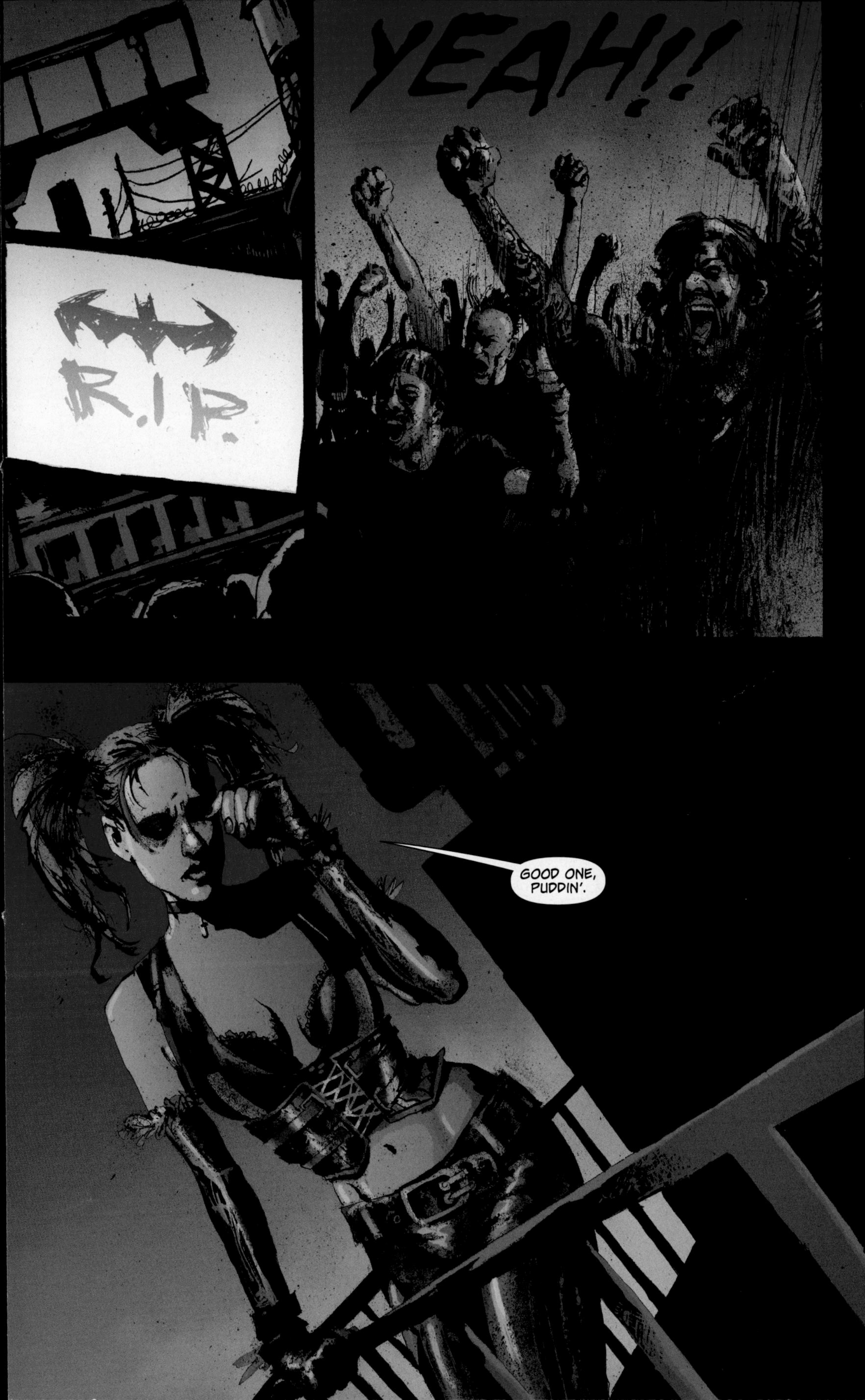
R.I.P.
YEAH!!
GOOD ONE, PUDDIN'.

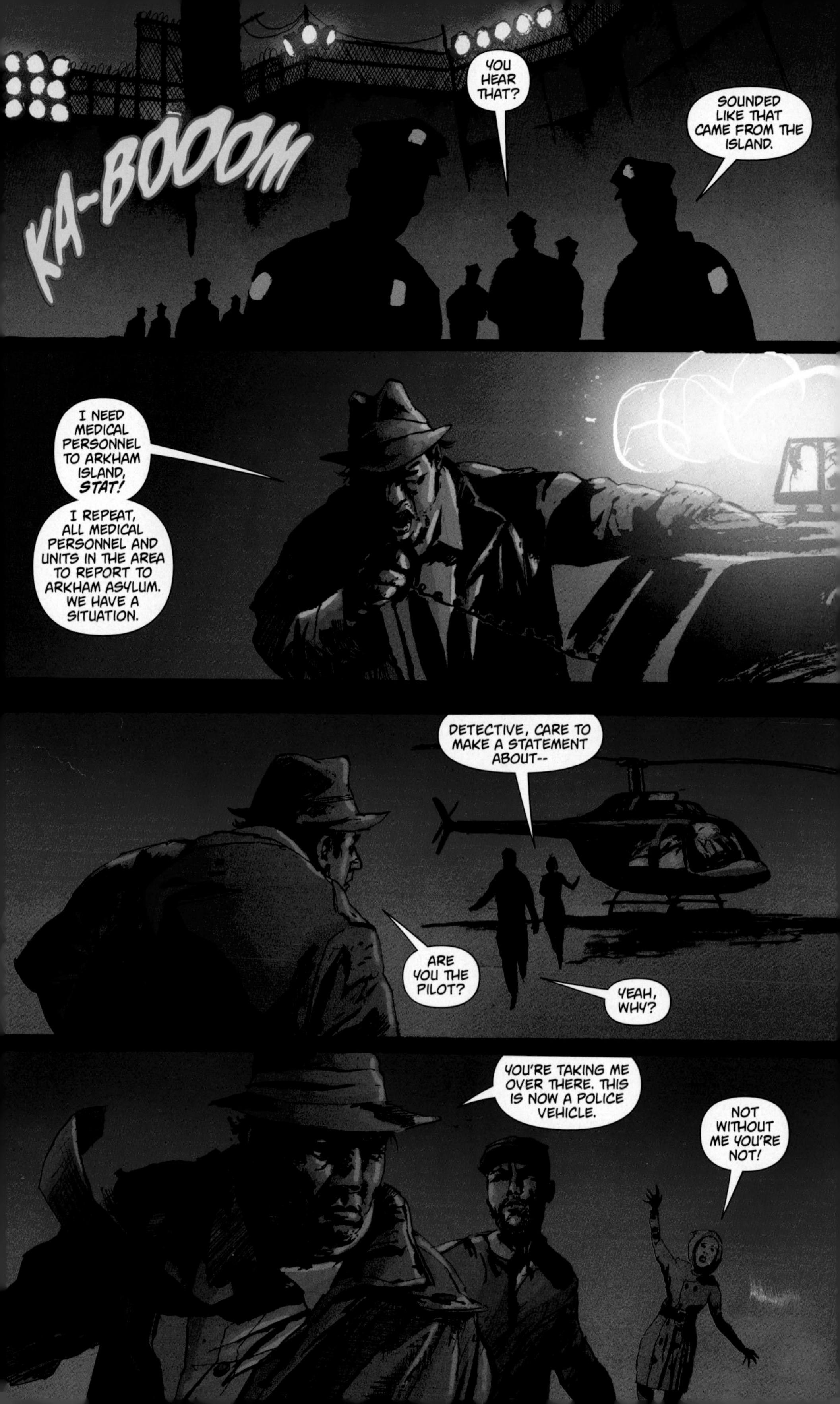
KA-BOOOM
YOU HEAR THAT?
SOUNDED LIKE THAT CAME FROM THE ISLAND.
I NEED MEDICAL PERSONNEL TO ARKHAM ISLAND, STAT!
I REPEAT, ALL MEDICAL PERSONNEL AND UNITS IN THE AREA TO REPORT TO ARKHAM ASYLUM. WE HAVE A SITUATION.
DETECTIVE, CARE TO MAKE A STATEMENT ABOUT--
ARE YOU THE PILOT?
YEAH, WHY?
YOU'RE TAKING ME OVER THERE. THIS IS NOW A POLICE VEHICLE.
NOT WITHOUT ME YOU'RE NOT!

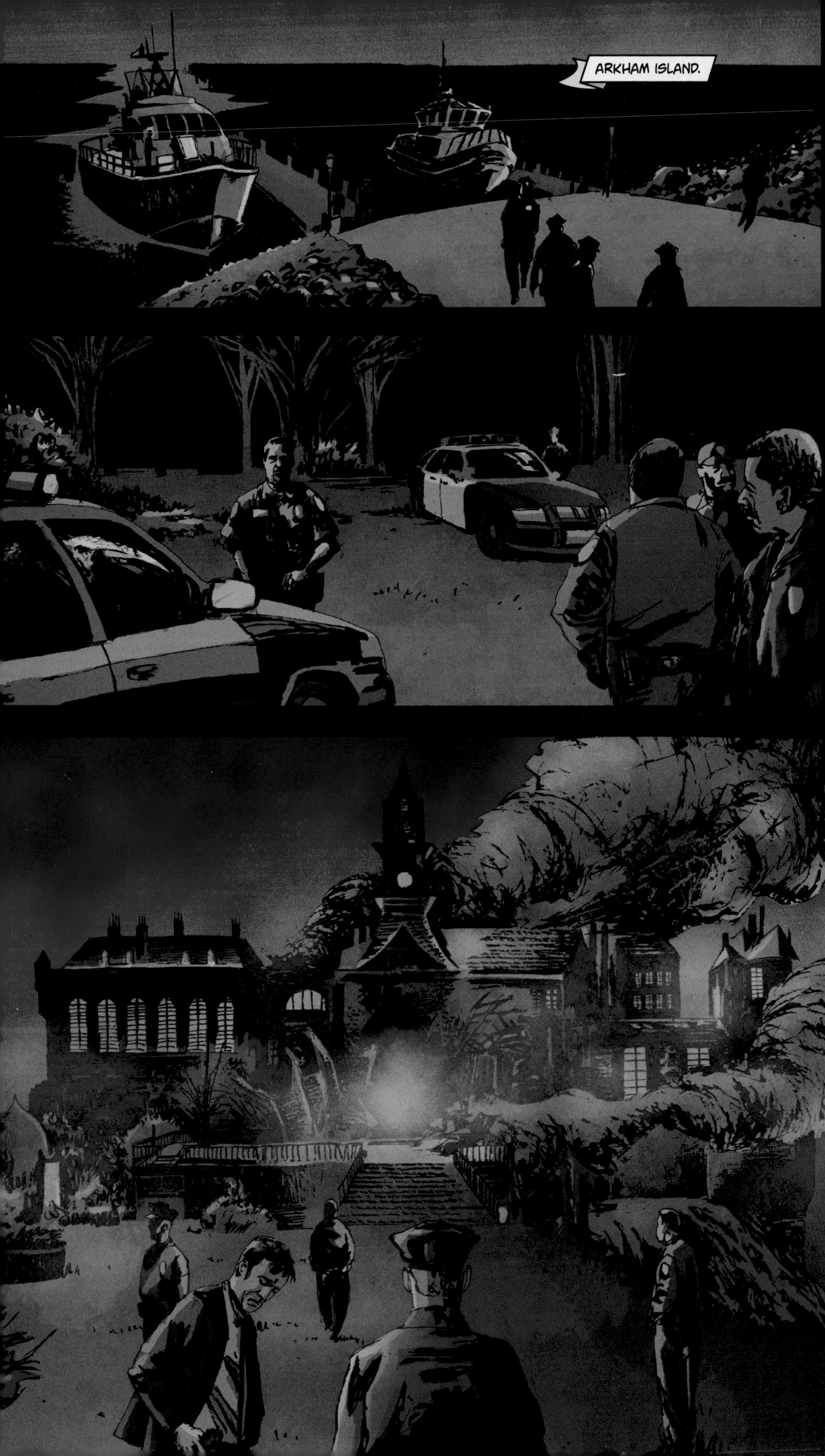
ARKHAM ISLAND.

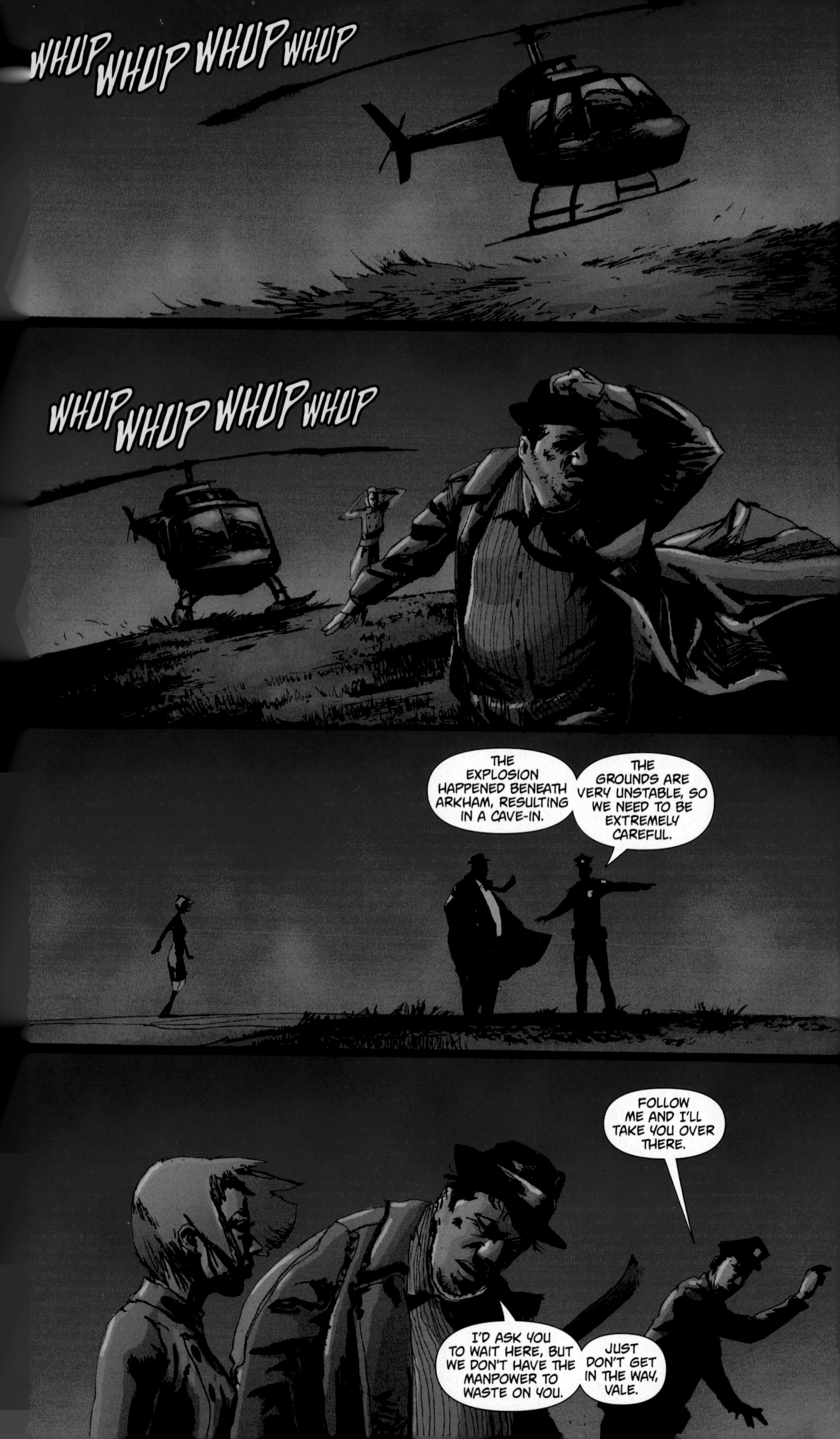
WHUP WHUP WHUP WHUP
WHUP WHUP WHUP WHUP
THE EXPLOSION HAPPENED BENEATH ARKHAM, RESULTING IN A CAVE-IN.
THE GROUNDS ARE VERY UNSTABLE, SO WE NEED TO BE EXTREMELY CAREFUL.
FOLLOW ME AND I'LL TAKE YOU OVER THERE.
I'D ASK YOU TO WAIT HERE, BUT WE DON'T HAVE THE MANPOWER TO WASTE ON YOU.
JUST DON'T GET IN THE WAY, VALE.

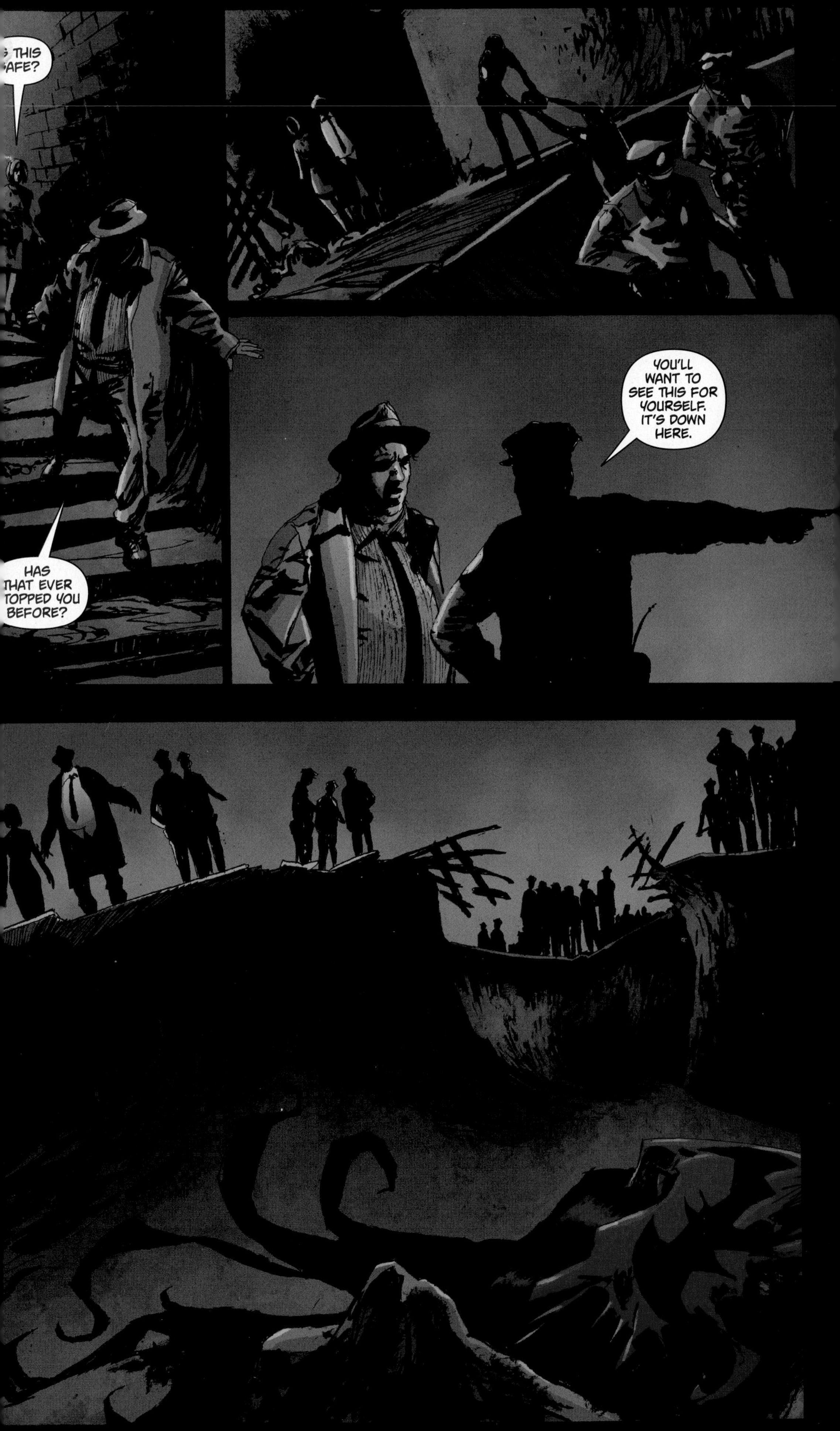

S THIS
SAFE?
HAS
THAT EVER
TOPPED YOU
BEFORE?
YOU'LL
WANT TO
SEE THIS FOR
YOURSELF.
IT'S DOWN
HERE.

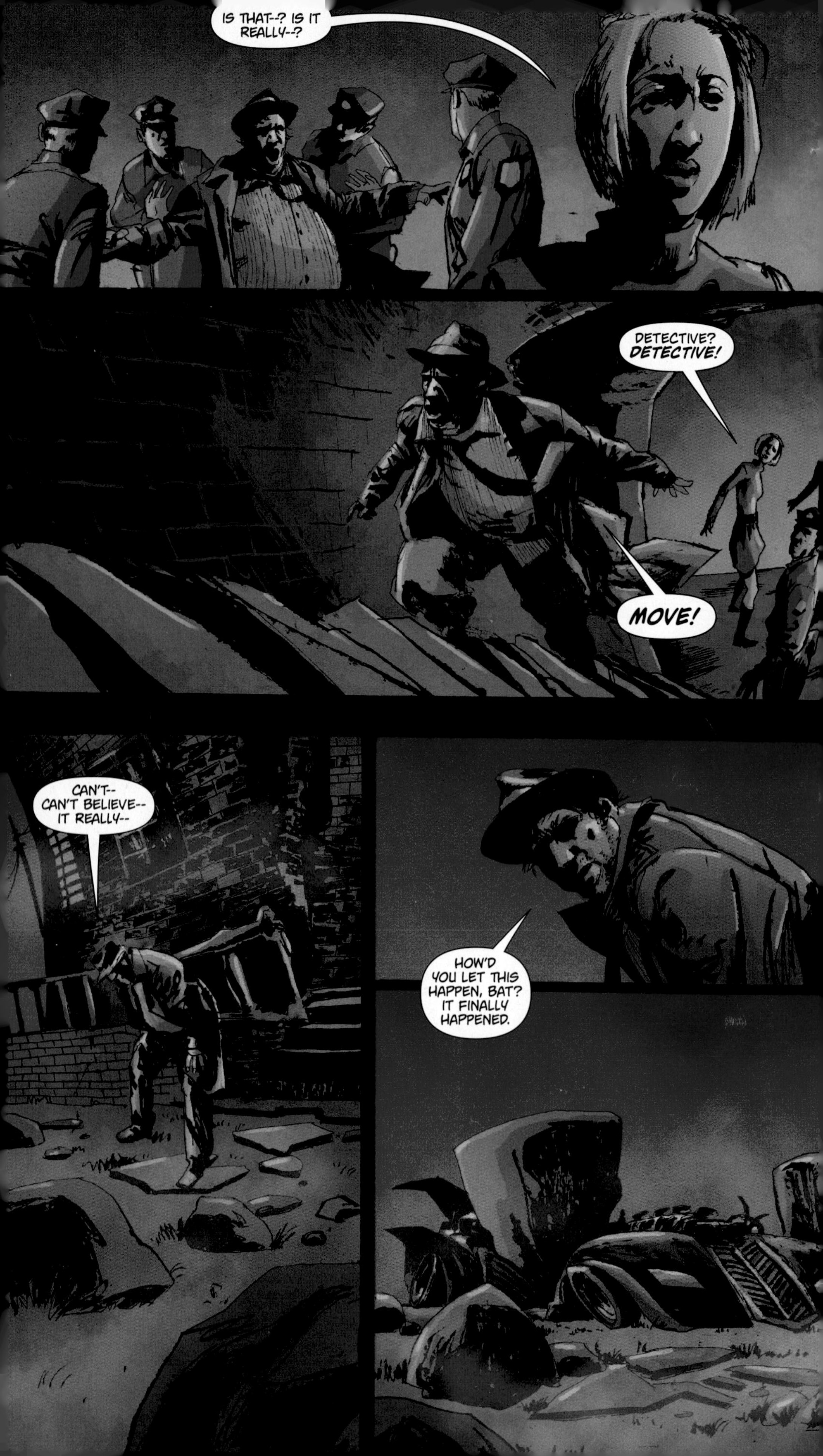
IS THAT--? IS IT REALLY--?
DETECTIVE? DETECTIVE!
MOVE!
CAN'T-- CAN'T BELIEVE-- IT REALLY--
HOW'D YOU LET THIS HAPPEN, BAT? IT FINALLY HAPPENED.

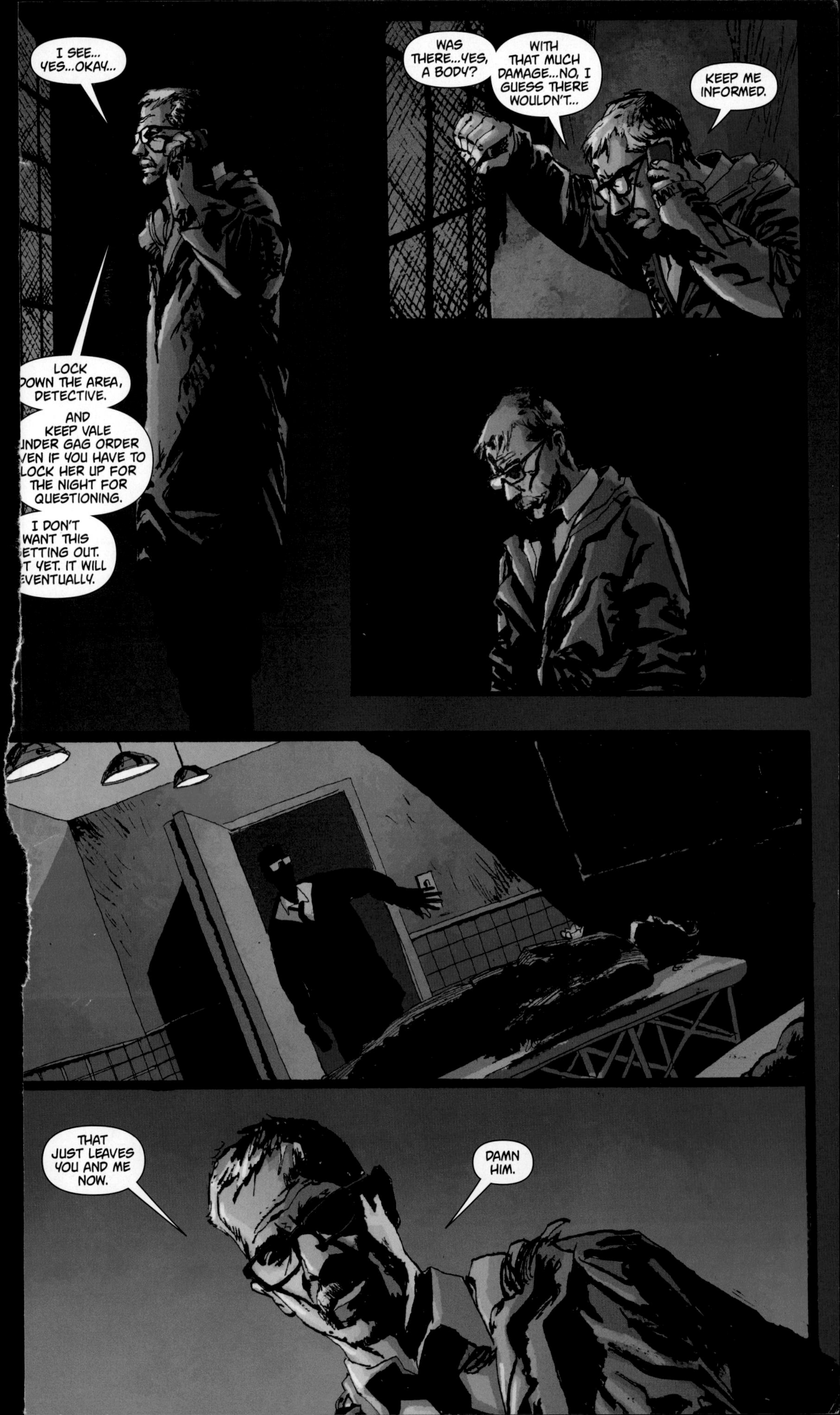
I SEE... YES...OKAY...
WAS THERE...YES, A BODY?
WITH THAT MUCH DAMAGE...NO, I GUESS THERE WOULDN'T...
KEEP ME INFORMED.
LOCK DOWN THE AREA, DETECTIVE.
AND KEEP VALE INDER GAG ORDER VEN IF YOU HAVE TO LOCK HER UP FOR THE NIGHT FOR QUESTIONING.
I DON'T WANT THIS ETTING OUT. T YET. IT WILL EVENTUALLY.
THAT JUST LEAVES YOU AND ME NOW.
DAMN HIM.

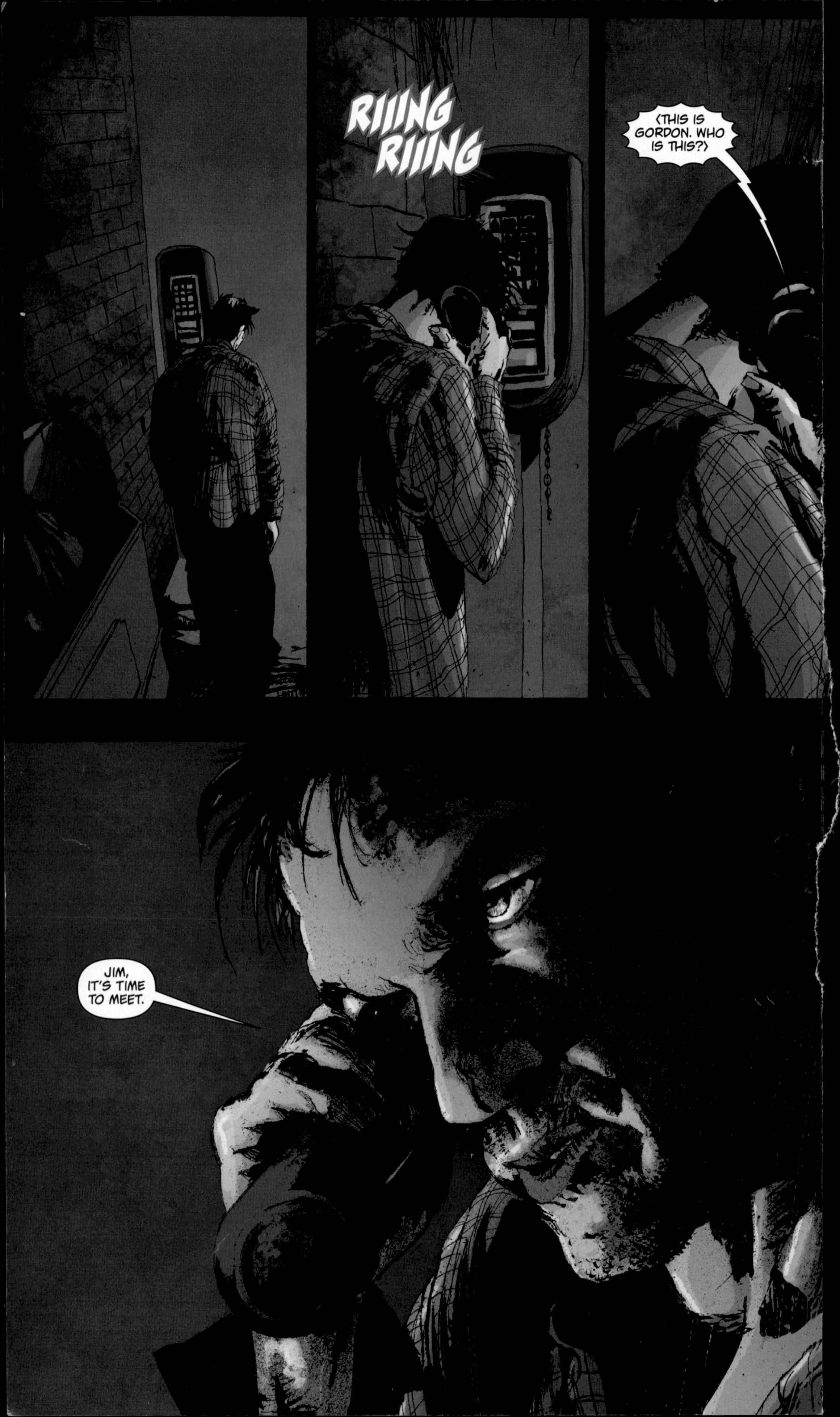
RIIING RIIING
(THIS IS GORDON. WHO IS THIS?)
JIM, IT'S TIME TO MEET.

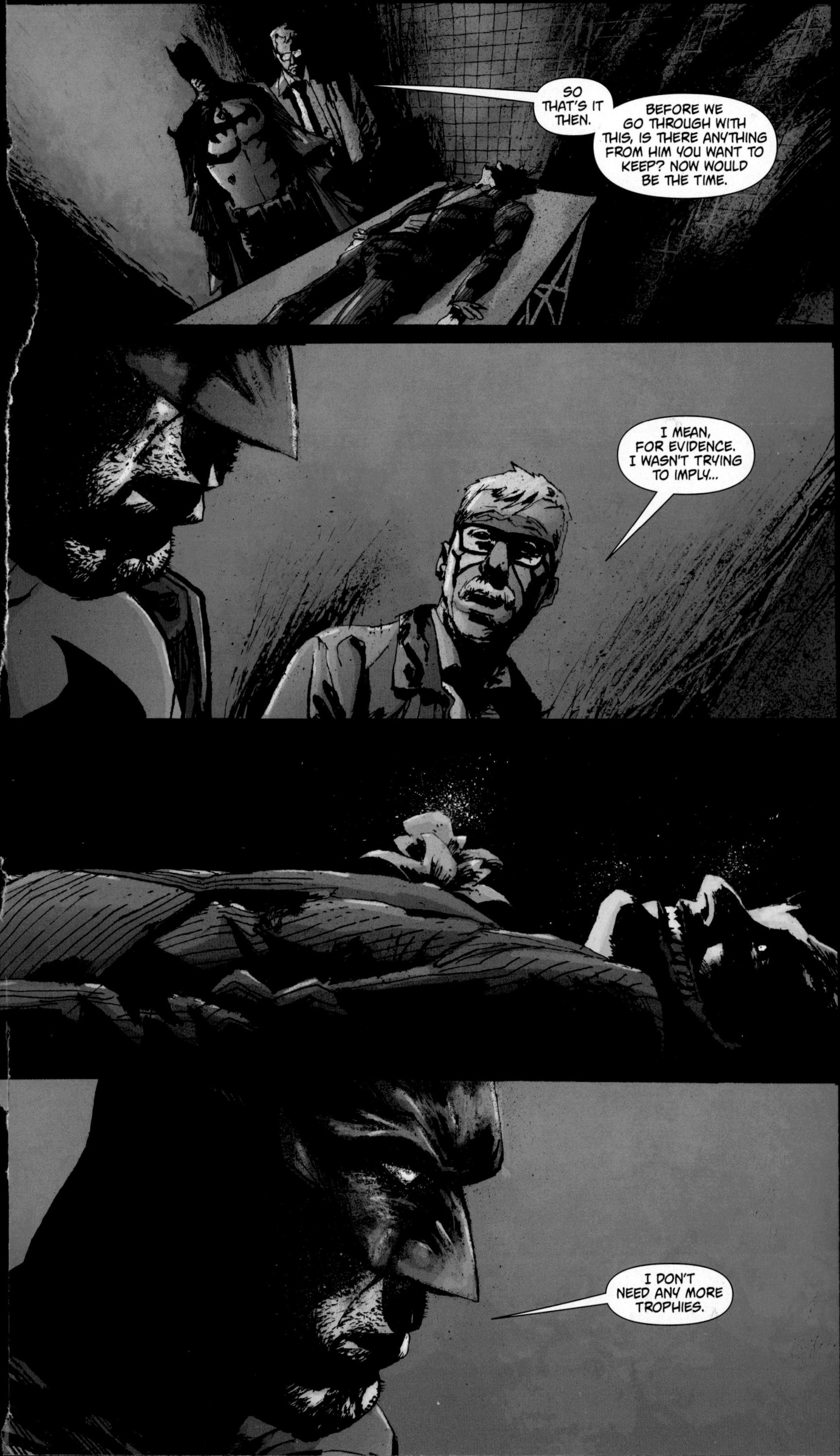
SO THAT'S IT THEN.
BEFORE WE GO THROUGH WITH THIS, IS THERE ANYTHING FROM HIM YOU WANT TO KEEP? NOW WOULD BE THE TIME.
I MEAN, FOR EVIDENCE. I WASN'T TRYING TO IMPLY...
I DON'T NEED ANY MORE TROPHIES.

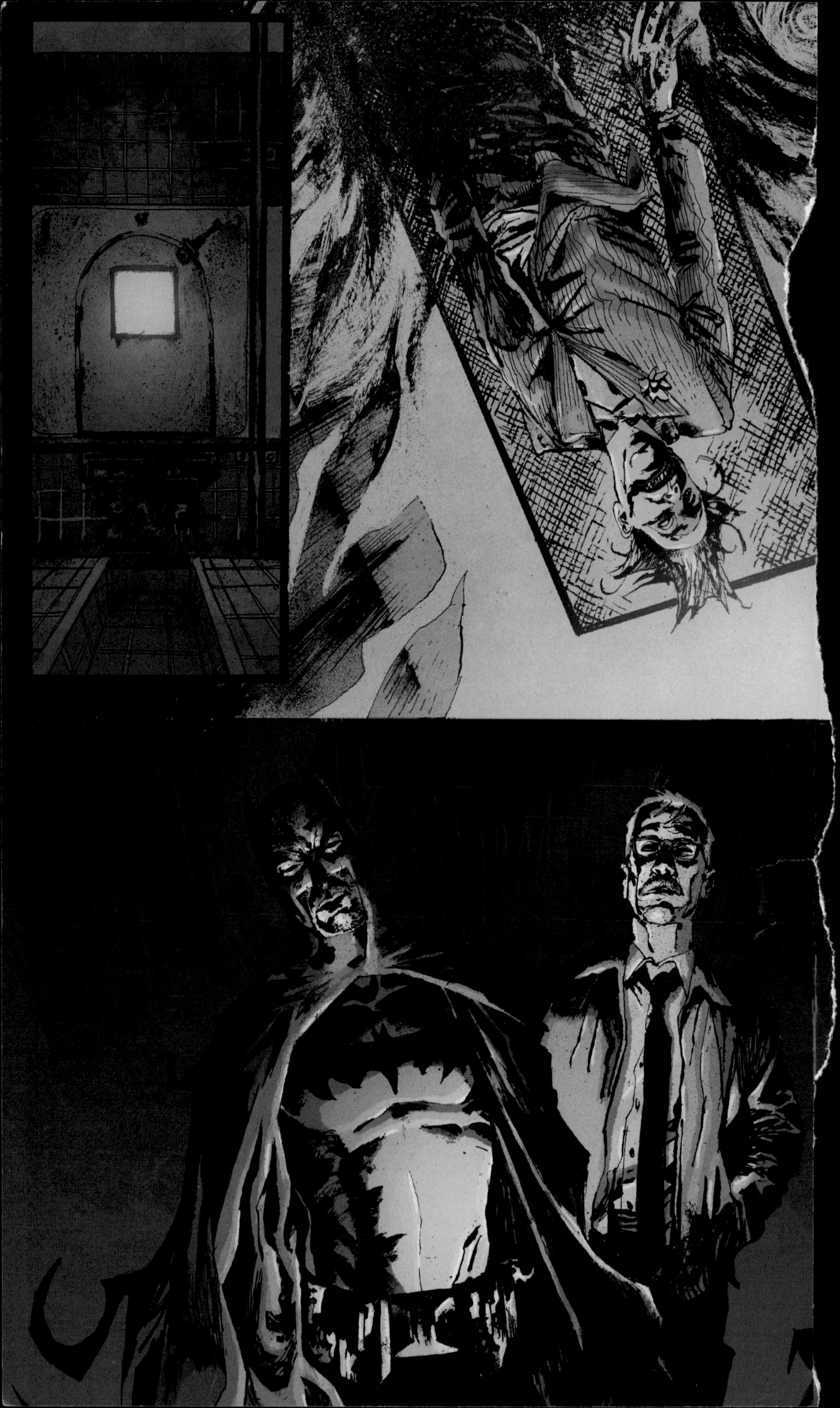

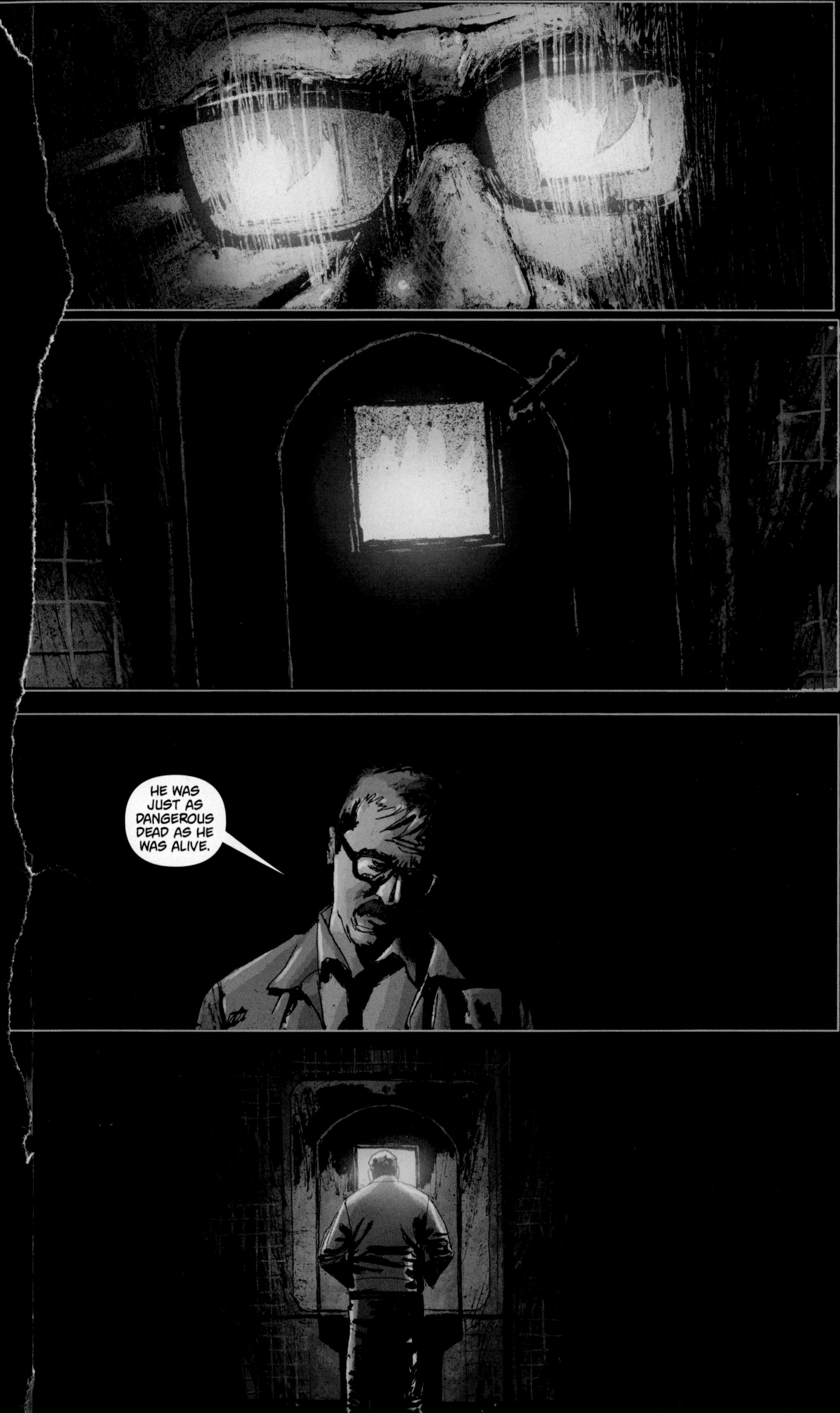
HE WAS JUST AS DANGEROUS DEAD AS HE WAS ALIVE.

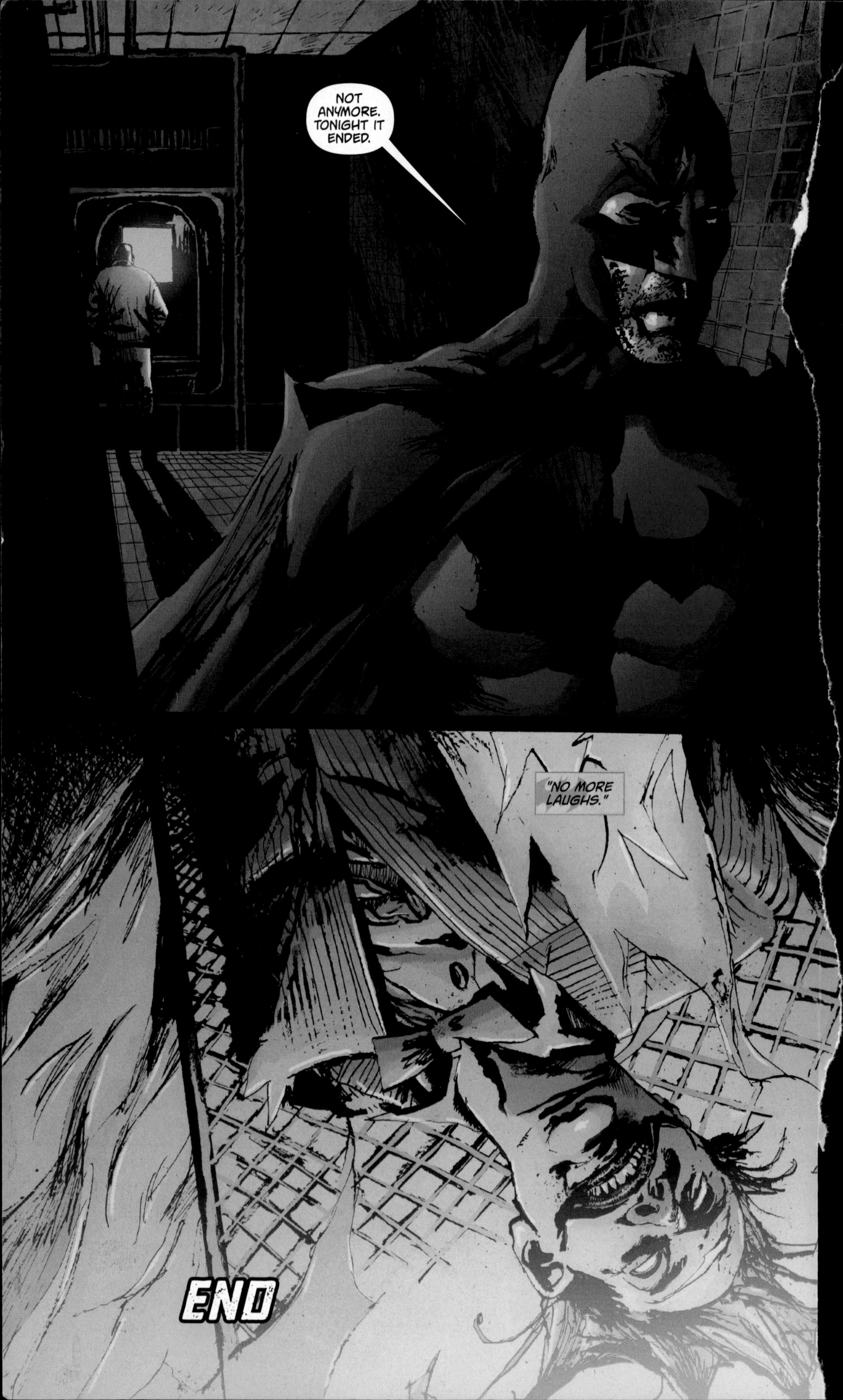
NOT ANYMORE. TONIGHT IT ENDED.
"NO MORE LAUGHS."
END

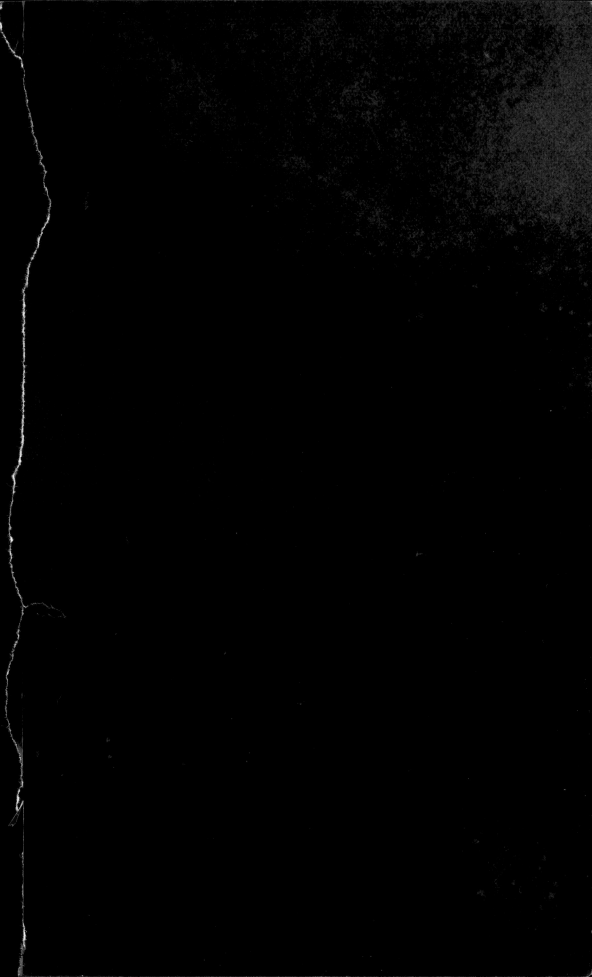

BATMAN – ARKHAM UNHINGED: END GAME #1
Full wrap-around cover by JASON SHAWN ALEXANDER & LEE LOUGHRIDGE

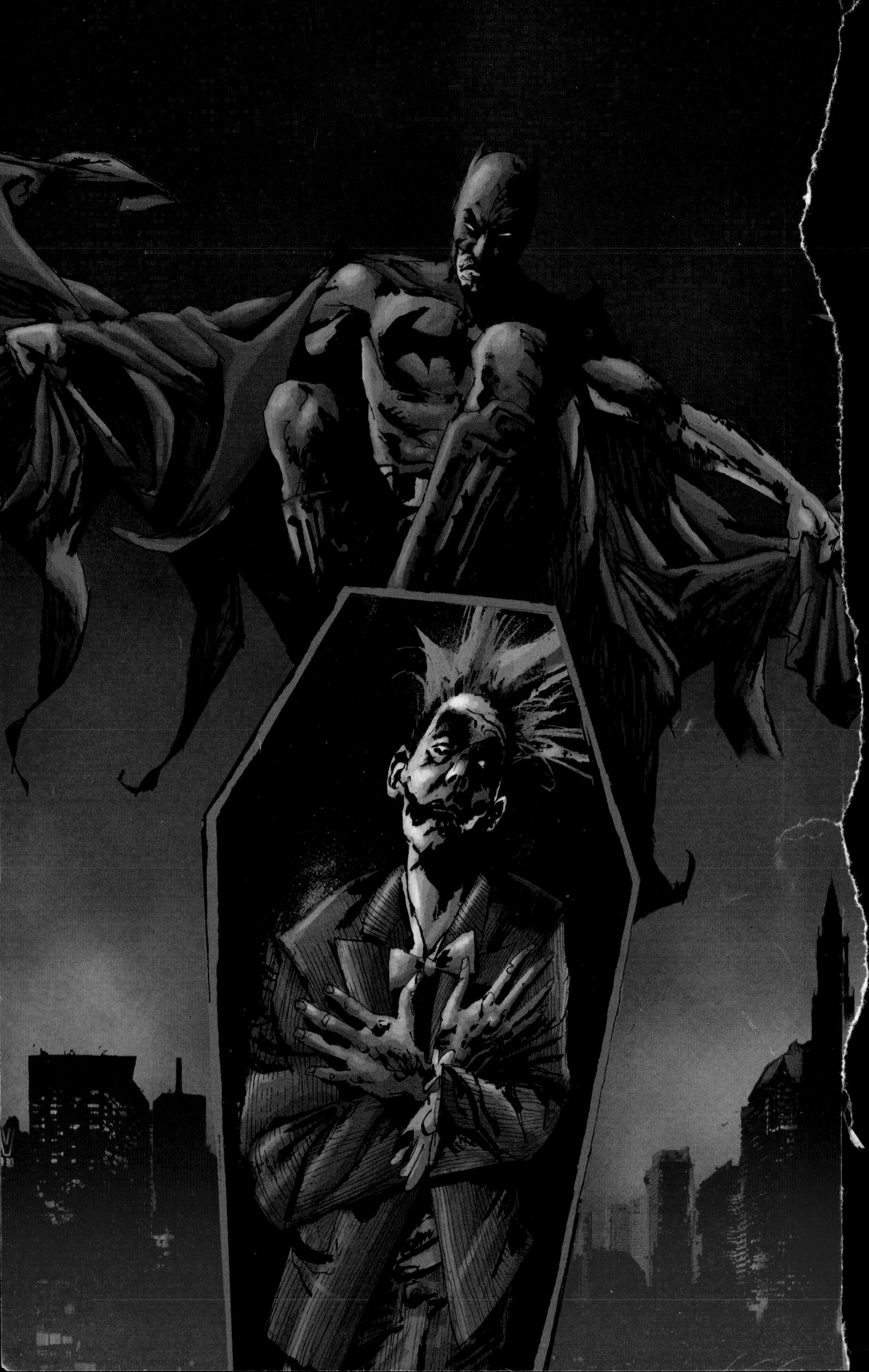

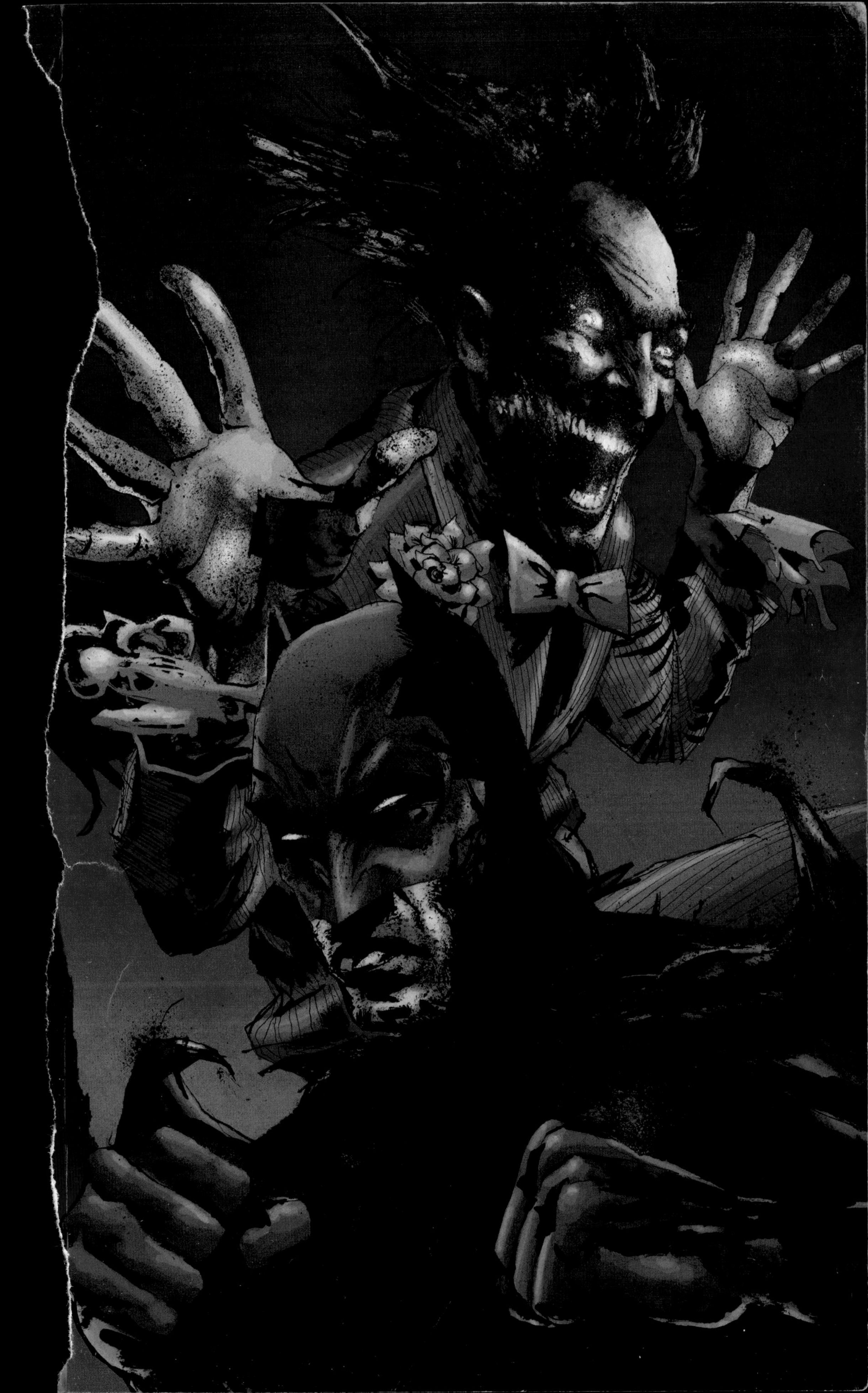

BATMAN – ARKHAM UNHINGED: END GAME #1
Full wrap-around variant cover by PAT GLEASON, DEREK FRIDOLFS & GABE ELTAEB

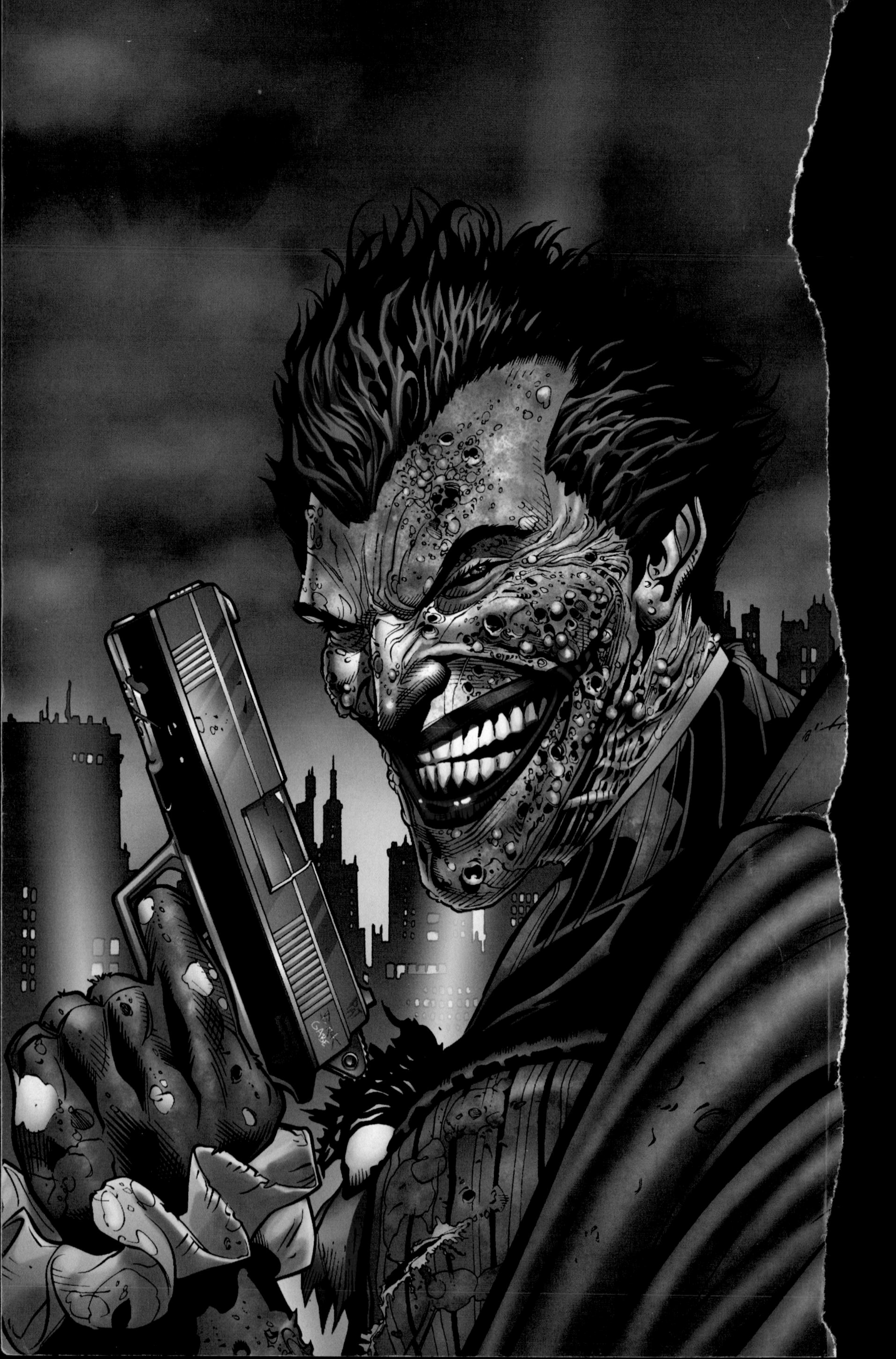

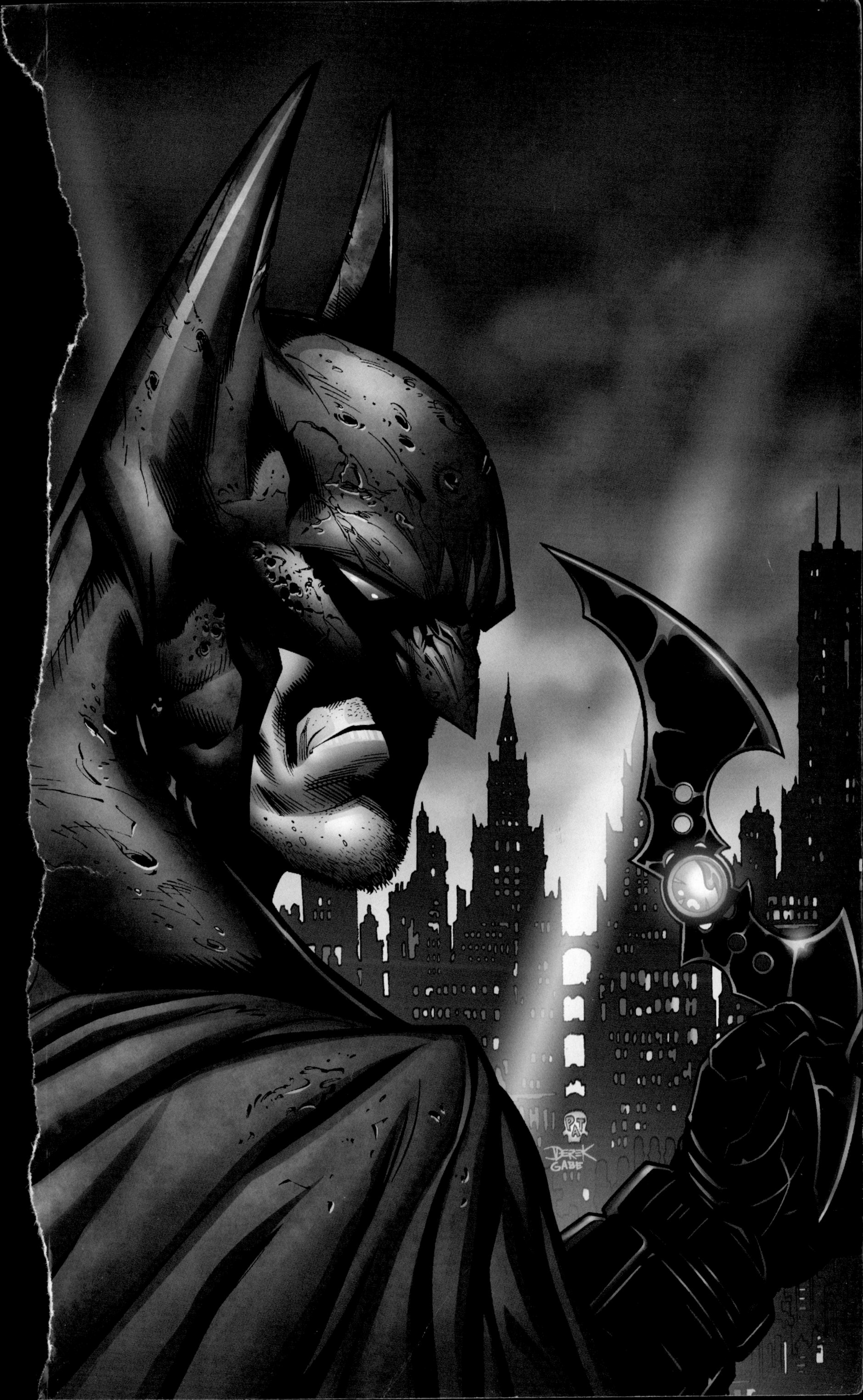
DEREK
GABE

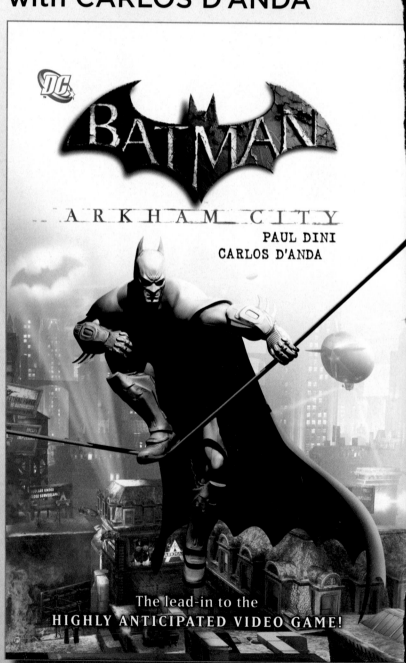